THE CAMBRIDGE COMPANION TO
BRITISH ROMANTIC POETRY

More than any other period of British literature, Romanticism is strongly identified with a single genre. Romantic poetry has been one of the most enduring,
best-loved, most widely read, and most frequently studied genres for two centuries and remains no less so today. This Companion offers a comprehensive
overview and interpretation of the poetry of the period in its literary and historical contexts. The essays consider its metrical, formal, and linguistic features;
its relation to history; its influence on other genres; its reflections of empire and
nationalism, both within and outside the British Isles; and the various implications of oral transmission and the rapid expansion of print culture and mass
readership. Attention is given to the work of less well-known or recently rediscovered authors, alongside the achievements of some of the greatest poets in the
English language: Wordsworth, Coleridge, Blake, Scott, Burns, Keats, Shelley,
Byron, and Clare.

JAMES CHANDLER is Director of the Franke Institute for the Humanities at
the University of Chicago.

MAUREEN N. MCLANE is Lecturer in the Committee on Degrees in History
and Literature at Harvard University.

THE CAMBRIDGE
COMPANION TO

BRITISH ROMANTIC POETRY

EDITED BY
JAMES CHANDLER and MAUREEN N. McLANE

CAMBRIDGE
UNIVERSITY PRESS

CAMBRIDGE UNIVERSITY PRESS

Cambridge, New York, Melbourne, Madrid, Cape Town, Singapore, São Paulo, Delhi

Cambridge University Press
The Edinburgh Building, Cambridge CB2 8RU, UK

Published in the United States of America by Cambridge University Press, New York

www.cambridge.org
Information on this title: www.cambridge.org/9780521680837

First published 2008

Printed in the United Kingdom at the University Press, Cambridge

A catalogue record for this publication is available from the British Library

Library of Congress Cataloguing in Publication data

The Cambridge companion to British romantic poetry / edited by James Chandler and
Maureen N. McLane.
p. cm.
Includes index.
ISBN 978-0-521-86235-6 (hbk.) – ISBN 978-0-521-68083-7 (pbk.)
1. English poetry – 19th century – History and criticism – Handbooks, manuals, etc.
2. English poetry – 18th century – History and criticism – Handbooks, manuals, etc.
3. Romanticism – Great Britain – Handbooks, manuals, etc.   1. Chandler, James K.
II. McLane, Maureen N.   III. Title.
PR590.C34   2008
821'.709145 – dc22   2008021913

ISBN 978-0-521-86235-6 hardback
ISBN 978-0-521-68083-7 paperback

CONTENTS

CONTRIBUTORS

ANDREW BENNETT is Professor of English at the University of Bristol. He has published widely on Romantic and post-Romantic literature, including three books with Cambridge University Press: *Keats, Narrative and Audience: The Posthumous Life of Writing* (1994), *Romantic Poets and the Culture of Posterity* (1999), and *Wordsworth Writing* (2007).

JAMES CHANDLER is Barbara E. and Richard J. Franke Distinguished Service Professor in the Department of English and in the Committee on Cinema and Media Studies at the University of Chicago, where he also serves as Director of the Franke Institute for the Humanities. His publications include *England in 1819* (1998) and *Wordsworth's Second Nature* (1984). He is co-editor of *Questions of Evidence* (1992) and *Romantic Metropolis* (2005). Most recently, he has edited *The Cambridge History of British Romantic Literature* (2008).

JEFFREY N. COX is Professor of English and of Comparative Literature and Humanities at the University of Colorado at Boulder, where he is also the Associate Vice Chancellor for Faculty Affairs. His work includes *Poetry and Politics in the Cockney School: Keats, Shelley, Hunt and Their Circle* (1998) and *In the Shadows of Romance: Romantic Tragic Drama in Germany, England, and France* (1987).

ADRIANA CRACIUN is Reader in Literature and Theory at Birkbeck, University of London. She is the author of *Fatal Women of Romanticism* (2003) and *British Women Writers and the French Revolution: Citizens of the World* (2005), and is currently writing a new book on multidisciplinary print culture and Arctic exploration, called *Northwest Passages*.

ANDREW ELFENBEIN is Morse-Alumni Distinguished Teaching Professor of English at the University of Minnesota–Twin Cities; he is the author of *Byron and the Victorians* (1995) and *Romantic Genius: The Prehistory of a Homosexual Role* (1999); his *Romanticism and the Rise of English* is forthcoming.

TIM FULFORD is Professor of English at Nottingham Trent University. He is the author of many books on Romantic-period literature and culture, most recently *Romantic Indians* (2006) and *Literature, Science and Exploration* (2004). He is currently editing Robert Southey's letters and poems for the first Collected Edition. His collection of essays (co-edited with Kevin Hutchings), *The Indian Atlantic*, also published by Cambridge University Press, appeared in 2008.

KEVIS GOODMAN is Associate Professor of English at the University of California, Berkeley, and the author of *Georgic Modernity and British Romanticism: Poetry and the Mediation of History* (Cambridge University Press, 2004). She has contributed articles on Milton, eighteenth-century verse, and Romantic studies to *ELH, Studies in Romanticism, South Atlantic Quarterly, European Romantic Review, The Wordsworth Circle*, and other journals.

NICK GROOM is Professor in English at the University of Exeter (Cornwall Campus) and Director of the Centre for Literatures of Identity and Place. He has written widely on national identity and authenticity in literature and culture – most recently in *The Union Jack* (2007) – and his edition of Percy's *Reliques* will be published shortly. He is currently writing a book on the cultural history of the British environment.

SIMON JARVIS is Gorley Putt Reader in Poetry and Poetics in the Faculty of English, University of Cambridge. He is the author of *Scholars and Gentlemen: Shakespearian Textual Criticism and Representations of Scholarly Labour* (1995); *Adorno: A Critical Introduction* (Cambridge University Press, 1998), and *Wordsworth's Philosophic Song* (Cambridge University Press, 2007).

WILLIAM KEACH is Professor of English at Brown University. His most recent book is *Arbitrary Power: Romanticism, Language, Politics* (2004); previous works include *Shelley's Style* (1984). He is currently working on determination and play in lyric poetry.

CELESTE LANGAN is an Associate Professor in the English Department at the University of California, Berkeley. She is the author of *Romantic Vagrancy* (Cambridge University Press, 1995, 2006) and several other essays on Romantic poetry. An essay on Scott's *Lay of the Last Minstrel* led to her ongoing interest in media theory and media archaeology. Her current book project, *Post-Napoleonism: Imagining Sovereignty after 1799*, interrogates Napoleon as, among other things, a figure of mass mediation.

MAUREEN N. McLANE is a Lecturer in History and Literature at Harvard University. She is the author of *Romanticism and the Human Sciences: Poetry, Population, and the Discourse of the Species* (Cambridge University Press, 2000, 2006), *Balladeering, Minstrelsy, and the Making of British Romantic Poetry* (Cambridge University Press, 2008), and *Same Life: Poems* (FSE, 2008).

ANN WIERDA ROWLAND teaches in the English department at the University of Kansas. She has published articles on Wordsworth, Scott, and the Romantic ballad revival, and is currently finishing a book on notions of childhood and Romantic literary culture.

SUSAN STEWART is the author of *Columbarium*, which won the National Book Critics Circle Award in Poetry in 2003, and the forthcoming *Red Rover*. Her prose works include *On Longing, Poetry and the Fate of the Senses*, and *The Open Studio*. She is a current Chancellor of the Academy of American Poets, a former MacArthur Fellow and the Annan Professor of English at Princeton University.

ACKNOWLEDGMENTS

This book was commissioned by Linda Bree, Senior Literature Editor at Cambridge, and she supervised each step of its development with steady, cheerful vigilance; her astute comments on these essays were invaluable. Maartje Scheltens handled a number of demanding editorial tasks at Cambridge with a consistent rigor and grace. Our thanks as well to Jo Bramwell, our eagle-eyed and most patient copy-editor, and to Elizabeth Davey, who kindly shepherded us through every phase of production. At crucial junctures, we benefited from the assistance of Mollie Godfrey and Andrew Yale at the University of Chicago. Gina DeGiovanni and Michael Meeuwis, also of the University of Chicago, did the lion's share of work on the Chronology. For helpful comments on the Introduction we thank Michael Chandler. And of course we thank our contributors for their patience with the process and for committing their considerable talents to the project in the first place: if the Romantics invented the conversation poem, our contributors made possible a richly collaborative conversation about Romantic poems.

CHRONOLOGY

1757   William Blake born
       Edmund Burke, *A Philosophical Enquiry into the Origin of our Ideas of the Sublime and the Beautiful*
       Thomas Gray, "The Bard"
1759   Robert Burns born
       Mary Wollstonecraft born
       Adam Smith, *The Theory of Moral Sentiments*
       Laurence Sterne, *The Life and Opinions of Tristram Shandy, Gentleman* (1759–67)
1760   Accession of George III
       James Macpherson's Ossianic *Fragments* published
1762   Joanna Baillie born
       Jean-Jacques Rousseau, *The Social Contract* and *Emile*
1763   Treaty of Paris ends Seven Years War
       Hugh Blair, *A Critical Dissertation on the Poems of Ossian, the Son of Fingal*
       Christopher Smart, *A Song to David*
       James Macpherson, *Temora*
1764   Ann Radcliffe (née Ward) born
       John Thelwall born
       Horace Walpole, *The Castle of Otranto*
1765   Thomas Percy, ed., *Reliques of Ancient English Poetry*
1766   Oliver Goldsmith, *The Vicar of Wakefield*
1767   Hugh Blair, *Heads of the Lectures on Rhetoric and Belles Lettres*
1768   Sterne dies
       Maria Edgeworth born
1769   Napoleon Bonaparte born
       Sir Joshua Reynolds, *Discourses on Art*
1770   Captain James Cook lands at Botany Bay
       Thomas Chatterton's suicide

Ludwig van Beethoven born
Georg Wilhelm Friedrich Hegel born
William Wordsworth born

1771   Walter Scott born
Dorothy Wordsworth born
James Beattie, *The Minstrel* (1771–4)
Henry Mackenzie, *The Man of Feeling*

1772   Mansfield Decision denies a legal basis for slavery in England
Samuel Taylor Coleridge born

1773   Anna Laetitia Barbauld, *Poems*

1774   *Donaldson* v. *Becket* reestablishes limits on copyright
Accession of Louis XVI of France
Robert Southey born
Goldsmith dies
Johann Wolfgang von Goethe, *The Sorrows of Young Werther*

1775   War begun with American colonies
Jane Austen born
Charles Lamb born
Joseph Turner born
Richard Brinsley Sheridan, *The Rivals*
Robert Wood, *An Essay on the Original Genius and Writings of Homer* (posthumous)

1776   American Declaration of Independence
John Constable born
David Hume dies
Smith, *An Inquiry into the Nature and Causes of the Wealth of Nations*

1777   Thomas Chatterton, "Rowley" Poems (posthumous)
Sheridan, *The School for Scandal*

1778   Franco-American Alliance signed at the Second Continental Congress
Britain declares war on France
William Hazlitt born
Rousseau dies
Frances Burney, *Evelina*

1779   Britain declares war on Spain
David Hume, *Dialogues Concerning Natural Religion*
Samuel Johnson, "Prefaces" to *The Works of the English Poets* (1779–81)
William Cowper and John Newton, *Olney Hymns*

1781 Friedrich Schiller, *The Robbers*
   Immanuel Kant, *A Critique of Pure Reason*

1782 Burney, *Cecilia*
   Edward Cowper, *Poems*
   Rousseau, *Confessions*

1783 American independence recognized at Peace of Versailles
   Blake, *Poetical Sketches*
   George Crabbe, *The Village*

1784 Pitt's India Act restricts the East India Company's autonomy
   James Leigh Hunt born
   Johnson dies
   Pierre Beaumarchais, *The Marriage of Figaro*
   Capt. James Cook, *A Voyage to the Pacific Ocean*
   Hannah More, *The Bas Bleu; or, Conversation*
   Charlotte Smith, *Elegiac Sonnets*
   Jacques-Louis David, *The Oath of the Horatii*

1785 Thomas de Quincey born
   Thomas Love Peacock born
   Cowper, *The Task*
   Thomas Warton appointed Laureate

1786 Burns, *Poems, Chiefly in the Scottish Dialect* published at
   Kilmarnock
   Mozart, *The Marriage of Figaro*

1787 Society for Effecting the Abolition of the Slave Trade founded
   American Constitution signed
   James Johnson, *The Scots Musical Museum* (1787–1803, with
   anonymous contributions from Burns)

1788 George III's first attack of insanity
   George Gordon (later Lord) Byron born
   More, *Slavery, a Poem*
   Ann Yearsley, *A Poem on the Inhumanity of the Slave-Trade*
   Charlotte Smith, *Emmeline*

1789 Convening of the Estates General to deal with financial crisis in
   France; the Tennis Court Oath; the Bastille falls; Declaration of
   the Rights of Man
   Jeremy Bentham, *Principles of Morals and Legislation*
   Blake, *Songs of Innocence* and *The Book of Thel*
   William Bowles, *Fourteen Sonnets Written Chiefly on Picturesque
   Spots during a Journey*
   Charlotte Brooke, *Reliques of Irish Poetry*

Olaudah Equiano, *The Interesting Narrative of the Life of Olaudah Equiano*

William Lisle Bowles, *Fourteen Sonnets, Elegiac* and *Descriptive*

1790   Blake, *The Marriage of Heaven and Hell*

Edmund Burke, *Reflections on the Revolution in France*

Wollstonecraft, *A Vindication of the Rights of Men*

Henry James Pye appointed Laureate

1791   American Bill of Rights ratified

Church and King Riots aimed at Joseph Priestley's beliefs concerning religious toleration and his political radicalism lead to the destruction of much property, including Priestley's house

Mozart dies

Louis XVI captured at Varennes

Boswell, *The Life of Samuel Johnson*

Paine, *The Rights of Man*

Radcliffe, *The Romance of the Forest*

1792   Royal Proclamation against seditious writings issued by George III; *The Rights Of Man* banned and Paine charged with sedition

Continental allies invade France; September massacres; declaration of the French Republic; imprisonment of French royal family

Wordsworth in France

Percy Shelley born

Burns, "Tam o' Shanter"

Charlotte Smith, *Desmond*

Samuel Rogers, *The Pleasures of Memory*

Wollstonecraft, *A Vindication of the Rights of Woman*

1793   Trial and execution of Louis XVI; France declares war on Britain; the Terror; execution of Marie Antoinette

Blake, *Visions of the Daughters of Albion* and *America: A Prophecy*

William Godwin, *Enquiry Concerning Political Justice*

Wordsworth, *An Evening Walk* and *Descriptive Sketches*

1794   Suspension of Habeas Corpus in England; reformers jailed without charges; Robespierre executed; end of the Terror; the Directorate established

Blake, *Songs of Innocence and Experience, Europe: A Prophecy*, and *The Book of Urizen*

Coleridge, "Monody on the Death of Chatterton"

Erasmus Darwin, *Zoonomia*

Godwin, *Caleb Williams*

Thomas Paine, *The Age of Reason*

Radcliffe, *The Mysteries of Udolfo*

1795   Thomas Carlyle born

John Keats born

Macpherson dies

Blake, *The Book of Los* and *The Book of Ahania*

Coleridge, *Conciones ad Populum*

Matthew Lewis, *Ambrosio, or The Monk*

More, *Repository Tracts* (1795–8)

Friedrich Schiller, *Letters on Aesthetic Education* and *On Naive and Sentimental Poetry*

Southey, *Poems*

1796   Attempted French invasion of Ireland

Robert Bloomfield, *The Farmer's Boy*

Burns dies

Burney, *Camilla*

Coleridge, *Poems on Various Subjects* and *The Watchman*

Mary Hays, *Memoirs of Emma Courtney*

Charlotte Smith, *Marchmont*

Mary Robinson, *Sappho and Phaon*

Southey, *Joan of Arc*

Thelwall, *The Rights of Nature Against the Usurpation of Establishments*

1797   Wordsworth and Coleridge become neighbours in Somerset, begin their historic collaboration

Burke dies

Wollstonecraft dies

Coleridge, *Poems*

Radcliffe, *The Italian*

1798   Irish Rebellion; French army lands in Ireland

The *Athenaeum* publishes fragments by founders Friedrich and A. W. Schlegel, and by Novalis, and Schleiermacher (1798–1800)

Baillie, *Plays on the Passions*

Coleridge, "Fears in Solitude," "France: an Ode," and "Frost at Midnight"

Thomas Malthus, *An Essay on the Principle of Population*

Wollstonecraft, *Maria, or the Wrongs of Woman*

Wordsworth and Coleridge, *Lyrical Ballads* (published by Joseph Cottle in Bristol)

Wordsworth launches the poem "on his own mind," a work that would be posthumously published as *The Prelude* in 1850

1799   French Directorate falls; Napoleon made First Consul
       Thomas Campbell, *The Pleasures of Hope*
1800   Act of Union with Ireland
       Cowper dies
       Anne Bannerman, *Poems*
       Edgeworth, *Castle Rackrent*
       Mary Robinson, *Lyrical Tales*
       Wordsworth and Coleridge, much expanded second edition of
       Lyrical Ballads
1801   George III refuses to support Catholic Emancipation; Pitt resigns
       James Hogg, *Scottish Pastorals*
       Southey, *Thalaba*
1802   Napoleon elected First Consul for life
       Erasmus Darwin dies
       Edinburgh Review begins publication; Francis Jeffrey christens
       the "Lake School of Poetry"
       William Cobbett begins the *Political Register* (1802–35)
       Bannerman, *Tales of Superstition and Chivalry*
       Coleridge, "Dejection: An Ode"
       Edgeworth, *Belinda*
       Amelia Opie, *Poems*
       Scott, *Minstrelsy of the Scottish Border*
       Wordsworth begins composition of what would become "Ode:
       Intimations of Immortality"
1803   Napoleon interns all British civilians in France; war resumed
       Erasmus Darwin, *The Temple of Nature*
1804   Henry Addington resigns; Pitt becomes Prime Minister
       Napoleon becomes Emperor
       Kant dies
       Blake, *Milton* and *Jerusalem*
       Edgeworth, *Popular Tales*
       Wordsworth completes the Immortality Ode
1805   Samuel Palmer born
       Scott, *The Lay of the Last Minstrel*
       Southey, *Madoc*
       Turner, *The Shipwreck*
       Wordsworth completes the thirteen-book version of what would
       later be called *The Prelude*
1806   Charlotte Smith dies
       Edgeworth, *Leonora*
       Sydney Owenson (Lady Morgan), *The Wild Irish Girl*

1807   Slavery abolished in England, but not in colonies; slave trade ended

Hazlitt, *A Reply to the Essay on Population*

Byron, *Hours of Idleness*

Hegel, *The Phenomenology of Spirit*

Charles and Mary Lamb, *Tales from Shakespeare*

Charles Maturin, *The Fatal Revenge*

Moore, *Irish Melodies*

Wordsworth, *Poems* (2 vols.)

1808   Hunt becomes editor of *The Examiner*

Goethe, *Faust* Part I

Felicia Browne (Hemans), *Poems, England and Spain*

Charles Lamb, *Specimens of the English Dramatic Poets*

Scott, *Marmion*

1809   Alfred Tennyson born

Charles Darwin born

Quarterly Review founded

Blake, *A Descriptive Catalogue*

Byron, *English Bards and Scotch Reviewers*

Campbell, *Gertrude of Wyoming*

Coleridge, *The Friend*

Wordsworth, *The Convention of Cintra*

1810   Scott, *The Lady of the Lake*

Percy Shelley, *Zastrozzi*

Southey, *The Curse of Kehama*

1811   Regency begins as George III is declared mentally unfit to rule

Luddite movement begins in response to mechanization of the textile industry

Austen, *Sense and Sensibility*

Barbauld, *The Female Speaker*

Hunt, "The Feast of the Poets"

Charles Lamb, "On the Tragedies of Shakespeare"

Scott, *The Vision of Don Roderick*

Percy Shelley, *On the Necessity of Atheism*

Mary Tighe, *Psyche* (privately printed 1805)

1812   America declares war on Britain

Robert Browning born

Charles Dickens born

Byron, *Childe Harold's Pilgrimage* (1812–18)

Crabbe, *Tales in Verse*

1817 Jane Austen dies
The Shelleys join Byron in Italy
Blackwood's Magazine founded
Byron, *Manfred*
Coleridge, *Biographia Literaria* and *Sibylline Leaves*
Hazlitt, *The Characters of Shakespeare's Plays*
Keats, *Poems*
Scott, *Rob Roy*
Southey, *Wat Tyler* (pirated)

1818 Austen, *Northanger Abbey* and *Persuasion*
Hazlitt, *Lectures on the English Poets*
Keats, *Endymion*
Scott, *The Heart of Mid-Lothian*
Mary Shelley, *Frankenstein*
Percy Shelley, *The Revolt of Islam*, "Ozymandias"

1819 Peterloo Massacre occurs outside Manchester when a large public
meeting calling for Parliamentary Reform is attacked by troops
Queen Victoria born
Walt Whitman born
John Ruskin born
Byron, *Don Juan* (1819–23)
Thomas Campbell, *Specimens of the British Poets* (7 vols.)
Hemans, *Tales and Historic Scenes in Verse*
Keats composes his Great Odes
John Polidori, *The Vampyre*
Scott, *The Bride of Lammermoor, The Legend of Montrose*, and
Ivanhoe
Wordsworth, *Peter Bell* and *The Waggoner*

1820 Accession of George IV
London Magazine founded
John Clare, *Poems Descriptive of Rural Life and Scenery* and *The
Village Minstrel*
Keats, *Lamia, Isabella, The Eve of St. Agnes, and Other Poems*,
and *Hyperion*
Peacock, "The Four Ages of Poetry"
Percy Shelley, "Ode to the West Wind" and *Prometheus
Unbound, The Cenci*
Scott, *The Abbott*, and *The Monastery*

1821 Greek War of Independence begins
Keats dies
Napoleon dies

Baillie, *Metrical Legends of Exalted Characters*
John Constable, *The Hay Wain*
De Quincey, *Confessions of an English Opium Eater*
Hazlitt, *Table-Talk*
Percy Shelley, *A Defence of Poetry*, "Adonais," and "Epipsychidion"
Scott, *Kenilworth*

1822   Matthew Arnold born
Percy Shelley dies
Byron, Hunt, and Percy Shelley publish in *The Liberal*

1823   Radcliffe dies
Hemans, *The Vespers of Palermo, The Siege of Valencia, and Other Poems, Tales and Historic Scenes* (2nd edn.)
Mary Shelley, *Valperga*

1824   Byron dies
Beethoven, Symphony No. 9 (Choral)
Hogg, *Private Memoirs and Confessions of a Justified Sinner*
Scott, *Redgauntlet*
Percy Shelley, *Posthumous Poems* (ed. Mary Shelley)

1825   Barbauld, *Works*
Hazlitt, *The Spirit of the Age, or, Contemporary Portraits*
Laetitia Elizabeth Landon, *The Troubadour: Poetical Sketches of Modern Pictures* and *Historical Sketches*

1826   Mary Shelley, *The Last Man*

1827   Beethoven dies
Blake dies
Wordsworth, *Poems* (5 vols.)
Scott acknowledges authorship of the *Waverley* novels

1828   Repeal of the Test and Corporation Acts permits Dissenters to hold official posts
University College London opens
Hemans, *Records of Woman with Other Poems*
Hunt, *Lord Byron and Some of His Contemporaries*
Carlyle, "Essay on Burns"
Coleridge, *Poetical Works*

1829   Honoré de Balzac, *Les Chouans*
Carlyle, "Signs of the Times"
Peacock, *The Misfortunes of Elphin*

1830   Death of George IV and accession of William IV
July Revolutions in France
Christina Rossetti born

Hazlitt dies
Carlyle, "On History"
Charles Lamb, *Album Verses*
Palmer, *Coming from Evening Church*
Tennyson, *Poems, Chiefly Lyrical*

1831 Lord John Russell introduces a Reform Bill in House of Commons
Charles Darwin departs on the *Beagle*
Coleridge's last meeting with Wordsworth
Benjamin Disraeli, *The Young Duke*
Hegel, *Lectures on the Philosophy of History*

1832 The Representation of the People Bill (First Reform Act) passes in Parliament
Scott dies

1834 Coleridge dies
Lamb dies
Thelwall dies

INTRODUCTION: THE COMPANIONABLE FORMS OF ROMANTIC POETRY

JAMES CHANDLER AND MAUREEN N. McLANE

> Only that film, which fluttered on the grate,
> Still flutters there, the sole unquiet thing.
> Methinks, its motion in this hush of nature
> Gives it dim sympathies with me who live,
> Making it a companionable form . . .
> Coleridge, "Frost at Midnight"[1]

It was, most immediately, the work of his own contemporaries that prompted Percy Shelley to proclaim, at the close of his *Defence of Poetry* (1821), that "Poets are the unacknowledged legislators of the world." The authority of those poets in the age we have come to call "Romantic," Shelley explained, derived not from their opinions, with which he often disagreed, but from their capacity to tap into a certain spirit – what he called "the spirit of their age." Shelley figured this with a metaphor taken from recent developments in the natural sciences: it is impossible to read these contemporaries, he wrote, without being struck by "the electric life that burns in their words."[2] "Electricity," for Shelley, is at once a modern scientific discovery and a theme that hearkens back to the ancient myth of Prometheus, the thief of divine fire. The prototypical writer of his age – the "Romantic poet" – thus became on Shelley's account a kind of modern Prometheus, a poet of the electric life of words. This view would not go unchallenged. Indeed, even before it was written down in the *Defence of Poetry*, Mary Shelley had published *Frankenstein: Or, The Modern Prometheus* (1818), a fable of "electric life" and monstrous ambition with more than casual application to her husband's grand schemes. In spite of such challenges, or because of them, a sense of verbal electricity in Romantic poetry has persisted through generations of readers and assured these writings a special place in British literature ever since.

This special place suggests that a Companion to Romantic poetry must do more than simply fill a gap between the Companions to eighteenth-century and Victorian poetry. It is true that all three of these ages differ each from the other in the historical particulars to which their poets had to respond. The Augustan poets and their immediate successors might be said to have responded to the new urban world of newspapers and coffee houses, to a new polite commercial order in Britain in the wake of the founding of the Bank of

England in the 1690s, to strife in Scotland, conflict with Holland and France, enlightenment in Europe. The Victorian poets, a dozen decades later, had to be responsive to a time of unprecedented growth in London, to industrialization on the one hand and art for art's sake on the other, to challenges aimed at traditional beliefs in geology, biology, and economics; to famine in Ireland and to the 1848 Revolutions on the Continent. By this same logic, one could reasonably say that poets of the Romantic period were responding, well, to the sorts of things that they themselves identified in their own time: the loss of the American colonies, uprising in Ireland, the emergence of mass literacy, wholesale reconfigurations of discourses of knowledge (e.g. history, moral philosophy, political economy, chemistry, physiology, electromagnetism), the new constitutional theories and reform movements in politics, and of course to the French Revolution, which many of them considered the most momentous event in post-biblical history.

To take seriously the Shelleyan formulation about the spirit of the age, however, is to see that the poets of this period were not simply responding to events and situations different from those of their Augustan and Victorian counterparts. Instead, they were responding to a new kind of historical horizon and a new sense of the power of poetry to speak to it. The special place of poetry in the Romantic period, furthermore, has implications for the place of this period in the history of poetry. As evidence of the latter, one need only consult standard anthologies of British poetry or British literature over recent decades, where the quantity of pages given to Romantic poets is out of all proportion to its brevity in years. As evidence of the former, consider how elevated a position poetry had in the hierarchy of cultural practice for Britain in this period – much as painting did in seventeenth-century Holland or music in eighteenth-century German-speaking countries. In Britain poetry attracted great talents that seem initially to be destined for other fields. Poetry harnessed energies that might have flowed elsewhere had British culture developed differently: noting the relative impoverishment of English music in the eighteenth and nineteenth centuries, Theodor Adorno mordantly suggested that Keats and Shelley – with their lyric virtuosities and ostentatious musicality – might be seen as the "*locum tenentes* of nonexistent great English composers."[3] Among the group of six male Romantic poets who until recently tended to dominate the anthologies, all were initially meant to be pursuing other careers: Blake in the visual arts, Wordsworth in law, Coleridge in the ministry, Byron in politics, Shelley in science, Keats in medicine. All came to see poetry as where the action was, even as they disagreed about what counted as poetry and what counted as action.

Thus no Companion aiming to do justice to "Romantic poetry" can simply and unreflectively take its place in a series of "genre in period" Companions.

Unlike "eighteenth-century," the adjective "Romantic" denotes not just a period, but a style, a movement, a way of thinking (an "ideology," some have said), even a way of being in the world. Some of this might be claimed for "Victorian," it is true. Yet, as a stylistic category, "Romantic" has sufficient conceptual force to be able to stand in ideational opposition to other concepts (e.g., "classical") in a way that not even "Victorian" can do. Poets writing long after the Battle of Waterloo might well think of themselves as "in the Romantic line." This too is a special feature of our subject, and one that we have attempted to address in the essays that follow.

There is yet another kind of indicator of the distinctive place of poetry in Romanticism and of Romanticism in poetry, made visible in the role that Romantic poetry has played in the development of modern criticism and of "English" as an academic discipline. The fate of Romantic poetry as a field of study has been closely tied to the fate of literary studies as a discipline and indeed has changed with shifting critical practices and altered paradigms. Certainly since the 1920s, soon after the English tripos was established at Cambridge and when I. A. Richards was conducting his famous experiments in "practical criticism," the writings of the Romantic poets have been central to debates over the way modern students of literature should go about their business. In 1934, Richards would align himself with a brand of Coleridgeanism in his *Coleridge on Imagination*, but the experiments in the interpretation of poetry that Richards undertook with students at Cambridge from 1925 to 1929 were already informed by fundamental poetic principles and cultural frameworks that he had avowedly drawn from Wordsworth, Shelley, and Coleridge himself. Over the course of the next decades, a surprising number of the scholars, critics, and theorists who followed Richards's ambitious shaping of practices and paradigms for literary study were also keen students of Romantic poetry. The names F. R. Leavis, Northrop Frye, M. H. Abrams, Harold Bloom, Geoffrey Hartman, and Paul de Man form only the beginning of a long litany of critics who drew far-reaching implications for the larger enterprise of literary studies from their engagements with Romantic poetry.

To recognize the interconnections between Romantic poetics and twentieth-century criticism, however, is to be in a position to see how the image of the former changes with the evolution of the latter. The poets we have mentioned thus far were part of the six-men-in-two-generations model of this field, and it is by no means irrelevant that all of the critics thus far invoked are men who dominated departments in a period when a scholar of poetry as talented and committed as Helen Vendler could not attend a research seminar at Harvard because of concern that her presence would disturb the sociality of the men who gathered at the home of the professor-convener.[4] We have so far also been representing Romantic poetry through a somewhat Richards-like sense of the autonomy of texts as objects of interpretation. Indeed, we have been talking as if Romantic Poetry still held the same high place in the study of literature from 1780 to 1835 as it did when Frye, Abrams, and Bloom were setting the scene for the field. Many observers of work being done in our period since 1975, however, have said that the case is otherwise. They declare that those times are past, and all their dizzy raptures are no more.

Recent scholarship has moved us far, if perhaps not far enough, beyond the once standard account of the big six. Walter Scott, Anna Barbauld, Joanna Baillie, Robert Burns, Thomas Moore, Charlotte Smith, Mary Robinson, and on the later end, Felicia Hemans and John Clare – these and other poets have benefited from the historicist and feminist inquiries since the early 1980s, as have the more familiar and much anthologized poets, who look quite different to us now. The challenge to the previous picture of the age of Romanticism came from several (often overlapping) constituencies in the last quarter of the twentieth century: from feminist criticism, which called attention to the great wealth of women's writing in a period when, after all, female authorship genuinely began to thrive in Britain; from scholars interested in the history of the novel, who rejected the idea that the seven decades from the death of Sterne to the publication of Dickens's *Pickwick* was a wasteland between two fertile eras of British fiction; from cultural studies and new historicism, which attempted to situate writing of the period (including poetry) in relation to various sorts of discursive and social frames of reference; from postcolonial criticism, which turned attention to writing in Scotland, Ireland, and elsewhere in the former Empire in an effort to integrate it more fully into the study of "English." These developments are well enough known in the critical literature and need not be rehearsed here.

Suffice it to say that, if we have been accustomed to reading Romantic poetry in light of its formal and generic features, or through the biographies of particular Romantic poets, lines of inheritance, affiliated communities (e.g., the Lake School, the "Cult of the South"), and various ideologies, we can now see that cultural nationalism might offer equally productive contexts for reading, say, Robert Burns's *Songs*, or Walter Scott's *Minstrelsy of the Scottish Border*, or his *Lay of the Last Minstrel*, or Thomas Moore's *Irish Melodies*, or Felicia Hemans's *Welsh Airs*. This Companion hopes to raise, if it cannot fully answer, the question of what is "British" about "British Romantic Poetry" – or more accurately, to address how "Britishness" itself recurs as a problem and a concern for poets. Scholarship in four-nations historicism allows us to see how poetry both assisted in the imagining of

"Britain" but also resisted her hegemony, carving out poetic territories in "Scottish ballads," "Irish melodies," "Welsh airs."

And further, the discovery of a long and deep history of "English" verse in the mid-eighteenth century (thanks to the efforts of Thomas Percy and Thomas Warton, among others) had enormous implications for the diversifying of Romantic versification; so too the excavation of other national poetic pasts (e.g., Macpherson's Ossian, Jones's Welsh bards, Irish antiquarians' even more vexed efforts) complicates our sense of what a *British* Romanticism in verse might be (as in the vexed case of Burns, or "dialect" poetry as a category). In addition to, or entwined with, a poetry-of-consciousness, of reflexive subjectivity, Romantic poetry emerges as a project of cultural inquiry, national fantasy, and sociopolitical critique as much as a poetry of self and nature: ethnopoetics meets psychology in this period in ways that still shape our own.

It is fair to say that, had this Companion been published a decade ago, in the late 1990s, the claims for the distinctiveness of a Companion on "Romantic Poetry" (much less a "British Romantic Poetry") would perhaps have been less evident. But over the course of the last decade – after the challenges from various quarters, after the expansion of the canon for this period, after efforts to displace "poetry" from its long-standing centrality to Romanticism, after some renewed questioning of the very concept of Romanticism itself – there have been a number of efforts to return to poetry and poetics in the period. These efforts have gone by various names: the new formalism, Adorno, the Frankfurt School, the new poetics. And they are still in some cases incipient gestures. Nonetheless, they suggest something on the horizon that, though not yet quite distinct, may move us in a new direction over the coming decades. What that direction might be is not easy to say, but, as a very rough stab at the problem, we speculate that poetry may reassert itself within Romanticism in either of two ways: either as a principle of indeterminate form or in multiple relation to other domains. We may think of this as the difference between "poetry as . . ." and "poetry and . . ."

Such a distinction perhaps informs Wordsworth's twofold wish in the sestet of the famous sonnet that celebrated its bicentennial in 2007: "The World is Too Much With Us":

> Great God! I'd rather be
> A Pagan suckled in a creed outworn;
> So might I, standing on this pleasant lea,
> Have glimpses that would make me less forlorn;
> Have sight of Proteus rising from the sea;
> Or hear old Triton blow his wreathed horn.

This is Wordsworth in what might be described as a quintessentially Romantic moment, catching himself in the act of wishing himself out of enlightenment, into re-enchantment, but just by virtue of having to wish it so, he acknowledges that the customary creed of the ancients cannot simply be put on again as if nothing had happened since. The creed is acknowledged as "outworn." But how interesting that he frames his wish to reinhabit this creed in terms of alternative siblings. These are two of the sons of Poseidon, god of the sea that, in this poem, seems to the poet standing on the lea to "bare . . . her bosom to the moon." Proteus, or "first born," is Poseidon's eldest son, but he is illegitimate. Triton is Poseidon's only legitimate son. Proteus responds to the world by assuming innumerable forms, thus remaining elusive to capture. He is the principle of poetry that Keats enshrined in the idea of the "camelion poet," the artist who enacts in his person the mimesis by which his art is constituted. Triton, by contrast, plays the world on his famous instrument.

The two sons of Poseidon suggest the double-sidedness of *poiesis*, a duality the Romantics compulsively explored. Able to inhabit any form, Proteus, we might say, embodies Shelley's polemically elastic conception of poetry as any great imaginative achievement, any triumph of *poiesis* as *making* (see his invocation of Plato's philosophy, the Roman Senate, the doctrines of Jesus, Bacon's science, and Dante's *Commedia*, all "poetry" in his 1821 *Defence*); whereas Triton, committed to his one powerful instrument, figures what Shelley called (in that same essay) "poetry in a more restricted sense," that is, metrical language.[5]

Poetry, in other words, retains its central role in the Romantic era because, in that age as perhaps in no other before or since, poetry came to mean (potentially) many different things and because it established itself in relation to so many different things. Poetry As (for example) Knowledge, Imagination, Truth, the Esemplastic Power; Poetry And (for example) Science, Philosophy, Religion, The Novel, Politics. The essays in this volume explore what we are provisionally calling the "Protean" and the "Tritonian" aspects of poetry. Many essays here follow the Romantics themselves by troubling the border between "poetry as" and "poetry and." Our contributors situate Romantic poetry in various matrices, contexts, and relations: *viz.* Nick Groom's exploration of poetry and antiquity; Susan Stewart on poetry and meter and form; Andrew Elfenbein on poetry and the standardization of English; Ann Rowland on poetry and the novel; Adriana Craciun on poetry and gender and sexuality; Tim Fulford on poetry and empire; Kevis Goodman on poetry and the science of nostalgia. Contributors also offer inquiries into poetry *as* a transformative and transformable power: poetry as a pantheon, in Jeffrey Cox's essay; as cognition, in Simon Jarvis's; as lyric inquiry into progress, in

James Chandler's; as a mode of resistance, in William Keach's account; as media, in Celeste Langan and Maureen McLane's; as an inheritance and a spur, in Andrew Bennett's essay.

Such lists, organized under an unstable opposition, cannot but grossly simplify the terms of the essays that follow, all of which are alive to the peculiar, multiple claims of poetries in this period. Wordsworth's Immortality Ode (as Chandler suggests) offers a movement unto itself that also gestures beyond itself. This doubleness – poetry-in-itself *v.* poetry-for-itself and -beyond-itself – is written into Romantic aspiration and into the essays here gathered. As Rowland observes, poetry and its ascendant lyric logic penetrated the novel so deeply that certain passages in fiction might be seen as poetry by other means (which in turn suggests to us one way to define all of Walter Scott's novels: balladry by other means); and certainly *Don Juan* has long been read as poetry's novelistic riposte to the novel. So too Nick Groom's discussion of poetry and antiquities reminds us that this period spawned all manner of poetic antiquities – works created to be or recovered as antiquities. Poetry *as* a vernacular antiquity: Scott's *Minstrelsy of the Scottish Border* (1802–3) as well as Chatterton's Rowley poems or Macpherson's Ossian poems. Indeed, the latter work reminds us that poetry could appear in this period *as prose*: a truly Protean transformation.

That the power of Romantic poetry is far from being "outworn" is evident in the electrified lines of influence we continue to find animating twenty-first-century poetry, politics, and media. It is no accident that one of the most lucid poets associated with Language Writing in the USA, Bob Perelman, opens his *Selected Poems* with a sly, witty "Fake Dream" starring Wordsworth:

> January 28: We were going to
> have sex in the stacks. We
>
> were in the 800s, standing eagerly
> amid the old copies of the
>
> Romantics. Looking at the dark blue
> spines of Wordsworth's *Collected*, I thought
>
> how the intensity of his need
> to express his unplaced social being
>
> in sentences had produced publicly verifiable
> beauty so that his subsequent civic
>
> aspirations seemed to have importance enough
> for him to become Poet Laureate . . .[6]

Poetry and critique, poetry as critique: Perelman revives Wordsworth in his full *avant-garde* and regressive dimensions, in a language and line as virtually transparent as the "real language of men." This complex critical engagement with Wordsworth (and with other Romantics) surfaces elsewhere in Perelman's volume, including a poem whose title takes wing from that famous phrase in Wordsworth's 1800 *Preface* to *Lyrical Ballads*: "The Real Language of Men." In the library, in dreams, in life, one discovers not only "the old copies of / the Romantics" but also that one might in fact *be* another copy of those old Romantics. Perelman reminds us, moreover, that any poet, however experimental, may end up filed in obsolete cataloguing systems – the Dewey Decimal system, for example – or slotted within those contingent taxonomic orders that produce pantheons and canons and indeed companions.

We believe, with many other readers, that the Romantics, their poems, and their diverse projects continue to be companionable: as Allen Ginsberg found inspiration in Blake's sunflower; as Seamus Heaney and Lisa Robertson differently plow Wordsworthian fields; as John Ashbery finds in John Clare an "other tradition"; as Geoffrey Hill finds Wordsworth's "Immortality Ode" an ongoing resource; as Paul Muldoon sends "90 Instant Messages to Tom Moore"; as Brian Kim Stefans reworks Blake's proverbs in *The Marriage of Heaven and Hell* into a species of digital-poetic "fashionable noise"; as Walter Scott moves to the multiplex.[7] It is no accident that Tom Leonard turned to Shelley when musing on "100 Differences Between Poetry and Prose": "poets are the unacknowledged thingwaybobs."[8] Leonard's poem illuminates the persistence of Romantic vexations as part of its social critique of the status of poetry (poetry *v.* prose, Shelley's "unacknowledged legislators" degraded). When Adrienne Rich gave a speech accepting the 2006 National Book Foundation Medal for Distinguished Contribution to American Letters, she launched her impassioned defense of poetry by quoting Shelley's *Defence of Poetry* as well as his *Philosophical View of Reform* and the "Ode to the West Wind." "Poetries are no more pure and simple than human histories are pure and simple," Rich observed. "And there are colonised poetics and resilient poetics, transmissions across frontiers not easily traced."[9] The essays here assembled hope to suggest the impure, complex riches of British Romantic poetry, and to offer usable maps and signposts as readers venture into territories and across frontiers both familiar and lesser known: for Romantic poetry, however deeply rooted in its historical and cultural moment, also remains "ever more about to be," in Wordsworth's phrase – ever ready to be reactivated and reimagined by the latest reader.

NOTES

1 Samuel Taylor Coleridge, *Complete Poetical Works*, ed. E. H. Coleridge, 2 vols. (Oxford: Oxford University Press, 1963), vol. 1, p. 240.

2 Percy Bysshe Shelley, "A Defence of Poetry," in *Shelley's Poetry and Prose*, ed. Donald H. Reiman and Neil Fraistat (New York: W. W. Norton, 2002), p. 508.

3 See Theodor W. Adorno, "Nations," in *Introduction to the Sociology of Music*, trans. E. B. Ashton (New York: Continuum, 1989), pp. 159–60.

4 See Rachel Donadio, "Profile: The Closest Reader," *The New York Times Sunday Book Review* (December 10, 2006), http://query.nytimes.com/gst/fullpage.html?res=9505E0D6113EF933A25751C1A9609C8B63, accessed June 27, 2007.

5 Shelley, *A Defence of Poetry*, p. 483.

6 Bob Perelman, "Fake Dream: The Library," in *Ten to One: Selected Poems* (Hanover, NH, and London: Wesleyan University Press, 1999), p. xiv.

7 See, e.g., Lisa Robertson's debt to *The Prelude* in *The Weather* (Vancouver: New Star Books, 2001); John Ashbery, *Other Traditions* (Cambridge, MA: Harvard University Press, 2000); Paul Muldoon, "Ninety Instant Messages to Tom Moore," in *Horse Latitudes* (New York: Farrar Straus, 2006); Brian Kim Stefans, *Fashionable Noise on Digital Poetics* (Berkeley, CA: Atelos, 2003).

8 In *Other: British and Irish Poetry since 1970*, ed. Richard Caddel and Peter Quartermain (Wesleyan University Press, 1999), 129.

9 Adrienne Rich, "Legislators of the World," *Guardian*, Saturday, 18 November 2006, file:///articles%20of%20interest%20poetry/Adrienne%20Rich%20on%20Poetry.html, accessed June 27, 2007.

I

JEFFREY N. COX

The living pantheon of poets in 1820: pantheon or canon?

As recently as the early 1980s, the definition of Romantic poetry would have been fairly clear and mostly non-controversial. Students explored Romanticism through the work of six major poets – Blake, Wordsworth, Coleridge, Byron, Shelley, and Keats – with primary attention being given to their lyric poetry or to the lyric qualities of their attempts at, say, epic. Yet a Romanticism defined by the "Big Six" male writers is very much a mid-twentieth-century creation contrasted with, for example, Thomas Humphry Ward's *English Poets* of 1880, which included the favored six (Blake, largely invisible during the Romantic period, had been recovered by his Victorian admirers) alongside "secondary" Romantic poets such as Thomas Love Peacock, "Barry Cornwall," and Leigh Hunt, popular writers of the period such as Sir Walter Scott, Thomas Moore, and Samuel Rogers, and women poets such as Anna Laetitia Barbauld, Joanna Baillie, and Felicia Hemans; George Benjamin Woods's 1916 *English Poetry and Prose of the Romantic Period* (still being reprinted in 1950) has a similar gathering of poets. Ernest Bernbaum's 1949 edition of his *Guide Through the Romantic Movement* continued to recognize sixteen major Romantic writers, though they are all male; but the path being taken by scholarship on Romanticism was signaled in the 1950 MLA publication *The English Romantic Poets: A Review of Research*, which included only five male poets, with Blake's absence corrected in later versions of this work. The most important anthology of the 1970s and 1980s, David Perkins's *English Romantic Writers* (1967), gives almost all of its pages to the core group, though it does sample other male poets.

Almost as soon as this consensus was achieved, it was challenged by developments within literary theory and by an expanded sense of the literary itself that has arisen through the reintroduction of the writing of women, people of color, the "lower" orders, and others who had seemed to vanish from literary history. As such writers have entered the classroom, as perhaps best seen in Anne K. Mellor and Richard E. Matlak's *British Literature*

1780–1830 (1996), we have in turn lost sight of the "minor," popular male British writers of the day.[1]

Our focus on a group of writers whom we have united under the banner of "Romanticism" – whether it involves only a few male poets or a broader gathering including women – can seem odd to those interested in other eras. While most periods are named for relatively neutral language features (Anglo-Saxon), rulers (Elizabeth or Victoria), or temporal aspects (modern or postmodern), the Romantic period is named for a particular trend in poetry, retrospectively applied. It is as if we would call the period of early modern English literature "metaphysical," using Dr. Johnson's later term for a particular group of poets to define all the work of that era. While we now conceive of the poetry between roughly 1789 and 1832 as part of a unified "Romanticism," at the time the poets we identify with Romanticism were grouped in a series of often opposing schools: for example, the Bluestocking circle of artistic and intellectual women who gathered in the second half of the eighteenth century; the Della Cruscans, who followed their leader Robert Merry in offering highly wrought and politically controversial poetry; the Lake School of Wordsworth, Coleridge, and Southey; the Cockney School of London intellectuals and artists, including Keats, Shelley, and Hazlitt, that centered on Leigh Hunt; or the Satanic School, Southey's derogatory name for the partnership of Byron and Shelley. Of course, Blake, so central to our sense of Romanticism now, stood apart not only from these schools but from the literary scene as a whole, though his engagement with the literature of the day is seen, for example, in his responses to Wordsworth and Byron. Not that "Romanticism" should be discarded as a period term: it describes a body of experimental work in the late eighteenth and early nineteenth centuries that points to larger trends in poetry beyond its confines. "Romanticism" enables us to gather together a group of poets who responded to a common moment of massive cultural, social, and political change with varying attempts to remake poetry and re-vision their world. As poetic innovators seeking to remake the world through their art, they both opened up the forms of poetry – think of Wordsworth's exploration of "lyrical ballads," Blake's turn to fourteeners or his dissent from the very means of literary production, the work on the sonnet of Charlotte Smith, Wordsworth, and Keats, or Hunt's assault upon the heroic couplet that would influence Shelley and Keats – and opened poetry upon the world, as they sought an art that could, like Keats's god of poetry, Apollo, in "Hyperion," "die into life," that is, leave behind the confines of art to build or remake the human community. While Wordsworth and Blake, Scott and Shelley, Byron and Hemans engaged in different kinds of aesthetic experiments for differing purposes, they all sought to make poetry new in ways that both impressed and puzzled their contemporaries and that continue to intrigue us. Of course, the presence of distinctly experimental verse points to the fact that much poetry in the period followed more conventional models or perhaps turned to roads not taken in the development of British literature. What we must remember is that the poetic field at the time was much larger than any canon we have yet assembled, and that Romanticism, while grounded in the work of the period and descriptive of its most challenging verse, is our creation, so that period labels such as "Laker" or "Cockney" serve to define fault lines within Romanticism even as we seek to separate the "Romantic" from other kinds of writing of the day.

Stuart Curran has called 1820 "the highwater mark for verse in the Romantic period,"[2] and indeed, with the publication of distinctive volumes by Shelley, Keats, Wordsworth, and Hemans, it is perhaps as key to our sense of Romanticism in its closing years as is 1798, with its publication of *Lyrical Ballads*, to our conception of the initial phase of Romantic poetry. The year 1820 also provides a point of entry into the story of the construction of Romanticism, as we can see how a quite broad field of varying kinds of poetry came to be defined by the work of a few favored writers, not necessarily recognized as central at the time or as members of a coherent movement, with this narrowing being corrected only in part when recently, the canon of the "Big Six" has been expanded to include other writers active in 1820, particularly women. As we turn to 1820's "pantheon of living poets," we should be alive to those poets who mattered to those living in 1820, to those poets who continue to live for readers and writers today, and simply to those poets who lived and wrote at the time. The term "pantheon," taken from a temple to all the gods in Rome, was most often used in the period to refer to encyclopedic accounts of the Greek and Roman (or Hindu, Chinese, or Egyptian) gods or to buildings modeled on the Pantheon, such as a place of entertainment with that name in London, or the Panthéon in Paris, which, with its memorials to the recently dead heroes of the Revolution, provides a model of a gathering of illustrious contemporaries. This attempt to reconstruct a poetic pantheon frames writing in a way different than efforts to define either a limited or an expanded canon, for a "heathen" pantheon, unlike a "sacred" canon, seeks to include all the "gods" of poetry, no matter how minor, how disparate, how heterodox.

England (and its poetry) in 1820

The year 1820 is not a "hot" date. It is not 1789, which opened the revolutionary era, or 1815, with Napoleon's return for the Hundred Days and Waterloo, or 1819, when widespread discontent and demands for Reform issued in the Peterloo Massacre. George III's long reign and the decade-long Regency did come to an end in 1820, but when Shelley's "old, mad, blind, despised and dying king" finally died, he was followed by George IV, one of the "Princes, the dregs of their dull race, who flow / Through public scorn, – mud from a muddy spring."[3] Upon taking the throne, the new George tried to divorce his old wife, sparking public outrage, street demonstrations, and an unprecedented pamphlet war; but widespread protest produced no change in the government, but instead marked the end of one era of radical resistance, with 1820's failed Cato Street Conspiracy to assassinate the whole cabinet turning many against Reform as violent resistance was used to justify the repressive policies that provoked the resistance in the first place. If 1819 seemed to open England to change, 1820 – which might have appeared, with a new king, a moment of transition – instead saw the confirmation of the powers that be.

We would not, then, expect 1820 to be immortalized as the prior year was in Shelley's "England in 1819," or as the Regency's opening in 1811, marked by economic distress giving rise to Luddite resistance and key events in the war with Napoleon, was immortalized in Anna Laetitia Barbauld's *Eighteen Hundred and Eleven.* Yet there did appear in London during 1821 *Eighteen Hundred and Twenty: A Poem*, probably by Alexander Hill Everett, an American diplomat then serving in The Hague, whose career, leading him to Spain, Cuba, and China, reminds us of that era's globalization, brought on by imperial efforts and the Napoleonic world war. Mixing an odal appeal to Spain's liberal revolution (which Shelley also celebrated in his 1820 "Ode to Liberty") with a couplet satire on the post-Napoleonic Restoration, the poem lampoons ultra-legitimatist monarchs, in part by suggesting that they see all the tribulations of their day arising from two early modern figures – Luther, identified with freedom of religious thought, who "from his desk at Wittenberg unfurled / The standard of revolt o'er half the world," and Faust, who

> with still deeper and more dangerous skill,
> Serving the purpose of the power of ill,
> Brought from the lower region's last recess
> That fatal engine of all our woe – the press.
>
> (pp. 26–7)

The devilish printing press is seen as inundating the world with uncontrolled information, a "flood of heresy and knowledge," so that "Knowledge – the apple with our ruin fraught, / Is now the cheapest fruit that can be bought" (p. 27). While here the main concern seems to be the journalistic pursuit of religious and political controversy, Coleridge had earlier lamented in the *Biographia Literaria*: "alas! the multitude of books, and the general diffusion of literature,"[4] and Z., the scourge of Hunt's Cockney School, attacked in *Blackwood's Edinburgh Magazine* the proliferation of poetry as a cultural disease, a "Metromanie" leading to an overproduction of books by "footmen" and every "superannuated governess in the island" (3 [August 1818], p. 519).[5] In 1820, as throughout the period, there is alarm over the sheer volume of material entering into print, and a deeper worry over who controls that material and, in particular, the cultural capital of verse. To understand 1820's literary scene, we must recognize first the quantity of verse being produced and then the fierce debate under way about the status of poetry, a debate that begins to narrow the pantheon of a multitude of books into a canon of authorized authors.

The reading nation and the writerly nation in 1820

During the period between 1770 and 1835, there were more than 4,000 writers producing poetry, of whom about 900 were women, as J. R. de Jackson's bibliographies have suggested.[6] 1820 saw the publication of around 200 new volumes or editions of poetry (57 by women), hardly any of which would be familiar to scholars today. Since the canon of Romantic verse has been smaller than that in other periods, there is something illustrative in simply listing the diversity of verse in 1820, even at the risk of appearing "metromaniacal"; the list, gesturing towards the encyclopedic, is a feature of the pantheon.

We have identified Romanticism's innovations with the lyric, but in 1820, narrative verse appeared the stronger genre, with Keats, for example, naming his new volume *Lamia, Isabella, The Eve of St. Agnes and Other Poems*, George Croly issuing *The Angel of the World; an Arabian Tale: Sebastian; a Spanish Tale: With Other Poems*, and "Barry Cornwall" (the pseudonym of Hunt and Keats's friend Bryan Waller Procter) offering *Marcian Colonna, An Italian Tale with Three Dramatic Scenes and Other Poems*. Even Wordsworth, whose *Lyrical Ballads* of 1798 proclaimed the desire to use the lyric to contest the popularity of narrative and the novelization of verse, published his *Peter Bell* (1819), originally written in 1798, not as a lyrical ballad but as a "tale." There were still works labeled as ballads, such as Robert Roscoe's *Chevy Chase: A Poem Founded on the Ancient Ballad*, but the term is also attached to pieces taken from plays, such as *Pity's Tear*, excerpted from Thomas Morton's *Henri Quatre; or, Paris in the Olden Times*, as well as to satires such as William Hone and George Cruikshank's *The Green Bag: "A dainty dish to set before a king;" A Ballad of the Nineteenth Century*, with such titles again suggesting the range of non-lyric verse. About 10 percent of new poetry volumes in 1820 were verse dramas, as devotees of the armchair theater could enjoy T. F. Barham's *Abdallah; or, the Arabian Martyr* or Henry Hart Milman's *The Fall of Jerusalem* in addition to Shelley's *Prometheus Unbound*.[7] With at least fifty-seven volumes of satiric verse issued in 1820 (including Wooler's *The Kettle Abusing the Pot*, Benbow's *Kouli Khan*, and an adaptation of Juvenal's seventh satire called *Patronage*), political satire, a genre only recently reclaimed for Romanticism, comprised the largest body of new verse published during a year marked by George IV's struggle with his wife that came to be known as the Queen Caroline Affair, a dispute to which Shelley added his *Oedipus Tyrannus; or, Swellfoot the Tyrant*. While Shelley's text would be withdrawn, the most popular volume of poetry in 1820, going through at least twenty-five editions, was certainly *The Man in the Moon* by the period's great satirist, William Hone.[8]

There was, as throughout the period, a fair sampling of religious poetry (e.g., Paul Thackwell's *Collection of Miscellaneous and Religious Poems* or R. Willoughby's *The Plaintive Muse, or Poems Sacred to Religion*), an important context for even the secularizing projects of a Hunt or a Shelley, and a sizeable gathering of juvenile verse, including *Poems for Youth*, a collaborative volume created by William Roscoe's family circle. Translation comprises another important block of verse in 1820, with Hunt's adaptation of Tasso's *Amyntas* reflecting an engagement with foreign literatures also seen in Bowring's *Specimens of the Russian Poets*, and translations of Goethe's *Faust*, Foscolo's *Sepulchres*, and Grillparzer's *Sappho*. Readers could experience a wide range of poetic forms: odes ranging from the celebratory (e.g., *A Pindaric Ode to the Genius of Britain* by Charles Ethelston) to the satiric (e.g. *Odes to the Pillory*); elegiac verses such as Margaret Sarah Croker's *Monody on His Late Royal Highness the Duke of Kent* and elegies on the death of George III by Hemans and Mary Cockle (Shelley would publish his elegy on Keats, *Adonais*, in 1821); epistolary poems (e.g., Joseph Cottle's *An Expostulary Epistle to Lord Byron* or John Wing's *Waterloo: A Poetical Epistle to Mr. Sergeant Frere*); and didactic works such as Elizabeth Hitchener's *Enigmas, Historical and Geographical* and the *Abridged History of the Bible, in Verse* by Sarah Richardson; as well as such volumes as *Comic Tales in Verse* (by "The Two Franks"), *Cottage Poems* (William Wight), *Hebrew Harmonies and Analogies* (William Coldwell), *Lines Written at Jerpoint Abbey* (Samuel Carter Hall), *Sacred Lyrics* (James Edmeston), and *Types of the Times* (Old Tom of Oxford), not to mention *Sultan Sham, and His Seven Wives: An Historical, Romantic, Heroic Poem in Three Cantos* by Hudibras the Younger.

Where do writers such as Wordsworth and Keats figure in this outpouring of verse? In defining what he calls the "reading nation,"[9] William

St. Clair has argued that during, say, Wordsworth's lifetime there was as yet no canon of Romantic poetry, as copyright law meant that access to works by living poets, initially printed in small numbers, was quite restricted. He does note that there was a canon of contemporary writers recognized for their literary merit – Byron, Campbell, Coleridge, Moore, Rogers, Scott, Southey, and Wordsworth – but he goes on to argue that only a few of these (most importantly, Scott and Byron) had a broad readership, and that this canon of prestige does not include such successful contemporary writers as the "peasant poet" Robert Bloomfield (two of his volumes were reprinted in 1820) and James Montgomery, a popular writer of hymns and author of such works as *The Wanderer of Switzerland and other Poems* (1806) and *Greenland* (1819), who had a three-volume edition of his works printed in 1820. While recognizing that there was a contemporary category of "living poets," St. Clair points to the centrality of an "old canon" of major poets from Chaucer to Cowper that, he argues, continued to dominate the reading of most of the populace; and 1820, for example, does see editions of Cowper, Gray, Goldsmith, and Gay from St. Clair's "old canon." Continued interest in that even older canon, the Greek and Latin classics, is seen in 1820 editions of Homer, Virgil, Horace, Aristophanes, and Anacreon.

St. Clair usefully reminds us of the larger world of poetry in 1820, comprising earlier writers, new "Romantic" writers, and other established, rising, or unsuccessful writers who stood opposed to Romanticism or simply apart from it. When readers took up a new volume by Wordsworth or Keats, they read it both alongside earlier writers, so that they might contrast Wordsworth with Pope or compare Keats to Spenser, and against contemporary rivals, so that they might ask whether Wordsworth offered the same pleasures as Bloomfield, the "Farmer Boy," or whether Keats's "The Eve of St. Agnes" could compete with Montgomery's "The Vigil of St. Mark" (1806). Even when we focus on innovative poetry, we need to recall that, of the "Big Six," only Byron was a bestselling author and that Scott, Campbell, Hemans, Rogers, and Moore would have had a stronger influence on what most readers considered to be "new" poetry than did Shelley or Coleridge. While our sense of Romanticism may follow a line of experimentation in the lyric that leads centrally from Wordsworth through Keats, at the time readers might have focused more on the development of narrative poetry from the widely read Scott, whose massive importance has come to be recognized in recent years,[10] to the popular Byron.

Still, there was a different kind of canon formed by what we might call the "writerly nation," composed not only of writers themselves but also of reviewers and others actively engaged in commenting on the writing of the day in, for example, letters, journals, and home-made miscellanies such as the Reynolds-Hood commonplace book.[11] Poets themselves indicated their engagement with contemporary poetry through direct or indirect imitation, opposition, and celebration. Byron had made a number of conspicuous dedications of his work to other contemporary poets – *The Giaour* to Rogers, and *The Corsair* to Moore – and in 1820 we find Shelley dedicating *The Cenci* to Hunt, and Hunt dedicating his *Amyntas* to Keats. Byron used a quotation from Moore for his epigraph to *The Giaour*, and, looking to 1820, we find others following suit. "Barry Cornwall" provided epigraphs for the three parts of his *Marcian Colonna*, Byron (*Lament of Tasso*, 1817) supplying the epigraph to the first part, Coleridge (*Sibylline Leaves* of 1817) and John Wilson (*Isle of Palms*, a Lake-Poet-influenced volume of 1812) supplying that to the second, and Wordsworth ("Vaudracour and Julia" just published in 1820 with *The River Duddon Sonnets*) supplying that to the third. Again, Jeremiah Holmes Wiffen included in his *Julia Alpinula; with The Captive of Stamboul and Other Poems* not only references again to Byron and Wordsworth but also a quotation from Cornwall's own *Marcian Colonna* published just a few months earlier. Shelley provided "Ode to Liberty," published with *Prometheus Unbound*, with an epigraph from Byron's *Childe Harold IV*; and John Abraham Heraud issued his *Legend of St. Loy With Other Poems* which included a sonnet praising Southey and which opened with "On First Reading the Remains of Henry Kirke White, 9th April 1819," celebrating Southey's edition of White, who had died in 1806. Even satires on contemporary poems are signs of their significance, as in Reynolds's and Shelley's parodies of Wordsworth's *Peter Bell*, where Wordsworth's delayed publication of what had originally been a lyrical ballad is now read as a betrayal of the poet's earlier experimental promise and as an embrace of the powers of political and religious reaction; and we might also note responses to Moore such as *The Fudger Fudged; or the Devil and T***Y M***E* (1819) and such take-offs of Byron as Lady Caroline Lamb's *A New Canto* (1819) or *Despair, A Vision. Derry Down and John Bull, A Simile. Being Two Political Parodies on "Darkness," and a Scene from "The Giaour," by Lord Byron* (1820). Celebrations and attacks begin to define what poets found innovative and disturbing in the work of their contemporaries.

We should also note the attention paid by reviewers to volumes of new verse. Shelley and Keats may not have sold many copies, but their poetry was reviewed – and thus excerpted – rather widely: one could, for example, read the entirety of "Ode to a Nightingale" in Hunt's *Indicator*. Keats's three volumes received at least eight, fifteen, and fourteen reviews respectively, and those reviews, positive and negative, appeared in key journals such as *The Monthly Magazine*, the *Quarterly Review*, *The Edinburgh Review*, the *Eclectic Review*, the *Examiner*, *Blackwood's Edinburgh Magazine*, and *The*

London Magazine. Other contemporary writers, in particular Byron, received broader exposure. While the *Quarterly Review* opposed the work of Shelley and Keats and while *Blackwood's* in part established itself through its Cockney School attacks, other journals clearly sided with innovative poetry, with Hunt's *Examiner* and *Indicator* both publishing and reviewing members of the Lake and Cockney schools, and John Scott's *London Magazine* in its first few issues setting forth its support of Wordsworth, Keats, Shelley, and Clare. While the circulation figures for Hunt's weekly *Examiner* (3,000–7,000) and *The London Magazine* (2,000) were not as high as the reactionary *Quarterly Review* (12,000–14,000) or *The Edinburgh Review* (12,000–13,000), with its mixed response to experimental poetry, they had considerable influence among the Reform-minded intelligentsia, and they were important enough to provoke vitriolic responses from conservative periodicals. The intensity of these reviews, pro and con, suggests how much was at stake for the "writerly nation" in these volumes of experimental verse. The new poetry was thus known, if only through the vicious attacks that were directed at it. It is this canon of what we call Romanticism which in the long run comes to dominate our sense of the period, for the institutionalization of the period through such mechanisms as school curricula and anthologies is finally structured by members of this "writerly nation."[12]

Certainly the most famous volumes of 1820 today are Keats's *Lamia, Isabella, The Eve of St. Agnes, and Other Poems*, and Shelley's *Prometheus Unbound: A Lyrical Drama in Four Acts, with Other Poems*. In retrospect, it was a significant year for the poets who have come to define Romanticism for us. Following the scandal and success of *Peter Bell* in 1819, Wordsworth not only issued a well-received new volume in 1820 (*The River Duddon, A Series of Sonnets: Vaudracour and Julia and Other Poems. To Which is Annexed, A Topographical Description of the Country of the Lakes, In the North of England*), but also prepared various volumes that presented his corpus anew to the public: a repackaging of the *River Duddon* volume to create volume III of Wordsworth's *Poems*, a second edition of *The Excursion* set uniformly with these three volumes, and a separate four-volume *Miscellaneous Poems of William Wordsworth*, not to mention an unauthorized reprinting of *Lyrical Ballads*, made up of sheets from the second volume of the 1800 and 1805 editions. Wordsworth was clearly reaching a larger audience. *Peter Bell* marked a turning point, with 1,000 copies (rather than the usual 500 for Wordsworth) being issued and with 700 being sold within about a month. *The River Duddon* sold 340 of its 500 copies in a month, and the four-volume *Miscellaneous Poems* was sold out by 1826. Where about half the run of 500 copies for the 1814 *Excursion* had sold within a year, with some copies still being remaindered in 1834, the 1820 edition sold out by 1824.[13] Stephen

Gill sees this work as marking an end to one phase in Wordsworth's life as a poet, with the *Ecclesiastical Sketches* begun shortly thereafter marking a new beginning;[14] in any event, it was a new opportunity for Wordsworth to construct himself as a poet, and, since there was a thirteen-year silence after 1822, this burst of activity in essence defined Wordsworth as he came to be widely recognized as the future Poet Laureate.[15]

While other poets may not have had the year Wordsworth did (though Crabbe, whose most popular volume, *Tales of the Hall*, was printed in 1819, saw new editions of *The Borough* [1810] and *Poems*, as well as a seven-volume edition of his poetical works), 1820 did see significant activity by writers who remain familiar. The year that saw Keats's last volume saw John Clare's first, as he issued *Poems Descriptive of Rural Life and Scenery*. Shelley produced three volumes, all reflecting his varied engagement with the drama. Hunt's translation of Tasso's *Amyntas* was one of several works sent forth by the Cockney School, with "Barry Cornwall" publishing two volumes, *Marcian Colonna* and *A Sicilian Story, with Diego de Montilla, and Other Poems*, John Hamilton Reynolds following up the success of his parody of *Peter Bell* with *The Fancy: A Selection of the Poetical Remains of the Late Peter Corcoran, Of Grey's Inn, Student At Law. With a Brief Memoir of His Life*, and Cornelius Webb, a minor but infamous member of the circle cited in *Blackwood's* attacks upon the group, issuing *Sonnets, Amatory, Incidental, & Descriptive; with Other Poems*. More established poets were well represented: there were three editions of the opening cantos of Byron's *Don Juan*, a twelve-volume edition of Sir Walter Scott's poetical works, an edition of the works of Burns along with new editions of four other pieces, and two pirated editions of Southey's *Wat Tyler*. Hemans's *Stanzas to the Memory of the Late King* was one example of elegiac pieces on the death of George III that would lead to Southey's adulatory *Vision of Judgment* the next year, and to Byron's riposte, which would satirize both the dead king and his Poet Laureate. Different views were also on offer. The "Quaker poet," Bernard Barton, issued *Poems* with lines critical of Shelley, and Walter Savage Landor produced a volume of Latin verse, *Idyllia Heroica Decem*, to which he attached an essay, "De cultu atque usu Latini sermonis," which took up modern poetry and contained criticisms of Byron. We can also see the arrival of writers who would help define future literary developments, with 1820 seeing the first volumes of poetry by Bulwer Lytton (*Ismael; An Oriental Tale. With Other Poems*) and Elizabeth Barrett (*The Battle of Marathon. A Poem*, with an epigraph from Byron) and with Laetitia Landon first achieving fame with the publication of her poem "Rome" in William Jerdan's *The Literary Gazette* of March 11, 1820. It was then a good year for experimental verse, though, of course, at the time, no one used "Romanticism" to identify the poetry of the day, and no one would have selected any of our Romantic canons as a guide through the complex landscape of contemporary literature.

Forging Romanticism in 1820

The preface to Barrett's epic *The Battle of Marathon* returns us to the problem of the explosion of verse, as Barrett writes of how "As the press pours forth profusion, the literary multitude eagerly receive its lavish offerings."[16] Out of this undifferentiated pantheon, what she calls "an inferior multitude of the common herd," Barrett identifies three "real Poets" among her contemporaries: Byron, Moore, and Scott. This little, unremembered act of canon formation and of love comes amid other efforts to discover what was truly alive and what would live among the work of the living poets. While most contemporary anthologies featured earlier verse, and while one might uncover other canons being formed in discussions of, say, religious poetry or "working-class" verse,[17] we can already see various moves to celebrate the poets we find central to Romanticism. These efforts to move from pantheon to canon were deeply contested as canons were formed on the mixed grounds of aesthetics, morality, religion, ideology, and political efficacy – Barrett, for example, not only celebrates "poetic excellence" (p. 3) but hopes to prove "that Poetry is the parent of liberty" (p. 9).

Most anthologies of the day featured not contemporary verse but the "old canon," with Thomas Campbell's massive seven-volume *Specimens of the British Poets* (1819) surveying poetry from Chaucer to Cowper and Beattie, and with others, designed for the schools or the "young" reader, focusing on the established canon, and particularly on works with a religious bent, as in Mant's *The Parent's Poetical Anthology: Being a Selection of English Poems primarily designed to assist in forming the taste and the sentiments of young readers* (1814, 1821). Still, there were various attempts to survey contemporary poetry, including John Pennie's *The Harp of Parnassus* of 1823, which offers Byron, Moore, Scott, Charlotte Smith, Mary Robinson, Campbell, Southey, and "Cornwall"; and George Croly's 1828 *Beauties of the English Poets*, which moves through a historical survey to include Keats and Hemans. We find something like the pantheon of living poets displayed in 1820 in *Beauties of the Modern Poets; Being Selections from the Works of the Most Popular Authors of the Present Day; Including Many Original Pieces, Never Before Published, and An Introductory View of the Modern Temple of Fame*, edited by David Carey. Carey's volume – like most such gatherings looking back to Knox's popular *Elegant Extracts* – offers an eclectic gathering of "Moral and Pathetic Pieces," "Narrative and Descriptive Pieces," "Amatory Pieces," and "Humorous and Amusing Pieces," and includes selections from, among others, Scott, Coleridge, Wordsworth and Southey, Byron and Moore, Rogers, Crabbe, Wilson, and Campbell, Montgomery and Bloomfield, the playwrights Thomas Dibdin, George Colman the Younger, and Sheridan, and most interestingly Joanna Baillie, Helen Maria Williams, and Mrs. Opie (there is also a poem by Ann Cuthbert Knight, from her 1816 *Keep-Sake*, but it is not ascribed to her). There is then an interesting mix of popular writers, experimental writers, women writers, and dramatists, which suggests again the range of work being produced at the time. There are also some largely lost names, such as the interesting polymath and world traveler John Leyden, the Reverend John Mitford, known for his editorial work, and Richard Westall, better known as a painter than as a very minor poet, along with such as yet unidentified figures as Finley and Fitz-Florian. Most poets are represented by one or two poems, with even the incredibly popular satirist "Peter Pindar" (the pseudonym of John Wolcot) receiving only one entry. Coleridge has three poems in the volume; Wordsworth, Southey, Crabbe, Scott, Rogers, and Campbell are represented by four to seven selections each; Moore has twelve; and Byron has the largest selection with sixteen poems or excerpts. Carey samples Byron's corpus, with a poem from his first volume, *Hours of Idleness*, passages from the oriental tales and *Childe Harold*, and excerpts from his new work, *Don Juan*, edited to de-emphasize the erotic and its most biting social and cultural commentary. Wordsworth's full career is also represented, from the 1800 *Lyrical Ballads* through *The White Doe of Rylstone* to *The Waggoner*, published in 1819, though we do not find the Wordsworth poems that most occupy our attention.

This volume gives us an important map of the field of contemporary poetry in 1820 as seen by someone familiar with a wide range of verse. At that moment, Byron was probably the central poet, with Moore, his friend and ally on the left, also commanding a great deal of interest. Standing alongside Byron and Moore in this volume but opposed to them in the culture wars of the day were the "Lake Poets," Wordsworth, Coleridge, and Southey. Montgomery and Bloomfield, identified by St. Clair as readers' favorites, receive less attention than Scott or Crabbe. Campbell and Rogers receive more space than in recent anthologies, in a sense occupying a place that would later be given to the younger, less established poets, Keats and Shelley. Women writers were at the time recognized as contributing to contemporary poetry as they would not be for most of the twentieth century but are again today; dramatists were seen as part of the world of poetry, with again the drama and theatre disappearing from our sense of the period until quite recently.

We can find the growth of a more specifically Romantic canon in works such as Hunt's often reworked *The Feast of the Poets*, as it evolves from its 1811 version, where Hunt creates a canon of contemporary popular poets comprising Campbell, Southey, Scott, and, first among equals, Moore, through the key 1815 edition, where he expands his list to include Byron, Coleridge, and, most prominently, Wordsworth, up through the 1860 version, where we find added Hunt's younger allies Keats, Shelley, and Procter, so that the poem offers an outline of what would come to be known as Romantic poetry. Galignani (a Parisian publishing house founded by an Italian who had spent time in London, indicating again that a cosmopolitan world of piracy and translation is important to the dissemination of the pantheon) offered during the 1820s a kind of library of Romanticism with editions of Scott, of Moore, of Crabbe, of Coleridge, Shelley, and Keats, of Wordsworth, of Southey, of Byron, of Rogers, Campbell, Montgomery, Lamb, and Kirke White, and of Milman, Bowles, Wilson, and "Barry Cornwall." Hazlitt's *Select British Poets, or New Elegant Extracts from Chaucer to the Present Time with Critical Remarks* (1824), created what is the closest thing to a contemporary model of what we think of as Romanticism, though, as Jeffrey Robinson has shown, the collection was reprinted the next year without the living poets, the assumption having been that the suppression of the 1824 volume arose over copyright issues, though Robinson suggests that this "Cockney" anthology "riled some member of the cultural police."[18] Including at first St. Clair's "old canon," Hazlitt's striking move is to gather contemporary writers in what Robinson has argued is a "Cockney" construction of Romanticism which "emphasizes poetic and thematic extravagance, poetic eroticism, and left-wing politics" (p. 243). For the first time we find Hunt, Charles Lamb, "Barry Cornwall," Shelley, and Keats appearing alongside their more established contemporaries such as Wordsworth, Coleridge, Southey, and Scott. While Hunt and Hazlitt, important figures in the "writerly nation" that would over time discover a Romantic movement in the period, may have begun to assemble a Romantic canon, it is important that such a gathering, familiar to us, was unusual enough at the time to lead perhaps to the suppression of Hazlitt's anthology; the "reading nation" was not, apparently, ready for a unified Romanticism. From our perspective, the major gap in Hazlitt's account of contemporary poetry is, as Robinson notes (p. 233), that he includes no poems by women, though some other volumes from the period, such as Carey's, Elizabeth Mant's *Parent's Poetical Anthology* (1814, 1821) and Elizabeth Scott's *Specimens of British Poetry* (1823), do include significant samplings from women writers of the late eighteenth and early nineteenth centuries. The lines between a masculine canon and a pantheon open to both men and women writers were already being drawn, with the gendering of literary production and of literary types occurring, as Margaret Ezell has shown, just at this moment.[19]

As Robinson's designation of Hazlitt's anthology as "Cockney" suggests, demarcations within the poetic field were volatile and at times violently disputed: the Bowles/Pope debate – in which criticism of Pope in *The Invariable Principles of Poetry* (1819) by the poet William Lisle Bowles, whose sonnets had influenced Coleridge, prompted a defense of the older poet by writers such as Byron and Campbell – indicates that even St. Clair's "old canon" was a matter of contention. The belittling names given to schools such as the "Bluestockings" and the "Cockneys" suggest the derision heaped upon experimental poetry. Aesthetically and/or politically conservative commentators within the "writerly nation" expressed deep reservations about the *avant-garde* poetry of the day: from *The Edinburgh Review*'s denigration of the Lakers to *Blackwood's* assault upon the Cockneys or Southey's blasts against Shelley and Byron, a great deal of energy is expended on trying to protect the reading nation, supposedly safely ensconced with Montgomery and Cowper, from this body of new poetry. Francis Hodgson, for example, the sometime friend and sometime critic of Byron, who published in 1820 *Sacred Leisure; or, Poems on Religious Subjects*, had the previous year issued *Sæculomastix; or, The Lash of the Age We Live In; A Poem, in Two Parts.*[20] Hodgson defends most of St. Clair's "old canon," though he identifies the decline of poetry (and religion) as beginning with Cowper (p. 78n.). His target is the work of Southey, Scott, Wordsworth, and Coleridge, all seen as contributing to a decline in style, with only the conservative Henry Hart Milman found to offer contemporary promise. Hodgson also expresses outrage over the religious valence of this poetry; he attacks Southey for allowing in *Thalaba the Destroyer* (1801) "the moral charms of Turks, / To tickle Christian ears" (p. 39), and finds Wordsworth and Coleridge offering a disturbing combination of "Classical learning with Gothic taste" (p. 89n.) and drawing upon Jacob Behme and Kant to create a dangerous pantheism (pp. 43–4). While the growing conservatism of Coleridge and Wordsworth on religious and other issues may have assuaged some critics, the religious threat posed by the Cockney writers was often noted. *The Quarterly Review* (18 [January 1818], p. 327), for example, saw Hunt, Shelley, and their contemporaries working to bring about a "systematic revival of Epicureanis . . . Lucretius is the philosopher whom these men profess most to admire, and their leading tenet is, that the enjoyment of the pleasures of the intellect and sense is . . . the great object, and duty of life". In a similar vein, the *Eclectic Review* (2nd series, 14 [September 1820], p. 169) attacked the mythological poems of Keats, Shelley, and Hunt as engaging in "grossness," as celebrating "the sensitive pleasures which belong to the animal." *Blackwood's* assault upon the religion of Hunt and his circle as "a poor tame dilution of the blasphemies of the *Encyclopædie*" is joined with criticism of their radical politics, seen as "a crude, vague, ineffectual and sour Jacobinism" (2 [October 1817], p. 39). New poetry, then, is found to be dangerous on stylistic, religious, and political grounds. The more general concern about the proliferation of print seems to focus on these purportedly obscure poets.

Opposition marked even the poetic attempts of the experimental poets to define an experimental poetry. Perhaps most famously, Byron in the first canto of *Don Juan* both defends a particular line within the old canon against what he sees as the unfortunate innovations of the Lakers and sets the liberal poets Rogers and Moore against the increasingly conservative Wordsworth, Coleridge, and Southey:

> Thou shalt believe in Milton, Dryden, Pope;
>   Thou shalt not set up Wordsworth, Coleridge, Southey;
> Because the first is crazed beyond all hope,
>   The second drunk, the third so quaint and mouthey:
> . . .
> Thou shalt not steal from Samuel Rogers, nor
> Commit – flirtation with the muse of Moore.
>
> (1.205)[21]

Byron, who elsewhere admits that the Lakers are "poets still" ("Dedication," l. 47), outlines here a liberal Romanticism that others would reject. Wordsworth certainly rejected Byron. In 1820, he called upon Henry Crabbe Robinson to urge the *Quarterly Review* to attack Byron after the publication of *Don Juan*: "What avails it to hunt down Shelley, whom few read, and leave Byron untouched? I am persuaded that Don Juan will do more harm to the English character, than anything of our time."[22] Joseph Cottle, Coleridge and Southey's old comrade, attacks Byron and Moore in his *Expostulatory Epistle to Lord Byron* (1820), a couplet satire on Byron and his "Liberal Don" (l. 110), while praising Southey in particular along with Wordsworth, Coleridge, Scott, Montgomery, Crabbe, Bowles, Rogers, Barton, and Campbell (ll. 162–75). Where we unite Byron and Wordsworth as part of Romanticism, at that moment they were defined as in opposition to one another and as allied with poets beyond the standard Romantic canon.

A more nuanced entry into the debate over the state of current poetry was offered by Felicia Hemans in her 1820 volume *The Sceptic*, a widely reviewed poem (and one often used to lead off later collected volumes of Hemans's poetry), which has been read as a critique of Byron's scepticism, and more broadly of a sceptical line of thinking that ran from Hume and certainly included Shelley.[23] Hemans is difficult to place aesthetically and ideologically (she had allies among Tory writers and critics such as William Gifford, Milman, and Reginald Heber, and was praised in the reactionary *Quarterly Review* of October 1821 by John Taylor Coleridge, but she also worked with Roscoe's Liverpool circle of cosmopolitan liberals), and her work is the site of productive debates about her stands and style; but, however we read her and her poetry, it is important to remember that in 1820 a woman writer could set out through a philosophical poem to define herself in debate and competition with the leading poet of the day. While increasingly the period came to be defined through an opposition between Byron and Wordsworth, in 1820 one might have considered mapping the poetic field along the fault lines between Hemans and Byron. And Byron himself certainly took notice, responding to Hemans's poem in a letter to his publisher John Murray of June 7, 1820,[24] where he also indicates his awareness of his immediate poetic context, commenting on other new work in 1820: William Herbert's *Hedin; or, The Spectre of the Tomb. A Tale. From the Danish History* (also published by Murray), the recent volumes of tales and "dramatic scenes" by "Barry Cornwall," and the translation of the first two cantos of Niccolò Forteguerri's *Ricciardetto*, another Murray product. Again, the contemporary debate over framing what we know as Romanticism occurred within a larger context that included women writers, dramatists, narrative poetry, and translations.

While Hemans points to an alternative construction of the period, the battle lines in 1820 were increasingly between the older poets of Romanticism and their younger contemporaries. We have here, however, less the standard story of two generations of Romanticism, with the "sons" of Wordsworth and his fellow Lakers learning from or struggling with the influence of the founding "fathers" of Romanticism, than a moment of struggle between two different versions of Romanticism, roughly between the Lakers and the Cockneys, though at times the battle seems to narrow to a struggle between Wordsworth and Byron as to who will define the course of modern poetry, an opposition that grew sharper over the decade, as seen in such events as a two-night debate in 1828, organized by John Stuart Mill at the London Debating Society, in which he defended Wordsworth against John Roebuck who championed Byron.[25] While Wordsworth had been a controversial, experimental poet, Hazlitt noted in *The Spirit of the Age* (1825) that "the tide has turned much in his [Wordsworth's] favour of late years. He has a large body of determined partisans,"[26] and by 1833 Bulwer Lytton, in *England and the English*, found Wordsworth's popularity rising at Byron's expense. Romanticism as we know it came into being when it could be identified with a particular (and not Wordsworth's) version of a Wordsworthian poetic, as Byron, the most popular of these writers, becomes increasingly marginal to a standard sense of the Romantic, as Keats and Shelley are recouped as poetic allies of Wordsworth rather than political comrades of Byron and Hunt, and as a masculine line of lyric verse comes to define an age filled with women writers, dramatists, and poetic tales. What occurred within the institutionalization of Romantic poetry was a victory of a Victorian version of a Wordsworthian vision of the period that enabled scholars not only to limit the list of important writers but also to limit the work even by those writers to a lyric encounter between the self and nature. While much good work has been done in reorienting Romanticism around Blake, and while we have seen recent attempts to rethink Romanticism from the position of a Byron or a Shelley or to redefine Romanticism to include the work of women writers, we have yet to arrive at a clear enough sense of how Romanticism arose in opposition not only to old or other modes of poetry but also to itself. As we continue to map the literary field within which Romanticism arose, we need to see that it was indeed a battlefield.

Hypercanonical Keats and the pantheon of living poets

All these long lists and old controversies might seem mere antiquarianism, an attempt to recover a body of work that serves no contemporary interest, aesthetic or otherwise. However, an awareness of the range of poetry available in 1820 can alter our understanding of even the most canonical of Romantic works, for example Keats's 1820 volume, *Lamia, Isabella, The Eve of St. Agnes, and Other Poems*. Placed back in its moment of production, Keats's book announces its connections to a broad range of poetry while staking out Keats's place as an innovator as he adopts a revisionary stance toward the popular tale, the canonically enshrined ode, and the epic, traditionally considered the highest form of poetry.

The poems we care most about in Keats's 1820 volume are the odes (and Shelley's 1820 *Prometheus Unbound* volume, while dominated by a drama, also included a sustained exploration of the ode in poems such as "Ode to Heaven," "Ode to the West Wind," and "Ode to Liberty"). But we might think about these odes differently if we did not place them in a tradition of the philosophical or sublime ode, marked by such masterworks as Wordsworth's Immortality Ode and "Ode to Duty," or Coleridge's "Ode to the Departing Year" and "Dejection: An Ode," but instead thought about them alongside the then better-known odes written for public occasions, such as Byron's "Ode to Napoleon Bonaparte," Wordsworth's Thanksgiving Ode of 1816, and the various odes Southey wrote in his position as Poet Laureate, including his "Ode for St. George's Day," written in 1820, with its celebration of the Hanoverian monarchs, George I to George IV – let alone such other 1820 offerings as "An Ode to Britain," attached to *An Illustration of the Dangerous Consequences Arising from Youth Listening to the Destructive Discourse of Atheists, Deists, and Freethinkers*, and "Ode on the King's Birthday," written on June 4, 1820, from New South Wales, by Michael Massey Robinson, the "First Poet Laureat of Australia," which seeks to "Retrace the Patriot-Chief's Career of Glory!" (l. 118). What have been seen as controversial claims for the political valence of Keats's odes[27] might strike us differently when we place his poems against a context in which one was less likely to read meditative odes to solitary birds than to read overly political poems such as the 1819 "Ode to Wellington," by Byron's acquaintance Robert Charles Dallas, who offers a sixty-two-page paean where the "muse Æolic" and "The living strains of Pindar's lyre" are invoked to sing "WELLESLEY'S martial name" (ll. 1, 3, 11), or Charles Bucke's Cockneyesque "Ode to the Nymph of the Fountain of Tears" (in *The Fall of the Leaf; and Other Poems* of 1819), where the Nymph weeps "When despots wield their giant powers / Against the sons of liberty" (ll. 3–4).

Most odes at the time were not Horatian moral meditations or sacred or sublime apostrophes to the natural or the supernatural, but instead amorous odes in the manner of Anacreon, as in Thomas Moore's *Odes of Anacreon* by "Thomas Little," or, even more strikingly, satiric odes. While Pindar was seen as the great exemplar of the "heroic" ode, the most popular writer of odes in the period was the satirist "Peter Pindar," John Wolcot (1738–1819), who first made his name with *Lyric Odes to the Royal Academicians for 1782* and who went on to write *Farewell Odes, Expostulary Odes to a Great Duke, and a Little Lord, Odes to Mr. Paine*, and *Ode upon Ode, or, A Peep at St James's*. At the height of his popularity he could sell 20,000 copies of a satire in a single day, and he was an influence not only on such imitators as "Peter Pindar, Jun." (who issued *The Old Black Cock and His Dunghill Advisers in Jeopardy; or, The Palace that Jack Built* as part of the Queen Caroline affair in 1820), "Philo Peter Pindar" (who published *The Field of Peter-loo, An Heroic Poem, in Two Cantos* [1820]), and C. F. Lawler (who also used the "Peter Pindar, Esq." pseudonym), but on Moore and Byron as well. At the time when Keats was publishing the great odes in his 1820 volume, Paul Thackwell released his *Collection of Miscellaneous and Religious Poems. To Which is Added a Series of Odes, on Various Subjects, Illustrated with Original Tales*. Given his main title, we might imagine Thackwell offering sacred, sublime odes, but instead we find odes to "Stupidity" and "Craft and Subtlety," to which are appended exemplary tales, as a satiric ode's subject is narrativized.[28]

Such a context might suggest different ways to think about Keats's odes, placed within a volume named for its narrative poems. The satiric turn of so many contemporary odes might make us alive to the punning, coinages, oxymorons, and other witty wordplay of Keats's poems, which, as contemporary reviewers noted, were "vivacious, smart, witty, changeful, sparkling, and learned" (*The Edinburgh [Scots] Magazine* [2nd series, 1 (October 1817), pp. 254–7]), and also "insolent," marked by a "bravado style" (*The London Magazine* 2 [September 1820], pp. 315–21).[29] The "Ode on Melancholy" might perhaps then be read as satirizing a tradition of courting melancholia, and even "Ode on a Grecian Urn" might be relieved of some of the utter seriousness that has accompanied its hypercanonicity.[30] Even if we do not embrace a thoroughgoing satirical reading of Keats, these odes offer daring language and startling patterns of thought that have led to a general agreement that these poems are engaged in both intellectual experimentation and an experiment with form, seen perhaps most clearly in accounts of the ways in which Keats creates his new odal stanzas out of his work on the sonnet. Given the place of the sonnet in Keats's 1817 *Poems* and noting Wordsworth's publication of his *River Duddon Sonnets* in 1820, we need to consider Keats's turn from the sonnet to larger lyric forms as a key feature of the 1820 volume.

We also need to remember that the great odes are placed within a volume named for and framed by narrative poems. Wordsworth famously stated in his "Preface" to the second edition of *Lyrical Ballads* that contemporary taste was being destroyed by "frantic novels, sickly and stupid German Tragedies, and deluges of idle and extravagant stories in verse";[31] beyond a concern that poetry is losing its place to the Gothic novel and to imported plays, Wordsworth stands against the rise of the poetic tale or romance that in many ways would define "Romanticism" for contemporary readers.[32] Keats, who at the time of finishing his 1820 volume was writing a "German" tragedy in *Otho the Great*, signals his sense that such romances are what readers want by labeling his book with his three poetic tales. As Stuart Curran, Peter Manning, and St. Clair have shown, romance was the dominant form in the era that ultimately would be called Romantic. As St. Clair puts it, "To contemporary readers the great poems of the Romantic age were not those that feature in modern university courses but *The Lay of the Last Minstrel, Marmion, The Lady of the Lake, Childe Harold's Pilgrimage, The Giaour, The Bride of Abydos, The Corsair, Manfred, The Pleasures of Hope*, and *Lalla Rookh*" (p. 215). We might add Southey's *Thalaba, A Rhythmical Romance* (1801) and *The Curse of Kehama* (1810), or Hunt's *The Story of Rimini* (1816), but that is just to expand the list of romances.

Even Wordsworth offered his own kind of counter to popular romances in *The White Doe of Rylstone; or, the Fate of the Nortons* (1815), and then in *Peter Bell*.

The poets of 1820 offered a host of different kinds of tales: Croly called his *The Angel of the World* an "Arabian Tale," and his *Sebastian* a "Spanish" one, which is how Mary Leman Grimstone also labeled her "Zayda." Hunt offered his translation of *Amyntas* as "A Tale of the Woods." Nodier's *Giovanni Sbogarro* was translated as "A Venetian Tale (Taken from the French)." Caroline Bowles Southey published her *Fitzarthur* as a "Metrical Tale." Bulwer Lytton's first volume of poetry opened with "Ismael, An Oriental Tale." William Herbert issued *Hedin; or, The Spectre of the Tomb. A Tale. From the Danish History.* John Roby published *Lorenzo, or The Tale of Redemption.* Mr. Frankly printed his *Omar and Zara, or, The Power of Truth, A Father's Tale in Verse.* John Brown released *Legitimacy, a Poem; or, Leonard and Louisa, A Tale for our Times*; and "Old Tom of Oxford" published *Solomon Logwood, A Radical Tale*, with satire again providing modal variations on other forms.

Keats, identified on the title page of the 1820 volume as the author of his poetical romance *Endymion*, does not provide his three opening poems with generic markers, but they have long been recognized as innovative interventions into the contemporary construction of the romance or tale, a point which, again, can be fully appreciated only if we return these poems to the larger pantheon of poetry into which they were introduced. Curran suggests that Keats's three tales provide a synoptic history of romance offering poems "in the mode of the Greek (in couplets), Italian (in *ottava rima*) and British (in Spenserian stanzas)."[33] Keats here may have been following Dryden, whose *Fables Ancient and Modern* (1700) also modernize classical (Ovid), Italian (Boccaccio), and English (Chaucer) romances, but he is also seeking to assert his experimental modernity by demonstrating that he can master and transform the entire range of romance. We see similar gatherings of tales covering a range of models, usually to point toward a kind of world or global literature, so that Croly offers both a "Spanish" and an "Arabian" romance, or Procter produces two stories from Boccaccio alongside "Gyges," a classical story in the style of Byron's *Don Juan*, "The Death of Acis," labeled "A tale Sicilian" (l. 2), and "Diego de Montilla. A Spanish Tale." Procter provides a particularly good point of comparison for his fellow Cockney, Keats, for both are engaged in exploring world literature's tales and more specifically in adapting Boccaccio, a project in which Keats would also be joined by Reynolds. Like Procter, Keats, whose "Fancy," also included in the volume, proclaims "Ever let the fancy roam, / Pleasure never is at home" (ll. 1–2), might be seen in these tales, including the *ottava rima* "Isabella," following Byron and his "Liberal Don" in using the tale to explore the world, rather than Wordsworth, who would rather be at home in Grasmere.

We can think of other juxtapositions. We might want to think of the sceptical "Lamia" alongside Hemans's *Sceptic*. We might want to consider "The Eve of St. Agnes" next to 1820's *Ivy Castle; or, The Eve of St. Agnes*, a prose work by Sarah Scudgell Wilkinson. "Isabella" is part of an extensive engagement with Italian literature that can be traced to Hunt's seminal romance, *The Story of Rimini*. We might also find new contexts for the volume's closing narrative poem, "Hyperion," called an "unfinished poem" in an "Advertisement" that Keats abjured, and often considered yet another example of a failed Romantic epic. This notion of the failed epic is essential to our construction of the Romantic movement as primarily lyric, but it is a notion that does not stand up to much scrutiny. Blake may have abandoned *The Four Zoas*, but he did complete long poems such as *Milton* and *Jerusalem*. If Wordsworth never finished the massive "Recluse" project, he was known at the time for the epic-length *The Excursion*, and he also completed *The Prelude*, though he left it to be published after his death. Byron completed his long romance of *Childe Harold*, and, though *Don Juan* is unfinished, that is because Byron died. Southey completed more epic-length poems than his critics thought wise; Scott finished long narrative poems, as did Moore, Shelley, Hunt, and many others. Now it may be that the Romantics did not write a poem to rival *Paradise Lost*, but while they certainly sought to rework that poem, it is not clear that their central goal was to replicate it rather than replace it. We might want to read "Hyperion" against contemporary epic attempts such as Barrett's *The Battle of Marathon*, but we can also see it as part of a Cockney effort to turn from the martial epic to the erotic and fanciful epyllion.[34] Again, we might note that the placement of this "Grecian" epic at the close of the volume parallels the inclusion of translations from the Greek and elsewhere at the end of volumes such as Hunt's *Foliage* (1818), or we might want to place it against projects such as Landor's 1820 *Idyllia Heroica Decem*, with its Latin poems. We might want to read "Hyperion," then, not as a failed attempt to return to Milton or Homer but as a successful modern, Cockney effort to open up British literature to the world and to open up the classics to the kinds of readers and writers that conservative protectors of the canon feared would dilute and dirty the pure waters of a Hippocrene of cultural capital.

With its unfamiliar pantheon of Titans, "Hyperion" might be seen – like Keats's 1820 volume as a whole – as another opening on to the pantheon of living poets in 1820. Even if we wish to celebrate the canonical Keats, we can do so only if we understand how his experimental verse defines itself against a larger body of alternative poetry. Whether we wish to argue that Keats eschews politics, ideology, and the everyday in his poetry, or whether we want, with Jerome McGann, to argue that these are deeply reactionary poems,[35] we need to see that his verse acquires some of its power from arising within a contemporary struggle over the power of poetry, both its aesthetic power and its power to change minds. No matter which canon we embrace, it should be understood as an interested act of replacing the encyclopedic pantheon of the living poets with the sacred book of the anthology which seeks to keep alive poets by interring them far from the affiliations and conflicts that gave their poetry life.

NOTES

1 On the issue of anthologizing Romanticism, see, e.g., the special issue of *Romanticism on the Net* 7 (August 1997).

2 Stuart Curran, "Romantic Poetry: Why and Wherefore?," in *The Cambridge Companion to British Romanticism*, ed. Stuart Curran (Cambridge: Cambridge University Press, 1993), p. 217.

3 Shelley, "England in 1819," in *Shelley's Poetry and Prose*, ed. Donald H. Reiman and Neil Fraistat, 2nd edn., (New York: W. W. Norton, 2002), pp. 1, 2–3. Subsequent references in the text.

4 Samuel Taylor Coleridge, *Biographia Literaria*, ed. James Engell and W. Jackson Bate (Princeton: Princeton University Press, 1983), vol. 1, p. 38.

5 Among other good work on print culture and Romanticism, see Kevin Gilmartin, *Print Politics: The Press and Radical Opposition in Early Nineteenth-Century England* (Cambridge: Cambridge University Press, 1996), and Paul Magnuson, *Reading Public Romanticism* (Princeton: Princeton University Press, 1998).

6 See J. R. de Jackson, *Annals of English Verse: A Preliminary Survey 1770–1835* (New York: Garland, 1985), and *Romantic Poetry by Women: A Bibliography 1770–1835* (Oxford: Oxford University Press, 1993).

7 On the importance of drama and theatre to the period, see, among other good work, Julie Carlson, *In the Theatre of Romanticism: Coleridge, Nationalism, and Women* (Cambridge: Cambridge University Press, 1994); Jeffrey N. Cox, *In the Shadows of Romance: Romantic Tragic Drama in Germany, England, and France* (Athens, OH: Ohio University Press, 1987); and Jane Moody, *Illegitimate Theatre in London, 1779–1840* (Cambridge: Cambridge University Press, 2000).

8 On Satire's importance to Romanticism, see Gary Dyer, *British Satire and the Politics of Style, 1789–1832* (Cambridge: Cambridge University Press, 1997), and Steven Jones, *Satire and Romanticism* (New York: St. Martin's Press, 2000).

9 William St. Clair, *The Reading Nation in the Romantic Period* (Cambridge: Cambridge University Press, 2004). See also Jon Klancher, *The Making of English Reading Audiences, 1790–1832* (Madison: University of Wisconsin Press, 1987).

10 See, e.g., James Chandler, *England in 1819: The Politics of Literary Culture and the Case of Romantic Historicism* (Chicago: Chicago University Press, 1998), pp. 303–49.

11 On "The Literary Diary; or, Improved Common-Place-Book" (Bristol Central Library), used by Reynolds, his sister Charlotte, Frances Hood, and Thomas Hood to collect poetry, among other writings, see Paul Kaufman, "The Reynolds-Hood Commonplace Book: A Fresh Appraisal," *Keats-Shelley Journal* 10 (1961), pp. 43–52; for other such gatherings made within the extended Keats circle, see Clayton E. Hudnall, "John Hamilton Reynolds, James Rice, and Benjamin Bailey in the Leigh Browne-Lockyer Collection," *Keats-Shelley Journal* 19 (1970), pp. 11–37. On writers and reviewers, see Barbara M. Benedict, "Readers, Writers, Reviewers, and the Professionalization of Literature," in *The Cambridge Companion to English Literature 1740–1830*, ed. Thomas Keymer and Jon Mee (Cambridge: Cambridge University Press, 2004), pp. 3–23; Marilyn Butler, "Culture's Medium: The Role of the Review," in Curran, *The Cambridge Companion to British Romanticism*, pp. 120–47; *British Romanticism and the Edinburgh Review*, ed. Massimiliano Demata and Duncan Wu (New York: Palgrave Macmillan, 2002); and Mark Parker, *Literary Magazines and British Romanticism* (Cambridge: Cambridge University Press, 2001).

12 Among the many studies of canon formation in this period, see John Guillory, *Cultural Capital: The Problem of Literary Canon Formation* (Chicago: University of Chicago Press, 1993); Michael Gamer, *Romanticism and the Gothic* (Cambridge: Cambridge University Press, 2000); Robert Crawford, *Devolving English Literature* (Oxford: Clarendon Press, 1992); David Simpson, "Romanticism, Criticism and Theory," in Curran, *The Cambridge Companion to British Romanticism*, pp. 1–24; and Natalie M. Houston, "Anthologies and the Making of the Poetic Canon," in *A Companion to Victorian Poetry*, ed. Richard Cronin, Alison Chapman, and Antony H. Harrison (Oxford: Blackwell Publishing, 2002), pp. 361–77.

13 St. Clair, *The Reading Nation*, pp. 660–4.

14 Stephen Gill, *William Wordsworth: A Life* (Oxford: Clarendon Press, 1989), pp. 330–7, 344.

15 On Wordsworth's efforts to create himself as the key poet of the day, see Lee Erickson, "The Egoism of Authorship: Wordsworth's Poetic Career," in *The Economy of Literary Form: English Literature and the Industrialization of Publishing, 1800–1850* (Baltimore: Johns Hopkins University Press, 1996), pp. 19–48.

16 Elizabeth Barrett, *The Battle of Marathon* (London: printed for W. Lindsell, 1820), p. 3.

17 See Michael Scrivener, *Poetry and Reform: Periodical Verse and the English Democratic Press 1792–1824* (Detroit: Wayne State University Press, 1992); Anne Janowitz, *Lyric and Labour in the Romantic Tradition* (Cambridge: Cambridge University Press, 1998); and Paul Thomas Murphy, *Towards a Working-Class Canon: Literary Criticism in British Working-Class Periodicals, 1816–1858* (Columbus: Ohio University Press, 1994).

18 Jeffrey C. Robinson, *Unfettering Poetry: The Fancy in British Romanticism* (New York: Palgrave Macmillan, 2006), p. 226. Subsequent references in the text.

19 Margaret J.M. Ezell, *Writing Women's Literary History* (Baltimore: Johns Hopkins University Press, 1993), pp. 66–131.

20 Francis Hodgson, *Sæculomastix; or, The Lash of the Age We Live In; A Poem, in Two Parts* (London: Porter, 1819).

21 Byron, *Don Juan*, in *The Complete Poetic Works*, ed. Jerome J. McGann, 7 vols. (Oxford: Clarendon Press, 1980–93), vol. v.
22 Wordsworth, letter to Henry Crabbe Robinson, late January 1820, in *The Letters of William and Dorothy Wordsworth: The Middle Years*, ed. Ernest de Selincourt, 2 vols. (Oxford: Clarendon Press, 1937), vol. ii, p. 579.
23 See *The Sceptic: A Hemans–Byron Dialogue*, ed. Nanora Sweet and Barbara Taylor: www.rc.umd.edu/editions/sceptic.
24 Byron, *Byron's Letters and Journals*, ed. Leslie A. Marchand, ii vols. (London: John Murray, 1973–9), vol. vii, pp. 113–14.
25 Mill, *Autobiography of John Stuart Mill* (London: Longmans, Green, Reader, & Dyer, 1873), ch. 5.
26 Hazlitt, *The Spirit of the Age*, in *The Complete Works of William Hazlitt*, ed. P. P. Howe, 21 vols. (London: J. M. Dent, 1930–4), vol. xi, p. 191.
27 See, e.g., Nicholas Roe on "To Autumn," in *John Keats and the Poetry of Dissent* (Oxford: Clarendon Press, 1997), pp. 253–65.
28 See Ann Rowland, "Romantic poetry and the novel," in this volume.
29 On Keats's striking language see Christopher Ricks, *Keats and Embarrassment* (Oxford: Clarendon Press, 1974); William Keach, "Cockney Couplets: Keats and the Politics of Style," *Studies in Romanticism* 25 (Summer 1986), pp. 182–96; Marjorie Levinson, *Keats's Life of Allegory: The Origins of a Style* (Oxford: Basil Blackwell, 1988); and Jerome J. McGann, *The Beauty of Inflections: Literary Investigations in Historical Method and Theory* (Oxford: Clarendon Press, 1988), pp. 17–65.
30 See Jeffrey N. Cox, *Poetry and Politics in the Cockney School: Keats, Shelley, Hunt and Their Circle* (Cambridge: Cambridge University Press, 1998), pp. 146–86.
31 Wordsworth, *Lyrical Ballads and Other Poems, 1797–1800*, ed. James Butler and Karen Green (Ithaca: Cornell University Press, 1992), p. 747.
32 On Wordsworth's statement, see Rowland, "Romantic poetry and the novel," below, pp. 120–1; and Gamer, *Romanticism and the Gothic*, pp. 90–126. While it is true that Wordsworth attacks "frantic," "sickly," "stupid," "idle," and "extravagant" versions of these genres rather than necessarily the genres themselves, this passage has often been read as a defense of the lyric against narrative and dramatic forms in ways that would shape various constructions of Romanticism.
33 Stuart Curran, *Poetic Form and British Romanticism* (Oxford: Oxford University Press, 1986), p. 150.
34 Cox, *Poetry and Politics in the Cockney School*, pp. 164–5.
35 McGann, *The Beauty of Inflections*, p. 53.

FURTHER READING

Fraistat, Neil, *The Poem and the Book: Interpreting Collections of Romantic Poetry* (Chapel Hill: University of North Carolina Press, 1985)
Mandell, Laura, and Michael Gamer, "The Canon and the Net," Special issue of *Romanticism on the Net* 10 (May 1998)
McGann, Jerome, *The Poetics of Sensibility: A Revolution in Literary Style* (Oxford: Clarendon Press, 1996)
Mellor, Anne, *Romanticism and Gender* (New York: Routledge, 1993)

Simpson, Erik, "Minstrelsy Goes to Market: Prize Poems, Minstrel Contests, and Romantic Poetry," *English Literary History* 71 (Fall 2004), pp. 691–718

White, Simon, John Goodridge and Bridget Keegan, eds., *Robert Bloomfield: Lyric, Class and the Romantic Canon* (Lewisburg: Bucknell University Press, 2006)

Wolfson, Susan, *Formal Charges: The Shaping of Poetry in British Romanticism* (Stanford: Stanford University Press, 1997)

2

NICK GROOM

Romantic poetry and antiquity

In "The Four Ages of Poetry" (1820), Thomas Love Peacock archly complained that contemporary poetry was absurdly derivative of ancient models of inspiration and composition: "While the historian and the philosopher are advancing in, and accelerating, the progress of knowledge, the poet is wallowing in the rubbish of departed ignorance, and raking up the ashes of dead savages to find gewgaws [toys] and rattles for the grown babies of the age."[1] He castigates Scott, Byron, Southey, Wordsworth, Coleridge, Moore, and Campbell for their cannibalistic and anachronistic efforts, which he sees as no more than patching together "disjointed relics of tradition and fragments of second-hand observation" to produce "a modern-antique compound of frippery and barbarism."[2] It was indeed confidently believed that ancient societies, whether British, Greek, or Roman, shared virtues of originality and genius, and that modern poets should mine these seams. Southey's preparation before writing his epic *Madoc* was to "study three works . . . the Bible, Homer, and Ossian," and Hazlitt argued that the four prototypes of poetry were, similarly, the Bible, Homer, Ossian, and Dante.[3]

There is of course nothing new in Peacock's attack: *The Dunciad Variorum* (1729) and the *Memoirs of Martinus Scriblerus* (1741) set the tone in the eighteenth century for satirizing the enervated taste of antiquarians and connoisseurs, and this mockery was carried through into the engravings of Hogarth and Gillray. But there *is* something new in Peacock's criticism of the ubiquity of the antique and the arcane. Rather than disappearing before the advance of science and the "march of mind," ancient esoteric mysteries seemed to have taken up permanent residence in the arts:

A poet in our times . . . lives in the days that are past. His ideas, thoughts, feelings, associations, are all with barbarous manners, obsolete customs, and exploded superstitions. The march of his intellect is like that of a crab, backward. The brighter the light diffused around him by the progress of reason, the thicker is the darkness of antiquated barbarism, in which he buries himself like a mole, to throw up the barren hillocks of his Cimmerian labours.[4]

Had poetry lost its way, becoming opaque or simply irrelevant to the "common readers of poetry," separated from humanity and the humanities? The clue is in Peacock's contrast of barbarity with the "civilized community." His template for this thinking is in the tension between the classical and the Gothic, the civilized and the savage, and the larger question of British identity (here disparagingly referred to as "Cimmerian" – an ancient barbarian race thought to be a proto-Celtic or proto-Germanic tribe). Throughout the discussions and deployments of antiquity during the period there is a rumbling anxiety over national identity: what does it mean to be British?

The contrast between the classical taste and the Romantic or Gothic taste had occupied critics for most of the eighteenth century – and continues to exercise opinions. The pioneering literary antiquarian Thomas Warton, for instance, had adapted his neoclassical training for the analysis and criticism of indigenous British literature, first outlined in *Observations on the "Fairy Queen" of Spenser* (1754) before being profoundly developed into an identifiable canon and recognizable national literary culture in his monumental *History of English Poetry* (published from 1774). Very early in his career Warton drafted possibly the first "Essay on Romantic Poetry" (1745), which asserts that Romantic taste is "entirely different" from the classical because it imitates "the actions of spir[i]ts, in describing imaginary Scenes, & making persons of abstracted things," although it had "more Judgement and less extravagance" than the writings of antiquity, by which Warton meant principally medieval romances.[5]

Eighty years later, Hazlitt was paraphrasing the German writer A. W. Schlegel on the same topic, identifying the classical with universal human associations, and the Gothic with the individual imagination: "A Grecian temple, for instance, is a classical object: it is beautiful in itself, and excites immediate admiration. But the ruins of a Gothic castle have no beauty or symmetry to attract the eye; and yet they excite a more powerful and Romantic interest from the ideas with which they are habitually associated."[6] And yet the two styles are often less opposites in the aesthetics of the period than different strands of antiquity twisted together. Percy Shelley's famous response to Peacock (his *A Defence of Poetry*, written in 1821) indicates as much. In a sense, Shelley confirms Peacock's criticisms by claiming that culture and hence artistic conception were accumulative and organic. Shelley called for an acknowledgment of and responsiveness to the literature of earlier cultures, arguing that the poetry of chivalric society came into being only after properly incorporating "the poetry and wisdom of antiquity," which he summed up as Platonism, Christianity, and Celtic mythology – in so doing combining ancient Greece with ancient Britain. "The result," he concluded, "was a sum of the action and reaction of all the causes included in it."[7]

In the first decades of the nineteenth century there seemed to be a great deal of history leading up to the present and following advances in a whole range of new fields – from archaeology to comparative religion, from pottery to vulcanology (the study of volcanoes). More history was being discovered all the time. Writers, artists, historians, and critics became sensitized to the inescapable presence of the past in everyday life – whether in the medieval rights-of-way and boundaries of London, or in the enigmatic standing stones and elusive oral folk traditions of the countryside. Moreover, history was happening every day, persistently felt and lived through in explosive international events such as the French Revolution and the ensuing upheaval of the Napoleonic Wars.

Antiquity in the general sense of "ancientness" therefore became integral to many features of intellectual and cultural life in the period – in politics, poetry, interior design, and even the erotic (the principal definitions of "antiquity" in Johnson's *Dictionary* [1755–6] are "1. Old times; time past long ago. 2. The people of old times; the ancients. 3. The works of remains of old times"). Antiquity therefore covers classical Greece and Rome (and Egypt), ancient Britain, and the medieval or Gothic. Considering the poetry of antiquity in this way presents a challenge to the proposition that Romantic poets rebelled against the neoclassical straitjacket of eighteenth-century Augustanism in a bid for the imaginative freedom of the Gothic – as if taste evolved "from a reptilian classicism, all cold and dry reason, to a mammalian Romanticism, all warm and wet feeling."[8] Critics today are in danger of replicating the split made at the time by commentators such as Hazlitt. Rather, classical taste and Gothic taste were less in competition to become the spirit of the age as complementary movements, both being literally rooted in the past, and in the idea and uses of the past. If Scott's comments in his *Minstrelsy of the Scottish Border* (1803) suggest an opposition between the Greeks and Romans on the one hand, and the Goths and Celts on the other, and in the next year Joseph Cottle remarked that "whoever in these times founds a machinery on the mythology of the Greeks, will do so at his peril," Byron had no qualms about combining, for example, Scotland with Homeric Greece in lines such as "And Loch-na-gar with Ida looked o'er Troy" ("The Island," Canto II, l. 291).[9] Classical literature was certainly valued differently at the end of the eighteenth century than at the beginning, but still formed part of the story of Britain and provided valuable commentaries on the activities of the so-called Goths and Celts.

"Gothic" has come to cover everything from the florid novels of Ann Radcliffe to the architectural visions of Augustus Welby Pugin, and it is still rapidly mutating today – as is clear from its ongoing popularity as an "alternative" fashion. Mid-eighteenth-century meanings of the term are, however, fundamental for understanding attitudes toward ancient Britain in the period and for the Romantic reception of ancient societies more generally, and the most appropriate place to begin an account of the Gothic aesthetic is of course in a graveyard. Thomas Gray's "Elegy Written in a Country Church-Yard" (1750) is particularly apt. Gray wrote much in the neoclassical style, and shares many of the same concerns as his contemporary, Pope, such as the death of meaning in the new age of capitalism and mass-print culture, and "universal darkness" covering all. But Gray does not share Pope's *Schaden-freude* at the descent of society into Dulness; rather, he fears this annihilation, and his fear becomes intensified through the lens of medieval history until he is facing utter extinction. Here is the genesis of the figure of the Romantic poet: writers gradually left their place within the witty and urbane circles of Augustan social commentary and became outsiders, haunted by an obsessive historical imagination.[10]

In the "Elegy," the poet's anxiety is expressed by the poem moving from the neverland of counterfactual or speculative English history (those "mute, inglorious Miltons" – what never was and what will never be) to an oral rhapsody, and finally to the written word carved on a stone in the country churchyard: "graved on the stone beneath yon aged thorn" (l. 116). The poem is itself an epitaph, and establishes a convention of mortal epigraphy in later Romantic poems, where, as we shall see, fragments of text are discovered and deciphered, either written on gravestones or other pieces of memorial furniture, or actually inscribed into the land in more suggestive ways. It is also a poem that struggles to find its own voice, and its expressly allusive style has been accused of being "an anthology of literary clichés available to every minimally educated reader."[11]

So already in Gray we have recognizable themes of what was to become characteristic of the Gothic: graves and funerary monuments, memory and loss, mortality and melancholia, all combining in an acute awareness of the transience of human endeavour, of loneliness, of the weight of the past, of antiquity, and of an inability to write. But Gray's most influential mouthpiece for this fear of history, and the strange terror of not-being and never-having-been, was the figure of the bard, who briefly stands proud of history atop Snowdon in one of the most spectacular images of the period – Thomas Jones painted "The Bard" in 1774, and the subject was still popular in 1817, when John Martin produced his iconic depiction. In Gray's poem "The Bard" (1757), the central speaker gives voice to Gray's fear in a wild fugue of inspiration. He is the last of his race, recording the extermination of his people – the Welsh druidic society – by the invading Anglo-Norman king Edward I, while also predicting the eventual extinction of Edward's line and the triumph of the Tudors. His is a lone voice in the devastation: no one will hear his death-song, but it will nevertheless reverberate, both a prophecy and a curse, through history. The poem finishes with the poet plunging suicidally from his mountaintop into "endless night" (l. 144).

This is the magnification of elegy to the level of apocalypse. Gray recognizes the savagery of English history, hitherto repressed. The need for a national British history posed fundamental questions about how the English, Scottish, Welsh, and Irish could write about the British past and the bloodshed that characterized it and that had made Great Britain. How could these social and cultural extirpations be described? Certainly human torture and sacrifice were already the stuff of poetry and art in many classical and biblical precedents – most obviously in the depiction of the crucifixion and other martyrdoms – but this sort of aesthetic material had yet to be tested in the British Isles. In other words, the Gothic is about much more than domestic horrors and melancholy lamentations: it is a historical theory, and Peter Ackroyd comes closest to it when he describes Gothic literature as "a rancid form of English antiquarianism."[12]

There are three elements to the Gothic imagination: the history of the Germanic tribes, an ensuing political ideology, and the medievalist aesthetic. Historically speaking, the Goths were a tribe who crossed the Danube in the fourth century CE on their way to sack Rome, and were therefore identified as the resistance to the Roman empire: rude Northern freedom-fighters overcoming the classical tyranny of the South. By the sixth century, the word was used to describe the Germanic tribes in general, and was applied to the Angles and Saxons settling in England, and to Hengist and Horsa, who allegedly landed in Kent in the fifth century. Gibbon noted that the sack of Rome presented the opportunity for Britain to separate itself from the Roman Empire, and hence Goths were considered to be constitutive of the nation, as distinguished from the Romano-British.[13] By similar means, they were also erroneously associated with the later pointed Gothic and English perpendicular architecture of the Middle Ages because of the apparent independence of these styles from classical models prevalent on the Continent.

In other words, the Goths seemed to represent an alternative historical dynamic to the classical movements revived in the Renaissance and Augustan periods. The Goths were considered to be the purest of the northern races, possessing an instinctive love of liberty that was antagonistic to the imperial pretensions of Rome, and later of other forms of despotic rule such as Catholicism. So it is not difficult to see how the Goths appealed to the emerging sense of English identity. Indeed, the English constitution's apparent progress through granting increased liberties and rights seemed to be in the Gothic spirit – hence episodes from the signing of *Magna Carta* to the "Glorious Revolution" of 1688 were presented as inherently Gothic.

Protestants stood up to Roman Catholics just as Parliamentarians had stood up to the absolutist claims of the monarch, and as the Anglo-Saxons had rebelled against the "Norman Yoke." It was as if the English constitution that emerged from these antagonisms was a product of the Gothic dynamic: negotiated in a spirit of compromise, balanced between extremes, latitudinarian, progressive, organic, pragmatic, responsive – what by the nineteenth century was known as the "Whig theory of history."

Yet there were also highly pejorative associations of the Gothic myth. The sack of Rome was a cultural and intellectual disaster that had resulted in the advent of the "Dark Ages," a term coined in the seventeenth century. The Goths did not replace the Roman system with one of their own – instead they simply laid waste to the civilization and displaced classical learning for a thousand years. Their taste was barbaric, crude, violent, obscure, and dark, and what monuments they did leave before the Middle Ages were inexplicable and eerie, carrying associations of death and destruction.

Neither did the bloodletting end there. The acknowledged liberal development of the English and subsequently the British constitution repressed the disturbing truth that it had come out of centuries of civil bloodshed on a terrible scale. The progress of British political freedoms – the "Whig" theory of history – was steeped in blood: it condoned, for example, the execution of Charles I and the ensuing Civil War; and even the so-called "Bloodless Revolution" of 1688, when William III and Mary II took the throne, saw protracted fighting in Ireland (the Battle of the Boyne was not fought there until 1690). Before the accession of James I and VI in 1603, England had been warring with Scotland for 300 years, and attempts to make the Welsh and the Scottish part of the union had been characterized by clinical state violence (such as the liquidation of Welsh culture dramatized by Gray's "Bard," or the Highland clearances of the eighteenth century) and acts of wild and capricious retaliation (such as the massacre at Glencoe).

Repressed guilt and horror therefore lie behind the aestheticization of the Gothic and medieval in the eighteenth century. Although Walpole may have commented that it was a relief for him to turn from politics to write his pioneering Gothic novel, *The Castle of Otranto* (1764), it was of course simply a displacement activity: a way of dealing with the butchery of the British constitution by condensing its violence into dreamlike scenes of medieval romance. Walpole might have been literally living in a fantastic pseudo-medieval mansion at Strawberry Hill (building began in 1748), but it should be remembered that he slept with a copy of the execution order for Charles I over his bedhead. By half-acknowledging the fearful slaughters at the heart of British identity, writers and artists began to explore how the imagination dealt with such fearsome cultural memories – often in the least expected places. Gothicism crept into gardens, for example, in the shape of uncultivated patches of "natural" wildness, into picturesque views as mock ruins, and into aesthetics in Edmund Burke's 1757 *An Inquiry into the Sublime and the Beautiful*, published in the same year as Gray's "Bard."

Burke's definition of the sublime was deeply rooted in the Gothic as a suggestive form of spectacle. Sublimity was characterized by terror and power, especially when somehow obscured. Of Milton's description of Death in *Paradise Lost*, Burke declares, "In this description all is dark, uncertain, confused, terrible, and sublime to the last degree":

> that shape had none
> Distinguishable in member, joint, or limb,
> Or substance might be called that shadow seemed,
> For each seemed either; black it stood as night.
> (Book II, ll. 667–70)[14]

The incomprehensibility of the passage works a strange alchemy, hinting at something vast, ineffable, and infinite. Hence obscurity in all things became the touchstone of the Gothic – in language, plot, psychology, clothing and materials, architecture, and even the weather: "An immense mountain covered with a shining green turf, is nothing in this respect, to one dark and gloomy; the cloudy sky is more grand than the blue; and night more solemn and sublime than the day."[15] The sublime signaled the limit of reason, and beyond that there were monsters.[16]

Burke was quick to recognize that the British landscape was dotted with sublime monuments – whether ruined abbeys and monasteries (victims of the Reformation) or megaliths (often called ancient cathedrals). Eighteenth-century antiquarians such as William Stukeley had already noticed that the country seemed to be laced with the physical traces of these other, earlier, more mysterious, perhaps even more terrible Britains, and had mapped both Stonehenge (*Stonehenge: A Temple Restor'd to the British Druids*, 1740) and Avebury (*Abury: A Temple of the British Druids*, 1743). These remains were like distant communications from another world, barely legible letters raised against the incessant depredations of time. And according to Roman historians, including Caesar in his memoirs, they had been temples of human sacrifice, whether conducted in terrifying wicker men and reed baskets (the victims were incinerated inside "figures of immense size . . . of twigs"), or on the rough altars at the centre of stone circles.[17]

The Gothic became intimately tied to British nationalism as a reminder of united Protestant resistance to Catholic Rome, or, it was believed, of the druidic resistance to imperial Rome. Pre-Roman monuments such as standing stones, rows, circles, and barrows were among the few things that gave

Great Britain and (after 1801) the United Kingdom a sense of shared history and common heritage, to the extent that they were consistently represented as part of a Gothic sense of identity. Thus in paintings and engravings, Stonehenge and other megaliths were, for example, usually shown against a dark sky obscured by clouds. In literature, this newly recognized communality emerged in the antiquarian aesthetic of *Ossian* (James Macpherson's third-century Celtic fragments and epics, first published in 1760) and the ballad revival inspired by Thomas Percy's *Reliques of Ancient English Poetry* (1765, which contained much lowland Scottish material and inspired subsequent collections by John Pinkerton, Joseph Ritson, and most notably Walter Scott and James Hogg). The medievalist ballad and verse romance derived from the models revived by Percy and his followers, and these significantly influenced the emerging historical novel. The pure lineaments of ancient society were discernible in the originality of its expression. As William Duff commented in 1767: "Original poetic genius will in general be displayed in its ultimate vigour in the early periods of society . . . and it will seldom appear in a very great degree in cultivated life."[18] Under the mantle of the Gothic, then, the ancient Britons provided the subject for hundreds of books, articles, letters, and papers written during the century, culminating in Sharon Turner's *History of the Anglo-Saxons* (1799); and, until the publication of Edward Davies's *Celtic Researches* in 1804, little distinction from the Celtic was made. The problem of course was that this original poetic genius was imagined to have been generated and cultivated by savage societies, and the present was formed on such savagery: civilization was raised on blood.

It is worth reiterating how many of the elements of this Gothic aesthetic are present in Gray's "Bard": the sublime, the melancholia, the fascination with the fading past, the savagery, and the political nation-building and "progress" through extermination. Gray's poetry here (and elsewhere) is a confrontation with the past in order to explore the social and cultural taboos of the present, and to answer the question: Where did Britain come from? Much of Gray's later poetry probes this ghastly problem further through the thrilling primitivism of Viking myth. "The Fatal Sisters" (published in 1768) tells of twelve weird sisters or Valkyrie weaving fate from human entrails weighted with decapitated human heads. This poetry is characterized by concrete nouns and active verbs, a collapse of the regular classical form into the irregular ode and freer forms of verse, the dissolution of time so that the past becomes literally omnipresent and haunts the present, and in mystical hints – the poet as a sorcerer, casting spells, as a bard weaving rhymes, as a druid. In this way, the poetry of Gray offers a compelling way of giving voice to an ancient landscape of Britain, whose only memorials were silent stones, once (it was believed – even hoped) stained with human blood. This is the poetry that makes those rugged monuments speak, that gives a voice to the dead, to ghosts, to nothingness, to what never was. In this, the poetry of antiquity goes far beyond the limits of elegy.

These mysterious ruins, then, like graveyards, served as the focus for meditations – the meditation being a form of restoration through hallucination. Warton's sonnet "Written at Stonehenge" (published in 1791), for instance, presents a series of meditative possibilities – or obscurities – for the "noblest monument of Albion's isle" (l. 1). Stonehenge is both an aid to pagan reflection and a tangle of riddles ("We muse on many an antient tale renown'd", l. 14).[19] In the eyes and mind of an antiquarian poet, the triliths could be any manner of – or all – things: a crossroads in the mystical imagination of the nation, a meeting place for myth, legend, and history, resounding in Warton's lines with memories of Merlin and Arthur, Hengist and Horsa, the druids, the Vikings, and Brutus, and are even the site of strange prehistoric coronations.

"Written at Stonehenge" can be seen as the prototype for later poetic restorations. The stones were a monument to the antiquity of the nation, evidence of its history, but reduced to suggestive ruins. The potential of ruins lay in their obscurity – their sublimity. The ruins of Tintern Abbey, for example, haunt Wordsworth's poem of the same name like an uneasy murmur or a shadow on a cloudless day, a presence of "The still, sad music of humanity" (l. 92). The poem is written "a few miles above" Tintern Abbey, and the picturesque ruin is therefore out of sight – it is the memory of a ruin (a Protestant ruin of a Catholic building) that is evoked.

Wordsworth's lines on an earlier ruin – Stonehenge – were written about the same time. By the time Wordsworth had incorporated this grim episode in the desolate landscape of Salisbury Plain into the 1805 *Prelude*, it had become an uncanny encounter with a ruin that attempts to frame the past by rebuilding the monument. Wordsworth falls into a reverie and sees the past – sees ancient Britons "With shield and stone ax, stride across the Wold" (Book XII, l. 323) to the place of sacrifice:

> It is the sacrificial Altar, fed
> With living men – how deep the groans! the voice
> Of those in the gigantic wicker thrills
> Throughout the region far and near.
> (Book XII, ll. 331–4)

There is perhaps a hint of the horror of recent political events – of the Bastille – in this ghastly vision, but, as with the revolution in France, something is learnt too. Wordsworth's attention shifts to the patterns of stones and circles, as if anticipating the twentieth-century cult of ley-lines (the supposed mystical alignment of ancient monuments) by making the stone patterns meaningful:

> 'twas my chance
> To have before me on the downy Plain
> Lines, circles, mounts, a mystery of shapes.
> (Book XII, ll. 338–40)

He is "charmed" by this "antiquarian's dream," sees the druids teaching, and hears their music – which was how the ancient Greeks described the druids. Wordsworth has reached beyond the Roman accounts of sacrifice to go further back into time. So, in an unnerving harmony, human sacrifice is twisted together with dulcet wisdom.

At the time when Wordsworth was meditating upon Salisbury Plain, Blake was imagining Stonehenge from his workshop in South Molton Street, near Tyburn, London's permanent gallows. His earliest influences had been, broadly speaking, Gothic: Macpherson's *Ossian*, Gray's reworkings of Norse myth, Percy's *Reliques* and his later translation of the *Edda*; and he was certainly aware of Stukeley's antiquarian researches. For Blake, Stonehenge was essentially a site of sacrifice, and therefore a monument of tyranny rather than of liberty. The druids who had been so romanticized by Stukeley (who actually described himself as a druid and took a druidic name) were to Blake authoritarian figures denying the humanity of man. The ancient poetry of the prophetic and inspired bard was therefore a voice in opposition to the authoritarian and hierarchical power of the druids, whose stone temples were so many "dark Satanic mills," the instruments of Blake's desolate lord, Urizen, and consequently antagonistic to lapsarian man, symbolized by the figure of Albion. Blake's epic *Milton* describes how "stony Druid Temples" grew from the ruins of Jerusalem (meaning London/Albion), while his dazzling follow-up *Jerusalem: The Emanation of the Giant Albion* (1804–7) details the building of Stonehenge. Having built "A building of eternal death: whose proportions are eternal despair" (pl. 66), the druids sacrifice their human victims, their own humanity, and the future of the race on the diabolical altar of progress.

Blake took the design of the megalithic temple on the final plate of *Jerusalem* from Stukeley's illustration of *Abury*'s serpent stones, and in doing so introduced further influences from antiquity. Ovid's fable of Cadmus and Harmonia – transformed into serpents for killing the dragon of Ares – was described by Stukeley as a possible source for the serpent temple he claimed was built at Avebury, demonstrating how, as Peacock observed, different elements of antiquity could be combined. Indeed, the resources of ancient

Greece in particular proved to be particularly apt for writers and artists of the period. As with the Gothic myth, past epochs may have been savage and barbaric, but they also constituted a golden age of pure thought and expression unsullied by the corruption of society, and ancient Greece (democratic, artistic, philosophic, and athletic) seemed to be exemplary in this respect.

In the late eighteenth and early nineteenth centuries, Greece was as much an idea – or rather a set of ideas – as it was a place, combining democracy, paganism, and individualism (or libertarianism). The Roman influence had held sway over the earlier part of the century, which in seeking to establish a state role for the arts consciously modeled itself on the court of Emperor Augustus (hence, "Augustan"); and even as late as Gibbon's *Decline and Fall of the Roman Empire* (1776–88), Greece was dismissed as simply a stage before the Roman Empire.[20] But a fascination with the ancient Greeks had begun to emerge with the discovery of Pompeii in 1748, buried when Vesuvius erupted in AD 79, and in the ensuing work of Johann Joachim Winckelmann, in particular his *History of Ancient Art* (1764). Pompeii had been a Greek colony, and Winckelmann chose to study the remains of Greek rather than Roman art there, arguing that Greek sculpture ideally achieved its beauty through the principle of harmony, and that this reflected the pure ideals of the society that had fostered it. As Shelley later put it in a letter to Peacock (January 23–4, 1819): "They lived in harmony with nature, and the interstices of their incomparable columns were portals as it were to admit the spirit of beauty which animates this glorious universe to visit those whom it inspired."

Greece had been under Turkish control since the fifteenth century and, like Britain, began to appreciate its own culture and history again only in the eighteenth century. Translations from the ancient Greek proliferated in the second half of the century, and Greek statues and vases became coveted by collectors, often obtained while traveling through Europe on the "Grand Tour." The Dilettanti Club first visited Greece in 1751, and by the time Byron arrived in Greece in 1810 he found it "infested" with English tourists.[21] Antiquity was in effect another destination on the itinerary, "a vast country separated from our own by a long interval of time," where connoisseurs sought not picturesque views or high society balls, but rather ancient *objets d'art* in their "attempts to discover unknown lands."[22] Gibbon had presented ancient history as a text, but it now emerged as a much more subtle aesthetic encounter that fed the imagination. There is a suggestive series of correspondences here: the past is a foreign country in chaotic disarray, but may be mapped by tracing the contours of its surviving works of art, and memorializing a nation in museums is, of course, a form of colonialism – a way of imposing imperial order.

Despite his oft-expressed antagonism to the classical – "Rome & Greece swept Art into their maw & destroyd it" – Blake was actually at the centre of the Greek Revival of the 1790s, which was encouraged with the first publication in 1788 of John Lemprière's *Bibliotheca classica* (*Classical Dictionary* – later a significant influence on Keats), and in 1790 of John Bell's *New Pantheon* of Greek and Roman myth.[23] Blake's patron George Cumberland and fellow artists John Flaxman and Henry Fuseli were instrumental in the Revival – Fuseli had himself translated Winckelmann as early as 1765, and Flaxman had worked with Josiah Wedgwood on his white bas-relief pottery since 1775. Wedgwood produced a copy of the renowned Portland Vase in 1790, and Blake engraved the artifact as one of a series for Erasmus Darwin's *Botanic Garden* (1791). Blake also later illustrated episodes from Greek myth, such as the Judgment of Paris (1805?), and used the story of Cupid and Psyche from Apuleius for *Vala*; more generally, the male nude as a figure of resistance to tyranny is a characteristic feature of his illuminated books.[24] Blake is also likely to have known and read "the English pagan," Thomas Taylor, who effectively attempted to revive Neoplatonism through his translations of Plotinus and his school, and through his *Orphic Hymns* (1787). And in a similar if less mystical vein, Jacob Bryant, president of the Society of Antiquaries, had turned his attention to comparative religion and was identifying fragments of Christianity in pagan mythology. A cult of new paganism began to grow. This fascination with primitive beliefs led to a revaluation of sexual taboos in Richard Payne Knight's scandalous *Account of the Remains of the Worship of Priapus* (1786), which provocatively argued that phallic worship formed the basis of all religions, and before long the Revival had exploded into a salacious Greekomania. This erotic mood was fueled by Emma Hamilton, wife of the connoisseur Sir William Hamilton, who scandalized society by modeling the provocative classical "attitudes" of ancient nude statues; she later embarked upon a notorious affair with Admiral Lord Nelson.

Taylor and Bryant made a profound impact on Blake's personal mythology, and their influence is also evident in the more fashionable apostasy of Shelley's *Prometheus Unbound*, as well as in Keats's *Endymion* (1818), whose "Hymn to Pan" was famously snubbed by the devout Wordsworth as "a Very pretty piece of Paganism."[25] Unlike Shelley, whose Hellenism (or "cult of the South") was intellectual and textual – he translated a number of ancient Greek works – Keats could not read Greek and even had trouble in pronouncing and scanning Greek names, reminding us that Greek was very much associated with the educated elite. Keats's Hellenism was more aesthetic than grammatical, inspired by artworks.[26] The Elgin marbles, for instance, which had been acquired during 1803–12 and purchased in 1816 for the British Museum at a cost of £35,000, give Keats "a most dizzy pain" when he gazes upon them ("On Seeing the Elgin Marbles," 1817). They are "Gothicized," mingling "Grecian grandeur with the rude / Wasting of old time" (ll. 11–13). His language collapses before the frieze, and his sonnet ends in fragments of its own: "– with a billowy main – / A sun – a shadow of a magnitude" (ll. 13–14).

These historical remains were for Keats necessarily only partially legible – objects for contemplation and interpretation; sometimes, like the Gothic relics of Britain, present, sometimes remembered. The metropolitan space of the museum or gallery therefore replaced mountains, lakes, and ruins as a place where the poet could experience these encounters with the "other," a place where the antique confronts the modern – where inspiration is primed to strike. The "Ode on a Grecian Urn" (1820) is the most notable instance of this museum effect and of a communion with the dead (it is a funerary urn), but the urn is also peculiarly silent. Its perfection cannot be articulated, but only suggested through Keats's describing the potential meanings of the scenes depicted. Keats's poem is therefore at a double remove from the object itself, which in any case does not of course physically exist. It is an elaborated memory, and in the absence of its own meaning becomes haunted by more sinister possibilities: "Who are these coming to the sacrifice?" (l. 31).

If in the "Urn" the marble figures are read by Keats in relation to real musicians, revelers, and lovers, in the first "Hyperion" (1820) the Titan Saturn himself is marmorealized. He begins the poem as if in ruins, like the colossal fragments of a great broken statue, reminiscent of Fuseli's chalk and sepia-wash sketch of "The artist in despair over the magnitude of antique fragments" (1778–80):

> Upon the sodden ground
> His old right hand lay nerveless, listless, dead,
> Unsceptred; and his realmless eyes were closed;
> While his bow'd head seem'd list'ning to the Earth,
> His ancient mother, for some comfort yet.
>
> (ll. 17–21)

But the scene is also Ossianic, and Saturn is explicitly associated with the Gothic when he shakes his "Druid locks" (l. 137).

"Hyperion" was itself subtitled "A Fragment," and its readers concurred. Byron called it a "fine monument," De Quincey compared it to a Greek temple adorned with Greek statuary, and Hunt considered it "a fragment – a gigantic one, like a ruin in the desert."[27] Hunt's comment obviously invites comparison with Shelley's sonnet "Ozymandias" (1818), which begins:

> I met a traveller from an antique land
> Who said – "Two vast and trunkless legs of stone
> Stand in the desert."
>
> (ll. 1–3)

In other words, this tiny fable on the fall of an Egyptian civilization evokes the megaliths of ancient Britain as well as orientalizing antiquity. But here there is a resolutely textual message: a carved inscription –

> "My name is Ozymandias, King of Kings
> Look on my Works, ye Mighty, and despair!"
>
> (ll. 10–11)

For Shelley, in comparison with Keats, the past is all too legible, and, in being so, is here fraught with chilling ironies of identity, being, and posterity. Similarly, in "Alastor," the "awful ruins of the days of old" (l. 108) are carved with signs that the poet can readily decipher:

> He lingered, poring on memorials
> Of the world's youth . . .
> And gazed, till meaning on his vacant mind
> Flashed like strong inspiration, and he saw
> The thrilling secrets of the birth of time.
>
> (ll. 120–8)

The legibility of antiquity for Shelley made it an appropriate vehicle for veiled political writing – *Cyclops* (written 1819), for example, can be seen as a response to the French Revolution, as can *Prometheus Unbound* (1820), which was in part an attempt to mystify the new orthodoxy of ancient Greece, making it strange again. Due to its prevalence in the education system, Greek culture was very much a pillar of the establishment, but it could just as well serve as a mouthpiece for radical and revolutionary views and, like the Gothic, could express anxieties or voice transgressive ideas. Indeed, ancient Greece had a famously democratic society that had nurtured the arts, aesthetics, philosophy, and even sciences, and could be promoted as the archetype for popular government at home. There were pressing contemporary political implications abroad as well: the philhellenes (lovers of Greece) supported Greek independence from Turkey. When the Greeks rebelled in 1821, this support went far further than the vocal or literary. Byron, a passionate philhellene, created the "Byron Brigade"; he died of fever at Missolonghi in 1824 as he waited impatiently to engage the Turks in the cause of freedom.

The British perspective on ancient Rome also had immediate political implications. Napoleon had taken Augustan trappings for his imperial style and was compared with the fourth-century Julian the Apostate, the last pagan emperor. The Roman model was again a two-edged sword: splendid and glorious, yet also condemned to decline and fall. Indeed, the process of history appeared to be quite manifestly cyclical in the example of Rome: a rise and fall, anticipating the whole notion of historical "revolution" that so gripped the age. Rome also had spectacularly legible ruins – stupendous remains, such as the Colosseum and the Forum, that worked like enormous versions of antique statues and vases. In the words of Byron's "Childe Harold" (1812),

> To meditate amongst decay, and stand
> A ruin amidst ruins; there to track
> Fall'n states and buried greatness . . .
> > (IV, xxv, 218–20)

For the Byronic experience of antiquity, one has to be present. He stressed the need to see these monuments *in situ*, and not in a museum or gallery – even (in Canto II) attacking Elgin's era-defining acquisitions.

Rome was wedded to the idea of impending catastrophe, but what is also revealing in Byron's descriptions is his combination of the different elements of antiquity. Here we see most clearly the blending of the Romantic with the classical. The panorama of Rome is one of Gothic sublimity, complete with "Cypress and ivy, weed and wallflower . . . arch crushed, column strown / In fragments, chok'd up vaults," and midnight owls, and the Colosseum even has "magic in the ruined battlement" (IV, cvii, 955–8; cxxix, 1159). The wreck is a vast *memento mori*, "the moral of all human tales . . . the same rehearsal of the past" (IV, cviii, 1–2). It is simultaneously a monument to the glory of Rome, a memorial to the blood of gladiators, slaves, and martyrs, and an echo of the megaliths. Byron also gave Peacock his central dismissive image, of the treasures of antiquity as "Glory's gewgaws shining in the van" (IV, cix, 979).

Rome was, then, like ancient Britain, a juxtaposition of the Christian and pagan, of the pure and the savage: a union of the Gothic with the classical. Braiding together the poetries of antiquity made the past new, and also gave it a resounding topical relevance. It enabled the poet to escape anxieties of influence or feelings of belatedness by recognizing that although the inevitable weight of history was massive, its dialogue with the present was forever fluctuating and changing – which made it always somehow original. A sense of the inescapability of British history had permeated its poetry; indeed, the awesome violence of the past now *needed* to be evoked to make the state of the nation comprehensible.

NOTES

1 *Peacock's Four Ages of Poetry, Shelley's Defence of Poetry, Browning's Essay on Shelley*, ed. H. F. B. Brett-Smith (Oxford: Basil Blackwell, 1921), p. 15.

2 Ibid., p. 16.

3 Southey to Grovesnor Bedford, May 27, 1795, in *The Life and Correspondence of Robert Southey*, ed. Charles Cuthbert Southey, 6 vols. (London: Longman, Brown, Green, & Longman, 1849–50), vol. I, p. 238; William Hazlitt, "On Poetry in General," in *The Complete Works of William Hazlitt*, ed. P. P. Howe, 21 vols. (London: J. M. Dent, 1930–4), vol. V, p. 18.

4 Peacock, *Four Ages*, p. 16.

5 David Fairer, "Organizing Verse: Burke's *Reflections* and Eighteenth-Century Poetry," in *Early Romantics: Perspectives in British Poetry from Pope to Wordsworth*, ed. Thomas Woodman (London: Macmillan, 1998), p. 10.

6 William Hazlitt, "Schlegel on the Drama," in *The Complete Works of William Hazlitt*, ed. Howe, vol. XVI, p. 61.

7 Percy Bysshe Shelley, *A Defence of Poetry*, in *Shelley's Poetry and Prose: Authoritative Texts, Criticism*, ed. Donald H. Reiman and Neil Fraistat (New York: Norton, 2002), p. 525.

8 Northrop Frye, "Towards Defining an Age of Sensibility," *English Literary History* 23 (1956), pp. 144–52, at p. 144 (reprinted in *Collected Works of Northrop Frye*, vol. XVII: *Northrop Frye's Writings on the Eighteenth and Nineteenth Centuries*, ed. Imre Salusinszky [Toronto: University of Toronto Press, 1995]).

9 Joseph Cottle, "Preface" to *Alfred*, 2nd edn., 1804 (London: Button & Son, 1816), p. xii.

10 *Thomas Gray and William Collins: Poetical Works*, ed. Roger Lonsdale (Oxford: Oxford University Press, 1977), pp. 115–16.

11 John Guillory, *Cultural Capital: The Problem of Literary Canon Formation* (Chicago: University of Chicago Press, 1993), p. 87.

12 Peter Ackroyd, *Albion: The Origins of the English Imagination* (London: Chatto & Windus, 2002), p. 374.

13 Edward Gibbon, *The History of the Decline and Fall of the Roman Empire*, ed. Betty Radice, 8 vols. (London: Folio, 1985), vol. IV, p. 135 (ch. 31).

14 Edmund Burke, *A Philosophical Enquiry into the Origin of our Ideas of the Sublime and Beautiful*, ed. Adam Phillips (Oxford: Oxford University Press, 1990), p. 55.

15 Ibid., p. 75.

16 Francisco Goya, "The Sleep of Reason Produces Monsters," *Los Caprichos*, pl. 43.

17 A. L. Owen, *The Famous Druids: A Survey of Three Centuries of English Literature on the Druids* (Oxford: Clarendon Press, 1962), p. 20.

18 William Duff, *An Essay on Original Genius* (London: Edward & Charles Dilly, 1767), p. 260.

19 Thomas Warton, *Poems on Various Subjects* (London: G. G. J. and J. Robinson, 1791), p. 108: Sonnet IV.

20 Gibbon, *Decline and Fall*, vol. I, p. 61 (ch. 2).

21 Robin Jarvis, *The Romantic Period: The Intellectual and Cultural Context of English Literature, 1789–1830* (Harlow: Longman, 2004), p. 157.

22 "Baron d'Hancarville," in *Antiquités Etrusques, Grecques et Romaines* (Naples, 1767–76), vol. III, p. 3: quoted in Ian Jenkins and Kim Sloan, *Vases and Volcanoes: Sir William Hamilton and His Collection* (London: British Museum, 1996), p. 40.
23 William Blake, "On Virgil," in *The Complete Poetry and Prose of William Blake*, ed. David V. Erdman, rev. edn. (New York: Doubleday, 1988), p. 269.
24 Kathleen Raine, *Blake and Antiquity* (Princeton: Princeton University Press, 1977), pp. 69–98.
25 *The Keats Circle: Letters and Papers, 1816–1878*, ed. Hyder Edward Rollins, 2 vols. (Cambridge, MA, 1948), vol. I, p. 144.
26 Jennifer Wallace, *Shelley and Greece: Rethinking Romantic Hellenism* (Basingstoke: Palgrave, 2001), pp. 3, 161–2.
27 Martin Aske, *Keats and Hellenism: An Essay* (Cambridge: Cambridge University Press, 1985), pp. 89, 84–6.

FURTHER READING

Bate, Walter Jackson, *From Classic to Romantic: Premises of Taste in Eighteenth-Century England* (New York: Harper & Row, 1946)
Brown, Marshall, "Romanticism and Enlightenment," in *The Cambridge Companion to British Romanticism,* ed. Stuart Curran (Cambridge: Cambridge University Press, 1993), pp. 25–47
Carabelli, Giancarlo, *In the Image of Priapus* (London: Duckworth, 1996)
Colley, Linda, *Britons: Forging the Nation 1707–1837* (New Haven and London: Yale University Press, 1992)
Hutton, Ronald, *The Image of the Druid* (Oxford: Oxford University Press, forthcoming)
Janowitz, Anne, *England's Ruins: Poetry and National Landscape, 1760–1820* (Oxford: Basil Blackwell, 1990)
Kidd, Colin, *British Identities before Nationalism: Ethnicity and Nationhood in the Atlantic World, 1600–2000* (Cambridge: Cambridge University Press, 1999)
  The Forging of Races: Race and Scripture in the Protestant Atlantic World, 1600–2000 (Cambridge: Cambridge University Press, 2006)
Levinson, Marjorie, *The Romantic Fragment Poem: A Critique of a Form* (Chapel Hill: University of North Carolina Press, 1986)
McFarland, Thomas, *Romanticism and the Forms of Ruin* (Princeton: Princeton University Press, 1981)
Piggott, Stuart, *Ancient Britons and the Antiquarian Imagination* (London: Thames and Hudson, 1989)
Raine, Kathleen, *Blake and Tradition*, 2 vols. (Princeton: Princeton University Press, 1968)
Simonsuuri, Kirsti, *Homer's Original Genius: Eighteenth-Century Notions of the Early Greek Epic (1688–1798)* (Cambridge: Cambridge University Press, 1979)
Smiles, Sam, *The Image of Antiquity: Ancient Britain and the Romantic Imagination* (New Haven and London: Yale University Press, 1994)
Stafford, Fiona, *The Last of the Race: The Growth of a Myth from Milton to Darwin* (Oxford: Clarendon Press, 1994)
Trumpener, Katie, *Bardic Nationalism: The Romantic Novel and the British Empire* (Princeton: Princeton University Press, 1997)

Webb, Timothy, *English Romantic Hellenism, 1700–1824* (Manchester: Manchester University Press, 1982)

"Romantic Hellenism," in Curran, *The Cambridge Companion to British Romanticism*, pp. 148–76

Whittaker, Jason, *William Blake and the Myths of Britain* (Basingstoke: Macmillan, 1999)

3

SUSAN STEWART

Romantic meter and form

Poetic meter is a pattern of marked linguistic features and their absence that shapes a poetic line. In English these features are most often stresses, and the pattern that emerges between marked and unmarked stresses eventually becomes the overall form that is the poem itself. Although meter is measurable, and to some degree predictable, once it has been established through a series of repetitions, the actual rhythm of a poem converges and departs from this pattern of meter, lending it texture and interest.

As early as Aristotle, such dynamic emergence, or entelechy, of form has been contrasted to structures, or finite shapes, and when we speak of poetic meters and the larger structures that are poetic forms, we must acknowledge their living dimension as well as the fixed repertoire of kinds of poems that we have inherited from literary history. Even in the two dominant forms of meter in English – accentual and accentual-syllabic verse – we find this tension between expected and emerging form. Accentual meter, which measures pure stresses alone, historically is associated with vernacular verse and song traditions, including British nursery rhymes, game chants, and ballads. Because English is isochronous, that is, it tends to have the same intervals of time between stressed syllables no matter how many unstressed syllables are between them, accentual meters follow the natural stresses of spoken language. The varying syllables of such meter, following the Anglo-Saxon line, often are characterized by four beats and a strong medial caesura. Accentual syllabic meters, however, unfold by means of an ideal pattern constituted by the relation between the number of feet, or groups of syllables, in a line and the number of stresses; in any given poem, the actual line may not supply that relation in the expected way, but the reader or listener will bear the ideal pattern in mind.

During the late eighteenth and early nineteenth centuries, the period we usually, and only retrospectively, designate as the "Romantic" era of British literature, issues of the fixed and living dimensions of meter became inextricably tied to questions of the connections between poetic forms and other life forms, the possibilities for representing emotion, and the role of poets' voices in an increasingly literate culture. Although "Romantic" poetry in England, and indeed throughout continental Europe, is often considered in terms of its recurring themes and the important revolutionary historical and political context that shaped them and was shaped by them, these themes were expressed in meters and forms of great variety – some reach back to antiquity, others were newly invented, and many were put to new occasions and uses. If meter tends to be a rather marginal aspect of the study of Romanticism today, we might remember that for eighteenth- and nineteenth-century poets themselves, characterizing their work often meant organizing books for publication under the headings of "sonnets," "eclogues," "metrical tales," "monodramas," and other forms, and they also often placed the name of the form directly in the title of the work. This is not to say that at the onset of the eighteenth century, genre distinctions for poetry were very clear. In a 1713 letter on song-writing printed in *The Guardian* (No. XVI) by Ambrose Philips, for example, writers of songs are called "sonneteers"; sonnets are called "little odes"; and the writer suggests that "a song should be conducted like an epigram."[1]

Eighteenth-century numbers

English Renaissance theorists focused upon the opportunities and difficulties that arose as poets tried to adapt the quantitative verse of Greek and Roman poetry, which, unlike English, has the resources of long and short syllables. The application of quantitative meters could not be successful, but it survived in the notion of the measured line, the poet's "numbers"; and in the early eighteenth century a certain idea about the regularity of classical forms led neoclassical poets to write with particular attention to the number of syllables in a line and the regularity of stresses. A tension between a system based on "natural" stress and one based on an ideal pattern thereby comes to underlie the historical dialectic between neoclassical and Romantic aesthetics, including values regarding meter.

From approximately 1639 to 1790, iambic pentameter became the dominant verse line for all British poetry, corresponding to the twelve-syllable alexandrine with a medial caesura that dominated French, and the fourteen-syllable line that dominated Spanish and Italian, neoclassical meter. A line like Alexander Pope's "Now SIGHS steal OUT, and TEARS beGIN to FLOW," from his "An Essay on Criticism," exemplifies exactly the line of ten syllables alternating between unstressed and stressed beats with a medial caesura. This variety of iambic pentameter, most often written in rhyming couplets, had developed out of Chaucer's use of ten-syllable lines and rhyming couplets, and was already flourishing by the sixteenth century. Chaucer's line had itself depended on the paired lines of the Latin elegiac distich, although classical pairs of this type use alternating hexameter and pentameter lines.[2] The ten-syllable "heroic line" was associated traditionally with epic, and poets of the eighteenth century used it for both epic and mock epic forms.

Edward Bysshe's *The Art of English Poetry*, published continually between 1702 and 1762, set out rules for the heroic line: strictly it should have ten syllables; accents should be on the second, fourth, and sixth syllables; trisyllabic feet, known as "substitutions," were prohibited – anapests and dactyls were to be used only for burlesque; "ed" endings should be contracted; alliteration, hiatus, and enjambment should be avoided.[3] Because spoken English tends to have more unstressed than stressed syllables, the evenly alternating stresses of this poetry have an artificial overall effect, and this was precisely what prosodists of the time admired about it: a poetic language distinguishable from an everyday language; a general scheme dominating the particular; moral rules overriding exception; clarity taking precedence over the ambiguities of symbol – such Augustan tenets were carried along quite literally by the structure of verse. Bysshe held that "A verse with an extra or a missing syllable . . . is either a faulty verse or, more properly, just a verse of a different kind. There are no feet in English poetry." Art was to be ideal, an opportunity to improve on nature and to speak to what was universal in human values.

Milton had written in his preface on "Verse" opening *Paradise Lost* that his "measure is English heroic verse without rhyme . . . rhyme being no necessary adjunct or true ornament of poem or good verse." His own aim would be to assure that "the sense [is] variously drawn out from one verse to another, not in the jingling sound of like endings." Admiring Milton's greatness, Samuel Johnson nevertheless followed Bysshe's tenets of regularity and found Milton's blank verse, use of enjambment, and distribution of caesuras across various positions in his lines an abomination. Johnson wrote: "the music of English heroic lines strikes the ear so faintly, that it is easily lost, unless all the syllables of every line co-operate together; this co-operation can be only obtained by the preservation of every verse unmingled with another as a distinct system of sounds; and this distinctness is obtained and preserved by the artifice of rhyme . . . Blank verse . . . seems to be verse only to the eye."[4] Johnson had objected to the irregularity of Spenserian stanza form, too,[5] and in his essay on "The Life of Cowley," Johnson took the opportunity both to name the "metaphysical" poets of the seventeenth century for the first time and to criticize the irregularity of their verse. He accused these poets of a lack of poetic, and personal, restraint. Complaining that they wrote with "an imperfect modulation and unrestrained wit," Johnson argues: "their thoughts are often new, but seldom natural; they are not obvious, but neither are they just; and the reader far from wondering that he missed them, wonders more frequently by what perverseness of industry they were ever found."[6]

The question of line endings in blank verse is also connected to the ongoing controversy of how to read enjambed lines. David Perkins has recently explained: "The older tradition, which Wordsworth still followed, observed the end of each line." Wordsworth wrote in an 1803 letter that such intonations and pauses are "not called out for by the passion of the subject, but by the passion of the meter," and Perkins records that Thomas Sheridan suggested that the speaker should use a "pause of suspension," holding the vowel of the final syllable a little longer.[7]

Nevertheless, a contrary reaction against any excessive regularity began very early in the eighteenth century, and not merely as a continuation of metaphysical aesthetics. In his *Horae Lyricae* of 1709, Isaac Watts argued: "It degrades the excellency of the best versification when the lines run on by couplets, twenty together, just in the same pace, and with the same pauses . . . the reader is tired with the tedious uniformity or charmed to sleep with the unmanly softness of the numbers, and the perpetual chime of even cadences."[8] Compared to the simplicity and directness of ballad and song forms, syllabic prosody, so prided for its smoothness and aptness, eventually came to be rejected on the basis of what might be called its semantic inelegance. In his 1831 preface to "The Lay of the Last Minstrel," Sir Walter Scott looked back to remark that the "Romantic" stanza, the measured short (tetrameter) line of "minstrel poetry" practiced by himself and his compatriots, could not be drawn out into the earlier heroic verse without using unnecessary epithets. He shows how Pope's translation of the *Iliad* has two syllables forming superfluous words in each line:

> Achilles' wrath to Greece the *direful* spring
> Of woes unnumber'd, *heavenly* goddess, sing;
> That wrath which sent to Pluto's *gloomy* reign,
> The souls of *mighty* chiefs in battle slain,
> Whose bones, unburied on the *desert* shore
> Devouring dogs and *hungry* vultures tore.[9]

Neoclassical regularity was to prove a historical exception rather than an enduring rule.

Transformations of feeling

Among the most important prosodic ideas that gradually took hold by the mid-eighteenth century was the contention that the content of the work should determine the shape of the form, and it is significant that such an early critique of heroic couplets had come from Isaac Watts, a prominent writer of hymns. There was a precedent for this, well known by Milton, in the classical idea that musical modalities had attached emotions: the Dorian scale vigorously masculine; the Lydian relaxed; the Phrygian wild.[10] Samuel Say's essays on prosody attached to his 1745 *Poems on Several Occasions* suggested that "'Tis reasonable . . . to assume a different Style, and Numbers far Different, when the Like Ideas, or the Like Passions are intended to be rais'd in Those that hear us," and he particularly admired the alternating active iambics and slow spondaics of *Paradise Lost*.[11]

St. Cecilia odes, often composed for an annual competition that was begun in 1683 by the London Musical Society, were important models in this light: with their effects of musical mimesis and varying metrical effects and forms, the Cecilia odes picked up on Pindaric irregularity and carried it over to forms of great originality and musicality, allowing various instruments to "raise and quell the passions." The mimetic effects of Wordsworth's "On the Power of Sound," and his libretto "Ode on the Installation of His Royal Highness Prince Albert as Chancellor of the University of Cambridge, July 1847," are much indebted to Dryden's and Pope's Cecilia odes.[12]

In 1789 William Lisle Bowles assembled a group of "Fourteen Sonnets, written chiefly on Picturesque Spots during a Journey." He recorded later: "I confined myself to fourteen lines, because fourteen lines seemed best adapted to unity of sentiment. I thought nothing about the strict Italian model; the verses naturally flowed in unpremeditated harmony, as my ear directed." He added: "The subjects were chiefly from river scenery . . . it will be recollected also, that they were published ten years before those of Mr. Wordsworth on the river Duddon."[13]

Bowles's decasyllabic poems used varied stress patterns, and, though they followed a Shakespearean rhyme scheme, they tended to divide between octave and sestet like a Petrarchan sonnet as they also introduced new rhymes in the second quatrain. His hybrid forms were themselves indebted to the popular, and irregular, *Elegiac Sonnets*, first published in 1784, of Charlotte Turner Smith – poems that had revived the possibilities of the sonnet for expressing interior emotion, whether experienced or invented. Bowles's innovation, however, was to link his emotions and thoughts to depictions of the landscape as he traveled in one journey from England to Scotland and in another journey across the North Sea to Ostend and up the Rhine. Yoking the long prospect poem with the sonnet, his poems proved to be a tremendous influence on the work of Blake, Coleridge, Wordsworth, and Byron because of their free expression of emotion. The Romantics looked to Milton's work, too, as a precedent for sonnets of public reflection; sonnets fit neatly into the space available in newspapers, and, after the craze for sentimental sonnets at the end of the eighteenth century, Coleridge's "Sonnets on Eminent Characters," Wordsworth's "Sonnets Dedicated to Liberty," and Shelley's "England in 1819," which literally turns Petrarchan convention upside down, were just some of the sonnets designed for political ends.[14] Wordsworth published 517 sonnets over his lifetime, and Keats, who gave up sonnet-writing just before he turned to his great odes of 1819, still managed to write sixty-four of them within a five-year period.[15]

The Romantic critique of eighteenth-century syllabic prosody was based not only in an idea about fidelity to the passions, but as well in an idea about fidelity to expression. What kind of expression was this? Perhaps, above all, it was one that had a realist bias – poetry was to represent the emotions and not to be an ideal and regulating force upon them; to this extent, arguments about poetic representation followed arguments about musical representation and led poets to become interested in the equal-time principles of accentual verse that linked the metrical foot and musical bar. And such feelings had to be located in the speaker/hearer relation – this placed a burden of authenticity on to the poet/speaker that could be alleviated only by means of imitation of others' voices.

Practices of ventriloquism in Romantic meter raise the possibility of sympathetic response conveyed through meter itself. The imitation of "mad" voices can be linked to chanting as a device of Romantic poetic composition. There are "mad song" elements in *Lyrical Ballads'* "The Idiot Boy" and "The Mad Mother," and in *Peter Bell*. Coleridge had a long interest in mad poetry, and, earlier, "mad songs" were an influence upon Thomas Percy's 1765 *Reliques*.[16] The imitation of the mad also figured, as we shall see, in the enormous contribution the mad poets of the eighteenth century made to Romantic prosody. And in the career of John Clare, issues of authenticity are magnified as the "mad" poet at times writes poems in the voices of Thomas Chatterton and Lord Byron.

The transfer of such feelings resulted in certain paradoxes, as when Wordsworth writes in the 1800 Preface to *Lyrical Ballads*[17] that poetry is at once "the spontaneous overflow of powerful feelings" (pp. 126–7) and "emotion recollected in tranquility" (pp. 148–9). In his 1850 version of the Preface, Wordsworth continued to think of meter as "superadded" (p. 137). Poetry is to be made of the "language really spoken by men," he wrote, explaining: "if meter be superadded thereto, I believe that a dissimilitude will be produced altogether sufficient for the gratification of a rational mind" (p. 137). For Wordsworth, "the distinction of meter is regular and uniform" (pp. 144–5) and, more than any other Romantic poet, he carried forward a sense of the eighteenth-century mandate toward regularity. Significantly, however, his thinking about blank verse's potential regularity arose from a sense that poets could make a painful content bearable by means of metrical ease: "The end of Poetry is to produce excitement in co-existence with an overbalance of pleasure" (pp. 146–7). In putting his tragic Lucy poems into simple ballad meter or laying out the sorrows of "The Female Vagrant" in Spenserian stanza, Wordsworth wrote in his 1850 text that he had explored the ways "more pathetic situations and sentiments, that is, those which have a greater proportion of pain connected with them, may be endured in metrical composition, especially in rhyme, than in prose" (p. 147).

Inevitably, because of their pathbreaking work on *Lyrical Ballads* and the enduring nature of their collaboration and involvement in each other's thought, Wordsworth and Coleridge are considered together in estimations of Romantic achievement. Yet their approaches to meter in theory and practice are quite different; Wordsworth's idea that meter is "superadded thereto" approaches the mechanical – the opposite of Coleridge's organic notions of meter as, following August Wilhelm von Schlegel's ideas of conscious and unconscious activity in creation, he outlined them in his 1808–19 Lectures on Literature. Coleridge contended that "One character belongs to all true poets, they that write from a principle within, nor originating in anything without," and he admonished: "Remember that there is a difference between form as proceeding, and shape as superinduced; – the latter is either the death or the imprisonment of the thing; – the former is its self-witnessing and self-effected sphere of agency."[18] In the *Biographia Literaria*, too, he suggested: "Could a rule be given from *without*, poetry would cease to be poetry, and sink into a mechanical art."[19]

Consequently, while Wordsworth states in the 1802 preface: "there neither is, nor can be, any essential difference between the language of prose and metrical composition" (134), Coleridge claims in the *Biographia Literaria*: "I write in meter because I am about to use a language different from that of prose."[20] In his essay "First Acquaintance with Poets," William Hazlitt famously recorded that these differences extended to the two poets' methods of composing: "Coleridge has told me that he himself liked to compose in walking over uneven ground, or breaking through the straggling branches of a copse-wood; whereas Wordsworth always wrote (if he could) walking up and down a straight gravel-walk, or in some spot where the continuity of his verse met with no collateral interruption."[21] This contrast persists, as a Miltonic legacy of enjambed blank verse remains the *métier* of the

Wordsworth of *The Prelude*, while Coleridge often seeks "lines" that reflect the emotion of their content. Meanwhile, a Spenserian legacy of accentual meters and song forms continues throughout both their careers.

Native sources

Poets in the second half of the eighteenth century and the beginning of the nineteenth tended to turn to such British roots for their practice, rather than, like Bysshe and others, looking to European, and particularly French, models. John Armstrong went so far as to imply, in his 1758 *Sketches*, that writers of excessively regular dramatic verse in the French style lacked patriotism.[22] The stately enjambed blank verse of William Cowper's "Yardley Oak" of 1791 links druid rituals to the oracle at Dodona, and the English fleet to Cowper's own translations from the *Iliad* (at ll. 159–60, he quotes from Book VI). John Aiken's 1774 *Essays on Song-Writing* claim that in ballads "the character of the nation displays itself in striking colours."[23] Percy's *Reliques* were the most evident source of the infusion of British ballad forms into poetry, but the poets of the mid-eighteenth century, confronted by the crisis in audience that the popularity of the novel, the extension of literacy, and the decline of local traditions and patronage posed, looked variously to the English, Welsh, Scots, and Irish minstrels, bards, and ballad-singers for models of their craft.[24] There are many thematic reasons for this, but there are as well formal ones since song forms untied many of the knots presented by the eighteenth-century prohibition on trisyllabic "substitutions."

Robert Burns wrote in 1785 in his *Commonplace Book*: "There is a certain irregularity in the old Scotch Songs, a redundancy of syllables with respect to that exactness of accent and measure which the English Poetry requires."[25] The stanza we now name for him, "Burns meter," is a six-line stanza form using a tail rhyme, or rhyme that unites the stanzas (in Burns stanza, *aaabab*); all the *a* lines are tetrameter and the *b* lines are dimeter. In "To a Louse" and other comic poems, Burns makes clever use of the comic surprise that the return of the *b* rhyme affords; inversely, Wordsworth creates, in his elegy, "At the Grave of Burns.1803. Seven Years After His Death," a sense of melancholy by turning to the serious task of mourning its maker. Here is the last stanza:

> Sighing I turned away; but ere
> Night fell I heard, or seemed to hear,
> Music that sorrow comes not near,
>   A ritual hymn,
> Chanted in love that casts out fear
>   By Seraphim.

In fact, this stanza has a medieval provenance; William of Poitiers used it in the eleventh century, and as "Scottish meter," derived from troubadour tradition, played a role in Romantic verse, so did medieval Irish accentual verse. Byron, who borrowed meters and forms widely and with a wild fluency, for example, adapted the Irish *ochtfhoclach*, with its complicated pattern of echoing stresses, assonance, and rhyme, in his 1819 "Stanzas."[26]

The emergence of accentual meter and effects of trisyllabic and trochaic substitution are perhaps even more readily evident in Blake's pioneering work in the *Songs of Innocence* (1789). In the first stanza of "The Little Boy Found," for example, we find both trochaic and anapestic substitutions:

> The little boy lost in the lonely fen,
> Led by the wand-ring light,
> Began to cry, but God ever nigh,
> Appeard like his father in white.

This is a traditional ballad stanza of 4343, rhyming *abcb*. It is the kind of ballad form Blake would have known from many sources, including his copy of Percy. There were of course other routes to song form – through returning to Ben Jonson, who wrote songs in 4444 common meter (as in "Song: To Celia I") and 4343 ballad meter (as in "Song: To Celia II"), and whose work influenced Percy's decisions regarding the printing of song texts. *The Shepheardes Calender* also was an important repertoire of song stanza forms.[27] The ballad collectors of the eighteenth century paid little attention to the living ballad tradition and tended to take two seven-beat phrases of ballad music and print them as a 4343 stanza; when we think of poets of the period using ballad form, we inevitably are looking at poetry influenced by printed collections.[28]

The widespread interest in hymns became a pervasive literary influence during the period as well. Congregational hymn-singing, which involves a collective group of people singing songs of individual, often paradoxically private, emotion, is closely associated with traditions of eighteenth-century Protestant nonconformism. Here another sense of the power of music and rhythm to sway thought was not lost on the didactic hymn-writers of the period, and we find many collections of hymns devoted particularly to children's voices, among them Watts's *Divine and Moral Songs Attempted in easy Language, for the Use of Children* of 1715. Blake's "A Cradle Song" is a direct imitation of Watts, and indeed all of *Songs of Innocence* and *Songs of Experience* forms a commentary upon this body of hymns.

Within the *Lyrical Ballads* of 1798, only "The Rime of the Ancyent Marinere" is strictly in 4343 ballad quatrains of *abcb*; "The Tables Turned" is in 4343 quatrains rhyming *abab* and "Lines" and "Expostulation and Reply" are written in common meter quatrains rhyming *abab*. But many poems in the volume are permutations on ballad, hymn, and common meter: "Goody Blake and Harry Gill" is written in an eight-line stanza form that doubles up two common-meter quatrains rhyming, with several exceptions, *ababcdcd*; "Simon Lee" is another eight-line form made of quatrains 44434343 rhyming *abbcded*; "Anecdote for Fathers" is 4443 *abab*. Everywhere the poems are constructed by various voices in call and response; they begin *in medias res*, often allowing an anonymous narrator to speak the words of others, often developing by means of incremental repetition – all techniques of the traditional British ballad.

However, this traditional ballad stanza does not exactly overlap with the metrics of the relatively more recent tradition of broadside ballads, which usually use stanzas of 4444 and frequently, unlike traditional ballads, begin at the beginning, with discursive sequential accounts and even rationales for action.[29] Broadside ballad structure and form are thus perfect to convey the immediacy of Shelley's *The Mask of Anarchy* – "Written on the occasion of the Massacre at Manchester" in August 1819. This political poem decries the killing, by drunken mounted soldiers, of a group of men, women, and children assembled to support Parliamentary reform. Shelley uses uncharacteristically low diction in the poem, designing it for a popular audience. Composed of tetrameter quatrains made of sets of rhyming couplets and occasional triplets, the poem was sent to be published in Leigh Hunt's *Examiner*, though Hunt, worried about prosecution, in fact did not publish it until 1832.[30]

The ballad revival was in part sparked by controversies over Homer's status as a bard,[31] and by James Macpherson's presentation of his 1761 epic pastiche, *Ossian*, as a genuine work of oral tradition rather than the literary composition it truly was. Macpherson's prose "translation" was a great influence on many of the Romantic poets, from Blake's construction of prose epics to Wordsworth's insistence that the best poetry, though distinguishable by its meter, would "in no respect differ from that of good prose" (p. 286). Macpherson's "translation" is organized around paragraphs of dialogue – here is a paragraph from "Fingal," Book I:

> He answered, like a wave on a rock, who in this land appears like me? Heroes stand not in my presence; they fall to earth beneath my hand. None can meet Swaran in the fight but Fingal, king of stormy hills. Once we wrestled on the heath of Malmor, and our heels overturned the wood. Rocks fell from their place; and rivulets, changing their course, fled murmuring from our strife. Three days we renewed our strife, and heroes stood at a distance and trembled. On the fourth, Fingal says, that the king of the ocean fell; but Swaran says he stood. Let dark Cuchullin yield to him that is strong as the storms of Malmor.[32]

Macpherson uses devices borrowed from classical epic, such as heroic epithets, hyperbole, and hyperbata, but it is his picturesque vertical effects of dizzying heights, falling rocks, and towering heroes, and his horizontal effects of vast seas and skies that became enduring techniques for representing the sublime. Wordsworth's late poem, "Written in a Blank Leaf of Macpherson's Ossian," part of his "Poems Composed or Suggested During a Tour in 1833," begins on a mountain height as a storm approaches, and ends by praising, in contrast to Macpherson, the authenticity of Milton. The Romantic aesthetic of poetic sublimity, inspired by nature and techniques of heightened rhetoric and intense meter at once, has a complex derivation out of Longinus' first-century treatise on the sublime, the eighteenth-century tenets of Edmund Burke, and Kant's "analytics" of the sublime and the beautiful. These issues can be seen to culminate in Shelley's "Hymn to Intellectual Beauty," with its urgent enactment of the mind's subreption via strings of similes as the speaker encounters and remembers his experiences of nature.

Ancient sources

The influences of Milton and Spenser, along with British song traditions, transformed a syllabic and heroic predilection to an accentual and lyric one, but Romanticism was itself another version of neoclassicism – and poets of the later eighteenth century simply began to draw on other resources of classical culture than those that occupied their immediate predecessors. Just as early eighteenth-century artists and architects mistakenly thought ancient buildings were unpainted, so did early eighteenth-century poets see rules of symmetry and heroic narrative in the dactylic hexameters of epic verse and the distiches of elegiacs. The uneven lines and stanza forms of Pindar's odes, the pounding heterometric stanzas of Sappho, Horace's practice of making each of his books anthologies of widely varying verse forms, were just some of the ancient poetic practices that came to the fore with the Romantic period. William Collins followed Milton's use of Horatian form; and the remarkable suspended syntax of Collins's Horatian "Ode to Evening" can be viewed as a precedent for the complex ambiguous syntax of Keats's odes. With its pronounced pauses in the final lines of its 4443 quatrains, Collins's "Ode to Peace"is an exact model for the haunting, curtailed "And no birds sing" refrains of Keats's "La Belle Dame Sans Merci."

With the significant exception of the Immortality Ode and a few other poems, Wordsworth also tends to the regularity of Horatian forms, as we can see in his juvenile translation of Horace's "O fons bandusiae," his "Ode to Duty," his "Ode to Lycoris," and his "Ode" of 1816 ("When the soft hand of sleep"), which begins with an epigraph from Horace's Book IV, 8: *Carmia possumus / Donare, et pretium dicere maneri.* And Coleridge, with the exception of his "Ode to Sleep" and "Ode to Tranquillity," tends to the unevenness of the Pindaric, as we can see in his "Dejection: An Ode," "Ode to the Departing Year," and "France: an Ode."

Self-taught in reading Hebrew, Greek, and Latin, Blake reported in 1799 that "to renew the lost Art of the Greeks" was "the purpose for which alone I live." Yet while he produced a visual art strongly influenced by Greek and Roman models, he excoriated classical culture for its militarism, writing in "On Homers Poetry": "the Classics, it is the Classics & not Goths nor Monks, that Desolate Europe with Wars," and in "On Virgil": "Rome & Greece swept Art into their maw & destroyd it a Warlike State never can produce Art . . . Gothic is Living Form."

Coleridge and Shelley, who had considerable Greek, continued to read English meters within a grid of classical metrics. We know, for example, that Coleridge described the line "I heard a voice pealing loud triumph today" as "amphibrach tetrameter catalectic": -/- -/- -/- -/ (that is, as four amphibrachs, the final one of which is catalectic, or incomplete).[33] The reception of the neoclassical poets themselves was not simply a matter of reversing their precepts. Bysshe and other strict syllabists had criticized Dryden, and Keats relied on him for *Lamia.* Wordsworth expressed his admiration for Pope's "Windsor Forest" as nature poetry; Byron praised the "softness, passion and beauty" of *Eloisa to Abelard* and the imagery of the *Epistle to Dr. Arbuthnot.*[34] The Romantics were able to read their own aesthetics back into neoclassical works.

Another important model for poetic form, once the heroic line gave way to enjambment and irregularity, was the Hebrew Bible. Christopher Smart's *Jubilate Agno,* composed during his confinement in a madhouse from 1756 to 1763, and his 1763 *A Song to David,* explicitly drew on Hebrew poetic traditions, particularly in their use of anaphora, syntactical parallelism, catalogues, and doubled sequences of phrases or clauses. Here is a stanza from *A Song to David:*

499	Glorious the sun in mid career;
500	Glorious th' assembled fires appear;
501	Glorious the comet's train:
502	Glorious the trumpet and alarm;
503	Glorious th' almighty stretch'd-out arm;
504	Glorious th' enraptur'd main:

In these lines Smart uses a pure accentual meter to create a song structure of 4a4a3b4c5c3b. The fifth line elegantly changes the dynamic between the falling dactyls of *Glorious* and rising iambs of those feet that follow to the literally stretched-out spondee of *out*. Smart's *Jubilate Agno*, not published until the twentieth century, was designed with alternating passages that would follow the antiphonal patterns of the scriptures.

Of course David had been a model for the figure of the poet during the metaphysical period as well, but when we look at the major genres of Hebrew poetry – the epithalamia of the Song of Songs, the hymns, the narrative poems of prophecy and the suffering of Job; the dirges on the destruction of Jerusalem in Lamentations and the aphorisms in Proverbs and Ecclesiastes – we find a map of much of Blake's work in *The Marriage of Heaven and Hell* and his songs, visions and prophecies, creation stories, and accounts of Jerusalem. In these lines (pl. 43, ll. 47–51) from Blake's *Jerusalem*, Chapter 2, we see a predominantly six-beat line focusing upon the meaning of a medial caesura that organizes a paradoxical relation between nothing and becoming nothing, withdrawing and releasing – a caesura first unmarked, then becoming stronger by means of punctuation from semicolon to colon to period:

> O I am nothing when I enter into judgment with thee!
> If thou withdraw thy breath I die & vanish into Hades
> If thou dost lay thine hand upon me behold I am silent:
> If thou withhold thine hand; I perish like a fallen leaf:
> O I am nothing: and to nothing must return again:
> If thou withdraw thy breath. Behold I am oblivion.

Here and elsewhere in his prophetic works, *The Book of Tel* and *Tiriel*, Blake uses the metrical line of the "fourteener," borrowing from its serious and elevated uses in the sixteenth-century translations of Arthur Golding's version of Ovid's *Metamorphoses* and George Chapman's version of Homer's *Iliad*. Golding and Chapman may have seen the fourteener as the closest equivalent to the dactylic hexameter of classical epic, and "poulter's measure," alternating twelve- and fourteen-syllable lines, gives some approximation of the rhythm of classical elegiac with its alternating lines of hexameter and pentameter. When two fourteeners are broken into hemistiches to form a quatrain of lines stressed 4343, rhyming *abab*, they resemble ballad meter and common meter, or common measure and other hymn forms. When a line of twelve syllables is followed by a fourteener, it can correspondingly be broken into a quatrain of 3343 – what we call short meter. There thereby seems to be an intriguing family resemblance between these meters, but it is important to note that the quatrain form makes a great difference in the sense of balance, pause, and emphasis that we find in these song meters.

Byron's *Hebrew Melodies* of 1815, written in the wake of Thomas Moore's tremendously successful *Irish Melodies* of 1808, are a mixture of lyric forms, many of them based on themes from the scriptures, including his poem of David, "The Harp the Monarch Minstrel Swept." This two-part lyric uses a ten-line stanza with four rhymes *ababbcdcdd*, and thus is a variation of French *ballade* form; each of its sets of nine tetrameter lines ends in a pentameter. Byron's use of discontinuous rhythm in "The Destruction of Sennacherib" is another innovation. The poem uses anapestic tetrameter rhyming couplets grouped into numbered quatrains. It is difficult to sustain the effect of the stanza, so Byron uses *And* anaphorically to begin nearly half the lines, sometimes with an unstressed syllable to continue the anapest and at other times using the conjunction as the first syllable of an iamb. These techniques add to the effect of biblical narrative, but also vary it. In the following stanza the quick leap to the iamb in the second line adds to the drama of *And breathed*, the central action of the stanza, rhyming internally with the consequence of this deadly breathing – the hearts that *heaved*.

> For the Angel of Death spread his wings on the blast,
> And breathed in the face of the foe as he passed;
> And the eyes of the sleepers waxed deadly and chill,
> And their hearts but once heaved – and for ever grew still!

With Byron's creation of Hebrew songs in imitation of Irish melodies, and Blake's extended biblical line borrowing from Renaissance translations of classical literature, we are in the thick of the syncretic dimension of Romantic meter and form. An age of prosodic simplicity gave way to an age of great prosodic texture – though simplicity, as admired in Italian madrigals by Coleridge and in the British ballads by everyone, is only one among many styles.[35] The metrical and formal nativism that for the most part kept Blake, Wordsworth, Keats, and Clare close to Milton, Spenser, and vernacular British forms yields to renewed influence from European literature with Coleridge's studies of German and Italian forms, with Shelley's *terza rima* of his "Ode to the West Wind" and "The Triumph of Life," and with Byron's *ottava rima* in *Don Juan* and "Beppo." In this sense the mandate that form should bear an intrinsic relation to content is reinforced and the liberty of the poet to choose a form increased. As Blake writes in the last paragraph of his preface to *Jerusalem*:

> When this Verse was first dictated to me I consider'd a Monotonous Cadence like that used by Milton & Shakespeare & all writers of English Blank Verse, derived from the modern bondage of rhyming; to be a necessary and indispensable part of Verse. But I soon found that in the mouth of a true Orator such monotony was not only awkward, but as much a bondage as rhyme itself. I

therefore have produced a variety in every line, both of cadences & number of syllables. Every word and every letter is studied and put into its fit place: the terrific numbers are reserved for the terrific parts – the mild & gentle, for the mild & gentle parts, and the prosaic, for inferior parts: all are necessary to each other.

Accentual inventions

Despite the epic poet's "dictation" from an invisible muse, Blake expresses both a novelistic sense of poetic form and a claim to a total art. Here one of the most important influences on the major Romantic poets is Thomas Chatterton (1752–70). Born five years before Blake and seven before Burns, he was the author of a number of works he acknowledged, as well as of his fake-medieval "Rowley" poems. The latter, composed between the ages of fifteen and eighteen, when he died a suicide, were attributed to imaginary others. Chatterton was a poet of astonishing inventiveness – not only in his creation of his medieval Bristol world, but as well in his facility with meter. The Rowley poems show him at work in a wide range of forms, including the traditional, and quite convincing, ballad structure of his "Bristowe Tragedie." An avid reader of Spenser, he also invented a number of stanza forms that can be seen as modifications of Spenserian stanza. When Horace Walpole recognized the anachronism of a "medieval" Spenserian form, Chatterton boldly claimed that the form in fact had been "in use 300 years before."

The most common of the Rowley stanzas, however, is a ten-line group *ababbcbcdd*. As in his "English Metamorphosis" by "T.[homas] Rowleie," Chatterton sometimes extends a last line of pentameter to hexameter, but more often his work is all in pentameter. Chatterton's influence upon Wordsworth is striking: the form of Wordsworth's "Resolution and Independence" is borrowed directly from Chatterton's "An Excelente Balade of Charitie (As Written by the Good Priest Thomas Rowley, 1464)": six lines of iambic pentameter with a seventh hexameter line, rhyming *ababbcc* – in other words, rhyme royal with a Spenserian alexandrine.[36] And although the comparison is less exact, there is a striking resemblance between the stanzas of varied lines in Chatterton's "Songe to Ælla, Lord of the Castle of Bristol in Days of yore," including the eight-line stanza:

> When Dacia's sons, whose hairs of blood-red hue,
> Like kingcups bursting with the morning dew,
>> Arranged in drear array,
>> Upon the lethal day,
> Spread far and wide on Watchet's shore;

> Then didst thou furious stand,
> And by thy valiant hand
> Didst sprinkle all the meads with gore

and the eight- and nine-line heterometric ode stanzas with which Wordsworth begins his Immortality Ode, and the eight-line stanzas of pentameter and tetrameter, with trimeter lines for emphasis, in Coleridge's "Monody on the Death of Chatterton" – a poem Coleridge worked on "for the whole of his life as a poet."[37] Chatterton's ten-line poems clearly have been an influence upon the various ten-line stanzas Keats invents for his "Ode to a Nightingale," "Ode on Melancholy" and "Ode on a Grecian Urn." Keats's *Endymion*, dedicated to Chatterton as "the stretched meter of an antique song," acknowledges his debt.

What does Keats mean by a "stretched meter"? In *Endymion*, which he considered an "endeavor" and sometimes wrote at a pace of fifty lines a day between the end of October and the end of November in 1817, the meter is iambic pentameter expressed in rhyming couplets, but the pentameter lines frequently shift to hexameter and often hold anywhere from eight to eleven syllables. Within this backdrop, Keats embeds in Book I his stanzaic "Hymn to Pan" (ll. 232–306) with its dramatic dimeter exclamations, and in Book IV, ll. 146–290, a "roundelay" built from alternations of dimeter and pentameter lines. As he gradually returns to the pentameter frame, he continues to interrupt the pentameter with dimeter and trimeter exclamations that give the effect of metrical echoes in the ensuing narrative.

Here the use of accentual meter to express various voices reflects both a view back to the pure stress meters of medieval verse and a more contemporary view of the possibilities of dramatic and written verse. The British ballad is sung traditionally as if the singer were possessed by alternating voices:

> Oh who sits weeping on my grave,
> And will not let me sleep?
> Tis I, my love, sits on your grave
> And will not let you sleep.
>
> ("The Unquiet Grave")
>
> What d'ye leave to your sister, my handsome young man"
> My gold and my silver: mother, mak my bed soon.
>
> ("Lord Randal")

Such call-and-response structures can stand alone as dramatic dialogues, or be embedded in narrative, as they are in most ballads and novels breaking into dialogue. One of the most important inventions of the period, the "conversation poem," as Coleridge labeled "The Nightingale" when it appeared in *Lyrical Ballads*, is indebted to this ballad technique. It is the innovation of "Tintern Abbey" and "Frost at Midnight" to have a silent auditor to the conversation, rather than voices existing in the presence of one another, and perhaps the conversation poem's ascendance explains why the epistolary poem, so popular during the earlier eighteenth century, almost disappears in the Romantic period.

Many of the long narrative poems of Romanticism rely on shifts of voice and meter such as those outlined in *Endymion*. As early as Bowles's 1798 blank-verse poem on the Elan Valley in Wales, "Coombe-Ellen," we find such embedding of voice and alternative meter as the expression of an interior monologue. The poet imagines "a pale minstrel" and then summons him via an invocation in ballad meter:

> Son of the magic song, arise!
> And bid the deep-toned lyre
> Pour forth its manly melodies.
> With eyes on fire.[38]

This multiplication of speakers and auditors also can be tied to the tendency of Romantic poets to ask questions in their poems – consider Keats's sublime "Do I wake or sleep?" with which he closes his "Ode to a Nightingale," or Coleridge's bizarre exchange in Part I of "Christabel": "Is the Night chilly and dark ? / The Night is chilly but not dark."[39]

The metrical romance, a poem situated in the margin between history and the imagination, allows for effects of surprise and drama to be heightened by the regularity of its beats. "He thought of her afar, his only bride: / He turn'd and saw – Gulnare, the homicide!" writes Byron in "The Corsair" (III, 1); "Yet they contrived to steal the basil-pot, / And to examine it in secret place. / The thing was vile with green and livid spot, / And yet they knew it was Lorenzo's face," goes the second climactic unburial in Keats's "Isabella, or the Pot of Basil" (LX, 473–6). The genre is most thoroughly rationalized by Coleridge in his introduction to "Christabel." There he claimed that "the metre of the Christabel is not, properly speaking, irregular, though it may seem so from its being founded on a new principle: namely, that of counting in each line the accents, not the syllables. Though the latter may vary from seven to twelve, yet in each line the accents will be found to be only four. Nevertheless, this occasional variation in number of syllables is not introduced wantonly, or for the mere ends of convenience, but in correspondence with some transition, in the nature of the imagery or passion."[40] Coleridge wrote to Byron in October of 1815: "I count by Beats or accents instead of syllables – in the belief that a meter might be thus produced sufficiently uniform and far more malleable to the Passion and Meaning."[41] Coleridge's claims of a "new" accentualism perhaps have more to do with the public acceptance of the form than anything else. In 1844, Leigh Hunt was still arguing for the metrical excitement of accentualism: "verse is the final proof to the poet that his mastery over his art is complete."[42] Widely circulated in manuscript for more than a decade before its publication in 1816, "Christabel" had been recited to Sir Walter Scott[43] and many others. Scott carried its equivalenced octosyllabic couplets and ballad meters within narrative verse over to his 1805 *The Lay of the Last Minstrel*, just as Wordsworth would use the form two years later to build the accentual tetrameter couplets of his "The White Doe of Rylstone." Even so, Coleridge is being either disingenuous or ironic in saying that accentual meter is a "new" principle; he was well aware that Spenser had used a four-stress line in the February, May, and September eclogues of his *The Shepheardes Calender*; he mentions the influence of Richard Crashaw's "Hymn to St. Teresa," also in pure stress meter, in his *Table Talk*; and Chatterton, Burns, and of course Blake had used accentual meter extensively.

Poetry as text

As many rubricated hymnals demonstrate, refrain and response can also be viewed as qualities of reading text. A call-and-response structure is employed by Blake across his book projects, so that the *Songs of Experience* echo and transform the *Songs of Innocence* and identical wording crosses *The Four Zoas*, *Milton*, and *Jerusalem*: passages are transposed with only place names changed.[44] Blake specialized in a poetry that repeated certain feelings in changing places, and we might say, thinking of "Tintern Abbey" and the title of the elegy to Burns, for example, that Wordsworth inversely specialized in a poetry that changed feelings in repeated returns to certain places. The demands the Romantic poets place on contexts of landscape and weather in their meditative odes are heavy and give evidence of poets who cannot fall back on the ritual structures of social life to put into motion traditional meanings either for poetry or for existence. Romantic poetry faced the need to generate its own occasions, and this alone may explain why so much of it was about poetry itself.

Some of the work of the Romantics remained a coterie poetry: if Coleridge often edited what was personal from his personal poems in order to publish them in the newspapers,[45] Shelley, making a clear separation between his public and his private poetry, never seemed to have planned to publish his lyrics addressed to individual living persons.[46] Yet in other ways, Romantic poetry is very much a textual poetry and poetry of the book, designed for an audience of strangers. Chatterton's illuminated manuscripts; the predilection of the later Romantics for epithets, epigrams, lines written on objects, and other forms of inscription;[47] Wordsworth's aesthetic of the fragment and habit of incorporating versions of one poem into versions of another; the marginalia of Coleridge's 1834 revision of "The Rime of the Ancient Mariner"; Charlotte Smith's discursive footnotes to her poems, including her sonnets; the "mental theater" of Byron's *Manfred* and *Cain*; Shelley's *Cenci* and *Prometheus Unbound* as closet dramas; Wordsworth's *The Borderers* "judiciously returned as not suitable for the stage";[48] Byron's hilarious asides to his readers in *Don Juan* – these are all some of the ways poets reinforced the printed materiality of their work. Indeed, the plethora of poems called simply "Lines," or using "Lines on" in their titles, speaks to the way blank verse is most easily discerned as verse by the eye, as Johnson had complained.

An important and unusual innovation of Blake's metrics was his consciousness of how meter might read visually amid his graphic art. Consider, for example, "The Sick Rose":

> O Rose, thou art sick.
> The invisible worm
> That flies in the night
> In the howling storm
>
> Has found out thy bed
> Of crimson joy,
> And his dark secret love
> Does thy life destroy.

Which we can depict metrically as follows:

> -/ --/
> -- / --/
> -/ --/
> --/ -/
>
> -/ --/
> -/ -/
> --/ --/
> --/ -/

Right side up, upside down, or backwards, this poem reveals a set of metrical repetitions (lines 1 and 5; 1 and 3; 4 and 8; 2 and 7) and reversals (lines 1 and 4; 5 and 8; 1 and 8; 4 and 5; 3 and 8), while the sixth line, "of crimson joy," remains unique – the damaged center of this little tightly wound bud of a poem.

The story of Romantic meter and form is often told within a liberation narrative that is rooted in Romanticism itself: it records how poets on or about 1798 awoke to shake off the chains of eighteenth-century prosody and expressed an individual passion through their newly invented meters and themes. To some degree, they did. But Romanticism was a European movement, and British poets cast widely in space and deeply in time for their models. Eighteenth-century syllabic theory was countered from the start; a number of the most dramatic innovations in Romantic metric were first put forward by the minor poets of the mid-eighteenth century; and Augustan neoclassicism turned out to be only one kind of neo-classicism. As Wordsworth implied, there is nothing particularly conservative or liberating about a meter – the regularity of a meter might sustain a poet expressing a nearly inexpressible content; the irregularity of meter might enliven and complicate a simple thought. Yet the great achievement of the Romantic poets' individual poems and books speaks to what is perhaps the most important and universal legacy of their work in theory and practice. Indeed, they created a domain where theory and practice are one as they insisted upon yoking conceptual and sensual life in the production of form.

NOTES

1 *Guardian* (London: J. Tonson, 1713), n.p.
2 C. B. McCully, "Writing Under the Influence: Milton and Wordsworth, Mind and Meter," *Language and Literature* 9/3 (2000), pp. 195–214.
3 Paul Fussell, *Theory of Prosody in Eighteenth-Century England* (New London: Connecticut College, 1954), pp. 13–14, and A. Dwight Culler, "Edward Bysshe and the Poet's Handbook," *PMLA* 63/3 (1948), pp. 858–86, at p. 872.
4 From "The Life of Milton," *Works of Samuel Johnson*, ed. Arthur Murphy, vol. II (New York: Harper, 1873), pp. 22–48, at p. 48. See also Johnson's essays from *The Rambler*, in *Works*, vol. I: "The danger of succeeding a great author: An introduction to a criticism on Milton's versification," p. 137; and "A Criticism of Milton's versification," p. 140.
5 Johnson, "The dangers of imitation: The impropriety of imitating Spenser," from *The Rambler*, *Works*, vol. I, p. 190.
6 Johnson, "The Life of Cowley," *Works*, vol. II, pp. 3–19, at p. 7.
7 David Perkins, "How the Romantics Recited Poetry," *Studies in English Literature 1500–1900* 31/4 (Autumn 1991), pp. 665–71.
8 Isaac Watts, *Horae Lyricae, or Poems Chiefly of the Lyric Kind*, 2nd edn. (London: J. Humfreys, 1709), p. xx.
9 Sir Walter Scott, *The Lay of the Last Minstrel* (New York: Thomas Crowell, n.d.), 1831 Introduction, text published in 1805. Italics original.
10 John Hollander, "Romantic Verse Form and the Metrical Contract," in *Vision and Resonance* (New Haven: Yale University Press, 1985), pp. 187–211, at p. 190.

11 Samuel Say, *Poems on Several Occasions, and Two Critical Essays* (London: John Hughes, 1745), p. 99, and, on Milton, p. 127. Fussell surveys Say's work in his *Theory of Prosody*, pp. 111–17.

12 Clifford Ames, "Variations on a Theme; Baroque and Neoclassical Aesthetics in the St. Cecilia Day Odes of Dryden and Pope," *English Literary History* 65/3 (1998), pp. 617–35, and Stuart Curran, *Poetic Form and British Romanticism* (New York: Oxford University Press, 1986), p. 65.

13 William Lisle Bowles, *The Poetical Works*, 2 vols. (Edinburgh: Ballantyne, 1855), with the preface to the 1837 edition, p. 2.

14 These comments follow Curran on the sonnet; *Poetic Form and British Romanticism*, pp. 29–55.

15 Lee M. Johnson, "Wordsworth and the Sonnet," *Anglistica*, vol. xix (Copenhagen: Rosenkilde & Bagger, 1973); Robert Gidding, *John Keats* (Boston: Little, Brown, 1968), p. 310; John Keats, *The 64 Sonnets*, ed. Edward Hirsch and Gary Hawkins (Philadelphia: Paul Dry Books, 2004).

16 J. C. C. Mays, "New Light on Wordsworth's Coleridge," *Wordsworth Circle* 29/1 (Winter 1998), pp. 9–20, at p. 12, and Brennan O'Donnell, *The Passion of Meter: A Study of Wordsworth's Metrical Art* (Kent, OH: Kent State University Press, 1995), pp. 163–5.

17 *The Prose Works of William Wordsworth*, ed. W.J.B. Owen and Jane W. Smyser, vol. 1 (Oxford: Clarendon Press, 1974). The 1800 Preface faces the 1850 one here. Page numbers in parentheses in the text refer to this edition.

18 Samuel Taylor Coleridge, *The Collected Works of Samuel Taylor Coleridge*, vol. v: *Lectures 1808–1819 on Literature*, ed. R. A. Foakes (London: Routledge & Kegan Paul; Princeton: Princeton University Press, 1987); see particularly the discussion of organic form in the 1811–12 *Lectures on Shakespeare and Milton*, p. 358 and n., and the 1812–13 *Lectures on Belles-Lettres*, p. 494.

19 Coleridge, *Biographia Literaria*, ed. James Engell and W. Jackson Bate, 2 vols., Bollingen series (Princeton: Princeton University Press, 1983), vol. ii, p. 83.

20 Ibid., p. 69.

21 "My First Acquaintance with Poets," in *The Complete Works of William Hazlitt*, vol. xvii: *Uncollected Essays*, ed. P. P. Howe (London: J. M. Dent, 1933), pp. 106–21, at p. 119.

22 Fussell, *Theory of Prosody*, p. 123.

23 John Aiken, *Essays on Song-writing; with a collection of such English songs as are most eminent for poetical merit* (London: Warrington, 1774), p. 27.

24 Maureen McLane, "The Figure Minstrelsy Makes: Poetry and Historicity," *Critical Inquiry* 29/3 (Spring 2003), pp. 429–52.

25 "The Commonplace Books," pp. 395–400; entry for August 1784, in *The Complete Works of Robert Burns* (Edinburgh: William P. Nimmo, 1865), p. 397.

26 In the Irish form, the first to the third, and fifth to seventh being hexasyllabic with a disyllabic final word, and the fourth and eighth being pentasyllabic with a monosyllabic final word. G. Murphy, *Early Irish Metrics* (Dublin: Royal Irish Academy, 1961), p. 70, cited in David Cooper, "Lámh Dearg: Celtic Minstrels and Orange Songsters," *Celtic Cultural Studies: An Online Journal* (1999).

27 Bruce Pattison, *Music and Poetry of the English Renaissance* (London: Methuen, 1948), p. 173, and John Thompson, *The Founding of English Metre* (New York:

Columbia University Press, 1961), pp. 88–9, provide catalogues of Spenser's song forms.

28 Albert Friedman, *The Ballad Revival: Studies in the Influence of Popular on Sophisticated Poetry* (Chicago: University of Chicago Press, 1961), pp. 238–46.

29 Leslie Shepard, *The Broadside Ballad: A Study of Origins and Meaning* (London: Herbert Jenkins, 1962), p. 143.

30 *Shelley's Poetry and Prose*, ed. Donald H. Reiman and Neil Fraistat (New York: W. W. Norton, 2002), notes, p. 326.

31 Friedman, *The Ballad Revival*, pp. 169–73.

32 James Macpherson, *The Poems of Ossian and Related Works*, ed. Howard Gaskill (Edinburgh: Edinburgh University Press, 1996), p. 55.

33 Coleridge, in *The Notebooks of Samuel Taylor Coleridge*, ed. Kathleen Coburn, 5 vols. (Princeton: Princeton University Press, 1957–2002), vol. II, entry 2224.22.15 (p. 38), and David Perkins, "Wordsworth, Hunt, and Romantic Understanding of Meter," *Journal of English and Germanic Philology* 93/1 (January 1994), pp. 1–17. For Coleridge's play with metrics see J. C. C. Mays, "Metrical Experiments," in *The Collected Works of Samuel Taylor Coleridge* vol. XVI: *Poetical Works II* (Reading Text) (Princeton: Princeton University Press, 2001), pp. 768–74; for his attempts to use Italian meters see Edoardo Zuccato, *Coleridge in Italy* (Cork: Cork University Press, 1996), p. 35.

34 Wordsworth, "Essay," in *The Prose Works of William Wordsworth*, ed. W. J. B. Owen and Jane Worthington Smyser (Oxford: Clarendon Press, 1974), vol. III, p. 73; and *The Letters of William Wordsworth and Dorothy Wordsworth, Arranged and Selected by the Late Ernest de Selincourt*, ed. Alan G. Hill (Oxford: Oxford University Press, 1979), Part II, pp. 236–9 and 259–60. Byron, "Letter to [John Murray] on the Rev. W. L. Bowles's strictures on the life and writings of Pope," in *Two Letters to XXXX XXXXXX* [John Murray] (London: John Murray, 1821), pp. 1–21.

35 *The Notebooks of Samuel Taylor Coleridge*, ed. Coburn, vol. II, text, May–August 1805, pp. 90–1.

36 Allen Grossman, "Wordsworth's 'The Solitary Reaper': Notes on Poiesis, Pastoral, and Institution," *TriQuarterly* 116 (Summer 2003), pp. 277–99.

37 J. C. C. Mays, head-notes for "Monody on the Death of Chatterton," in *The Collected Works of Samuel Taylor Coleridge*, ed. Coburn, vol. XVI: *Poetical Works I* (Reading Text), p. 139.

38 William Lisle Bowles, *The Poetical Works*, 2 vols. (Edinburgh: Ballantyne, 1855), with the preface to the 1837 edition, p. 115; on "corrections," p. 2.

39 See Susan Wolfson, *The Questioning Presence: Wordsworth, Keats, and the Interrogative Mode* (Ithaca: Cornell University Press, 1986). In her later *Formal Charges: The Shaping of Poetry in British Romanticism* (Stanford: Stanford University Press, 1997), pp. 39–43, Wolfson explores further dimensions of Romantic form, including the connection between blank verse and the visual experience of the line.

40 Mays, ed., *Poetical Works I*, pp. 482–3.

41 Coleridge to Byron: *Collected Letters*, vol. IV, p. 603.

42 "Verse," from *Imagination and Fancy: Essays and Sketches by Leigh Hunt*, ed. R. Brimley Johnson (London: Oxford University Press, 1912), pp. 121–2, at p. 121.

43 Scott, 1805 Introduction to *The Lay*; and Rachel Crawford, "Thieves of Language: Coleridge, Wordsworth, Scott, and the Contexts of 'Alice du Clos'," *European Romantic Review*, 7/1 (Summer 1996), pp. 1–25.

44 William Kumbier, "Blake's Epic Meter," *Studies in Romanticism* 17/2 (1978), pp. 170–1.

45 Susan Stewart, "What Praise Poems are For," *PMLA* 120/1 (January 2005), pp. 235–45.

46 G.M. Matthews, "Shelley's Lyrics," in *The Morality of Art: Essays Presented to G. Wilson Knight by His Colleagues and Friends*, ed. D. W. Jefferson (London: Routledge & Kegan Paul, 1969), pp. 195–209, at p. 198.

47 Geoffrey Hartman, "Wordsworth, Inscriptions, and Romantic Nature Poetry," in *Beyond Formalism: Literary Essays 1958–1970* (New Haven: Yale University Press, 1970), pp. 206–30, and Marjorie Levinson, *The Romantic Fragment Poem* (Chapel Hill: University of North Carolina Press, 1986).

48 *The Borderers by William Wordsworth*, ed. Robert Osborn (Ithaca: Cornell University Press, 1982), p. 814: "The Fenwick Note," 1843.

FURTHER READING

Barfield, Owen, *Poetic Diction: A Study in Meaning* (Middletown, CT: Wesleyan University Press, 1987)

Hartman, Geoffrey, *Wordsworth's Poetry, 1787–1814* (Cambridge, MA: Harvard University Press, 1987)

Lacoue-Labarthe, Philippe, and Jean-Luc Nancy, *The Literary Absolute: The Theory of Literature in German Romanticism* (Albany: State University of New York Press, 1988)

Peckham, Morse, *Man's Rage for Chaos: Biology, Behavior, and the Arts* (Washington, DC: Maisonneuve Press, 2004)

Praz, Mario, *Romantic Agony*. Trans. Angus Davidson (Oxford: Oxford University Press, 1985)

Warnock, Mary, *Imagination* (London: Faber, 1980)

Wolfson, Susan, *Formal Charges: The Shaping of Poetry in British Romanticism* (Stanford: Stanford University Press, 1997)

4

ANDREW ELFENBEIN

Romantic poetry and the standardization of English

Rather than trying to understand the historical relation between present-day English and English of the Romantic period, literary scholars have rarely thought much about English at all. Instead, they have concentrated on more abstract and seemingly weightier issues, such as Romantic debates about how language originated and how it related to the operations of the mind. This philosophical focus on language masks the fact that Romantic poets did not necessarily share contemporary critics' ability to take English as a given. They confronted considerable uncertainty about just how to write in English because the ways that the language was defined, taught, analyzed, judged, and printed changed dramatically in the second half of the eighteenth century. Linguistic historians usually describe these changes as "standardization" or "prescriptivism," the process whereby philologists, grammarians, lexicographers, and orthoepists (codifiers of correct pronunciation) developed rules about right and wrong English usage. While guides to English had existed for centuries, they had largely been designed for foreigners wanting to learn English. The eighteenth century saw the rise of books of usage for native speakers. They aimed to teach readers not how to speak and write English, but how to speak and write English correctly.

Great Britain during this period was an unstable political entity, sometimes subject to violent internal divisions, as in the American War of Independence and the 1798 Irish rebellion, and more generally characterized by significant and widespread variation from region to region, and even from county to county. As Linda Colley has noted, this variety meant that "active commitment to Great Britain was not, could not be a given. It had to be learnt; and men and women needed to see some advantage in learning it."[1] The standardization of English seemed to eighteenth-century writers one of the most advantageous sites for teaching such commitment. The pioneering elocutionist Thomas Sheridan, for example, described the advantages it would offer:

> An uniformity of pronunciation throughout Scotland, Wales, and Ireland, as well as through the several counties of England, would be a point much to be wished; as it might in great measure contribute to destroy those odious distinctions between subjects of the same king, and members of the same community, which are ever attended with ill consequences, and which are chiefly kept alive by difference of pronunciation, and dialects.[2]

Sheridan argues that "pronunciation, and dialects," more than any other factors, distance people from one another, and hopes that imposing a standard will allow those in England, Scotland, Ireland, and Wales to believe that they are really "members of the same community." One might have imagined that such factors as religion or economic disparity would be treated as far greater roadblocks to unity, but Sheridan concentrates on language alone. There was an obvious reason for this focus: of all possible modes of creating national unity, linguistic standardization seemed the most achievable. The institutional infrastructure necessary for such standardization, including a functioning public sphere, a book trade that reached throughout Great Britain, a widespread system of education, and a commitment to the liberty of the press, made Sheridan's vision seem not like a utopian dream but a practical goal.

While many languages were spoken in Great Britain during this period, English dominated print: no utopian upheavals were needed to create print monolingualism. This pervasiveness of English grew even as other aspects of reading changed. J. Paul Hunter has noted that by the beginning of the eighteenth century, authors wrote as if they had to make up for the lack of a previous connection with their readers, through such devices as introductions, direct addresses, and appeals to common interest.[3] As other sources of common ground between writers and readers faded, English was left to become the chief and possibly the only bond that authors could assume they would share with readers. Instead of writing for particular readers, authors faced a more amorphous general public, of whom little could be known beyond the fact that it read in English. As a result, the stakes in believing that a common linguistic ground really existed became more important than ever before, and the standardizers of English worked hard to make it a reality.

Nothing better attests to the perceived political urgency of developing standardized English than the energy and dedication with which eighteenth-century writers tackled the project. John Walker, in his *Critical Pronouncing Dictionary* (1791), noted that "the greatest abilities in the nation have been exerted in cultivating and reforming [English]; nor have a thousand minor critics been wanting to add their mite of amendment to their native tongue."[4]

In his hands, standard English appears as a vast cooperative project, joining together greater and lesser talents in a common goal of perfecting the language. Walker could have added that many of those "abilities" did not belong to natives of England. While it would be an overstatement to claim that standardized English was invented by the non-English, many of those not born in England had a high stake in it because it held out the possibility of creating an equal footing for all Britons. Thomas Sheridan may have been particularly sensitive to the internal divisions of Great Britain because he himself was from Ireland. Hugh Blair, whose *Lectures on Rhetoric and Belles Lettres* (1783) sold approximately 18,500 copies during the Romantic period, was Scottish; his lectures, which became one of the best-known guides to English style, originated in his courses at the University of Edinburgh. Lindley Murray, whose *English Grammar* (1795), along with his other textbooks, had estimated sales of 3 million in the first half of the nineteenth century, was born in Pennsylvania.[5] As Robert Crawford has noted, "while the metropolis and English Court may have taken it for granted that their own standards should be adopted as universal, it was none the less Scots, and generally 'provincials,' who encouraged other Scots and provincials to adopt these standards."[6]

Even standardizers native to England spent significant parts of their careers outside of it. Before becoming an elocutionist, John Walker was an actor on the Dublin stage; Robert Lowth, whose *Short Introduction to English Grammar* (1762) was the most prevalent grammar before Murray's, had ecclesiastical appointments in Ireland; and William Cobbett, who wrote a grammar designed for the laboring classes, lived in the United States from 1792 until 1800; most of the copyists who helped Samuel Johnson compile his famous dictionary were Scottish. Admittedly, books by these writers either do not mention the English of Scotland, Ireland, or the United States, or denigrate it as obviously incorrect; they usually assume that the English they disseminate is the variety spoken in England itself. Nevertheless, while their introductions often claim to reflect general usage, the writers' specific decisions usually arise from their own sense of what they like. Given their own biographies, these somewhat undefined linguistic preferences should be treated not as the record of a preexisting English of England, but as a mosaic arising from collective experiences of a variety of Englishes from throughout Great Britain.

While the codification of English had been in progress for decades before the Romantic period, the Napoleonic Wars gave particular urgency to the need for national unity in the face of imminent threat. More than ever before, standard English became a symbol for national pride. To speak non-standard English was not simply to offend against linguistic rules: it was a kind of political treason, an offense against the nation. In *Belinda* (1801), by Maria Edgeworth, for example, Harriot Freke, dangerous supporter of French ideas, speaks markedly sloppy English: "And how d'ye go on here, poor child? . . . I hope you're of my way o' thinking . . . now we talk o'looks." The virtuous Belinda, in contrast, speaks in perfectly composed, almost exaggeratedly formal sentences: "Is it possible, sir . . . that you should suspect me of such wretched hypocrisy, as to affect to admire what I am incapable of feeling?"[7] Standardized English acquired remarkable power in the Romantic period to create dividing lines between the empowered and the marginal, the polite and the vulgar.

Nevertheless, standardization never became as rigid as it was in other countries, such as France, which had an actual academy to determine proper usage. Although Jonathan Swift imagined the benefits of such an academy for English, it never materialized. Instead, monuments of usage like Samuel Johnson's *Dictionary of the English Language* (1755) or the works of Lowth, Sheridan, Walker, Murray, and others, came from no single, centralized institution. They were the work of enterprising individuals with differing backgrounds, levels of education, professions, and links to the book trade. Nothing prevented the marketing of competing works, stopped writers from disagreeing with one another, or denied the power of individual usage.

Strange as it may seem, the resistance to standardization was loudly defended by the standardizers themselves. In the "Preface" to his *Dictionary*, Samuel Johnson wrote, "I, who can never wish to see dependence multiplied, hope the spirit of English liberty will hinder or destroy" the establishment of "an academy . . . for the cultivation of our style."[8] This is a remarkable claim: in the preface to the most influential work of English standardization ever written, Johnson protests against an academy that might standardize English too completely. Similarly, grammarians often avoided rhetoric that might seem too fanatical. John Fell noted that "the laws of our speech, like the laws of our country, should breathe a spirit of liberty."[9] Standardization might be a good thing, but it had to be careful to appear as an organized reflection of the best usage, not as a tyrannical set of arbitrary rules.

The result was a provocative tension in relation to the standardization of English. Non-standard English, like that given by Maria Edgeworth to Harriot Freke, could be seen as a rebellion against the nation, a refusal to accede to the signifiers of real Englishness. At the same time, too slavish an adherence to the niceties of grammar could also seem un-English, a pedantic rejection of traditional English liberty and custom. In practice, this tension was resolved less by actually making English uniform than by selecting a few points of usage that all standardizers agreed were wrong. Policing certain linguistic rules, such as the prohibition on double negatives and the incorrect use of "h" and "r," became shorthand dividing acceptable and unacceptable English. Good English arose less from a formal institution than from selected markers of practice that became a social code for those with the right education.

For poets, standardization had immediate practical effects. They could expect their manuscripts to be altered to fit a publisher's sense of correct English; if corrections were not made, critics were quick to attack perceived faults. Indeed, they would pounce on mistakes that were not especially obvious. Even worse, standardization destroyed the long-held belief that great poets molded a nation's language. Eighteenth-century standardizers of English let it be known that, whatever had happened in the past, for the future, standardizers, not great writers, would determine the language. As a result of their work, great poetry no longer defined English, but manuals, handbooks, dictionaries, and other guides to usage did. Admittedly, these books often cited literary texts for examples, and the list of their most frequently cited sources gives a good indication of their canon: Swift, the New Testament, Hume, Addison, Pope, *The Spectator*, the Old Testament, Shakespeare, Dryden, and Milton.[10] Of the poets on the list, all were dead – in some cases, long dead – as if whatever the English language needed to get from poetry, it had gotten long ago. Existing authorities provided enough examples of standard and non-standard English to make all future English superfluous as a source of models.

William St. Clair describes the "old canon" as a set of poets dominating anthologies and collections from the late eighteenth century until the middle of the nineteenth century; this canon overlapped substantially with the writers quoted by the grammarians.[11] By the Romantic period, English had a canon, a standard language, more than enough exemplars of good and bad usage, and a decided bias toward prose, especially Addison's. There hardly seemed any pressing need for poetry at all. In seeming to exclude contemporary poetry from shaping English, the standardizers were creating more than a linguistic challenge. Given the importance of standardized English to the politics of nationhood, they were also implicitly removing poetry by living writers from a significant role in Great Britain's future. In response, late eighteenth-century poets had two choices: they could admit defeat and follow tamely the standardizers' prescriptions, or they could fight back by developing forms of English that supposedly provided a truer link to the nation than that of the standardizers. Many of the most compelling poets of the second half of the eighteenth century made the second choice, and ushered in one of the most dramatic, exciting periods of linguistic experimentation in English poetry.

Typically, as is often true of radical aesthetic experiments, these proceeded under the banner of archaism: new developments pretended to revive old ones. Hugh Blair had raised the stakes for such archaisms by claiming, in his *Lectures on Rhetoric and Belles Lettres*, that modernity was the age of prose. The early bard sang "indeed in wild and disorderly strains; but they were the native effusions of his heart"; however, in "after ages," poets "composing coolly in their closets . . . endeavoured to imitate passion, rather than to express it."[12] The prospects for modern poets seemed dim if they were doomed to produce tepid pseudo-emotion. Late eighteenth-century poets responded by inventing modes of English that were meant to be perceived as antedating its eighteenth-century codification. Archaic English could be seen as reviving the "wild and disorderly" language of true poets, reaching back to a more genuine, though less polished, form of expression.

In terms of the politics of these archaic Englishes, they resisted the fiction of a unified Great Britain. If the standardizers were trying to invent a cosmopolitan, transnational version of English that could supposedly unite England, Scotland, Wales, Ireland, and North America, archaic poetic English refused the union into Great Britain by privileging individual nations within it and focusing on local areas within them. It created a set of polarities that set Addison and Pope against archaic English, urban cosmopolitanism against provincial culture, Great Britain against nationalism, and Latinity against Anglo-Saxon or Gaelic.

The most famous example of pseudo-archaic English came from Thomas Chatterton, a poor seamstress's son from Bristol. He invented for himself an identity as a fifteenth-century poet, Thomas Rowley, along with a fantasy of what Rowley's English would look like, as in the opening of this "Mynstrelle's Song" from *Aella: A Tragycal Enterlude* (1777):

> O! synge untoe mie roundelaie,
> O! droppe the brynie teare wythe mee,
> Daunce ne moe atte hallie daie,
> Lycke a reynynge ryver bee;
>> Mie love ys dedde,
>> Gon to hys death-bedde,
>> Al under the wyllowe tree.[13]

Since Rowley was supposed to be a Bristol native like Chatterton, Chatterton's poetry located this archaic English not in London but in a provincial English city. Especially striking in Chatterton's "Bristol" English is its etymological art: most of his words have roots in Anglo-Saxon or Norman French, unlike the more Latinate diction of Chaucer, the most famous medieval poet. The fictional Rowley's etymological relation to Chaucer was a cover for the real Chatterton's relation to Pope, the Latinate paragon of standard English in poetry. This etymological battle had a political edge because the Latinity of poets like Pope represented for outsiders like Chatterton the entrenched power of a poetic establishment nurtured on the classics and on an elite educational system (though, interestingly, Pope himself had had an oblique relation to this system because, as a Catholic, he could not attend Oxford or Cambridge). It also challenged the tendency on the part of eighteenth-century standardizers to use Latin models for English grammar. The aggressive Englishness of Chatterton's vocabulary created the fantasy of a more pure, original mode of English. Hence, John Keats would later write that Chatterton "is the purest writer in the English Language. He has no French idiom, or particles like Chaucer – 'tis genuine English Idiom in English words."[14] For Keats, who, like Chatterton, was rebelling against the class implications of the standardizers' cosmopolitan English, Chatterton, far more than Chaucer, was the well of English undefiled, even though Chatterton's English was a forgery.

Another challenge to the standardizers' English came from the ballads that Thomas Percy published in *Reliques of Ancient English Poetry* (1765). This collection was a hodgepodge of actual ballads, original compositions of Percy's, and hybrid works in which Percy altered or rewrote existing ballads. Ballads in the eighteenth century occupied the lowest rung of literature. They were sensational, often bawdy works associated with illiterate or barely literate classes; many of them were hundreds of years old.[15] Percy cleaned up his ballads by excluding their characteristic bawdry, omitting occasional notes of political protest, and presenting his collection as a work of antiquarian scholarship into the authentic roots of English literature. As in Chatterton, this connection with true Englishness pitted the local against transnational Britishness; Percy particularly favored ballads about Northumberland because he dedicated the collection to Elizabeth, Countess Percy, wife of the Earl of Northumberland, who subsequently became his patron. Through Percy's collection, "bad" English could be revalued as a mark of vigor, originality, and a true English spirit, rather than mere illiteracy.

Another influential form of localism was the move away from England altogether to the Celtic fringe. Before English was spoken in the British Isles, the chief language was Celtic. James Macpherson, a Scottish writer, wrote a series of supposed "translations" from the works of the ancient bard Ossian (1760–3). He had researched Ossian in the Scottish Highlands, but his texts were less strict translations than imaginative elaborations upon some themes and motifs from Ossianic ballads. Strikingly, Macpherson rendered Ossian's supposed poetry as prose, but prose that shared few characteristics of the English approved by the standardizers. The ideal English prose promoted by

Scottish academics like Hugh Blair, Adam Smith, and George Campbell was clear, error-free, purged of obvious rhetorical figures, and smooth. Macpherson's Ossian was just the opposite: as Hugh Blair noted, the style had "no artful transitions, nor full and extended connection of parts"; instead, the narration was "concise, even to abruptness."[16]

Blair championed Ossian nevertheless precisely because Ossian's roughness created a neat divide between ancient poetry, open to aesthetic appreciation, and modern prose, designed for practical goals. While standardized British English was neutral, prosaic, polished, and contemporary, the Ossianic English of Scotland was expressive, poetic, rough, and ancient. This division allowed Blair and others to retain an arena for Scottish cultural nationalism even as they were simultaneously creating a transnational British identity. As Crawford notes, the Ossianic poems, especially as interpreted by Blair, are "a skilled effort at cultural translation, turning Scottish material of an unacceptable kind into a form acceptable to a new British audience."[17]

If Blair and Macpherson's Ossian located the pseudo-Celtic in the legendary past, the Scots of Robert Burns insisted on the continuing vitality of non-standard language varieties. In 1786, he published *Poems, Chiefly in the Scottish Dialect*, which demonstrated his mastery both of standard English and of Scots, though it was the poems in "the Scottish Dialect" for which he became famous. If standardizers agreed on the need to preserve some "liberty" in usage, they also agreed that this liberty did not include Scottish or Irish. In most guides to grammar, one of the most cutting comments about errors was that they were "Scottish." Burns transformed the despised Scottish dialect from the prime example of bad English into the pure voice of supposedly natural poetry. There had been peasant poets before Burns, but they typically did not write in dialect; there had been dialect poets before Burns, but they did not claim to be unlettered peasants. Burns for the first time linked dialect to a peasant persona (though his actual class position was far more complex than this phrase implies), and, in so doing, provided another alternative to standardized English. Burns's early reviewers regretted his use of Scottish dialect; Henry Mackenzie noted that in Scotland, his dialect "is now read with a difficulty which greatly damps the pleasure of the reader" and that in England "it cannot be read at all."[18] Yet Burns's dialect, actually a hybrid of standard English and a range of Scottish language varieties, was quickly revalorized as one of his prime attractions.

Such alternatives to standardized English could be seen as inherently radical insofar as they challenged the presumed universality of standardized English and its ability to represent a unified Great Britain. Yet, as I have noted, the standardizers always insisted on the importance of maintaining a degree of liberty: in some ways, writers like Chatterton and Burns could be understood less as rebelling against standardization than as taking seriously the standardizers' praise of British liberty. Moreover, the exaltation of alternative Englishes could turn into a quite condescending celebration of the perceived simplicity and primitivism of other times and cultures, as a conservative retreat from the supposed evils of modernity. As a result, the politics of language use was never simple or unidirectional: the same choices could occupy quite different places in the political spectrum.

Nevertheless, in the eighteenth century, many proponents of alternative English were indeed associated with reformist politics; Burns, for example, was an ardent champion of the French Revolution. In addition, one of the most energetic reformist movements of the late eighteenth century, abolition, drew heavily on dialect poetry in which slaves were made to speak. In these poems, slaves' non-standard English made them not contemptible or laughable figures, but ones deserving the protection and sympathy of the British nation. Tellingly, however, such English could appear only in works written by white writers; when actual African writers, like Phillis Wheatley or Olaudah Equiano, published their works, they used flawless standard English as a means of demonstrating their right to be taken seriously.

Traces of late eighteenth-century experiments with English can be found throughout Romantic poetry. Coleridge in *The Rime of the Ancient Mariner* (1798, 1817), Scott in *The Lay of the Last Minstrel* (1805), Byron in the first canto of *Childe Harold's Pilgrimage* (1812), and Keats in *The Eve of St. Agnes* and *La Belle Dame Sans Merci* (1820) all employ moments of pseudo-medieval English that recall Chatterton. Blake and Coleridge imitated Ossian's prose poetry, and Blake took over Ossianic names, as when Ossian's "Oithona" became "Oothoon" in *Visions of the Daughters of Albion* (1793). Wordsworth and Coleridge's decision to entitle their joint volume *Lyrical Ballads* was in part a nod to Percy's *Reliques*, although their results were quite different from anything that Percy had written; Coleridge also took the name "Christabel" from Percy's collection. Scott followed Burns's lead by collecting Scottish ballads in his *Minstrelsy of the Scottish Border* (1802–3); James Hogg wrote poetry in Scots; and Hemans adapted some Welsh ballads in her *Selection of Welsh Melodies* (1822).

Yet the most striking aspect of Romantic poets' relation to English is how consistently they abandoned the more flagrant oddities of eighteenth-century experimentalism. For example, Coleridge rewrote *The Rime of the Ancyent Marinere* as *The Rime of the Ancient Mariner* to omit many of its most obvious archaisms, as in the altered title. His changes to the following stanza suggest the results:

> She doth not tack from side to side –
>   Hither to work us weal
> Withouten wind, withouten tide
>   She steddies with upright keel.
>
> See! see! (I cried) she tacks no more!
> Hither to work us weal;
> Without a breeze, without a tide,
> She steadies with upright keel![19]

Removing the quaintness of the earlier version increases the stanza's emotional intensity as well, as if the veil of archaism keeping the poem's events at a safe distance from the reader had been suddenly removed. The neutral formality of "She doth not tack from side to side" becomes the more immediate, personal, and urgent, "See! see! (I cried) she tacks no more," an urgency so great that Coleridge even sacrifices to it the "side/tide" rhyme in his first version. He modernizes the faux-archaic "withouten wind, withouten tide" to the more pointed and concrete "without a breeze, without a tide." Chatterton's excitement came from sustaining his weird fake Middle English; Coleridge's, from stripping away his pseudo-Gothic vocabulary.

On the whole, a distinguishing mark of Romantic English is its counter-rebellion against an earlier, late eighteenth-century search for pseudo-archaic alternatives to standardized English. Coleridge is not alone in cleaning up his poetry to make its English look less strange. When Wordsworth wrote a romance set in the sixteenth century, *The White Doe of Rylstone* (1815), he did little to create a mock-Tudor English; the poem's English is for the most part that of his other poetry. Although Byron began *Childe Harold's Pilgrimage* with a sprinkling of faux Spenserianisms (imitations of the English used by Edmund Spenser in *The Faerie Queene* [1590–6]), these fade by the end of the 1812 version, and he did not return to them in Canto III (1816) or Canto IV (1818); Percy Shelley's *Adonais* (1821) uses the Spenserian stanza (a nine-line stanza rhyming *ababbcbcc*, in which the first eight lines are in iambic pentameter and the last in iambic hexameter) but pointedly does not employ pseudo-archaic English. For all Scott's interest in Scottish balladry, romance, and history, little of his poetry uses Scots vocabulary, as opposed to its extensive presence in his novels. Even Keats, despite his admiration for Chatterton, follows a similar pattern; although he died quite young in his career, the language of his later poems like *The Fall of Hyperion* (1819) and *Lamia* (1820) is far less aggressively experimental than that of his earlier work.

Yet if Romantic poets steered away from markedly strange English, they did not exactly embrace standardization. Indeed, since the standardizers' prototypical mode was prose, doing so would have meant artistic suicide. Instead, Romantic poets continued to experiment with new possibilities for English, but more subtly than late eighteenth-century poets had done. Their English can be thought of as a brilliant interlanguage that combines the prescriptions of standardized English with certain select archaisms (such as the widespread use of "thou" and its associated verb forms for the second-person singular), and distinctive personal twists. In all cases, these interlanguages situate the poets in relation not only to linguistic debates but also to political ones. Through their English, Romantic poets explore the larger question of what role the poet can have in the nation, if poetry is no longer a privileged site for producing the national language. Their poetry transforms a loss of authority into a new source of freedom in which to explore the public role of poetry and to question if it had one at all.

Of all Romantic poets, William Wordsworth most explicitly confronted the newfound status of prose as the privileged medium for standardized English. He famously claimed in his "Preface" to *Lyrical Ballads* that "some of the most interesting parts of the best poems will be found to be strictly the language of prose when prose is well written."[20] By insisting on the value not simply of prose, but of prose when it was "well written," Wordsworth linked his ideas to those of writers like Hugh Blair, who had defined well-written prose at length. Blair held up Joseph Addison as an ideal, and offered as a model such Addisonian sentences as these:

> This [sense of beauty] consists either in the gaiety or variety of colours, in the symmetry and proportion of parts, in the arrangement and disposition of bodies, or in a just mixture and concurrence of all together. Among these several kinds of Beauty, the eye takes most delight in colours.[21]

These sentences are not simply grammatically correct: they also follow certain dictates of style. The vocabulary is heavily Latinate; the sentence structure favors parallel phrases; and the sentences retain a trace of Latin periodicity by saving their climax for the end. These stylistic traits link Addison's English to a particular social network: an urban elite of educated gentlemen who had learned Latin and whose English was heavily influenced by the classics.

By invoking prose when it was "well written" in his *Preface*, Wordsworth sets the reader up for Latinate, neatly turned English like Addison's. What he produces is something quite different, as this excerpt from *Michael* suggests:

> UPON the Forest-side in Grasmere Vale
> There dwelt a Shepherd, Michael was his name,
> An old man, stout of heart, and strong of limb.
> His bodily frame had been from youth to age
> Of an unusual strength: his mind was keen,
> Intense and frugal, apt for all affairs,
> And in his Shepherd's calling he was prompt
> And watchful more than ordinary men.[22]

Next to the spectacular experiments of writers like Chatterton and Burns, Wordsworth's poetry seems studiously ordinary. He avoids strange or unusual words, flashy rhetorical devices, and loud deviations from standard grammar. His vocabulary is not aggressively Anglo-Saxon like Chatterton's, or Scots like Burns, but combines words with varying etymological roots, all of which had long been in the language.

Yet if Wordsworth resists the dazzle of late eighteenth-century experiments with English, his poetry is still far from what his contemporaries might have considered prose when it was "well written." Unlike Addison's neatly analytical sentences, Wordsworth's are loosely organized piles of attributes. In particular, eighteenth-century standardizers insisted that a good writer should *"dispose of the capital word, or words, in that place of the sentence, where they will make the fullest impression,"* usually near the beginning or end.[23] A sentence following such a prescription might read as follows: "An old shepherd named Michael, who had a stout heart and strong limbs, dwelt upon the forest-side of Grasmere Vale." Rather than writing such a sentence, Wordsworth breaks down information into discrete units that he lists: "There dwelt a Shepherd, Michael was his name, / An old man, stout of heart, and strong of limb." He creates a slow-moving, almost rambling sentence quite unlike the tight, precise prose most admired by eighteenth-century authorities. His meter even contracts the pronunciation of the words "bodily" and "unusual" as if to give them a casual, unassuming tone.

Moreover, despite Wordsworth's desire to bring poetry closer to prose, *Michael* includes constant reminders that it is not actually prose. Most obviously, it does not look like prose because of the way the lines are arranged, and the pulse of the iambic pentameter meter distinguishes it from prose rhythms. In addition, Wordsworth freely shifts conventional word order, as when he concludes with "he was prompt / And watchful more than ordinary men" instead of "he was more prompt and watchful than ordinary men." Forms of rhetorical amplification elevate the diction: "body" becomes "bodily frame"; "unusually strong" becomes "of an unusual strength." The strong rhythmic alliteration of a phrase like "stout of heart, and strong of limb" stands out against the prose-like rhythms elsewhere. While such devices are not intrinsically alien to prose, they were treated as such by eighteenth-century standardizers, who aimed for a clear, dry, abbreviated style. The fact that Wordsworth retains them tugs against the neutral, expository style favored by the standardizers by raising his English to a more solemn, dignified tone.

Wordsworth thus develops his English as a hybrid medium, poised between conventions of prose and of poetry. As such, it becomes part of *Michael*'s more general aim of representing an almost archetypal image of English moderation: for all that Wordsworth subtitles the poem "A Pastoral," Michael is less a pure figure of nature than a middle ground between poetry and prose, nature and culture, myth and history. On one hand, Wordsworth believed that the poem was so historically urgent that he sent a copy to Britain's Prime Minister, Charles James Fox, as an example of the difficulties facing the rural poor in the early nineteenth century. Nevertheless, he introduces the poem not with loud political anger but with the recollection that stories such as this led him, when he was young, to "think / At random, and imperfectly indeed / On man, the heart of man, and human life" (ll. 31–3). This hybridity unsettles our sense of the larger significance of Michael's story: it is both about England in a particular time and place, and about human suffering that cannot be confined to topical specificity. This balance between the historical specificity of the poem as a document of actual conditions and the mythic associations it acquires as a local legend parallels the balance between prose and poetry in English.

Within the plot of the poem, the middle ground between history and myth is shattered: the cruelty of history takes over, in the form of the debt that Michael must pay and the subsequent breakdown of his family. In response, the more that history invades Michael's life, the more he becomes a myth for his local community: "I have convers'd with more than one who well / Remember the Old Man and what he was / Years after he had heard this heavy news" (ll. 460–2). Devastatingly, by the end of the poem, most of the concrete traces of Michael's life are wiped out, with only the ruined sheepfold remaining. Yet Wordsworth's English sustains the middle ground between poetry and prose that his poem's plot does not. To the end, at least in this poem, language can be an alternative to the outrages of history because of its ability to maintain a fragile poise: the poem's message and its code diverge in ways that suggest that English maintains Englishness in a way that history cannot.

Not all writers were as subtle as Wordsworth in creating their relation between English and the nation. William Blake became a printer to produce his own illuminated poems that broke down the distinction between words and pictures. A side benefit was that he avoided a disapproving editorial eye.

Given his deep mistrust of his country's governing institutions, it was not surprising that English liberty appears in Blake's work through the liberties he takes with English. Whereas Chatterton identified Rowley's patriotism with a particular region, Bristol, Blake's patriotism takes the form of radical individualism: he stands for England by being himself. As a result, he bypasses conventions of grammar, spelling, and punctuation to develop his own peculiar idiolect.

For example, in "The CLOD & the PEBBLE" in *Songs of Innocence and of Experience* (1794), he writes,

> Love seeketh not Itself to please,
> Nor for itself hath any care;
> But for another gives its ease,
> And builds a Heaven in Hells despair.[24]

As "Hells despair" indicates, Blake has little time for the niceties of standard punctuation. Less noticeable but perhaps more strange, Blake suddenly modernizes his verb conjugations in mid-stanza. The Clod begins in lines 1–2 with archaic forms of third-person singular verbs ("seeketh," "hath") yet by lines 3–4, it suddenly updates them ("gives," "builds," instead of "giveth," "buildeth").

Such moments pose a challenge to the interpreter about how to explain their source. Should this switch be understood as part of Blake's characterization of the Clod: is the Clod too cloddish to control his grammar? Or is this grammatical shiftiness part of Blake's vision of Experience, a comment on its uneasy, jarring shifts between archaic and modern? Or do we treat it as a product of Blake's more general grammatical-political rebellion against standardization, which leads to unpredictable eruptions of odd English? Or does it have less to do with Blake than with some uncertainty at the end of the eighteenth century about how to form negative statements, since both the archaic forms appear in negated clauses? How much does the poem's English belong to the poem as an individual unit, to a peculiar authorial idiolect, or to the state of English in the 1790s?

Such questions are particularly vexing because Blake's oddities never arose merely from ignorance; he could use finer points of English grammar precisely, as in this dialogue from *The Marriage of Heaven and Hell* (1793):

> An Angel came to me and said. O pitiable foolish young man! O horrible! O dreadful state! consider the hot burning dungeon thou art preparing for thyself to all eternity, to which thou art going in such career.
> I said. perhaps you will be willing to shew me my eternal lot & we will contemplate together upon it and see whether your lot or mine is most desirable.[25]

The tone of this dialogue hinges on a tiny detail that is easily missed: Blake's second-person pronouns. The Angel addresses Blake with "thou" and "thyself," while Blake addresses the angel with "you" and "your." In earlier centuries, "thou" and its derivatives had been used for the second person singular; "you," for the second person plural and as a formal, elevated marker of the second person singular. Yet by Blake's day, "thou" and its derivatives had largely fallen out of common usage except in two cases: in exalted poetic language, and in debased language used to inferiors. A 1754 grammar, for example, described using "thou" as an "ungenteel and rude" form of address.[26]

Blake's dialogue teeters between the different possibilities for employing the second-person pronoun. Initially, it may seem that the angel employs a formal tone by using "thou." But Blake's response, in which he uses "you," may suggest retrospectively that he, at least, has heard the angel's "thou" as an insult, so that his "you" appears exquisitely polite. At the same time, his "you" could also be a refusal of the angel's formality, an insistence on moving the dialogue to a more demotic idiom. Blake adapts the uncertainty around the tone of the second-person pronoun as a metaphor for what he calls the marriage of heaven and hell, the coexistence of contraries that refuses absolute solutions. His adaptation reminds his audience of possibilities of nuance and register in English that standardization was erasing. In Blake's hands, it is as if English, by becoming more standard, had become less English, because less able to contain the interpretive freedom represented in miniature by his ambiguous pronouns. In his poetry's non-standard English, he wages a one-man campaign to maintain English liberty.

Byron occupied a social position as far removed from Blake's as possible; where Blake was a poor, radical artisan, Byron was a baron with wealth, education, and social connections. Yet, with regard to standard English, it might seem that extremes met: Byron, like Blake, was notorious for his offenses against the language. Yet the stakes were quite different for the two poets. Blake's unusual English was a sign of his independence, like his control over book production: since he (with the help of his wife) created, produced, and marketed his work, he could adopt whatever punctuation, spelling, and grammar he chose. Whereas Blake painstakingly constructed his illuminated poetry, Byron, as an aristocrat, made sure that he did not seem to work too hard: to do so would be to lower himself to the status of a mere craftsman. Early in his career, he took no money for his poetry, to signal that, for him, it was not work, but a hobby. A bourgeois work ethic would demand grammatical exactness; an aristocratic one would not. In Byron's hands, if a particular phrase or word choice did not follow the standardizers' rules, too bad for the rules.

This indifference accompanied a more cosmopolitan outlook than that of writers who identified their language with particular locales, like Chatterton and Burns. Byron fashioned himself as a citizen of the world, and his most famous poems were set far from England. To seem too English would, for Byron, seem too like the middle classes, too willing to abdicate the aristocracy's traditional superiority to national boundaries. Byron's solecisms are a continual reminder that his English is not tethered to England, as if he were developing a strange global English, one that moved beyond national boundaries by showing itself above prescriptivism.

For example, Byron's most notorious solecism appears in his address to the ocean concluding Canto IV of *Childe Harold's Pilgrimage* (1818). He accuses the ocean of toying with the shipwrecked mariner:

> The vile strength he wields
> For earth's destruction thou dost all despise,
> Spurning him from thy bosom to the skies,
> And send'st him shivering in thy playful spray
> And howling, to his Gods, where haply lies
> His petty hope in some near port or bay,
> And dashest him again to earth: there let him lay.[27]

The final verb should be "lie." Eighteenth-century standardizers had clarified the difference between "lie" and "lay," and Byron's passage became a much quoted warning that famous literature was no guide to good usage.[28]

Yet, to be fair to Byron, in the poem's context, the solecism is much less glaring than it is often supposed to be. The rhyme scheme of the Spenserian stanza (*ababbcbcc*) sets the reader up for a word that will rhyme with "spray" and "bay," so that "lay" has a felt inevitability that moderates its grammatical wrongness; in addition, the alliteration of "let" and "lay" makes the error less prominent. The fact that Byron's publisher, John Murray, allowed the mistake to slip by means that Byron's supposedly glaring errors may have been less troublesome than later readers have sometimes claimed. Usually, Byron adheres to standard English; his slips feel less like programmatic rebellions than the result of putting grammatical perfection low on his list of poetic priorities. What counts for him is a vivid emotional climax; if standard English needs to be sacrificed to achieve it, so be it. Byron's non-standard English becomes a metaphor for international English because it insists that the particularities of a national grammar are less important than the usefulness of a language as means of expression. So long as he can convey the feeling that supposedly lies behind his English, it does not matter if small rules of usage are broken.

John Keats, in contrast, fashioned his English at the level of style, not grammar, as in this passage from the "Ode to Psyche" (1820):

> 'Mid hush'd, cool-rooted flowers, fragrant-eyed,
>   Blue, silver-white, and budded Tyrian,
> They lay calm-breathing on the bedded grass;
>   Their arms embraced, and their pinions too;
>   Their lips touch'd not, but had not bade adieu,
> As if disjoined by soft-handed slumber,
> And ready still past kisses to outnumber
>   At tender eye-dawn of aurorean love.[29]

Although nothing in the passage counters the rules for English grammar, spelling, or punctuation, everything in it counters the rules for what made a good English style. Lindley Murray's *English Grammar*, for example, included detailed advice about "promoting perspicuity in speaking and writing." It advised students to strive for "purity" by avoiding words and phrases that were "*obsolete*, or *new-coined*, or *ungrammatical*, or *not English*." He advocated a clean, unfussy style that avoided any flashiness and promoted sentences characterized by "1. *Clearness*. 2. *Unity*. 3. *Strength*."[30]

For clearness, Keats substitutes lush sensuality; for unity, a pile-up of choice phrases; for strength, a post-orgasmic laxity. In terms of his English, he treats Murray's comments about stylistic purity as if they were of a piece with prudish demands for sexual purity. Keats belonged to a circle of writers eager to rebel against the aristocratic appropriation of classical literature to inculcate ideals of military heroism and masculine virtue. Keats's counter-classicism used mythological figures as vehicles for glorifying sexual pleasure. He writes as if Murray's rules about stylistic purity supported the same repressiveness as the aristocratic use of the classics. In response, he makes the classics impure thematically by writing about erotic abandon in a markedly oppositional style. If avoiding the "*obsolete*" and "*new-coined*" produced "pure" English, then Keats's English does the opposite. The "Ode to Psyche" packs its lines with such novelties as "cool-rooted," "fragrant-eyed," "silver-white," "eye-dawn," "aurorean," and "soft-handed." Whereas Murray warned against obsolete words, Keats preserves the full pronunciation of the "-ed" suffix in words where this suffix had long ceased to be a separate syllable, as in "embraced" and "disjoined." Keats's style gleefully effeminizes the implicit sexual politics of Murray's mandates.

What made Keats's English so dismaying to his first reviewers was that such stylistic abandon was not the result, as in Byron, of carelessness; it was too systematic. Keats had unforgivably manipulated English usage to create a distinctive style, complete with marked tics and peculiarities. Standardized

English had striven to eliminate the need for such distinction: Addisonian prose was to stand for all times and places as the model of good style. Keats shattered the illusion of consensus on which such prescriptions were based by showing that different populations might develop different Englishes. As his reviewers recognized, his style belonged to a particular sociopolitical group, the "Cockney" circle surrounding Leigh Hunt: lower middle-class men with radical political sympathies who explored an aesthetics of pleasure and liberation from strict Evangelical mores that stressed self-control, sexual discipline, and the value of hard work. Conservative reviewers of Keats blasted his poetry precisely because of what they perceived to be its distasteful link between English style and politics. In time, however, the politics of Keats's style faded, leaving the more influential precedent of a poet who seemed to recreate English entirely as a reflection of his genius. By the end of the nineteenth century, Keats's precedent would make it incumbent upon poets to strive for stylistic originality, as if doing so were a prerequisite to writing poetry at all. Poets could be appreciated less for the content of their poetry or for the purity of their English than for their ability to shape English into an original style that supposedly demonstrated the power of genius to bend language to its will.

During the Romantic period itself, the poet who may have most success-fully handled the challenges of adapting standardized English was Felicia Hemans. Traditionally, men had targeted women for using bad or vulgar English, since women's educational opportunities were far more restricted than men's. The grammatical slips that in Byron would be treated as mere carelessness were liable to be seen as signs of incompetence in a woman writer. It might seem, therefore, that a writer like Hemans would be partic-ularly eager to adhere to all the prescriptions of the standardizers and write in perfectly pure English.

Yet her response was not quite so simple, since, as I have noted, the standardizers emphasized that the model of perfect English was Addiso-nian prose, not poetry. Wordsworth's prosaicism had been treated as an odd experiment; Keats's demolition of standard English style had been widely scorned. Hemans's solution was to use standard English (with certain con-ventional archaisms, such as the second-person "thou"), but to avoid pro-saicism through a dramatic use of punctuation, as in this excerpt from "Evening Prayer at a Girls' School" (1826):

> Gaze on, 'tis lovely! – childhood's lip and cheek,
>   Mantling beneath its earnest brow of thought!
> Gaze, yet what seest thou in those fair and meek
>   And fragile things, as but for sunshine wrought?

> – Thou seest what grief must nurture for the sky,
> What death must fashion for eternity![31]

The eighteenth-century standardization of English had focused not only on grammar, spelling, and pronunciation, but also on punctuation. Hemans's poetry loudly exploited this new resource. This relatively short stanza contains three exclamation points, two dashes, and one question mark. About exclamation points and question marks, Lindley Murray noted that they were "indeterminate as to their quantity of time, and may be equivalent in that respect to a semicolon, a colon, or a period, as the sense may require."[32] Their indeterminacy stood for a kind of freedom within the larger structures of standardization because it was up to the reader to determine how much time should be taken for each mark, and what tone each created. A similar indeterminacy surrounds the odd dash before "Thou seest." Dashes typically marked an abrupt break within a sentence; one between sentences, as in the quotation's penultimate line, was peculiar because terminal punctuation, like the question mark in the previous line, should be enough to indicate a pause. Hemans, however, signals a further pause with the dash, as if to make sure that it is not passed over. Such marks insist on the presence of the real or imagined reading voice, as if the poetry could be fully realized only through oral performance.

This vivid use of punctuation allows Hemans to carve out a particular kind of English characterized by its close connection with punctuational signals of strong emotion. While not offending against any rules of the standardizers, it nevertheless insists on poetry's special relation to English as a site for emotion, sound, and voice, as opposed to prose's neutrality, silence, and print. Through her insistent exploration of themes and motifs associated with femininity, Hemans gendered this special English as a peculiarly feminine one. This was a risky strategy, since, as I have noted, any uses of English that seemed particularly feminine had been traditionally despised. Hemans successfully reinvented feminized English not as non-standard English but as a distinctive hybrid of archaisms, standard grammar, and a foregrounded use of standard punctuation.

Hemans's vocal English also had a telling relationship to the nation. Whereas Byron's English flouted the standardizers to enable the expression of strong emotion supposed to emanate from Byron himself, Hemans instead imagined her English as a universal channel for emotion. In poems such as her *Records of Women* (1828), she represents woman of all times and places as speaking in English, and in exactly the same kind of English. The peculiarly gendered relation to standardized English that she perfected becomes a utopian vehicle for global unification: whereas men's languages represent the aftermath of Babel, for women, all emotions in all cultures can be funneled through Hemans's English. It overflowed the boundaries of Great Britain to encompass universal femininity.

If the English of late eighteenth-century writers opposed that of the standardizers, that of the Romantic poets ended up in a tense complementarity with it. Standardization had on its side the prestige of Great Britain, the precedence of the best authors like Pope and Addison, and huge distribution through textbooks and anthologies, but it also had the drawback of its potential for almost instant obsolescence. Romantic poetry, on the other hand, represented the cutting edge of English usage, in part because much of it did not become widely accessible until quite late in the nineteenth century. The standard approach to Romantic poetry has been to focus on it as representation: to examine the poets' treatments of such topics as subjectivity, nature, the imagination, or even language. Yet doing so tends to forget that poetry is not just about what it represents: any poem also makes a statement about the possibilities of the language in which it is written. For Romantic poets, the uncertainty of these possibilities became the occasion for an often hidden drama that nonetheless lay at the heart of their poetic projects.

NOTES

1 Linda Colley, *Britons: Forging the Nation, 1707–1837* (New Haven: Yale University Press, 1992), p. 295.
2 Thomas Sheridan, *Course of Lectures on Elocution* (1762), facs. edn. (Menston: Scolar Press, 1968), p. 206.
3 J. Paul Hunter, *Before Novels: The Cultural Context of Eighteenth-Century English Fiction* (New York: W. W. Norton, 1990), pp. 156–61.
4 John Walker, *A Critical Pronouncing Dictionary and Expositor of the English Language* (1791), facs. edn. (Menston: Scolar Press, 1968), p. iii.
5 Information on Blair and Murray from William St. Clair, *The Reading Nation in the Romantic Period* (Cambridge: Cambridge University Press, 2004), pp. 581, 137.
6 Robert Crawford, *Devolving English Literature*, 2nd edn. (Edinburgh: Edinburgh University Press, 2000), p. 38.
7 Maria Edgeworth, *Belinda* (1801), ed. Kathryn J. Kirkpatrick (Oxford: Oxford University Press, 1994), pp. 225, 236.
8 Samuel Johnson, "Preface to *A Dictionary of the English Language*" (1755), in *Johnson on the English Language*, ed. Gwin J. Kolb and Robert DeMaria, Jr. (New Haven: Yale University Press, 2005), p. 108.
9 John Fell, *An Essay Towards an English Grammar* (London: C. Dilly, 1784), p. xi.
10 Bertil Sundby, Anne Kari Bjørge, and Kari E. Haugland, *A Dictionary of English Normative Grammar, 1700–1800* (Amsterdam: John Benjamins, 1991), p. 35.

Since Addison wrote many of *The Spectator* essays, his combined total is higher than Swift's.

11 St. Clair, *The Reading Nation*, pp. 122–39.

12 Hugh Blair, *Lectures on Rhetoric and Belles Lettres* (1783), ed. Harold F. Harding, 2 vols., facs. edn. (Carbondale: Southern Illinois University Press, 1965), vol. II, pp. 322–3.

13 *The Complete Works of Thomas Chatterton*, ed. Donald S. Taylor and Benjamin B. Hoover, 2 vols. (Oxford: Clarendon Press, 1971), vol. I, p. 210, ll. 961–7.

14 *The Letters of John Keats*, ed. Hyder Rollins, 2 vols. (Cambridge, MA: Harvard University Press, 1958), vol. II, p. 167.

15 See St. Clair, *The Reading Nation*, ch. 17.

16 James Macpherson, "A Preliminary Discourse on the Poems of Ossian, the Son of Fingal," in *The Poems of Ossian, and Related Works*, ed. Howard Gaskill (Edinburgh: Edinburgh University Press, 1996), p. 354.

17 Crawford, *Devolving English Literature*, p. 36.

18 Quoted in *Robert Burns: The Critical Heritage*, ed. Donald A. Low (London: Routledge & Kegan Paul, 1974), p. 69.

19 *The Complete Works of Samuel Taylor Coleridge*, vol. 16: *Poetical Works I–III*, ed. J. C. C. Mays (Princeton: Princeton University Press, 2001), vol. I, Part I, pp. 384–7.

20 William Wordsworth, "Preface to the Second Edition of *Lyrical Ballads* (1800)," in *Lyrical Ballads, and Other Poems, 1797–1800*, ed. James Butler and Karen Green (Ithaca: Cornell University Press, 1992), p. 748.

21 Blair, *Lectures*, vol. I, p. 442.

22 William Wordsworth, *Lyrical Ballads, and Other Poems, 1797–1800*, p. 254, ll. 40–7.

23 Lindley Murray, *English Grammar* (1795), facs. edn. (Menston: Scolar Press, 1968), p. 205. Italics original.

24 *The Complete Poetry and Prose of William Blake*, ed. David V. Erdman, rev. edn. (New York: Doubleday, 1982), p. 19, ll. 1–4.

25 Ibid., p. 41, pl. 17.

26 *Dictionary of English Normative Grammar*, p. 221.

27 *Lord Byron: The Complete Poetical Works*, ed. Jerome J. McGann and Barry Weller, 7 vols. (Oxford: Oxford University Press, 1980–93), vol. IV, p. 180.

28 See *Dictionary of English Normative Grammar*, p. 223.

29 *The Poems of John Keats*, ed. Jack Stillinger (Cambridge, MA: Harvard University Press, 1978), pp. 364–5, ll. 13–20.

30 Murray, *English Grammar*, p. 191. Italics original.

31 *Felicia Hemans: Selected Poems, Letters, Reception Materials*, ed. Susan J. Wolfson (Princeton: Princeton University Press, 2000), p. 436, ll. 7–12.

32 Murray, *English Grammar*, p. 170.

FURTHER READING

Aarsleff, Hans, *From Locke to Saussure: Essays on the Study of Language and Intellectual History* (Minneapolis: University of Minnesota Press, 1982)
    The Study of Language in England, 1780–1860 (Minneapolis: University of Minnesota Press, 1983)

Bailey, Richard W., *Nineteenth-Century English* (Ann Arbor: University of Michigan Press, 1996)

Barrell, John, *English Literature in History, 1730–80: An Equal, Wide Survey* (New York: St. Martin's, 1983)

Bewell, Alan, *Wordsworth and the Enlightenment: Nature, Man, and Society in the Experimental Poetry* (New Haven: Yale University Press, 1989)

Butler, Marilyn, "Burns and Politics," in *Robert Burns and Cultural Authority*, ed. Robert Crawford (Iowa City: University of Iowa Press, 1997), pp. 86–112

"Romanticism in England," in *Romanticism in National Context*, ed. Roy Porter and Mikuláš Teich (Cambridge: Cambridge University Press, 1988), pp. 37–67

Cohen, Murray, *Sensible Words: Linguistic Practice in England, 1640–1785* (Baltimore: Johns Hopkins University Press, 1977)

Crowley, Tony, *Language in History: Theories and Texts* (London: Routledge, 1996)

Keach, William, *Arbitrary Power: Romanticism, Language, Politics* (Princeton: Princeton University Press, 2004)

McKusick, James, *Coleridge's Philosophy of Language* (New Haven: Yale University Press, 1986)

Michaelson, Patricia Howell, *Speaking Volumes: Women, Reading, and Speech in the Age of Austen* (Stanford: Stanford University Press, 2002)

Miller, Thomas P., *The Formation of College English: Rhetoric and Belles Lettres in the British Cultural Provinces* (Pittsburgh: University of Pittsburgh Press, 1997)

Mugglestone, Lynda, *"Talking Proper": The Rise of Accent as Social Symbol* (Oxford: Clarendon Press, 1995)

Romaine, Suzanne, ed., *The Cambridge History of the English Language*: vol. IV, *1776–1997* (Cambridge: Cambridge University Press, 1998)

Smith, Olivia, *The Politics of Language, 1791–1819* (Oxford: Clarendon Press, 1984)

Turley, Richard Marggraf, *The Politics of Language in Romantic Literature* (New York: Palgrave Macmillan, 2002)

5

SIMON JARVIS

Thinking in verse

In his *Biographia Literaria* Coleridge took issue with the ideas about meter which Wordsworth had expressed in the "Preface" to the *Lyrical Ballads*. For Coleridge, Meter's chief function was a symbolic one. "I write in metre, because I am about to use a language different from that of prose."[1] Meter is a sign, which produces certain expectations about other linguistic features of the poem. If these expectations are disappointed, a kind of bathos will ensue. For Wordsworth, on the other hand, meter is not primarily a sign but, instead, is essentially connected to the fundamental organization of human knowing itself. We might characterize these accounts of meter, broadly speaking, as "symbolic" and "cognitive" respectively. For Coleridge's kind of account, the effects of meter are dependent upon recognition of a convention; for Wordsworth's kind of account, they depend upon the organization of consciousness itself.

What should be noted at once is that scholarship is still not in a position to settle this argument. For one kind of approach to meter, it is a metacommunicative feature of poetic discourse. In this approach it is imaginable that we can, for example, identify "iambic" pentameter as "a hegemonic form . . . a sign which excludes and includes, sanctions and denigrates, for it discriminates the 'properly' poetic from the 'improperly' poetic, Poetry from verse."[2] For other kinds of approach, meter is connected to the rhythmic organization of consciousness itself.[3] The terrain remains disputed because, despite the startling developments of twentieth-century linguistics, there is still no science of verse.

Absent such a science, the often fragmentary formulations in which poets themselves try to make sense of the practice of verse take on a peculiar importance. They remain items of current theoretical interest, because the field to which they contribute remains disputed.

For each of the poets whom I will centrally consider – Blake, Shelley, Wordsworth – thinking was not something which naturally first of all happened in prose, and which then had somehow to be put into verse. It was instead something which could happen in verse too, and would happen differently if it did. Each of these poets took a deep and profoundly formative interest in fundamental questions of philosophy. Yet none offers us a versified system; each matters precisely because of the intensity of their absorption in the verse material itself and the specific interferences, distortions, mutilations, and mutations *of thinking* which that absorption made possible. Each, by the same token, finds a quite singular path through and out of what they think of as a false opposition between knowledge and inspiration, to the extent that the resulting bodies of work are entirely unassimilable to each other, marked much more visibly by their conspicuous antagonisms than by this deeper filiation of their insistence on thinking in verse. In the case of each, their fragmentary accounts of the relation between versifying and thinking are at once documents of essential importance and also, as always in the relation between poetical theory and practice, partial ciphers of a much more complex practice. This chapter cannot interpret their verse practice, not only for the usual reasons (shortness of space, etc.), but because it contends that no approach which might make this technique of the body interpretable as a mode of *thinking* has yet been fully elaborated. Instead the chapter is a contribution to the history of ideas about verse. It tries to follow closely the actual words used by three important poets of this period to describe their experiences, theories, and judgments about verse. In doing so, it hopes to suggest that thinking about – and *in* – verse might be a topic still in its infancy. The period covered by this volume is one of particular importance for this thinking, because so many of its most important writers of verse were also quite clearly major thinkers, and because they worked at a historical moment when certain neoclassical modes of thinking about these questions were in the course of breaking up. The present chapter attempts to open up a little our sense of how some of these poets themselves thought about thinking in verse, so as to suggest the possibility that, far from having been read to death or superseded, their thought and work may remain far in advance of any literary-critical apparatus which has so far been brought up to decode them. It aims, in the longer term, to begin opening up the possibility that verse is not merely a kind of thinking but also a kind of implicit and historical *knowing*: the possibility that the finest minutiae of verse practice represent an internalized mimetic response to historical changes too terrifying or exhilarating to be addressed explicitly.[4]

"Pish!"

Donald Reiman records the following conversation which, according to an "Eye Witness," Shelley once had with Byron.

SHELLEY. . . . Is not a line, as well as your outspread heroics, or a tragedy, a whole, and only as a whole, beautiful in itself? as, for instance, "How sweet the moonlight sleeps upon this bank." Now, examining this line, we perceive that all the parts are formed in relation to one another, and that it is consequently a whole. "Sleep," we see, is a reduplication of the pure and gentle sound of sweet; and as the beginning of the former symphonizes with the beginning s of the latter, so also the l in moonlight prepares one for the l in sleep, and glides gently into it; and in the conclusion, one may perceive that the word "bank" is determined by the preceding words, and that the b which it begins with is but a deeper intonation of the two p's which come before it; sleeps upon this slope, would have been effeminate; sleeps upon this rise, would have been harsh and inharmonious.

BYRON. Heavens! do you imagine, my dear Shelley, that Shakspeare had any thing of the kind in his head when he struck off that pretty line? If any one had told him all this about your p's and s's, he would just have said, "Pish!"

SHELLEY. Well, be that as it may, are there not the coincidences, I suppose you would call them, that I showed in the line?

BYRON. There are. But the beauty of the line does not lie in sounds and syllables, and such mechanical contrivances, but in the beautiful metaphor of the moonlight sleeping.

SHELLEY. Indeed, that also is very beautiful. In every single line, the poet must organize many simultaneous operations, both the meaning of the words and their emphatic arrangement, and then the flow and melting together of their symphony; and the whole must also be united with the current of the rhythm.

BYRON. Well, then, I'm glad I'm not a poet! It must be like making out one's expenses for a journey, I think, all this calculation!

SHELLEY. I don't say that a poet must necessarily be conscious of all this, no more than a lady is conscious of every graceful movement. But I do say that they all depend upon reason, in which they live and move, and have their being; and that he who brings them out into the light of distinct consciousness, beside satisfying an instinctive desire of his own nature, will be more secure and more commanding. But what makes this metaphor beautiful? To represent the tranquillity of moonlight is the object of the line; and the sleep is beautiful, because it gives a more intense and living form of the same idea; the rythm [sic] beautifully falls in with this, and just lets the cadence of the emphasis dwell upon the sound and sense of the sweet word "sleep;" and the alliteration assimilates the rest of the line into one harmonious symmetry. This line, therefore, is it not altogether a work of art?[5]

We cannot be sure whether just this conversation took place, although there is no particular reason to doubt it. Whether it is a precise transcription, a loose reconstruction, or a flight of fantasy, it tells us something important about how some people understood poetry in our period. Although the conversation is widely familiar, its terms repay close scrutiny.

The "Pish!" uttered by "Byron" is attractive. A good deal of the best recent commentary on Romantic poetry might almost have taken its cue from it. Yet the skin and bones of any reader's experience of verse are made up largely of the kind of consideration addressed here by "Shelley." "Byron" cuts into those speculations with a sharp opposition between art and craft. Under this regime, sounds and syllables are "mechanical contrivances." To this machinery is then joined an opposition between the generous and the venal. Syllable-catchers are also penny-pinchers. The response of "Shelley" to this is remarkable. The first move is obvious enough: the poet need not do any of this consciously. The second is much more surprising: "I do say that they all depend upon reason, in which they live and move, and have their being; and that he who brings them out into the light of distinct consciousness, beside satisfying an instinctive desire of his own nature, will be more secure and more commanding." This claim decisively rejects the assignation of prosody to the sub-field of craft. Instead it develops a difference between "reason" and "distinct consciousness." The latter is to be understood in the tradition of the philosophical opposition between "clear and distinct" ideas and "obscure and vague" ones. "Distinct consciousness" does not merely refer to sentience as such, but to reflective consciousness. To bring these "operations" into "distinct consciousness" is to make them explicit. Reason, conversely, is understood as the very element or condition of possibility of these "symphonic" operations. These symphonic operations, that is, live and move and have their being in reason, and yet they are not necessarily or ordinarily visible to distinct consciousness. (The atheist poet, "Shelley," alludes here to St. Paul, who, on the Areopagus, offered to identify for the pagans the unknown god to whom their altar was inscribed. Prosodic artifice may, Shelley implies, be thought of as that element in which our communication lives, whether we choose to thematize it or not.) They are, this is to say, a form of prereflective cognition. Far from being essentially mechanical contrivances or calculations, these operations are forms of knowledge. Moreover, an undecidability creeps in as to the status of these operations. It would be common sense to think that they are mental operations. Yet what is said is that the operations are in the line. All this raises the possibility – a possibility more uncanny than any melodrama of emptiness – that the poem might know something we don't; so that when "Shelley" reverts to his primary claim, "This line, therefore, is it not altogether a work of art?," we can see how much more this means than it seemed to mean before. The line is *altogether* a work of art, not only in the sense that it is a work of art when taken together, as a whole, but in the sense that it is a work of art to the very cartilage of its letters, words, and syllables, and not merely in the spirit of its thoughts, feelings, metaphors, etc. Each line is a cognitive artifact.

Thinking in verse

In the last few decades some brilliant scholarship has made us keenly aware of how easily the superimposition of large and inflexible philosophical or theoretical frameworks over the verse of this period can erase its specificity, complexity, and variety. Yet such reductions can also be brought about by the opposite procedure – by insisting that philosophy has nothing in particular to do with poetry, and that it was a prejudice only of a certain generation of Romanticists to link the two. In our period, many poets, critics, and readers understood philosophy and poetry to be necessarily and intimately connected, and they imagined that connection in as many different ways as they imagined philosophy and poetry. This was not a peculiarly "Romantic" view. One important motor for it, indeed, was currents of *classical* scholarship whose development had accelerated in the course of the eighteenth century. Close attention to dating and chronology meant that ancient verse was much less likely to be understood as an essentially unified body of cultural monuments, and more likely to be understood in relation to its own changing social and political contexts. One set of currents in classical scholarship strongly emphasized the fact that much of the knowledge available to archaic Greek society, for example, had in fact been transmitted in verse. So the assumption self-evident to our epoch, that philosophy and other forms of knowledge naturally fall into prose, became self-evident only after what one classical scholar has called "the invention of prose."[6] The historical differentiation of literary history which was taking place in the eighteenth century allowed this false self-evidence to be opened up to questioning; just as, we may think, the revolutionary work of our own generation of classicists demands a rethinking not merely of literary history but also of literary theory, of our conception of what verse itself might be.[7]

In such a climate it began to be possible to develop alternatives to the blunt option with which Socrates faces Ion in the dialogue of that name: "Choose, then" (as Shelley translates it), "whether you will be considered false or inspired?" Gianvincenzo Gravina could entitle his widely influential treatise "Of Poetic *Reason*" (emphasis mine), and explain that "poetry is an enchantment (*maga*), but a salutary one, and a delirium which clears delusions. It is well known what the ancients fabled of Amphion and Orpheus, of whom we read that one with his lyre moved stones, the other beasts; from which fables it may be collected that the great poets with the sweetness of their singing were able to entrap the rough genius of men, and to conduct them back to civil life."[8] Certainly, it is not difficult to find ancestors of the "Byronic" "Pish!" George Campbell, the author of the *Philosophy of Rhetoric*, believed that "versification . . . is more to be considered as an appendage, than as a constituent of poetry. In this lies what may be called the more mechanical part of the poet's work, being at most but a sort of garnishing, and by far too unessential to give a designation to the kind."[9] But elsewhere, and especially where historically informed classical scholarship met enlightened speculation on the rise and progress of languages, a different view could be found. Hugh Blair insisted in his *Lectures on Rhetoric and Belles Lettres* that "among the Athenians, there was what was called the Nomic Melody; or a particular measure prescribed to the public officers, in which they were to promulgate the laws to the people; lest, by reading them with improper tones, the laws might be exposed to contempt."[10] Laws and tones, in such a view, do not stand in a merely indifferent or arbitrary relation to each other, but are instead intimately interconnected. Such a power of melodious speech was by many, including Blair himself, considered as something lost to modernity. Remarking on that period of a Roman rhetorician supposed by its sheer musicality to have prompted spontaneous acclamation, Blair adds: "I cannot believe that an English Sentence, equally harmonious, would, by its harmony alone, produce any such effect on a British audience, or excite any such wonderful applause and admiration, as Cicero informs us this of Carbo produced."[11]

Shelley had himself translated one of the inaugural documents of the long withdrawal of cognition from poetry, Plato's *Ion*. The eponymous rhapsode is a late and weak representative of the notion that poetry is magically efficacious speech. In the dialogue Socrates easily makes Ion look ridiculous. Socrates' decision that all knowledge falls under one special expertise or another is faced by nothing stronger than Ion's belief that he knows about military strategy because he knows what Homer says about it. Defeated, Ion is made at the close to accept the consolation prize that, although he knows nothing, he is indeed "inspired." Shelley admired Plato and certainly would not have wished to reverse this outcome. Yet he could see, as not all others did, the extent to which the idea of poetry as magically efficacious speech was a part, not of the early history of poetry alone, but also of the prehistory of science. After that apparently definitive sundering, we are not in the event left with two perfect opposites, one disenchanted science, the other fanciful poet-ery; instead, poetry lies buried alive inside systems of imaginary disenchantment, suppressed and stigmatized, or supplementary and aesthetic, certainly, but in truth one condition of their practicability and intelligibility alike. "The poetry in these systems of thought, is concealed by the accumulation of facts and calculating processes."[12] Most of the discussion of this part of Shelley's thinking has concentrated on metaphor. No less important to Shelley, though, was prosody. When Shelley writes that "language is arbitrarily produced by the imagination, and has relation to thoughts alone,"[13] we need to notice precisely what this says. It does not say that the relation between signifier and signified is an arbitrary one, but only that language is arbitrarily produced by the imagination. As his *Defence* proceeds, it becomes clear that Shelley in fact thinks the relation between signifier and signified is not arbitrary in any strict sense of that adjective. "Sounds as well as thoughts have relation both between each other and towards that which they represent, and a perception of the order of those relations has always been found connected with a perception of the order of the relations of thought."[14] The argument that Plato was a poet, that Bacon was a poet, that Christ was a poet, is meant more directly than recent exegesis has always wanted to see. When Shelley argues that "every great poet must inevitably innovate upon the example of his predecessors in the exact structure of his peculiar versification," he means not only Homer's versification, Dante's versification, Milton's versification, but also Plato's versification, Bacon's versification, Christ's versification. How is this possible? Because "the distinction between poets and prose writers is a vulgar error."[15] It is so, not in the usual banal sense that versification is no essential part of poetry, but in the directly contrary sense that melody or its absence is an ineradicable dimension of prose. The oblivion of this dimension of language is not a natural fact but a long historical tide. When Shelley says that "the distinction between philosophers and poets has been anticipated,"[16] what he means is that it has been dated historically too early: Plato has been regarded as clearly a philosopher rather than a poet, although in Shelley's view "Plato was essentially a poet – the truth and splendour of his imagery, and the melody of his language, are the most intense that it is possible to conceive. He rejected the harmony of the epic, dramatic, and lyrical forms, because he sought to kindle a harmony in thoughts divested of shape and action, and he forbore to invent any regular plan of rhythm which would include, under determinate forms, the varied pauses of his style."[17] Essential to what makes Plato essentially a poet are melody, harmony, and rhythm.

Several of this period's most consequential verse authorships, then, found ways to refuse the false choice between falsehood and inspiration offered to Ion by Socrates.

The line of beauty

When Blake was asked to make an inscription in William Upcott's "autograph album" he took the occasion to consider what an autograph might be:

I do not think an Artist can write an Autograph, especially one who has studied in the Florentine & Roman Schools, as such an one will Consider what he is doing; but an Autograph, as I understand it, is writ helter skelter like a hog upon a rope, or a Man who walks without considering whether he shall run against a Post or a House or a Horse or a man, & I am apt to believe that what is done without meaning is very different from that which a Man does with his Thought & Mind, & ought not to be Call'd by the Same Name.

I consider the Autograph of Mr Cruikshank, which very justly stands first in the Book, & that Beautiful Specimen of Writing by Mr Comfield, & my own, as standing [in] the same Predicament: they are in some measure Works of Art & not of Nature or Chance.[18]

Blake's distrust of the very idea of the autograph album is of a piece with his broader thinking. Autograph collectors, Blake suspects, think they are getting an access to the essential character of the signatory, precisely in that the signatory does not deliberate the act of writing. The autograph is supposed to reveal character through spontaneity. It is supposed to be an unconscious revelation of the artist's inner nature. But for Blake this rests upon a confusion. An artist does nothing without meaning to do it. Whenever an artist writes, the writing will be a work of art, and not of nature.

Whether and how to sign one's name in an album seems like a small question. Yet for Blake, it brings into play some of the central energies of his thought. Thinking, knowing, and execution – whether in painting, writing, or versifying – are intimately connected:

Ideas cannot be given but in their minutely Appropriate Words, nor can a Design be made without its minutely Appropriate Execution. The unorganized Blots & Blurs of Rubens & Titian are not Art, nor can their Method ever express Ideas or Imaginations any more than Pope's Metaphysical Jargon of Rhyming.[19]

Others besides Blake in this period emphasized, though usually in different language, the identity of design and execution, conception and expression. Stranger to our ears, perhaps, is the idea that Pope's versification is a "Metaphysical Jargon." Blake draws a strict consequence from his premise – the identity of conception and expression – to the view that errors in technique must also be errors in thinking. Pope's versification, in other words, is objected to not simply on aesthetic grounds, but also, and most centrally, on cognitive ones. In a peculiar yet arresting analogy, Pope's verse technique – which is to say his verse thinking or, precisely, *failure* of thinking – is compared to the painterly technique of the Venetian colourists. Titian or Rubens, in Blake's view, in their emphasis on color, lack the "hard and wiry outline" which alone confers determinate form. Lacking this, their art lacks determinacy of any kind. By comparing it to Venetian coloring or to the work of certain British engravers whose work he detests on kindred grounds – not fleetingly, but throughout the "Public Address" – Blake is claiming that Pope's and Dryden's versification lacks determinacy. The claim is that like the work of these engravers, the verse is at once over-elaborated and monotonous: "Now let Dryden's Fall & Milton's Paradise be read, & I will assert that every Body of Understanding [will *del.*] must cry out Shame at such Niggling & Poco-Pen as Dryden has degraded Milton with. But at the same time I will allow that Stupidity will Prefer Dryden, because it is in Rhyme [but for no other cause *del.*] & Monotonous Sing Song, Sing Song from beginning to end."[20] For Blake, clarity and determinacy of outline are not set against concretion and vivid immediacy, but rather make it possible. Without such determinacy, nothing has its own shape, and everything is then able to merge into everything else.

We need to follow the centrality of this motif of determinacy through a little further in order to decode its significance for Blake's thinking about verse. Blake's maxims about "the outline" do not merely constitute technical remarks, but lie also at the centre of his very conception of "life itself":

> The great and golden rule of art, as well as of life, is this: That the more distinct, sharp and wiry the bounding line, the more perfect the work of art; and the less keen and sharp, the greater is the evidence of weak imitation, plagiarism, and bungling . . . How do we distinguish the oak from the beech, the horse from the ox, but by the bounding outline? How do we distinguish one face or countenance from another, but by the bounding line and its infinite inflexions and movements? What is it that builds a house and plants a garden, but the definite and determinate? What is it that distinguishes honesty from knavery, but the hard and wiry line of rectitude and certainty in the actions and intentions? Leave out this line, and you leave out life itself; all is chaos again, and the line of the almighty must be drawn out upon it before man or beast can exist.[21]

This remarkable passage from Blake's "Descriptive Catalogue" incises the outline, counterintuitively, as the condition of the possibility of concrete and living variety. Firm outline is not only the right way to draw, paint, and engrave. It is also the only way of knowing anything. Without the line, we literally cannot tell one thing from another. Discrimination drops out of cognition. (It is all the more unfortunate that Blake has so often been commended for "blurring" conceptual boundaries.) Yet there is more. The outline is not only fundamental to cognition, but also to justice (to the distinction of honesty from knavery), and indeed to the existence of "anything at all and not nothing," as Leibniz's question put it. The artist's line is also the knower's line and the just man's line and the line of creation itself. It is all these things because it distinguishes what is alive – the "Spiritual Body," as Blake has it elsewhere – from what is not. "Leave out this line, and you leave out life itself."

These claims are deeply considered. They have a powerful epistemological lineage behind them: the lineage of Berkeley's attack on Locke. Blake's detestation of indeterminacy is directly informed by Berkeley's attack on the indeterminacy of Locke's "idol," matter – but matter devoid of any of those attributes which make matter matter: taste, color, smell, and so on. The "solid without fluctuation" for which Urizen has despairingly sought is, like the "Even Tint" which is "not in Nature", a descendant of Locke's colorless, odorless, tasteless volumes.[22] This attack is the primary source for Blake's insistence on "Minute Particulars". These last are not the sheer givennesses of empiricism, but rather the musculature of the *spiritual* body. Minute particulars are known because they are us, that body which we do not "have," but are. Blake does not "subvert" dualism. He refuses the wrong kind of dualism – that between the evacuated soul, on the one hand, and the phenomenalized object, on the other, a dualism of nothing meeting nothing. The opposition between the spiritual body – that at once affective and cognitive body which I am – and everything else, on the contrary, is not to be blurred, but sharpened, exacerbated, and deepened.

This puts us in a better position, I think, to see why Blake might be able to think of Pope's versification as a "Metaphysical Jargon." Rhyme may presumably issue in "Song," and not only in "Sing-Song." But Pope's, for Blake, does not. Lacking determinacy, it presents to us "a Piece of Machinery of Points of Light to be put into a dark hole." Its failure of technique is also a failure of imagination and a failure of thinking. It thinks something abstract and general, which is to say that it does not, properly speaking, in Blake's or in Berkeley's sense, think at all. It would "turn that which is Soul & Life into a Mill or Machine", because the absence of this determinacy is the absence of "life itself."[23]

I would rather own up to what Blake calls "Stupidity" than share his opinion of Pope. But that opinion lets us see what kind of thinking Blake imagined his own verse to be undertaking. His verse is "Living Form," not "Mathematic Form," precisely because it is not the form of an object, but the musculature of a spiritual body.[24] What kind of connection might there be between the cut line and the verse line? Clearly, the two are not the same. Yet behind Blake's thinking about both lies the same thought about the identity of inspiration with execution. The two cannot be separated for Blake. When introducing his long prophetic poem *Jerusalem*, Blake explained his practice of verse in the following way: "When this verse was first dictated to me I consider'd a Monotonous Cadence like that used by Milton & Shakspeare & all Writers of English Blank Verse, derived from the modern bondage of Rhyming; to be a necessary and indispensible part of Verse. But I soon found that in the mouth of a true Orator such monotony was not only awkward, but as much a bondage as rhyme itself. I therefore have produced a variety in every line, both of cadences & of number of syllables."[25] The opposition to the bondage of meter and rhyme is not an abstract freedom to do whatever you like, but instead the true vision dictated to the true orator. What Blake discovered that he had to abandon was precisely any idea that the content of his prophecies might be divinely dictated, but that their form would be a matter of the poet's craft: the idea that one might somehow "put" these dictations "into" metrical cadence without changing anything essential about them. Both thoughts and numbers become equally essential to what the poet knows. Inspiration does not stop somewhere in the cerebral cortex, but travels right "down the Nerves of my right arm."[26] Blake's verse, line after line, thinks of itself as cutting the line of the almighty – who is, after all, only we ourselves in so far as we are "honest" – out on what would otherwise be chaos, over and over again, and thereby as restoring us, over and over again, to that life which we habitually keep disowning. To scan Blake's line would demand a metrics that does not yet exist, or, better, would require scrutiny of the concept of "scansion" itself. Scansion offers to make a diagram out of an experience. It is what Blake would have considered a form of graven image. "Nature & Fancy are Two Things & can Never be joined; neither ought any one to attempt it, for it is Idolatry & destroys the Soul."[27]

The transparent veil

Wordsworth, of course, was precisely someone whom Blake could have thought of as idolatrously joining nature and fancy. The stark differences between Wordsworth and Blake over meter not only are matters of technical preference but reach right down to fundamental differences in their mental universes.

Wordsworth wrote a number of poems lamenting the slow disappearance of spinning-wheels from rural cottages. Here is one of them:

> Grief, thou hast lost an ever ready Friend
> Now that the cottage spinning-wheel is mute;
> And Care – a Comforter that best could suit
> Her froward mood, and softliest reprehend;
> And Love – a Charmer's voice, that used to lend

More efficaciously than aught that flows
From harp or lute, kind influence to compose
The throbbing pulse, – else troubled without end:
E'en Joy could tell, Joy craving truce and rest
From her own overflow, what power sedate
On those revolving motions did await
Assiduously, to sooth her aching breast;
And – to a point of just relief – abate
The mantling triumphs of a day too blest.[28]

The sonnet appears at first to be chiefly preoccupied with the topic of consolation. The spinning-wheel is valuable, and its loss lamentable, because it is a "Friend" to grief and "Comforter" to care. Yet as the poem proceeds, its focus shifts. The spinning-wheel also offers to compose the throbbing pulse of – what we might not at first think we need any refuge from – "Love." So that, by the time we have reached the sestet, the spinning-wheel's rhythms, its "revolving motions," are protecting us not from extremes of sorrow or pain, but rather from those of *joy*: "Joy craving truce and rest / From her own overflow." The preoccupation with how we may be protected from excessive or overflowing bliss – "the mantling triumphs of a day too blest" – is wholly characteristic of one current of Wordsworth's verse from about the middle of the first decade of the nineteenth century onwards. High mountings to delight tend to be followed by correspondingly deep descents into dejection. Wordsworth becomes concerned with how brief and transient exaltation may be made to settle into the fabric of daily life, rather than passing rapidly and throwing us into subsequent misery.

How does the spinning-wheel protect us from this? Perhaps in this way: "the co-presence of something regular, something to which the mind has been accustomed when in an unexcited or a less excited state, cannot but have great efficacy in tempering and restraining the passion by an intertexture of ordinary feeling."[29] This, of course, is part of the account of meter given in Wordsworth's "Preface" to *Lyrical Ballads*, and the sonnet, in fact, is not only about spinning-wheels, but also about meter. The connections are not merely thematic, but also lexical. "Poetry is the spontaneous overflow of powerful feelings"; this overflow is tempered and restrained by the co-presence of something regular. Just so, here, joy craves truce and rest from its own "overflow," and finds it in the "power sedate" of the spinning-wheel's revolutions.

Put in this way, meter might seem to have a primarily conservative function, the function of curbing an enthusiasm which might otherwise prove dangerous. It might feel like a development of Wordsworth's earlier celebration of the restrictions which the sonnet form itself imposes: "Nuns fret not at their convents' narrow room."[30] But the often overlooked corollary of Wordsworth's account of meter as tempering or restraining excessive passion is that it induces or increases passion where the latter is insufficient. Indeed, although most critical attention has devolved upon the first of these functions, Wordsworth himself seems to regard the second as more often pertinent:

> – On the other hand (what it must be allowed will much more frequently happen) if the Poet's words should be incommensurate with the passion, and inadequate to raise the Reader to a height of desirable excitement, then, (unless the Poet's choice of his metre has been grossly injudicious) in the feeling of pleasure which the Reader has been accustomed to connect with that particular movement of metre, there will be found something which will greatly contribute to impart passion to the words, and to effect the complex end which the Poet proposes to himself.[31]

In this passage meter's role is the reverse of that which Wordsworth is sometimes thought solely to ascribe to it: here meter, far from restraining or tempering passion, imparts it. Wordsworth, in fact, as Brennan O'Donnell has shown in a fine study, does not find "passion" to inhere only in what words refer to, but also in meter itself. In a later letter to John Thelwall, the friend of Liberty who had developed an anti-metrical theory of verse rhythm, Wordsworth further developed his account of verse as a productive collision between the "passion of the sense," that is the meaning of words, and the "passion of metre." The productivity of the collision can be seen at work in another of Wordsworth's poems about the spinning-wheel:

> There, too, did *Fancy* prize the murmuring wheel;
> For sympathies, inexplicably fine,
> Instilled a confidence – how sweet to feel!
> That ever in the night calm, when the Sheep
> Upon their grassy beds lay couched in sleep,
> The quickening spindle drew a trustier line.[32]

The sestet takes a pleasure characteristic of Wordsworth's verse in its play with the distribution of polysyllables and monosyllables, a play which culminates in the tensions held in the final line. Most eighteenth-century prosodists would have demanded that this line be performed with two elisions, "quick'ning" and "trust-yer", so as to make clear its conformity to meter. A Thelwallian approach would require this line to be spoken as twelve syllables, arguing that any elision of this kind would be a violent imposition of a "verse mouth" on to the rhythms possessed by the words themselves. Wordsworth's position, as O'Donnell is able to show, gives rights to both metrical *and* rhythmic requirements. It thus implies the need for a performance in which both sorts of norms are acknowledged.[33]

Wordsworth's friend Coleridge was later to develop an account of meter in which its function was primarily (though not exclusively) symbolic, delivering notice to the reader that the poet was about to use a kind of language different from that used in prose. But Wordsworth's step was to imagine the possibility of detaching diction from meter entirely, to see that meter need not in any aprioristically necessary way carry any implications whatever for the poet's lexicon. Thus, for example, a blank-verse style, partly developed from the striking advances in informality made by predecessors such as William Cowper and Charlotte Smith, was able, emboldened by this insight, to achieve lines of an astonishing fearlessness in the face of still powerful preconceptions of the necessary connectedness between meter and register. A line such as "of the low wall in which the pales were fixed" must needs have been, for another kind of taste, an instance of a verse "where ten low words oft creep in one dull line."

But what kind of "passion" is meter? How does it achieve the effects attributed to it by Wordsworth? Wordsworth retains throughout his authorship a sense that this question is one to which we do not yet know the answer. Verse remains, for him, what it is taken to be in the "Preface" – not a cut and dried question of forms, meters, and patterns, but rather a mode of experience in which the most fundamental and least understood powers of the human mind are in operation. Wordsworth's verse itself continually explores, explicitly as well as implicitly, the question of what verse is. I want to finish by following two of these explorations, contributions to the theory of verse not less important but only less discussed than Wordsworth's remarks in his "Preface."

In "Home at Grasmere," Wordsworth breaks off from a narrative of a widow's fond recollections of her dead husband with the following interjection:

> Is there not
> An art, a music, and a stream of words
> That shall be life, the acknowledged voice of life?
> Shall speak of what is done among the fields,
> Done truly there, or felt, of solid good
> And real evil, yet be sweet withal,
> More grateful, more harmonious, than the breath,
> The idle breath of sweetest pipe attuned
> To pastoral fancies? Is there such a stream,
> Pure and unsullied, flowing from the heart
> With motions of true dignity and grace,

Or must we seek these things where man is not?
Methinks I could repeat in tuneful verse
Delicious as the gentlest breeze that sounds
Through that aerial fir-grove, could preserve
Some portion of its human history
As gathered from that Matron's lips and tell
Of tears that have been shed at sight of it.

In "a stream of words" what matters is not only the individual words. In "Resolution and Independence" the leech-gatherer's speech becomes "like a stream" to the poet precisely at the point where word-boundaries disappear, and what is heard, instead, is only the intonation contour: the leech-gatherer's prosody.[34] Here, Wordsworth is taking up again with the question of what kind of thing meter might be. Is it a natural rhythm, something like a pulse or like breathing in and out? Or is it a violence imposed, something beaten out upon words? Our current theories of meter tend clearly to opt for one of these choices. Meter can be understood either as something naturally cognitive, hard-wired into brain structure, or as something symbolic, an achievement of culture. It is a quality of Wordsworth's thinking in general to pay attention to the slipperiness and subtle intermediatedness of nature and culture, and upon no topic more so than meter. He wishes for "an art . . . that shall be life," and knows how much he is wishing for. The model for it is that "human history" possessed not, as it happens, only by some human beings, but by a clump of trees. It would be a music whose human character would reside not in its ability to work the world over, filling it with human meanings, but in its capacity to *receive* meaning. And it would be able to do this just because meter itself cannot confidently be assigned, from a Wordsworthian view, either to nature or to culture. Contemporary metrics might have something to learn from this refusal to class the cabinet of our sensations.

This unclassifiability of verse thinking is developed still more powerfully in a passage towards the end of Book V of Wordsworth's "Prelude":

Visionary power
Attends upon the motions of the winds
Embodied in the mysteries of words;
There darkness makes abode, and all the host
Of shadowy things do work their changes there
As in a mansion like their proper home.
Even forms and substances are circumfused
By that transparent veil with light divine,
And through the turnings intricate of verse
Present themselves as objects recognized
In flashes, and with a glory scarce their own.[35]

Wordsworth is picking up here a thought begun in the "Preface." Meter, he said there, tends "to throw a sort of half consciousness of unsubstantial existence over the whole composition." Here this is a "transparent veil." This verse discussion is still more complex than that earlier prose one. But Wordsworth was never that kind of poet who thinks that you can say anything you like in verse, provided that it sounds good: and we should treat these as "words of reason deeply weighed" until driven to suppose otherwise. What Wordsworth is trying to get at here is the experience of the materiality of language. Words are not pure tokens, but also have sounding bodies. In the bodies of words some troubling powers seem to have come to rest: "darkness," and "all the host / Of shadowy things." These powers are the powers of meter. They work changes: they make the words work differently from the way in which they would work without meter, yet in a way which Wordsworth finds almost impossible to specify. These changes affect not only the outer surface of meaning. They are not decorative. "Even forms and substances are circumfused." Verse changes something essential to writing. Does verse obscure, or reveal? It seems to do both: these dark and shadowy powers, strangely, light up forms and substances. Yes, these last appear with a glory "scarce their own." Yet still, in this light, they "present *themselves*." The possibility is opened that these forms and substances may be more fully encountered in the strange light cast on them by verse, than when we think that we see straight into them, as though language were to interpose no veil of any kind. It is as though verse opens up, not just meter and rhythm, but the materiality of language itself as a possible domain of experience.[36]

If we like, we can see the kinds of thinking about verse which I have been pursuing in this chapter as a kind of mystification. In such a view, they might be chapters in an old story about the specialness of poetry and the specialness of poets. But in order to support such an opinion, we would need to know that we already know all about what verse is, and that there is nothing at all uncertain about it. Happily or unhappily, this is not the case. There is no satisfactory consensus even at the most basic descriptive level among literary scholars today about what meter is, what rhythm is, what a stress is, or how scansion should work.[37] Still less is there any consensus about how verse works: about the nature of the experiences, performances, and practices concerned. Meanwhile, the question is continuously set aside by being called one of "form," when really it is one of the essential and intimately historical matter of whatever these poems are. In this context, it is essential to revisit the fragmentary evidence of how the most significant thinkers *in* verse thought *about* verse. This evidence constitutes a precious yet fragile inheritance, because it is so tempting to assimilate their figures, concepts, and gestures for verse to what we think we already know about it. What we may find, if we instead read these fragments to the letter, is the possibility that their verse, and their thinking about it, present difficulties to literary criticism which literary criticism has only just begun to consider.

NOTES

1 Samuel Taylor Coleridge, *Biographia Literaria*, ed. Nigel Leask (London: Dent, 1997), p. 222.
2 Anthony Easthope, *Poetry as Discourse* (London: Methuen, 1983), p. 65.
3 For example, Richard D. Cureton, *Rhythmic Phrasing in English Verse* (London: Longman, 1991).
4 That is to say, "cognition" is used here in the sense in which art is understood as a form of implicit and mimetic historical *knowledge* in the aesthetic theory of Theodor W. Adorno. For a more detailed account of this idea, see S. Jarvis, *Adorno: A Critical Introduction* (Cambridge: Polity Press, 1998).
5 "Byron and Shelley on the Character of Hamlet", *New Monthly Magazine and Literary Journal* 29/2 (183), pp. 330–1, quoted from "'The Triumph of Life': A Variorum Edition," in *Shelley's "The Triumph of Life": A Critical Study*, ed. Donald Reiman, Illinois Studies in Language and Literature, 55 (Urbana: University of Illinois Press, 1965), pp. 135–225, at pp. 99–100.
6 Simon Goldhill, *The Invention of Prose* (Oxford: Oxford University Press, 2002).
7 I think in particular of the work of Gregory Nagy, especially *Pindar's Homer: The Lyric Possession of an Epic Past* (Baltimore: Johns Hopkins University Press, 1990); and of Marcel Detienne, *The Masters of Truth in Archaic Greece*, trans. Janet Lloyd (New York: Zone Books, 1996).
8 Gianvincenzo Gravina, *Della Ragion Poetica e della Tragedia* (Cosenza: Brenner, 1992), p. 11. Translation mine.
9 George Campbell, *The Philosophy of Rhetoric*, 2 vols. (London and Edinburgh, 1776), vol. 1, p. 15.
10 Hugh Blair, *Lectures on Rhetoric and Belles Lettres*, 2 vols. (London and Edinburgh, 1783), vol. 1, p. 253.
11 Ibid., pp. 254–5.
12 Percy Bysshe Shelley, *A Defence of Poetry*, in *Shelley's Poetry and Prose: Authoritative Texts, Criticism*, 2nd edn., ed. Donald H. Reiman and Neil Fraistat (London and New York: W. W. Norton, 2002), pp. 480–508, at p. 502.
13 Ibid., p. 483.
14 Ibid., p. 484.
15 Ibid.
16 Ibid.
17 Ibid.
18 William Blake, "Inscription in the Autograph Album of William Upcott," in *Complete Writings*, ed. Geoffrey Keynes (Oxford: Oxford University Press, 1972), pp. 781–2.
19 William Blake, "[Public Address] From the Note-Book," in *Complete Writings*, ed. Keynes, pp. 591–603, at p. 596.

20 Ibid., p. 600.

21 William Blake, "A Descriptive Catalogue of Pictures, Poetical and Historical Inventions, Painted by William Blake in Water Colours," in *Complete Writings*, ed. Keynes, pp. 563–86, at p. 585.

22 "Solid without fluctuation": "The First Book of Urizen," in *Complete Writings*, ed. Keynes, pp. 222–37, at p. 224; "Even Tint": "Public Address", additional passage, p. 603.

23 Ibid., pp. 599, 603.

24 William Blake, "On Homer's Poetry and On Virgil," in *Complete Writings*, ed. Keynes, p. 778.

25 *The Poetry and Prose of William Blake*, ed. David Erdman (New York: Doubleday, 1968), p. 144.

26 William Blake, "Milton, a Poem," in *Complete Writings*, ed. Keynes, pp. 480–535, at p. 481.

27 William Blake to Thomas Butts, July 6, 1803, in *Complete Writings*, ed. Keynes, pp. 823–6, at p. 824.

28 William Wordsworth, *Shorter Poems 1807–1820*, ed. Carl H. Ketcham (Ithaca: Cornell University Press, 1989), pp. 109–10.

29 William Wordsworth, "Preface" to *Lyrical Ballads* (1800) in *"Lyrical Ballads" and Other Poems, 1797–1800*, ed. James Butler and Karen Green (Ithaca: Cornell University Press, 1992), pp. 741–65, at p. 755.

30 William Wordsworth, *"Poems, in Two Volumes" and Other Poems, 1800–1807*, ed. Jared Curtis (Ithaca: Cornell University Press, 1983), p. 133.

31 Ibid., p. 756.

32 William Wordsworth, "Through Cumbrian wilds," in *Shorter Poems 1807–1820*, ed. Carl H. Ketcham (Ithaca: Cornell University Press, 1989), pp. 109–10.

33 Brennan O'Donnell, *The Passion of Meter: A Study of Wordsworth's Metrical Art* (Kent, OH: Kent State University Press, 1995), pp. 26–37.

34 William Wordsworth, in *"Poems, in Two Volumes,"* pp. 123–46, at p. 128, l. 114.

35 William Wordsworth, *The Thirteen-Book Prelude*, ed. Mark L. Reed, 2 vols. (Ithaca, NY: Cornell University Press, 1991), vol. 1, p. 177 (Book V, ll. 619–29).

36 For an illuminating commentary on this passage, see Neil Hertz, "Voices of Two or Three Different Natures," in *Under Criticism: Essays for William H. Pritchard*, ed. David Sofield and Herbert F. Tucker (Athens, OH: Ohio University Press, 1998), pp. 226–39.

37 For some of the most important studies currently available, each valuable and each using entirely different methods of scansion and employing widely differing conceptions of meter, rhythm, and the relations between them, see Marina Tarlinskaia, *English Verse: Theory and History: Translated from Russian*, De proprietatibus Litterarum, Series Practica 117 (Paris and The Hague: Mouton, 1976) (four-value stress system); Derek Attridge, *The Rhythms of English Poetry* (London: Longman, 1982) (system of "demotion" and "promotion" of non-ictic stresses and ictic non-stresses respectively); and George T. Wright, *Shakespeare's Metrical Art* (Berkeley: University of California Press, 1989) (sophisticated deployment of traditional foot-scansion).

FURTHER READING

Adorno, Theodor W., *Aesthetic Theory*, trans. Robert Hullot-Kentor (London: Athlone, 1996)

Attridge, Derek, *The Rhythms of English Poetry* (London: Longman, 1982)

Brogan, T. V. F., *English Versification, 1570–1980: A Reference Guide* (Baltimore and London: Johns Hopkins University Press, 1981)

Curran, Stuart, *Poetic Form and British Romanticism* (New York: Oxford University Press, 1986)

Grimaud, Michel, "Versification and Its Discontents: Towards a Research Program," *Semiotica* 88/3–4 (1992), pp. 199–242

Hollander, John, *Vision and Resonance: Two Senses of Poetic Form*, 2nd edn. (New York: Oxford University Press, 1985)

Jarvis, Simon, *Wordsworth's Philosophic Song* (Cambridge: Cambridge University Press, 2007)

Keach, William, *Shelley's Style* (London and New York: Methuen, 1984)

Perkins, David, "How the Romantics Recited Poetry," *Studies in English Literature 1500–1900* 31/4 (1991), pp. 65–71

Stewart, Susan, *Poetry and the Fate of the Senses* (Chicago: University of Chicago Press, 2002)

6

ANN WIERDA ROWLAND

Romantic poetry and the romantic novel

Readers interested in the relationship between poetry and the novel in the Romantic period have long been charmed by the scene of the autumnal walk in Jane Austen's *Persuasion* (1818). Keeping each other begrudging yet compulsive company, the extended family circle at Uppercross sets out on a "*long* walk," and Anne Elliot must once again witness at close hand the flirtations of her beloved Captain Wentworth and the Musgrove sisters. Finding pleasure in this walk requires a deliberate effort on Anne's part: she thus turns to the mental discipline of "repeating to herself some few of the thousand poetical descriptions extant of autumn, that season of peculiar and inexhaustible influence on the mind of taste and tenderness, that season which has drawn from every poet, worthy of being read, some attempt at description, or some lines of feeling." But while Anne occupies her mind "as much as possible in such like musings and quotations," she cannot help, when "within reach of Captain Wentworth's conversation," but try to hear it. And so the scene unfolds as a drama of what Anne overhears when unable to "fall into a quotation."[1]

With its retrospective structure and its attention to feeling and subjectivity, *Persuasion* is often called the most "Romantic" of Austen's novels. This particular scene is beloved for its "lyric" qualities and structure, and its interest in subjectivity, landscape, colloquy, and voiced and unvoiced emotion, justifies such comparisons. Barbara Hardy once described the episode as resembling an "Ode to Autumn in three stanzas,"[2] and, for Romanticists, Keats's as yet unwritten ode lends an uncanny charge to Austen's evocation of autumn's poetry. While we, perhaps, cannot resist reading this Romantic novel through our subsequent theories of Romantic poetry, Austen uses the form of the novel to frame the verse of her day, to present and critique the cultural circulation and subjective work of poetry in the early nineteenth century. And poetry, in her novels, often works in ways that do not conform to our early twenty-first-century expectations.

Set in the most elegiac of seasons, for example, this scene uses poetry to guard against feeling even as it defines poetry as "lines of feeling." Anne's intimate knowledge of poetry proves her mind to be one of "taste and tenderness"; yet the packaging of that taste into reiterated "musings and quotations," the proliferation of tenderness into a "thousand poetical descriptions extant," suggests that the feelings of poetry come rather cheap. Later in the novel Captain Benwick's habit of reciting the poetry of Scott and Byron warns of a possibly superficial or self-indulgent emotional life. Quoting poetry – excerpting it, repeating it, inserting it elsewhere – changes its value, changes what poetry is and how it works; lines of lyric can work to block or mute consciousness rather than bring it into full articulation. Poetry is certainly central to *Persuasion*'s exploration of what is often called "lyric consciousness," but in this novel they are by no means equivalent. Indeed, when Anne recommends a "larger allowance of prose" to Captain Benwick mid-way through the novel, the stage seems set for Austen's demonstration that prose – perhaps even the novel itself (although Anne prefers letters and memoirs) – is the superior vehicle for the "lyric" representation and composition of consciousness.

Taking its direction from the "and" of its title, this essay will explore how poetry and the novel can and should be read together in this period and how these two broad generic categories defined themselves in and through each other. Streamlined narratives describing the "rise of the novel" or the "ascendancy of the lyric" cannot adequately account for the vigorous mixing and jostling of genres in these years, and we have increasingly realized the need for literary histories that describe how the formal and social categories of Romantic literary genre took shape through persistent acts of both differentiation and appropriation. Novels and poetry, in particular, have a lot to say about each other in a period when the cultural status of both was in dramatic flux. There were more new volumes of poetry published in the years 1780–1830 than there were new novels, but in their material and social aspects (as book commodities of a certain size or price, as cultural products associated with certain levels of class and prestige), these two literary forms were beginning to follow inverse trajectories: the novel on a slight upwards course and poetry on an equally slight decline.[3]

In all aspects, however, these two literary categories were entirely entangled with each other in these years and not necessarily in ways our current understandings of these terms would predict. A significant number of writers – Charlotte Smith, Ann Radcliffe, Matthew Lewis, Mary Robinson, Sydney Owenson, Walter Scott, Amelia Opie, James Hogg – wrote and published in both poetic and novelistic forms. Capacious in structure and voracious in appetite, many novels of the period contain and reflect on poetry to such an extent that they may best be described as composite or even multimedia forms. The long verse romances of the period are also mixed forms, typically including extensive prose notes that interrupt, historicize, and otherwise frame the poetic lines. Critical histories of literature and language written during the Romantic period used the generic and modal markers of "poetry" and "novel" in ways that often seem counterintuitive to us today, writing "histories of fiction" that included poetry or tracing the "poetic" qualities of a novel. Subtitles, such as that of Anna Seward's *Louisa: A Poetical Novel in Four Epistles*, or Amelia Opie's *The Father and Daughter, A Tale, In Prose*, suggest the flexibility of generic markers in moving between and bringing together verse and prose, poetry and the novel.

When we examine poetry through the prose frame of scholarly footnotes or novelistic narrative, when we try to recover what the Romantics meant when they distinguished or failed to distinguish between poetic and prose writing, we confront a variety of challenges to our current valuations of literary categories and modes. The Romantic lyric, for example, changes significantly when read in relation to Gothic romance, the national tale, the historical novel or the novel of manners, looking less and less like the triumphant emergence of psychological individualism than a careful marker of sentimental subjectivity or the elaboration of a historical sensibility. Indeed, when we approach the poetry and novels of this period together, we are immediately reminded that most of the poetry written and read in these years was not lyrical, but narrative – epics, tales, and romances, collections of old and new ballads. Romantic narratives tell a variety of social stories about sentiment, national culture, domesticity, and gender. But they also unfold as acts of cultural framing and generic staging, reflecting on the relations of poetry or the novel to society and the social action of literary forms.

Literature of feeling and imagination

Tracing poetic forms and legacies in the novel, as many have done in *Persuasion*, is not, of course, a recent development in literary criticism. Anna Letitia Barbauld, a well-respected Romantic poet, essayist, and educator, begins the introductory essay to her edition of *The British Novelists* (1810) by describing a "good novel" as an "epic in prose."[4] Given the remarkable resurgence of epic poetry in the early years of the nineteenth century, Barbauld may be tapping into a current literary craze to promote the novel. But, of course, she also follows a well-worn formula for enlisting the prestige of poetry on behalf of the novel. About sixty years earlier, Henry Fielding famously described *Joseph Andrews* as a "comic epic poem in prose,"[5] claiming a respectable lineage for a disreputable, upstart genre and launching a tradition of novel criticism that dominated much of the eighteenth century.

Central to Fielding's claim is his classical assumption that poetry may be "likewise either in Verse or Prose"(p. 4). But whether or not a "work of fiction and imagination," written "according to the rules of the epic poem" *but in prose*, "may deserve the name of Poem, or not," became a significant question of mid-eighteenth-century criticism.[6] Richard Hurd, whose *Letters on Chivalry and Romance* (1762) was so influential in the Gothic revival of the late eighteenth century, answers that question elsewhere with an emphatic negative, insisting that an epic must be written in verse, and condemning prose novels and romances as "hasty, imperfect and abortive poems." To "mix and confound" genres may be a "literary luxury," he insists, but such "half-formed pleasures" ultimately betray the "vitiated, palled and sickly imagination – that last disease of learned minds, and sure prognostic of expiring letters."[7] Other critics were less convinced that the end was nigh. Lord Monboddo describes Fielding's *Tom Jones* in triumphant, nationalist terms. "There is lately sprung up among us a species of narrative poem, representing likewise the characters of common life," he notes: "we have, in English, a *poem* of that kind, (for so I will call it) which has more of character in it than any work, antient or modern that I know."[8] James Beattie uses "poetical" to classify the modern romance or novel, what he calls the "poetical prose fable": "*poetical*, from the nature of the invention; and *prose*, because it is not in verse." Anticipating later Romantic arguments about the commonality of poetry and prose, Beattie insists that "Prose and Verse are opposite, but Prose and Poetry may be consistent."[9] Under the category of "poetical prose fable," Beattie discusses *Robinson Crusoe*, the novels of Richardson and Smollett, as well as those of Fielding, which he terms "comic epick poems."[10]

Most eighteenth-century critics treated prose fiction as "poetry without the ornament of verse."[11] To some extent they were simply adapting an inherited critical lexicon to new and unfamiliar literary forms. But the emergence and popularity of novels within the literary scene made it necessary for a number of old questions and terms to be asked and defined anew in the years of the Romantic period. If, for example, prose can be "poetry without the ornament of verse," what then is poetry?

Wordsworth has one of the Romantic period's most famous answers to this question in his "Preface" to the *Lyrical Ballads*. Significantly that answer is ventured with the novel in mind. In fact, it is with an acute sense of the novel's growing cultural influence that Wordsworth positions his new and experimental poetry over and against the "frantic novels, sickly and stupid German Tragedies, and deluges of idle and extravagant stories in verse." The target of Wordsworth's criticism here is less specifically the "frantic novel," than the "degrading thirst after outrageous stimulation" that characterizes the age encouraged by such literature. Wordsworth is not invested in the formal distinctions between "frantic novels" and "extravagant stories in verse"; instead he groups them together according to the taste and sentiments they represent and inspire. His exemplary definitions of poetry and prose follow the same rationale:

> Is there then, it will be asked, no essential difference between the language of prose and metrical composition? I answer that there neither is nor can be any essential difference . . . They both speak by and to the same organs; the bodies in which both of them are clothed may be said to be of the same substance, their affections are kindred and almost identical, not necessarily differing even in degree; Poetry sheds no tears "such as Angels weep," but natural and human tears; she can boast of no celestial Ichor that distinguishes her vital juices from those of prose; the same human blood circulates through the veins of them both.[12]

Poetry and prose share the same body, blood, and organs and thus produce the same bodily affects: "natural and human tears." Wordsworth's rhetoric draws on eighteenth-century empirical philosophy (with its emphasis on sensation and bodily impressions) as well as on the culture of sensibility and sentiment (with its conventions of tears and quotations).

Such traditions allow Wordsworth not only to make connections between poetry and prose, but to define poetry as an imaginative and emotional, rather than a formal, category of writing. Meter is indeed the only "strict antithesis to Prose," but poetry is not restricted to meter. Poetry, famously, is the "spontaneous overflow of powerful feelings," and the poet is a "man endued with more lively sensibility," an "ability of conjuring up in himself passions," and a "greater readiness and power in expressing what he thinks and feels." Wordsworth's expressive and passionate idea of poetry – so often read as the clarion call of Romanticism's new day – in fact continues an eighteenth-century tradition of defining poetry as, in Hugh Blair's influential words, "the language of passion, or of enlivened imagination." Blair's *Lectures on Rhetoric and Belles Lettres*, a popular account of literary history and style reprinted in Britain and America well throughout the nineteenth century, describes the passionate language of poetry as "formed, most commonly, into regular numbers," but again the convention of meter is not presumed to constitute the essence of poetry. Like Wordsworth several decades later, Blair insists that the "primary aim of a Poet is to please, and to move; and therefore, it is to the Imagination, and the Passions, that he speaks."[13]

This emphasis on the strong and passionate language of poetry is a hall-mark of Enlightenment and Romantic primitivism, which insisted on the ancient origins of poetry and located its "manly" language in the most primitive figures: in the "savage tribes of men," for example, who are "governed by imagination and passion, more than by reason" and whose speech must be "deeply tinctured by their genius."[14] But as we have already begun to note, the more feminine-encoded influence of sensibility is also at work in this discourse of poetic language as one of feeling. Indeed, by tracing Wordsworth's definitions of poetry and the poet back to the culture and conventions of Enlightenment history and eighteenth-century sensibility, we draw stronger lines of continuity and influence between sentimentalism and romanticism as well as between the eighteenth-century novel and romantic poetry. By the turn of the nineteenth century, the novel was laying an increasingly larger claim to the category of imaginative and affective literature, and if both poetry and prose shed "natural and human tears," tears were coming to be recognized as the novel's specialty.

This widely accepted notion of poetry as passionate and imaginative language thus gradually shifted the relationship between poetry and the novel, providing new ways of understanding the novel as poetical, of finding poetry in prose, or defending the prose in poetry. By the end of the eighteenth century, the "poetical" quality of Richardson's *Clarissa* was debated, for example, as a question of the "passions" provoked by the novel, rather than of its adherence to a classical model. And in an 1821 essay on Smollett, Walter Scott, the most esteemed poet-novelist of the Romantic period, comments that "every successful novelist must be more or less a poet, even although he may never have written a line of verse."[15] Again for Scott, it is the "quality of imagination" and the power of "examining and embodying human character and human passion" that characterize the poet novelist.[16]

Scott's description of the successful novelist-poet is a bit ironic given William Hazlitt's criticism of Scott's own novels for lacking feeling and passion. Hazlitt wrote and lectured on both "The English Poets" and "The English Novelists" in 1818, and he uses strikingly similar terms in discussing these different literary categories. "Poetry is the language of the imagination and the passions," Hazlitt writes, "the universal language which the heart holds with nature and itself." All "great art," he comments in the essay on novels, is stamped by an "*instinct of the imagination*" which is the "intuitive perception of the hidden analogies of things."[17] When Percy Bysshe Shelley writes his *A Defence of Poetry* a few years later, his definition of poetry as "the expression of the Imagination" and of poetic language as "vitally metaphorical," marking "the before unapprehended relations of things," resonates as strongly with Hazlitt's account of the novel as with that of poetry. For Shelley, "the distinction between poets and prose writers" can now be dismissed as simply a "vulgar error."[18]

In gathering together the words and phrases Romantic-period writers used to represent poetry and the novel, we are arguably tracing the emergence of our modern conception of "Literature," a category of writing that narrowed over these years to mean, in Clifford Siskin's words, "special kinds of deeply imaginative writing."[19] What qualified as the depths or heights of this writing, what sort of subjectivity or character it supported, how it mapped feeling on to personal memory and national, cultural forms, emerged not in poetry alone, or in the novel alone, but in their various acts of mutual poaching and appropriation. Poetry laid claims beyond the borders of versification by staking out the sentimental grounds of the novel, while the novel redescribed its ambitions through a rhetoric of poetry and "poetical" writing. If "Literature" was "invented" in these years, it was largely a product of the elision of formal distinctions between poetry and prose, poetry and the novel.

Traditional forms and genres did not disappear, but their cultural value changed. Many Romantic writers championed those literary productions that *seemed* to elude or slip free of the "artificial" constraints of genre, meter, and other literary conventions. In his "Essay, Supplementary to the Preface" of 1815, Wordsworth conveys his contempt for the poets featured in Samuel Johnson's *Lives of the Most Eminent English Poets* by dismissing them simply as "metrical writers." In a 1796 essay entitled "Is Verse Essential to Poetry?," William Enfield describes versification as "artificial" and "mechanical," a literary "charm" or "embellishment" by no means essential to "the sublime operation of poetic invention." Provoking his essay is the "arrogant assumption" of poets who, considering themselves a "privileged order," inhabit a "consecrated enclosure" and look down upon the "prose-men" as a "vulgar, plebian herd." Enfield defines poetry in the familiar terms of passion, imagination and sensibility, and he exploits the flexibility of that definition to bring a host of "prose-men," including novelists, into the ranks of "poetical writers."[20]

Popular, national and domestic literature

Although collected editions such as Barbauld's *The British Novelists* and Scott's *Ballantyne's Novelists Library* suggest that the novel had a recognized and marketable canon by the beginning of the nineteenth century, critical discussions of novels in this period (and the prose-men and women who wrote them) continue to grapple with their "vulgar," "plebian" or "popular" status. "A Collection of Novels," Barbauld comments, "has a better chance of giving pleasure than of commanding respect." Promoting novels meant confronting the contradictions of popular literary culture: "books of this description are condemned by the grave, and despised by the fastidious; but their leaves are seldom found unopened, and they occupy the parlour and the dressing-room while productions of higher name are often gathering dust upon the shelf."[21]

Often in these years, the reading and writing of novels were discussed and critiqued as a question of national taste and morals, if not of high or serious literature. Hugh Blair devotes a chapter of *Lectures on Rhetoric and Belles Lettres* to "Fictitious History," that "species of composition in prose, which comprehends a very numerous, though, in general, a very insignificant class of writings, known by the name of Romances and Novels." Blair justifies his attention to such "insignificant" writings by quoting Andrew Fletcher on national ballads: "Mr. Fletcher of Salton, in one of his Tracts, quotes it as the saying of a wise man, that give him the making of all the ballads of a nation, he would allow any one that pleased to make their laws."[22] Novels, Blair suggests, have replaced ballads in shaping "the morals and taste of a nation." Barbauld echoes this point almost verbatim in the conclusion to her essay:

> Some perhaps may think that too much importance has been already given to a subject so frivolous, but a discriminating taste is no where more called for than with regard to a species of books which every body reads. It was said by Fletcher of Saltoun, "Let me make the ballads of a nation, and I care not who makes the laws." Might it not be said with as much propriety, Let me make the novels of a country, and let who will make the systems?[23]

The "ballads of a nation" stand as a privileged site of "popular literature" for the Romantics: they establish the popular as primitive, national, original, and representative of the people. Novels, on the other hand, evoke the more troubling aspects of the popular, that of an alienated, artificial, and mass culture. By replacing ballads with novels as the current national form, both Blair and Barbauld make strong claims for the authenticity and importance of the novel. It becomes the literary form that most directly reflects and influences the manners of the current stage of society.

Enlightenment and Romantic histories of language and literature treated poetry as the original and most ancient form of writing and literature, the natural expression of primitive social states. Other social stages favored other literary forms: prose, for example, was an advanced development. "It is always late before prose and its beauties come to be cultivated," writes Adam Smith in his *Lectures on Rhetoric and Belles Lettres*.[24] According to Smith's influential stadial theory, prose is the preferred style of modern commercial or capitalist society – "No one ever made a Bargain in verse," he quips – and the novel, the most recent prose form, represents the highly refined manners and sensibilities that are the social expression of capitalism. Defending the sentimental novel's attention to the fine gradations of emotion and the even finer distinctions of social life, Henry Mackenzie (the author of one of the most popular eighteenth-century sentimental texts, *The Man of Feeling*) demonstrates this sense of the novel's close connection to contemporary culture:

> Those who object to [novels] as inculcating precepts, and holding forth examples, of a refinement which virtue does not require, and which honesty is better without, do not perhaps sufficiently attend to the period of society which produces them. The code of morality must necessarily be enlarged in proportion to that state of manners to which cultivated eras give birth . . . the necessary refinement in manners of highly-polished nations creates a variety of duties and of offences, which men in ruder, and, it may be (for I enter not into that question), happier periods of society, could never have imagined.[25]

Of course, the refinements of "highly-polished nations" can be quickly suspected of decadence: "If it be true, that the present age is more corrupt than the preceding," wrote Vicesimus Knox, "the great multiplication of Novels has probably contributed to its degeneracy."[26] Literary styles and genres are both cultural cause and symptom, determining and depicting the manners of their age. To critique the "modern Novel" in the Romantic period was to critique the current age.

In close but uneasy connection to the refinements and corruptions of the modern novel were its undemanding, readily available pleasures. "Reading is the cheapest of pleasures: it is a domestic pleasure," wrote Barbauld. "Poetry requires in the reader a certain elevation of mind and a practised ear . . . But the humble novel is always ready to enliven the gloom of solitude."[27] Here Barbauld extends her earlier image of novels lying open around the parlours and dressing rooms of the house, connecting the cheap and popular pleasures of novel-reading with domesticity, women, and the bodies of women readers. Such associations were standard in a period in which women were thought to make up the majority of the novel-reading public, and in which women's reading, as Ina Ferris has demonstrated, was often represented as a form of sensual appetite and pleasure. "Books, merely entertaining, produce the same effect upon the mental faculties, which a luxurious diet does upon the corporeal frame," a critic in the *Lady's Magazine* warned.[28] Critics began to review, and thereby attempt to regulate, the "merely entertaining" or "humble" novel not because of its perceived literary merits, but out of a growing sense of the growing numbers of particularly impressionable readers relishing or luxuriating in novels, and the deep and lasting effects such indiscriminate reading might have on the moral character and taste of the larger public.

Barbauld, however, does something more with women and the pleasures of novels. Not only is she more confident in women readers and their ability to read the "merely entertaining" with discrimination and intelligence, but she also credits women writers with elevating the novel in the early years of the nineteenth century.[29] While other reviewers in these years tend to bemoan the novel as exhausted and degraded from the mid-eighteenth-century glory days of Richardson and Fielding (a narrative that has held sway well into our own day), Barbauld takes another tack. Admitting that "a great deal of trash is every season poured out upon the public from the English presses," she nevertheless insists that the present age is a great one for novels. "We have more good writers in this walk living at the present time, than at any period since the days of Richardson and Fielding," she declares, adding furthermore that "a very great proportion of these are ladies."[30] Indeed, women novelists such as Burney, Edgeworth, Inchbald, and Radcliffe have only improved the taste and morals of the country, and it is largely due to their efforts, Barbauld suggests, that "our national taste and habits are still turned towards domestic life and matrimonial happiness."[31] Here Barbauld discovers other rhetorical resources in the humility of the novel, transforming its low and easy pleasures from those that proliferate wantonly into those that respectfully reproduce domestic habits and morals. The novel's representations of domestic life can thus stand as representations of national life.

There is no doubt that the novel helped to make the domestic and every-day one of the more privileged settings for Romantic literature. The novel, as opposed to the romance, was typically defined as committed to representing the ordinary and the probable. In 1750, Samuel Johnson describes the novel as "exhibit[ing] life in its true state, diversified only by accidents that daily happen in the world, and influenced by passions and qualities which are really to be found in conversing with mankind."[32] Johnson's definition of the novel strikingly anticipates Wordsworth's description of his experimental poetry, which sought "to chuse incidents and situations from common life, and to relate or describe them . . . in a selection of language really used by men."[33] Hazlitt very famously attributes Wordsworth poetic style to the revolutions of the age: "the political changes of the day were the model on which he formed and conducted his poetical experiments."[34] Yet, as Gabrielle Starr has recently argued, he might just as easily have attributed Wordsworth's experimental style to the influence of the novel. Indeed, his description of the poetry – "his style is vernacular: he delivers household truths" – places Wordsworth squarely in the domestic terrain of the novel.[35] Household truths, common life, and the daily happenings of the world increasingly became privileged topoi in both poetry and the novel as writers used the discourse of domesticity to locate and secure an emerging vernacular literature.

Composite orders, or poetry *in* the novel

By the end of the eighteenth century and the early decades of the nineteenth century, novels were, in fact, reviewed and discussed regularly in the growing number of monthly periodicals. But often the literary productions called novels seemed very far from the salutary categories of either popular or serious literature: the national and domestic, or the imaginative and passionate. What could one make of the "contemporary scandals and *causes célèbres*, lightly dished up in 'two curious *open-worked* volumes'; fictitious or semi-fictitious biographies of statesmen, actresses and prostitutes; secret histories; travels and memoirs of uncertain value . . . and other obscure blends of fact and fiction," all of which "counted as 'novels' in the book lists of the day"?[36] Critics in the last years of the eighteenth century seemed without any new resources for evaluating the heterogeneous novel than those of complaint. In 1810, for example, Walter Scott reserves praise for the novels of Charlotte Smith and Maria Edgeworth but condemns other novelists as the "lowest denizens of Grub-street narrating, under the flimsy veil of false names, and through the medium of a fictitious tale, all that malevolence and stupidity propagate."[37] Half-formed mixtures, false names, and curious blends: the popular novel of the Romantic period was frequently derided as a debased composite form.

Whether claiming the status or name of an epic poem, stitching together a variety of other poetic and prose forms, or swallowing other texts wholesale, the novel in the eighteenth century certainly took shape by bumping up against, breaking down, and appropriating other genres and forms. That bumping is typically understood as rough and tumble, even aggressive. Here it might be useful to remember Mikhail Bakhtin's observation that "the novel gets on poorly with other genres." Indeed, Bakhtin's narrative of the novel's ascendancy entails the dramatic decline or "novelization" of other genres. "There can be no talk of a harmony deriving from mutual limitation and complementariness," he declares.[38] The novel parodies, incorporates, squeezes out or levels all other literary forms, becoming the very force of generic change and formal incoherence in literary history. Alternately celebrated for its democratic freedoms of form and subject or criticized for its totalitarian and imperial aggressions, the novel "can do what it wants with literature." Critics in this tradition have done what they want with the novel, finding "description, narration, drama, the essay, commentary, monologue, and conversation . . . fable, history, parable, romance, chronicle, story and epic" in the novel either "in turn or at once." Even verse is fair game, as we have seen in the Romantic period specifically. As Marthe Robert has observed: "The only prohibition [the novel] generally observes, because it defines its 'prosaic' nature, is not even compulsory for it can include poetry at will or simply be 'poetical.'"[39]

This tradition of defining the novel around its formal fluidity has roots in German Romantic theory, which celebrated the novel as the paradigmatic romantic form precisely because of its generic mixings. "A novel is a romantic book," Friedrich Schlegel wrote, because it is a "mixture of storytelling, song and other forms."[40] Discussion of the novel in Britain for much of the nineteenth and twentieth centuries has been far less tolerant of generic instability, a stance that significantly contributed to earlier accounts of the Romantic period as a striking interruption in the otherwise steady "rise of the novel" and as a period almost exclusively devoted to reviving and revising the lyric. Indeed, our bifurcated focus on the novel or the lyric has obscured our understanding of many of the period's most influential literary forms, including that which arguably gave these years their name: the romance.

Romances and tales dominated the contemporary canon as the most popular publications, as well as the best literature of the most respected writers. Scott's *The Lay of the Last Minstrel* follows "the plan of the ancient metrical romance." His *Marmion, A Tale of Flodden Field, A Romance in Six Cantos*, and Byron's *Childe Harold, A Romaunt*, as well as his Oriental tales, such as *The Giaour: A Fragment of a Turkish Tale*, were all subtitled "romances" or "tales," as were Thomas Moore's *Lalla Rookh: An Oriental Romance*, Thomas Campbell's *Gertrude of Wyoming: A Pennsylvanian Tale*, and Robert Southey's *Thalaba, A Rhythmical Romance*. Volumes of shorter poems also adopted these generic markers of romance, such as Mary Robinson's *Lyrical Tales* or Felicia Hemans's *Tales, and Historic Scenes, in Verse*. And, of course, many "novels" of the period referred to themselves as "romances" or "tales," as in the case of Ann Radcliffe's *The Mysteries of Udolpho, A Romance*, Matthew Lewis's *The Monk, A Romance*, Sydney Owenson's *The Wild Irish Girl, A National Tale*, or *The Missionary, An Indian Tale*.

With its fascination for older times and exotic places, its habitual, self-reflexive structure of historical and cultural juxtaposition, and, significantly, its freedom to cross poetic and prose forms, the romance that emerged in the late years of the eighteenth century is a multifarious, composite form. Romances in verse typically included extensive prose notes, such as Byron's notes to *The Giaour* or Southey's notes to *Thalaba*, which add ethnographic and imperial frames to the poetic tales thereby contained. The prose romance, on the other hand, almost always featured ballads, songs, and other poetic inserts. The "Table of the Poetry" in the preliminary matter of *The Monk* calls attention to Lewis's poetical offerings scattered throughout the narrative, and the title pages of Ann Radcliffe's Gothic romances typically advertised that the narratives were "*Interspersed with some Pieces of Poetry.*" Literary histories of the day discussed romances and novels (whether in verse or prose) as "fictitious narratives" with primitive or ancient origins, taking oral or written, poetic or prose form. Clara Reeve's introduction to her novel *The Old English Baron* (1778) is standard: "Fictitious Stories have been the delight of all times and all countries, by oral tradition in barbarous, by writing in more civilized ones." New romances and tales were celebrated as revivals of old forms, continuing the tradition of the medieval romances that the antiquarians of the day were busy recovering and publishing; together these new and rediscovered texts formed a "romance revival" that defined Britain's emerging national, vernacular literary tradition. Mixing genres became a deliberate strategy to represent the different periods of that tradition: the prose footnotes of a verse romance or the excerpted ballad within a national tale stage the progress and development of literary history and genres within a single, culminating, and all-inclusive form.

The sentimental novels of the period also included verse to such a degree that they must be seen as a major force in shaping the cultural position of poetry in these years, a framing device that, in particular, challenges many of our entrenched notions about lyric subjectivity. Charlotte Smith's novels follow the literary conventions of sensibility by quoting lines of poetry within their narratives and by representing their characters as reading, writing, and discussing poetry. As Leah Price has demonstrated, such novels reveal their affinities to commonplace books and anthologies, excerpting and collecting literary bits and pieces, drawing on and constructing a literary archive assumed to be shared and familiar.[41] Quoting Shakespeare, Thomson, or the old ballads in a novel may also be seen as a strategy for mapping the world of that novel on to the world of the readers, as characters and readers alike read and repeat the same texts. Lyric lines within a novel thereby take on a much greater social function than we may expect.

For example, when Orlando, the hero of Smith's *The Old Manor House* (1794), finds the windows of his lover's room dark and empty, Smith describes his reaction first from the perspective of external observation: "he stopped, and gazed mournfully on the place which perhaps no longer contained the object of his affection."[42] She then evokes a generally recognized degree of pain, effectively locating Orlando's emotion outside Orlando:

"There is hardly a sensation more painful than the blank that strikes on the heart, when, instead of the light we expect streaming from some beloved spot where our affections are fondly fixed, all is silent and dark."[43] The sentence moves from an action in the world – "the blank that strikes" – into the shared "heart" of "our affections," but this heart – both a conventional marker of sensibility and one "fixed" to a "beloved spot" – still remains outside any single, interior subjectivity.

In case we have missed the implicit invitation to move "our affections" into the novel or to transpose Orlando's "sensations" into our own, the text next models such an interaction. Still standing outside the dark house, Orlando, who is "passionately fond of poetry," recalls the ballad of Hardyknute:

> "Theirs nae licht in my lady's bowir,
> Theirs nae licht in the hall;
> Nae blink shynes round my fairly fair – "

And, like the dismayed hero of the song,

> "Black feir he felt, but what to fear
> He wist not zit with dreid."[44]

Even as it quotes the "simply descriptive stanza" of this popular ballad, Smith's own descriptive prose is anything but simple. She persists in leaving the sentiments which are the central focus of this extended passage unspecified, bound neither to a single subject nor, here, to a specific object: "but what to fear / He wist not zit with dreid." The tenor and quality of Orlando's feelings are given shape first by evoking familiar and commonly shared emotion and then by embodying that emotion in familiar and commonly shared lines of poetry through the act of quotation. Orlando's interiority is, in fact, a communal construct crafted in a series of movements out into a shared social world.

Poetry here organizes and signals certain emotions through a kind of suggestive shorthand. Its quotability and reiteration, its capacity to refer to and work for varieties of occasions and individuals, to evoke without overly specifying, make it invaluable to the novel's project of representing and inserting itself into a recognized cultural field. Such a scene also tells its readers what to do with poetry: together the quoted lines and the novelistic frame suggest that poetry (and perhaps all "serious literature") represents and works through heightened emotional moments.

Of course Orlando does not simply recollect and repeat poetic lines at moments of heightened emotion. Like any romantic hero worth his salt, he also composes his own poems. Such poems register and express the passions of the moment: sensations "so much under the influence of fancy" which the *reading* of poetry alone cannot compose often assume "poetical form" (allowing Smith to insert and showcase her own poetical work).[45] In the sentimental novel, the reading and writing of poetry becomes a therapy, a system of emotional regulation or pedagogy of taste. Smith also uses such poetical moments to organize the significant geography and memories of her central character. Orlando's "poetic effusions" either occur in or evoke the park of Rayland Hall, the "old manor house" of the title which he hopes one day to inherit. Orlando spends much of the novel crossing these grounds, hurrying to see his lover in the old hall, or racing to reach home again before his absence is discovered. Poetry becomes a literal "pause" in his walking, as well as in the narrative progression of the novel, a pause for retrospective or prospective reflection in which the natural world seems to conspire:

> It was a cold but clear evening . . . a low wind sounded hollow through the firs and stone-pines over his head, and then faintly sighed among the reeds that crowded into the water . . . Orlando had hardly ever felt himself so impressed with those feelings which inspire poetic effusions: – Nature appeared to pause, and to ask the turbulent and troubled heart of man, whether his silly pursuits were worth the toil he undertook for them?[46]

Orlando's "silly pursuits" are about to lead him into the army, across the Atlantic to America, and away from this beautiful scene of "rural beauty and rural content."[47] On the verge of departure, he sees and claims this place as his "native country." But Orlando will return to this path and park, as well as to such moments of poetic "pause," repeatedly throughout the novel. Poetic effusion thus not only gives form to emotion and memory; it also gives embodiment and place to his emotional life, constructing and restoring him to his "original self" and "native country."

The ways in which the novel frames poetry for Romantic literary culture can be traced in volumes of poetry as well. Here again the example of Charlotte Smith is instructive. Smith's *Elegaic Sonnets* went through nine ever-expanding editions between 1784 and 1800, years in which she also wrote ten novels. By writing a number of sonnets "Supposed to be Written by Werter," as well as including numerous poems from the pages of her novels (and the pens of her characters), Smith crafts sonnets intimately involved in a novelistic world. It is, however, the extensive apparatus of the volume – the series of prefaces, the frequent footnotes, the author portrait and other illustrations – that primarily provides these lyric sonnets with a novelistic frame. On the margins of the page and at the periphery of the volume, Smith relates an autobiographical tale of pecuniary and legal distress, detailing the suffering of herself and her children in rhetoric heavily indebted to the conventions of the sentimental novel. The plot of a novel and the plight of her life merge to form the backdrop and motivating context for each single, solitary lyric episode. The lyric organization of emotion in the sonnets is thus set within the novelistic organization of sentiment in the framing apparatus.

One might read the "pauses" of poetry within a novel as teaching readers how to read – to pace themselves in their rush through the plot with pauses for reflection and sentiment – or as teaching readers how poetry fits into the rest of what one does – poetry as the experience of intense emotion that interrupts the business of living and transports one to the native landscapes of memory. The personal, ethnographic, and historical notes that typically frame a collection of sonnets, old ballads, or other lyric poems in this period also work both to establish the difference of poetry as an emotional experience and form apart from ordinary life and discourse, as well as to demonstrate that poetry's difference participates in and remains a function of the social and historical world it seems to reject. That sense of poetry as the experience of revelatory emotional and perceptual moments that disrupt ordinary life has been central to ideas of the Romantic lyric. But it is a myth of poetry that has significant origins in the novel, staged by the insertion of lyric lines into the novel's narrative frame. This is another way of understanding the novel's impact on other genres, or what Bakhtin considered the "novelization" of other literary forms in the wake of the novel's emergence. It is not so much that poetry begins to resemble the novel as that the novel shapes poetry's difference from itself, providing the frame that sets poetry apart from prose and giving poetry and poetry-readers their distinct work and status.

NOTES

1 Jane Austen, *Persuasion*, ed. Janet Todd and Antje Blank (Cambridge and New York: Cambridge University Press, 2006).
2 Barbara Hardy, *A Reading of Jane Austen* (New York: New York University Press, 1976), p. 58.
3 William St. Clair, *The Reading Nation in the Romantic Period* (Cambridge: Cambridge University Press, 2004), pp. 175–6.
4 Anna Letitia Barbauld, *Selected Poetry and Prose*, ed. William McCarthy and Elizabeth Kraft (Peterborough, Ont.: Broadview Press, 2002), p. 378.
5 Henry Fielding, *Joseph Andrews*, ed. Martin C. Battestin (Middletown, CT: Wesleyan University Press, 1967), pp. 3–4.
6 Richard Hurd, *Dissertation on the Idea of Universal Poetry* (London: A. Millar, 1766), p. 20.
7 Ibid., pp. 21–2.
8 James Burnett, Lord Monboddo, *The Origin and Progress of Language* (London: T. Cadell, 1786), vol. III, pp. 134–5.

9 James Beattie, *Dissertations Moral and Critical* (London: T. Cadell, 1783), p. 518.

10 Ibid., p. 571.

11 Ioan Williams, *Novel and Romance, 1700–1800: A Documentary Record* (London: Routledge & Kegan Paul, 1970), p. 2.

12 William Wordsworth, *Lyrical Ballads and Other Poems, 1797–1800*, ed. James Butler and Karen Green (Ithaca: Cornell University Press, 1992), pp. 747, 749–51, 756.

13 Hugh Blair, *Lectures on Rhetoric and Belles Lettres*, ed. Harold F. Harding, 2 vols. (Carbondale: Southern Illinois University Press, 1965), vol. II, p. 303.

14 Ibid., vol. I, p. 283.

15 In Ioan Williams, *Sir Walter Scott on Novelists and Fiction* (New York: Barnes & Noble, 1968), p. 67.

16 Ibid., p. 67.

17 William Hazlitt, *Selected Writings of William Hazlitt*, ed. Duncan Wu (London: Pickering & Chatto, 1998), vol. V, p. 116; vol. II, p. 165; vol. V, p. 100.

18 Percy Bysshe Shelley, *Shelley's Poetry and Prose*, ed. Donald H. Reiman and Neil Fraistat (New York: W. W. Norton, 2002), p. 514.

19 Clifford Siskin, *The Work of Writing: Literature and Social Change in Britain, 1700–1830* (Baltimore: Johns Hopkins University Press, 1998), p. 6.

20 William Enfield, "Is Verse Essential to Poetry?," *The Monthly Magazine* (2 July 1796) (London: R. Phillips), pp. 453–6.

21 Barbauld, *Selected Poetry and Prose*, p. 377.

22 Blair, *Lectures on Rhetoric*, vol. II, p. 303.

23 Barbauld, *Selected Poetry and Prose*, pp. 416–17.

24 Adam Smith, *Lectures on Rhetoric and Belles Lettres*, ed. J. C. Bryce (Indianapolis: Liberty Fund, 1985), pp. 135, 137.

25 Henry Mackenzie, *The Lounger* 20, Saturday June 18, 1785.

26 Vicesimus Knox, "On Novel Reading," in *Essays Moral and Literary* 15 (1778), excerpted in Williams, *Novel and Romance*, p. 304.

27 Barbauld, *Selected Poetry and Prose*, p. 407.

28 Claudia Johnson, "'Let Me Make the Novels of a Country': Barbauld's *The British Novelists* (1810/1820)," *Novel* (Spring 2001), p. 171.

29 *Lady's Magazine* 43 (1812), p. 222; quoted in Ina Ferris, *The Achievement of Literary Authority: Gender, History, and the Waverley Novels* (Ithaca: Cornell University Press, 1991), pp. 38–9. See Ferris, *The Achievement*, 30–45.

30 Barbauld, *Selected Poetry and Prose*, p. 414.

31 Ibid., pp. 414–15.

32 Quoted in Jay Clayton, *Romantic Vision and the Novel* (Cambridge: Cambridge University Press, 1987), p. 53.

33 Wordsworth, *Lyrical Ballads*, p. 743.

34 William Hazlitt, *The Spirit of the Age: or Contemporary Portraits* (1825), in *Selected Writings of William Hazlitt*, ed. Wu, vol. VII, p. 161.

35 Gabrielle Starr, *Lyric Generations: Poetry and the Novel in the Long Eighteenth Century* (Baltimore: Johns Hopkins University Press, 2004), pp. 159–201.

36 J. M. S. Tompkins, *The Popular Novel in England, 1770–1800* (Lincoln: University of Nebraska Press, 1961), p. 4.

37 In Williams, *Sir Walter Scott on Novelists*, p. 206.

38 Mikhail M. Bakhtin, *The Dialogic Imagination*, ed. Michael Holquist (Austin: University of Texas Press, 1981), pp. 4–5.

39 Marthe Robert, *Origins of the Novel*, excerpted in *Theory of the Novel: A Historical Approach*, ed. Michael McKeon (Baltimore: Johns Hopkins University Press, 2000), p. 58.

40 Friedrich Schlegel, *Dialogue on Poetry* (1799–1800), translated, introduced, and annotated by Ernst Behler and Roman Struc (University Park: Pennsylvania State University Press, 1968), pp. 101–2.

41 Leah Price, *The Anthology and the Rise of the Novel* (Cambridge: Cambridge University Press, 2000).

42 Charlotte Smith, *The Old Manor House*, ed. Jacqueline M. Labbe (Toronto: Broadview Press, 2002), p. 250.

43 Ibid.

44 Ibid.

45 Ibid., pp. 317–18.

46 Ibid., pp. 181–2.

47 Ibid., p. 182.

FURTHER READING

Chandler, James, *England in 1819: The Politics of Literary Culture and the Case of Romantic Historicism* (Chicago: University of Chicago Press, 1998)

Clayton, Jay, *Romantic Vision and the Novel* (Cambridge: Cambridge University Press, 1987)

Curran, Stuart, *Poetic Form and British Romanticism* (Oxford: Oxford University Press, 1986)

Favret, Mary, *Romantic Correspondence: Women, Politics and the Fiction of Letters* (Cambridge: Cambridge University Press, 1993)

"Telling Tales About Genre: Poetry in the Romantic Novel," *Studies in the Novel* 26/3 (October 1994), pp. 281–300

Ferris, Ina, *The Achievement of Literary Authority: Gender, History, and the Waverley Novels* (Ithaca: Cornell University Press, 1991)

Gilroy, Amanda, and Wil Verhoeven, eds., *The Romantic-era Novel: A Special Issue, Novel* (Spring 2001)

Hofkosh, Sonia, *Sexual Politics and the Romantic Author* (Cambridge: Cambridge University Press, 1998)

Johnson, Claudia, "Let Me Make the Novels of a Country": Barbauld's *The British Novelists* (1810/1820)," *Novel* (Spring 2001), pp. 163–79

Labbe, Jacqueline, *Charlotte Smith: Romanticism, Poetry and the Culture of Gender* (Manchester: Manchester University Press, 2003)

McLane, Maureen N., *Romanticism and the Human Sciences: Poetry, Population and the Discourse of the Species* (Cambridge: Cambridge University Press, 2000)

Pinch, Adela, *Strange Fits of Passion: Epistemologies of Emotion, Hume to Austen* (Stanford: Stanford University Press, 1996)

Price, Leah, *The Anthology and the Rise of the Novel* (Cambridge: Cambridge University Press, 2000)

St. Clair, William, *The Reading Nation in the Romantic Period* (Cambridge: Cambridge University Press, 2004)

Siskin, Clifford, *The Work of Writing: Literature and Social Change in Britain, 1700–1830* (Baltimore: Johns Hopkins University Press, 1998)

Starr, Gabrielle, *Lyric Generations: Poetry and the Novel in the Long Eighteenth Century* (Baltimore: Johns Hopkins University Press, 2004)

Todd, Janet, *Sensibility: An Introduction* (London: Methuen, 1986)

Tompkins, J. M. S., *The Popular Novel in England, 1770–1800* (Lincoln: University of Nebraska Press, 1961)

Trumpener, Katie, *Bardic Nationalism* (Princeton: Princeton University Press, 1997)

Zimmerman, Sarah, *Romanticism, Lyricism, and History* (Albany: State University of New York Press, 1999)

7

JAMES CHANDLER

Wordsworth's great Ode: Romanticism and the progress of poetry

Having agreed that this volume should include a chapter on a single Romantic poem, and that I would write it, I chose the lyric that came to bear the unwieldy title "Ode: Intimations of Immortality from Recollections of Early Childhood," first published in 1807. Wordsworth composed this poem over two intensive periods of work in 1802 and 1804, the heart of his great decade of creativity. The two-year gap after the composition of the Ode's first four stanzas can perhaps be taken as a measure of the challenge it posed to him. The result of his labors, in any case, is arguably the most important lyric poem of an age known for its lyric poetry. Furthermore, it forms a crucial link in several canonical chains of English poetry that run through the period. For later lyric poets in the nineteenth century, Wordsworth's "second selves," as he once called them, the Ode loomed as large as anything he ever wrote, including the more professedly experimental poems of *Lyrical Ballads* and the longer, more ambitious works such as *The Excursion* and his posthumously published autobiographical poem, *The Prelude*. In seminal lyrics by Keats, Shelley, and Browning, the Ode set the very terms of poetic engagement with Wordsworth and what he came to stand for.[1] At the same time, the Ode also connected allusively to some important poems of the century before, including to lyrics written in the post-Augustan genre known as the "progress poem." This latter point, about the progress poem, has not been much addressed in modern critical commentary on the Ode, and I want to suggest that it is crucial for understanding how the Ode establishes its exemplary role in British Romantic poetry and its own place in the history of the lyric, both retroactively and proactively.

There are perhaps few notions more vexed within the period we call Romantic than the notion of progress. This notion is indeed crucial for many of the ways one would want to talk about Romanticism – especially in relation to "enlightenment," a period or concept against which the Romantic period is often defined. The question of progress is both a central and intractable issue for this poem, as it was for Romanticism more generally.

The poem might even be said to offer an anticipation of Ernst Haeckel's notion that ontogeny recapitulates phylogeny, that the development of an individual restages the collective development from which that individual has emerged. The central stanzas of the Ode trace the growth of the poet's sentiments in relation to a larger story of European poetry. What makes the question of progress so vexed for the Ode, however, is that its implicit narrative of how a poet's personal sentiments develop over time does not readily square with its implicit history of poetry. The relation of those two implicit narratives in the Ode will be my subject in the second half of this chapter, but my commentary on the poem will be more intelligible after some more general discussion of some of the ways in which sentiment came to matter to both poetry and progress in the period.

On some readings, the Age of Wordsworth comes right in the middle of the age of progress. According to perhaps its best-known historian, Robert Nisbet, the so-called "idea of progress" actually "reached its zenith" in "the Western mind" in the period from 1750 to 1900, a chronology that would locate Wordsworth's most productive years on the ascent toward the zenith point of 1825.[2] Nonetheless, there is reason to be skeptical about Nisbet's story – even apart from the questionable scheme that has an "idea" of this sort moving up and down in "the Western mind." Romanticism richly complicates the case. To see how, we need look no further than Hazlitt's attempt to do justice to the Romantic period in *The Spirit of the Age*, a collection of critical portraits of Hazlitt's contemporaries that was in fact published in that very year, 1825. For if there ever was a book that made trouble for claims to progress in its own time – possibly even for the very idea of progress – it was this one.

Readers who know *The Spirit of the Age* will recall that one of the most basic interpretive principles in Hazlitt's various essays – on Mr. Godwin, Mr. Wordsworth, Mr. Bentham, and so on – is the (for him) axiomatic truth that a person's distinctive strengths are closely matched with corresponding obverse weaknesses. The fact that Mr. Coleridge can see every side of an issue is just the flip side of his never getting anything accomplished. The fact that Sir Walter Scott extends his imagination generously toward a variety of past objects great and small is just the flip side of his refusal to think about the future. What holds true on the level of the individual character also holds true for the larger character of the age itself. The era's interest in abstraction, for example, is a great strength that enabled a new kind of thought and practice in society and politics, but it also evacuated thought and politics of life and gusto. It is true that Hazlitt declared – a few short years later in his *Life of Napoleon* – that the widening horizon of public scrutiny made possible by the expansion of the public press in its turn made possible a greater diffusion of justice and equity in contemporary society. It was in this sense that Hazlitt could proclaim that the French Revolution could be understood as "the remote but inevitable result of the invention of the art of printing."[3] Yet Hazlitt tended to see his age's gains as ultimately offset by its losses. To speak particularly of the fine arts – his own areas of special concern – Hazlitt tended to see every advance in technology and civil society as occasioning a decline in the quality of poetry and painting.

Hazlitt addressed this issue often in his work, and sometimes explicitly, as in the essay fragment entitled "Why the Arts are not Progressive," a piece that probably owes something to Jean-Jacques Rousseau's prize-winning First Discourse (". . . on the Arts and Sciences"), which had already challenged certain prevailing assumptions about human progress when it was published in 1750. Nothing could be further from the truth, Hazlitt writes, than "the supposition that in what we understand by the fine arts, as painting and poetry, relative perfection is only the result of repeated efforts, and that what has been once well done constantly leads to something better" (vol. 1, p. 161). What Hazlitt calls "our sanguine theories" about gradual improvement in the arts are simply not consistent with the facts of the case as he sees them, which he states as follows:

> The greatest poets, the ablest orators, the best painters, and the finest sculptors that the world ever saw, appeared soon after the birth of these arts, and lived in a state of society which was in other respects, comparatively barbarous. Those arts, which depend on individual genius and incommunicable power, have always leaped at once from infancy to manhood, from the first rude dawn of invention to their meridian height and dazzling lustre, and have in general declined ever after. This is the peculiar distinction and privilege of each, of science and of art; of the one, never to attain its utmost summit of perfection and of the other, to arrive at it almost at once. (Ibid.)

This is partly an anti-academic position – in that particular sense of anti-"arts academy." It is thus reminiscent of some of Blake's spirited annotations to Joshua Reynolds's lectures on painting. Hazlitt himself mentions Reynolds by name. What complicates the politics of the case, however, is that Hazlitt's is also an anti-Godwinian position. In his influential *Enquiry Concerning Political Justice*, described by Hazlitt in *The Spirit of the Age* as a philosophic meteor over the 1790s, Godwin had seemed to posit the possibility, nay the necessity, of dramatic long-term improvements in virtually every aspect of human life. This pan-progressivism, as we might term it, is what called down Thomas Malthus's wrath on Godwin's head in the *Essay on the Principles of Population* in 1798. For Hazlitt, characteristically, both Godwin's strength and his weakness inhered in the optimistic ambition of his program. Hazlitt wrote of him in his portrait for *The Spirit of the Age* that "he carried with him the most sanguine . . . understandings of the time" (vol. 4, p. 201). And such sanguine understandings formed part of Hazlitt's target in the essay on why the arts are not progressive.

One young disciple of Godwin's well known to Hazlitt, Percy Shelley, produced a sanguine vision of a progressive future toward the end of his closet drama, *Prometheus Unbound* (1820), a vision very much supported by belief in progress in the fine arts. This vision appears at the end of Act 3, when Prometheus and Asia look forward to the later stages of the process of global millenarian renovation they have set in motion:

> And lovely apparitions, dim at first
> Then radiant . . .
> Shall visit us, the progeny immortal
> Of Painting, Sculpture and rapt Poesy
> And arts, though unimagined, yet to be . . .
> (3.iii.49–56)[4]

It might seem that these apparitions constitute a utopian norm, rather than a scheme of progress, especially given the Platonic overtones of the appositional construction offered in the next lines:

> The wandering voices and the shadows these
> Of all that man becomes . . .
> (ll. 57–8)

But to this appositional phrase is added another, that makes the progressive cast of the vision quite unmistakable:

> the mediators
> Of that best worship, love, by him, and us
> Given and returned, swift shapes and sounds which grow
> More fair and soft as man grows wise and kind,
> And veil by veil evil and error fall.
> (ll. 58–62)

We recall, moreover, that in *A Defence of Poetry*, Shelley's progressive account of the arts – the intertwining of the story of poetry and the story of human liberty – is itself intertwined with the question of human affection. In the *Defence*, Prometheus' claim about how reciprocities of human love develop hand-in-hand with the growth and proliferation of the arts appears in Shelley's central statement about the moral imagination: "for the great secret of morals is love, the capacity to put ourselves in the place of another, and of many others."[5] This is a principle that Mary Shelley had already

appropriated for her account of the "Modern Prometheus," Victor Frankenstein, and that she subtly turned against Percy himself in suggesting that, like
Victor, he may have discovered the secret of life at the expense of forgetting
the secret of love.[6]

In one of Percy's own texts that closely parallels *Frankenstein* in its ambiva-
lent representation of monstrosity, *Peter Bell the Third*, Shelley offered an
allegorical account of Wordsworth, at once critical and sympathetic toward
its subject, in which he suggested that the moral imagination was precisely
what was missing in the author of *The Excursion*:

> He had as much imagination
>   As a pint pot: – he never could
> Fancy another situation
> From which to dart his contemplation,
>   Than that wherein he stood.
>
> (ll. 298–302)

For Shelley, this capacity – let us call it sympathetic imagination – is what
makes the unperverted practice of the arts progressive. Like Godwinian
"foresight," it will, left unfettered, expand with the extension of experience.[7]

The notion of such a capacity belongs to the line of moral sense philosophy
that we associate with David Hume and Adam Smith – whose own connections with Godwinian social theory are well documented. This capacity is
indeed the fundamental premise and crucial starting point of Smith's *The
Theory of Moral Sentiments* (1759): our ability not to feel what others feel
but to feel what we would feel in their place, our capacity to bring their case
home to our own bosoms. In these Scottish theorists, moreover, this talent
already belongs very specifically to a scheme of progress. Their so-called
"philosophic history" posited a four-stage process all peoples undergo –
under the auspices of increasingly secure social arrangements – in developing from hunter-gatherer societies, to pastoral, to agricultural, and then to
commercial societies. The commercial is the most advanced phase in this
stadial progression, and it is the one marked increasingly by its reliance
on a developed capacity for putting oneself in the place of another, as any
merchant must do to negotiate successfully. Smith was explicit in suggesting that the later stages of commercial growth in his own society would be
marked by a decreased dependence on casuistical rules and an increasing
reliance on a sincere exchange of views in the widening sphere of social
intercourse.

The Jesuitical notion of the case, with its rules and logic-chopping, is
explicitly rejected in the closing pages of *The Theory of Moral Sentiments*.
In its stead, Smith advocates the social practice of mutual identification by

way of his notion of the sentimental case, a situation from which to dart our contemplation, as Shelley put it, other than the one wherein we stand – a virtual point of view from which to *imagine* ourselves undergoing experience, to imagine ourselves feeling. Thus sentiments, on this account, are feelings processed through this kind of reflective mediation of point of view. It was this linkage of reflection with the sentimental that Friedrich Schiller pointed to in 1795 when he distinguished the naïve from the sentimental in poetry as a difference between a poetry of unreflective sensations that produced degrees of a single feeling and a poetry of reflection that produced "mixed feelings."[8]

Eighteenth-century writers in this line – and even some post-Romantic writers like Charles Dickens and Harriet Beecher Stowe – tended to take a "progressive" view of the sentimental. The philosopher Annette Baier titles her study of Hume *A Progress of Sentiments* precisely to emphasize this feature of the moral sense school in Scotland. To put the matter briefly, the practice of reflection "improves" in a way that calculated rule-following does not. And this holds true across *both* domains of sentimental theory. It holds true for the interpersonal domain, in which we reflect on one another's cases "as it were holding a mirror up to ourselves," to use a metaphor employed by both Hume and Smith. It is also true of the internal domain, in which, according to this epistemology, the ideas we form from affective impression can themselves return as second-order affect: what in Hume's technical vocabulary are called "impressions of reflection." Baier is, I think, the first commentator to identify the category of sentiment closely with this technical concept in Hume.[9] Both domains of the sentimental involve the negotiation of virtual points of view to establish something that is known in this line of philosophy as a "general point of view," a concept that answers to *right perception* in epistemology, *good taste* in aesthetics, and, in ethics, *sound moral judgment* (thanks to the impartial spectator, who embodies, but virtually embodies, this concept of the general point of view). For all his putative rationalism, this set of sentimental arguments was deeply important to Godwin's program for social progress in the 1790s. Shelley picked it up and gave it a more aestheticist inflection, linking its fate most particularly to what, in the end, he called "poetry."

All of this runs directly against the grain of Hazlitt's thinking about progress in this period, and indeed might well have formed part of its target. For while Hazlitt could not have known the unpublished *Defence*, he surely knew *Prometheus Unbound*. Indeed, in his essay on why the arts are not progressive, Hazlitt's pithiest formulation of the principle on which he explains the issues turns implicitly on a distinction between the useful arts and the fine arts, as follows:

What is mechanical, reducible to rule, or capable of demonstration, is progressive, and admits of gradual improvement: what is not mechanical or definite, but depends on genius, taste, and feeling, very soon becomes stationary, or retrograde, and loses more than it gains by transfusion.   (vol. 1, p. 161)

This formulation, so much at odds with what I have described as the Hume-Smith-Godwin-Shelley line on sentimental progress, seems in its turn to be contradicted outright in the text on which Shelley drew when he wrote *A Defence of Poetry, A Philosophical View of Reform*, the text in which Shelley elaborated his own account of what he called "the spirit of the age" six years before Hazlitt's volume appeared. The *View*, of which Shelley finished three sections, concludes its first section with the famous paragraph about how poets are the unacknowledged legislators of the world, but then goes on to shape a transition to what are called "less abstracted considerations" with an appeal in the form of a question: "Has there not been [asks Shelley] and is there not in England a desire of change arising from the profound sentiment of the exceeding inefficiency of the existing institutions to provide for the physical and intellectual happiness of the people?"[10] This question introduces the second of the essay's three parts, titled "On the Sentiment of the Necessity of Change," in which Shelley attempts both to "state and examine the present condition of this desire," and "to elucidate its causes and its object."[11] Here, in short, Shelley turns to the language of sentiment – of desire, affect, and feeling – to describe the very engine of social progress. The progress of society is a function of the state of its sentiment, and the state of its sentiment is a function of the state of its poetic activity. Shelley even seems to suggest that poetry's sentimental advance counts for *more* than the advances of the useful arts. For him, the constitutional experiment under way in America is the embodiment of the principle of utility – and the progress of the USA in that vein has been more dramatic than any prior nation's. But Shelley explicitly states his preference for England's long-term chances, exactly because of England's advances in poetry, its fostering of writers who are able to represent the general will as it should be, rather than just producing an efficient mechanical representation of the will as it is. They reflect the normative dimension of sentiment that discloses the inadequacy of existing institutions to general human well-being.

Intriguingly, then, between Hazlitt and Shelley, perhaps the two earliest explicators of the notion of the spirit of the age in the age of progress, we find some sharp discrepancies. Though each writer's work embodies contradictions of its own, these positions on the progress of poetry, on the relative merits of the naïve and the sentimental, can be taken as two poles for purposes of contextualizing poetic treatment of these issues. Indeed, they help us to see that such questions are at stake in poetic texts where we might not have thought to look for them at all.

Close to the time when Shelley first drafted his account of the progress of sentiment, his friend Keats set out his own scheme of progress in a letter to his brother and sister-in-law in America. Like many schemes of progress, Keats's sags in the middle. Keats posited three large changes in British history: one for the better, leading to the English Revolution of the 1640s; one for the worse, commencing with the Restoration of 1660; one for the better again, culminating in the French Revolution of 1789. The current struggle in England, as he saw it, was to rid society of the Christian superstition that was being exploited to roll back the gains associated with the French Revolution. Poetry could be a part of that struggle, as he explained a few months earlier, because poetry could help develop a "system of salvation" that might comfort without deluding. His great Odes were conceived very much within this scheme of progress and his sense of poetry's place in it – an improvement in the nation's feeling soul, a progress of sentiments, but not unproblematically so.

This is not the place to rehearse in detail an account of the "Ode to Psyche" as Keats's poem about the history and historicity of the human soul.[12] The bare-bones version of that argument is that when Keats examines the late emergence of the Psyche myth in the first century CE – late in respect to the "fond believing lyre" of Homer's Olympian gods – he sees in her human apotheosis a counterfactual possibility to the dark history of the West under Christianity. What I would like to add to that account now, however, is the suggestion that the "Ode to Psyche" is itself about the question of whether the arts are progressive. It is itself, that is, an exercise in the manner of the kind of Ode whose topic was the "progress of poetry."

Keats's Ode dramatizes its own apotheosis in reverse. In it, Keats reworks the myth of the woman whose curiosity toward her divine lover costs her his love but whose steadfastness in making amends earns her promotion to divinity. In Keats's account, divinity is humanized in the course of Psyche's uneven development toward Keats's very recognition of her in this poem. This would seem indeed to be a march of progress, and one apparently attended by progress in the fine art of poetry. These two advances are mutually reinforcing, perhaps even mutually defining. Certainly, the form of divinity that takes shape in the light of the frankly acknowledged mythopoeic function of poetry is superior to that faded Olympian hierarchy of the "fond believing lyre" – superior in its truth and in its egalitarianism. Conversely, when poetry is revealed as the source of all we know of divinity within ourselves, it achieves a status – so a Keatsian like Wallace Stevens would argue – superior to all that came before it. Keats had earlier still acknowledged this kind of complex progress in his famous letter about life as a passage through a "Mansion of Many Apartments":

> The first we step into we call the infant or thoughtless Chamber, in which we remain as long as we do not think – We remain there a long while, and notwithstanding the doors of the second Chamber remain wide open, showing a bright appearance, we care not to hasten to it; but are at length imperceptibly impelled by the awakening of the thinking principle – within us – we no sooner get into the second Chamber, which I shall call the Chamber of Maiden-Thought, than we become intoxicated with the light and the atmosphere.[13]

The letter itself is a kind of progress text, with Shakespeare and Milton assuming their places in a long poetic development. The figure who most immediately preceded Keats himself in this sequence was, of course, Wordsworth. "To this point was Wordsworth come."[14] It does not take a great deal of work to show that allusions to Wordsworth are pervasive in the "Ode to Psyche" – echoes of words and phrases and motifs and larger patterns, especially to the Immortality Ode. I will turn to some of these presently, but now I would like to return to the Ode itself. For I have not yet even made the case for why we should think of it as a progress poem in the first place.

There are a number of ways in which to see the Immortality Ode as addressing the progress of poetry and of a poet. The narrative middle section of the poem, read carefully, declares itself more than the story not just of a generalized first person plural agent, us – "our birth is but a sleep and a forgetting" (l. 59) – though these pronouns are all the more striking after all those first-person singular pronouns through the first four stanzas. This section simultaneously offers itself as an account of a poet's development, the growth of his mind. And it is in this sense that the Ode is rightly understood as a kind of miniature of Wordsworth's self-portrait in *The Prelude*.

We know, in the first place, that this is in fact the story of a poet because the story of this young "philosopher" in stanzas 5–8 of the Ode is a story of poetic activity. The full flowering of the boy's genius comes when we are told that he has begun to "fit his tongue" (98) to certain forms and discourses taken from the world as he imagines it.[15] This emphasis on the role of the tongue in the boy's story tells us how to read that later line about his acting as if "his whole vocation / Were endless imitation" (ll. 107–8). Thus prepared, in other words, we are encouraged to read this as a reference to *poetic* imitation, to mimesis in the Aristotelian sense. Moreover, the reference to "endless imitation" sums up a passage in which the child's play is cast in Shakespearean terms. The child mimics the character types from all those stages of life that the misanthrope surveys in *As You Like It*, a passage in the Ode that quotes the Shakespearean source outright:

> The little Actor cons another part;
> Filling from time to time his "humorous" stage
> With all the Persons, down to palsied Age,
> That Life brings with her in her equipage;
> > As if his whole vocation
> > Were endless imitation.
>
> > > (ll. 103–8)

Jaques had allegorized the human trajectory as a cycle in which our end – "sans teeth, sans eye, sans taste, sans everything" (2.vii.166) – spells a return to our infantile beginnings.[16] In Wordsworth's extraordinary lines, Jaques's anti-progress is reframed within the larger narrative of progress that constitutes this second movement of the Ode. This reframing is achieved first by virtue of the narrative of the child's ontogenetic development, and secondly by virtue of the larger allusive structure of this second movement, which suggests not only an ontogenetic development but a phylogenetic one as well. The entire allusive structure of this middle movement of the Ode, in other words, confirms that we are being offered an account – albeit in allegorical form – of the progress of poetry.

It now becomes crucial to recognize that the Ode signally echoes such eighteenth-century progress poems as James Beattie's "The Minstrel: Or, the Progress of Genius" or Thomas Gray's "The Progress of Poesie: A Pindaric Ode." In Gray, for example, after poesie progresses from Greece to Latium and then finally arrives in England, we are treated to a brief biography of the childhood of Shakespeare, a narrative addressed to mother England. This narrative is introduced in the following terms:

> Far from the sun and summer-gale,
> In thy green lap was Nature's Darling laid
> > . . . The dauntless Child
> Stretched forth his little arms, and smiled.
> > (ll. 83–8)[17]

Beattie's "Minstrel" seems already to be refitting Gray's lines to Wordsworth's purposes.[18] In a mood of interrogative bewilderment which distinctly anticipates that of the speaker of Wordsworth's Ode, Beattie's speaker asks his Minstrel prodigy:

> O how canst thou renounce the boundless store
> Of charms which nature to her votary yields
> ... and hope to be forgiven!
> (ll. 91–9)[19]

Is it possible that one can know these poems as well as Wordsworth and his readers would have known them and not be reminded of them at the opening of the stanzas recounting his Shakespearean child-poet's relation to nature?

> VI
> Earth fills her lap with pleasures of her own,
> Yearnings she hath in her own natural kind ...
> (ll. 78–9)

And:

> VII
> Behold the Child among his newborn blisses,
> A six years' Darling of a pygmy size.
> (ll. 86–7)

Wordsworth, I suggest, has merged Gray's and Beattie's texts to show a connection between them that is not otherwise evident, rather along the lines of T. S. Eliot's idea that every poem added to a tradition effects a reordering of that tradition.[20] It seems clear from this particular act of synthesis that the Immortality Ode means to recompose the progress of poetry, and that it means to do so in, as it were, a new key. It also seems clear that Keats recognized as much in his turn when he recomposed the Ode as the "Ode to Psyche."

Keats recognized something else in the Immortality Ode as well, something that inheres in the broader form of the meditative lyric as Wordsworth developed it, though it achieves perhaps its most fully elaborated shape in the Immortality Ode. Viewed in terms of the 1800 "Preface" to *Lyrical Ballads*, the Wordsworthian lyric is defined, in the first instance, by powerful emotion recollected in tranquility. But, alternatively, reinvoking Schiller's distinction, we can think of it as involving a shift from a stage in which things are apprehended naïvely – apprehended *in sense* – to one in which they are apprehended sentimentally – through reflection (or "thought," to use the Wordsworthian shorthand). Looking at the Wordsworthian lyric paradigm this way, it seems easy enough to see, first of all, that both Keats's and Wordsworth's Odes chart roughly such a course for themselves. Keats's lyric begins with a puzzled account of Psyche in her bower, and then, after its meditation on her history, it concludes with an account of "all soft delight / That shadowy thought can win" (ll. 64–5) for Psyche in a bower now understood as a work of the poetic imagination, a product of the mind's engagement with language.[21]

Wordsworth begins the Immortality Ode, for his part, with a series of vexing scenarios, all of them apparently false starts, including an apparently failed pastoral exercise. By the conclusion of the poem, however, he can announce (at the beginning of stanza 10):

> X
> Then sing, ye Birds, sing a joyous song!
> And let the young lambs bound
> As to the tabor's sound!
> We *in thought* will join your throng.
>   (ll. 169–72, italics added)

We find something similar in "Tintern Abbey," when the mature Wordsworth concludes that he now looks on a landscape such as that of the River Wye "not as in the hour / of thoughtless youth" (ll. 89–90) but with properly humanized reflection.[22] "Thought," it needs to be emphasized, acquires a quasi-technical status within the Humean idiom that Wordsworth bequeathed to Keats. It is a term that was of course duly glossed in the sentimental epistemology of the "Preface" to *Lyrical Ballads*, where Wordsworth explains the work of "reflection" as a process in which our continued influxes of feeling are modified and directed by our thoughts, which are themselves indeed the representatives of our past feelings – a fairly straightforward paraphrase of Hume's account of how impressions are modified by ideas which are themselves indeed the representatives of past impressions.

We thus discover in the Immortality Ode – especially as illuminated by Keats's rewriting of it in "Psyche" – two key formal structures: one involves the progress of poetry, the other a shift from the naïve to the sentimental. But the relationship between these two dominant lines is anything but straightforward. This problem is worth detailed attention for any serious reader of the Ode and, given the centrality of the Ode, for any serious student of Romantic poetry. The remainder of my commentary is an attempt to address this relationship with some care and precision.

It will be helpful to stipulate a few basic points about the Ode for the sake of the argument. First, as I have already suggested, the eleven numbered stanzas of the Ode fall roughly into three movements: stanzas I–IV, V–VIII, and IX–XI. (In this respect, indeed, it has a structure like that of Gray's "Progress of Poesy.") I will assume further that the questions that appear at the end of each of the first two movements mark a quandary that the ensuing moments of the poem, respectively, attempt to address. So we have the famous questions at the end of stanza IV that seem to stop the poet's progress (we know from the biography that the poem literally stopped at this point for two years): "Whither is fled the visionary gleam? / Whither is it now, the glory and the dream?" (ll. 57–8). The resumption of the poem with stanza V – with the beginning of the second movement – attempts to answer this question by way of the collective autobiography of the Western poet as growing boy. This narrative runs aground with the new interrogative at the end of stanza VIII, when the speaker raises the question (so very close in spirit to Gray's question) about why the child seems so eager to accommodate himself to the forms of the adult world:

> Why with such earnest pains dost thou provoke
> The years to bring the inevitable yoke,
> Thus blindly with thy blessedness at strife?
>
> (ll. 124–6)

The last three stanzas of the poem constitute a response to this second puzzle, and by implication also the first puzzle. I have suggested that this response reworks the conclusion of "Tintern Abbey," in which the once thoughtless is revisited in thought. I have also suggested that this conclusion is emulated in Keats's conclusion to the "Ode to Psyche," where he tells us that Psyche will at last have her accouterments, but only those that "shadowy thought" can win. And finally, I would like to enter as "assumed" that the ninth stanza of the poem – the one that effects the transition that leads to the resolution – is the crucial one.

With these points considered as given, then, we can examine the crucial transition at stanza IX. Like the transition at stanza V, this one seems to mark a new beginning, a phoenix-like rising from the ashes of a prior skepticism. In the case of stanza IX, however, it is, somewhat astonishingly, the skepticism itself that is acknowledged as the reason to celebrate life anew. The lines are tortuous, and not always well understood, in spite of a certain dogged explicitness in their formulation:

> IX
> O joy that in our embers
> Is something that might live,
> That nature yet remembers
> What was so fugitive!
> The thought of our past years in me doth breed

Perpetual benediction: not indeed
For that which is most worthy to be blest;
Delight and liberty, the simple creed
Of Childhood, whether busy or at rest,
With new-fledged hope still fluttering in his breast: –
    Not for these raise I
    This song of thanks and praise;
But for those obstinate questionings
Of sense and outward things,
Fallings from us, vanishings;
Blank misgivings of a Creature
Moving about in worlds not realized,
High instincts before which our mortal Nature
Did tremble like a guilty Thing surprised.
(ll. 130–48)

This is a dazzlingly complex passage, and one point it is crucial to be clear about is just how the speaker of the Ode claims to find redemption from the vexing fugitivities of stanzas I–IV ("whither is fled the visionary gleam?") and from the puzzlements of the story that unfolds in stanzas V–VIII ("Why . . . dost thou provoke the years . . . ?). He does so not by recalling the naïve faith ("simple creed") of the child, but by recalling the child's doubts, his (as it were) philosophical skepticism about the world of sensation. This is the skepticism that is indicated by way of the child's "obstinate questionings / Of sense and outward things" (ll. 146–7).

If we ask what this skepticism refers to, where it gains its purchase in the collective narrative of the child in the poem's second movement, I think the best answer we can make is one that points to the child's tendency to wish to grow up too fast, the tendency that was so mystifying and vexing to the speaker toward the close of the poem's second movement in stanza VIII. In the second movement of the poem, these tendencies are couched as accommodations of his language arts to the forms of life inherent in human usage – dialogues of business, love, and strife – and in the fundamental ritual practices of human society:

A wedding or a festival,
A mourning or a funeral.
(ll. 94–5)

That the child's dream – his plan or chart of life – should aim at the customary world of adult practice remains puzzling to the speaker until – in a moment that (like the best Aristotelian plots) unites reversal and discovery – he comes to understand that this appetite for human ritual is not so much a hastening on of the familiarizing film of custom as a deep expression of dissatisfaction with the merely sensual order of the world. If this point has so long been misrecognized by even many of the poem's shrewdest readers, including M. H. Abrams, this may have to do with the influence of Coleridge's account of *Lyrical Ballads* in the *Biographia Literaria*, where Coleridge pursues a Kantian line, imposing on Wordsworthian "anthropology" (British in provenance, empirical in method, moral-sense in orientation) on an implicitly transcendental critique.[23]

To follow this line of argument another step, we can turn to the relation between the first and last of the poem's three parts. We can recognize that the first part not only terminates in a stymied confusion, but also is largely constituted of a series of apparent false starts, in which the poet seems to try on first one and then another of a series of various poetic styles and modes. These are in their turn discarded as obsolete, superannuated, unable to overcome the debilitating sense of the passage of time. Viewed from the point of view of part 3, however, these forms are all redeemed. Skepticism about them has been replaced by a recognition that they themselves amount to so many expressions of skepticism about the world as taken in by the senses. They are some of the ways in which the poet of a "mature age" – in both senses of the term – has fitted his tongue to the forms of culture. The forms are now seen, one might say, in the light of the sentimental and the positive dimension of reflection, rather than in the light of superannuated naïvety. This is perhaps most easily recognizable in that reprise of the pastoral mode in stanza X, when, reclaiming the young lambs bounding to the tabor's sound again, the speaker declares he will join their throng *in thought*.

My suggestion, then, is that the styles and forms attempted in what seem to be the poem's various false starts constitute not only the point of departure for a progress narrative but also its end point, or at least the stage that the mature poet has so far managed to achieve. The logic is the same as we find with the opening lines of "Tintern Abbey," where the poet's reflections on the vagrant dwellers in the houseless woods or the speculation about the hermit sitting by his fire represent not only the occasion of his meditation but also the upshot of his maturation, the sobering shift from the naïve to the sentimental. In "Tintern Abbey," these reflections supply the proof, as it were, that the poet now, in 1798, no longer seeks thoughtlessly after nature's objects but rather has attuned his perception to the still sad music of humanity. The poet of the first four stanzas of the Ode, by the same token, turns to the varied forms of poetic expression because the sensory world is not enough for him. Those apparently failed attempts to start the poem are the proof of that dissatisfaction, that dubiety. On this reading, then, the poem amounts to a sentimental redemption of a sentimental problem, a problem of mixed feelings at one level (let us call this level "deep almost as life") being redeemed by mixed feelings at another level – one "too deep for tears" (ll. 133, 208).

But what does such a reading imply for an account of the Ode as a progress poem for an age in which, as I noted at the start, progress – especially the progress of the fine arts – is such a highly charged question? Perhaps one key to addressing this issue can be found in the poem's celebrated epigraph:

> The Child is Father of the Man;
> And I could wish my days to be
> Bound each to each in natural piety.[24]

"Piety" is the term that stands out in the present context since it is not normally taken to be a virtue associated with progress. Piety is religious devotion and, in its modern sense, the kind of respect that a child owes a parent – a father, say. By making his child a father, Wordsworth has apparently turned a structure of tradition on its head. He has also internalized the notion of tradition, however, in the sense that piety's binding of generation to generation over a long duration is translated into the binding of days in a single lifespan. In natural piety, one day owes the respect to its predecessor that one generation owes to *its* predecessor. But of course, if the poem is a progress poem of the kind that I have suggested it is – that is, if the life of the child allegorizes a collective story about the development of poetic art – then these two readings are no longer in conflict.

If this does prove to be the case, what would it mean to understand the opening stanzas as the work of the mature poet as *modern* rather than the mature poet as *adult*? That is, what would it mean to understand it as the work of a poet who comes late in the collective progress of poetry? It might mean – I offer this as a speculation – that the expression of pain on the part of the solitary individual ("to me alone there came a thought of grief") was a part of the contemporary form of life, part of modern poetry. There is some evidence that Wordsworth himself took such a view of his own achievement in the Ode when he returned to rework the terms of the great ninth stanza for a late but influential ode on "The Power of Sound." That, however, is a subject for another essay.

If the older progress poems of the eighteenth century involved a westering movement of poetry (say) from place to place, Wordsworth's is a progress poem of an age when progress has been largely recast in temporal terms. He himself casts it, in part, as the growth of a child. There is, of course, a marked and structurally important westering movement in the Immortality Ode, but it is that of the sun, that primordial measure of time's passing. Interestingly, both metaphors appear in Hazlitt's comment, as I quoted it earlier, about "Why the Arts are Not Progressive":

> Those arts, which depend on individual genius and incommunicable power, have always leaped at once from infancy to manhood, from the first rude dawn of invention to their meridian height and dazzling lustre, and have in general declined ever after.

Wordsworth's sentimental progress poem seems to undo both of Hazlitt's conceits before the fact. He insists on a narrative of maturation, not of overleaping, even as he finds the end of this narrative in its beginning. And, as for spatial progress and decline, Wordsworth opposes the radiant clouds of orient dawn and occidental dusk *alike* to the colorless meridian light of common day.

Is Hazlitt invoking Wordsworth's metaphorical structure allusively? It certainly would not be the only time in his work that he does. Does the Ode amount to a proleptic rebuttal of Hazlitt's claim that the fine arts are not progressive? Perhaps. But it is certainly possible to draw another conclusion: that the "idea" of progress is so profoundly transformed in the Ode as to reconstitute Hazlitt's question, for his own age and perhaps for ours. As the Immortality Ode enters its third century of engagement with thoughtful students of Romantic poetry, there is no reason to imagine that it will not continue to provoke the years with its obstinate questionings of sense, or that it will cease to tease us with answering yet always elusive sentiments.

NOTES

1 On how the Ode provoked later poets to take its terms as exemplary, see my "'Wordsworth' after Waterloo," in *The Age of William Wordsworth*, ed. Kenneth Johnston and Gene Ruoff (New Brunswick: Rutgers University Press, 1987), pp. 84–111.
2 Robert Nisbet, *History of the Idea of Progress* (New York: Basic Books, 1980), p. 171.
3 *The Complete Works of William Hazlitt*, vol. XVII: *Uncollected Essays*, ed. P. P. Howe (London and Toronto: J. M. Dent, 1931), p. 38. Subsequent references in the text.
4 *Shelley's Poetry and Prose*, ed. Donald H. Reiman and Neil Fraistat (New York: W. W. Norton, 2002), p. 260. Subsequent references to Shelley's poetry by line number to this edition.
5 Ibid., p. 517.
6 In writing *A Defence of Poetry*, Shelley undertook to respond to an essay by Thomas Love Peacock, *The Four Ages of Poetry*, in which Peacock had actually produced a narrative of long-term decline since the heyday of the ancients. Hazlitt's "Why the Arts are Not Progressive" can thus be seen as mediating a larger dispute.

7 William Godwin, *Enquiry Concerning Political Justice, and its Influence on General Virtue and Happiness*, 2 vols. (Dublin: printed for Luke White, 1793), vol. 1 pp. 273–6.

8 Friedrich Schiller, *Naïve and Sentimental Poetry* and *On the Sublime: Two Essays*, trans. Julius A. Elias (New York: F. Ungar Publishing Co., 1967).

9 Annette Baier, *A Progress of Sentiments: Reflections on Hume's Treatise* (Cambridge, MA: Harvard University Press, 1991), pp. 180–1.

10 *The Complete Works of Percy Bysshe Shelley*, ed. Roger Ingpen and Walter E. Peck, 10 vols. (London: Ernest Benn, 1926–30), vol. VII, p. 20.

11 Ibid.

12 For a fuller treatment of these questions see my *England in 1819: The Politics of Literary Culture and the Case of Romantic Historicism* (Chicago: University of Chicago Press, 1998), pp. 389–440.

13 To J. H. Reynolds, May 3, 1818, in *Letters of John Keats, 1814–1821*, ed. Hyder Rollins, 2 vols. (Cambridge, MA: Harvard University Press, 1958), vol. I, pp. 280–1.

14 Ibid., vol. I, p. 281.

15 *The Poetical Works of William Wordsworth*, ed. Ernest de Selincourt and Helen Darbishire, 5 vols. (Oxford: Clarendon Press, 1940–9), vol. IV, p. 282. Subsequent references by line number in the text.

16 William Shakespeare, *The Complete Works*, ed. Stanley Wells and Gary Taylor (Oxford: Clarendon Press, 1998), p. 638.

17 Thomas Gray, *Odes by Mr. Gray, Author of An Elegy in a Country Church-yard* (Dublin: printed for G. Faulkner and J. Rudd, 1757), p. 6.

18 On Beattie's treatment of the "minstrel" theme, see Maureen McLane, "The Figure Minstrelsy Makes: Poetry and Historicity," *Critical Inquiry* 29/3 (Spring 2003), pp. 429–52.

19 James Beattie, *The Minstrel; or, the Progress of Genius, Book the First* (London: printed for E. and C. Dilly, A. Kincaid, and J. Bell, 1771), p. 6.

20 T. S. Eliot, "Tradition and the Individual Talent," in *The Sacred Wood: Essays on Poetry and Criticism* [1920] (London: Methuen, 1928), pp. 47–59.

21 John Keats, *The Poems of John Keats*, ed. Jack Stillinger (Cambridge, MA: Harvard University Press, 1978), p. 366.

22 *The Poetical Works of William Wordsworth*, ed. de Selincourt and Darbishire, vol. II, p. 261.

23 See my *Wordsworth's Second Nature* (Chicago: University of Chicago Press, 1984), pp. 74–81, 234–65.

24 *The Poetical Works of William Wordsworth*, ed. de Selincourt and Darbishire, vol. IV, p. 279.

FURTHER READING

Abrams, M. H., "Structure and Style in the Greater Romantic Lyric," in *From Sensibility to Romanticism: Essays Presented to Frederick W. Pottle*, ed. Frederick W. Hilles and Harold Bloom (New Haven: Yale University Press, 1965), pp. 527–60

Bennett, Andrew, *Wordsworth Writing* (Cambridge: Cambridge University Press, 2007)

Bradley, A. C., *Oxford Lectures on Poetry* (London: Macmillan, 1909)

Brooks, Cleanth, "Wordsworth and the Paradox of the Imagination," in *The Well-Wrought Urn: Studies in the Structure of Poetry* (New York: Harcourt Brace & World, 1947), pp. 124–50.

Ferguson, Frances, *Wordsworth: Language as Counter-Spirit* (New Haven: Yale University Press, 1977)

Fry, Paul H., *The Poet's Calling in the English Ode* (New Haven: Yale University Press, 1980)

Hartman, Geoffrey, *Wordsworth's Poetry: 1787–1814* (New Haven: Yale University Press, 1964)

Jarvis, Simon, *Wordsworth's Philosophic Song* (Cambridge: Cambridge University Press, 2006)

Levinson, Marjorie, *Wordsworth's Great Period Poems* (Cambridge: Cambridge University Press, 1986)

Liu, Alan, *Wordsworth: The Sense of History* (Stanford: Stanford University Press, 1989)

McLane, Maureen N., *Romanticism and the Human Sciences* (Cambridge: Cambridge University Press, 2000)

Simpson, David, *Wordsworth's Historical Imagination* (New York and London: Methuen, 1987)

Spadafora, David, *The Idea of Progress in Eighteenth-Century Britain* (New Haven: Yale University Press, 1990)

Trilling, Lionel, "The Immortality Ode," in *The Liberal Imagination: Essays on Literature and Society* (New York: Viking, 1950), pp. 129–59

Vendler, Helen, "Lionel Trilling and the Immortality Ode," *Salmagundi* 42 (Spring 1978), pp. 65–85

8

ADRIANA CRACIUN

Romantic poetry, sexuality, gender

The herald, companion, and follower of an "affective revolution" as significant to modernity as its accompanying political revolutions, Romanticism is deeply concerned with questions of sexuality and gender. In its lyric intensity, introspection, powerful emotions, and luxuriant language, Romantic poetry has played a critical role in our enduring notions of poetry as expressive of a deep self. Sexuality, and the self-knowledge and liberation that sexuality seems to promise, are central to this expressive hypothesis associated with Romantic poetry. We are familiar with readings of canonical Romantics that emphasize their celebrations of politicized sexual liberty; building on this work, I would like to broaden the spectrum of poets considered, and most importantly, to engage with the emerging consensus in the history of sexualities. Approaching the question of Romantic poetry's relationship to sexuality and gender in more historically charged ways allows us to consider how categories of sexuality and gender operate through both content and form – as significant to the intellectual and aesthetic work of the poetry as to the material and commercial properties of poetic production.

The revolutionary fervor of late eighteenth-century Europe destabilized both gender and sexual roles in unprecedented ways, unleashing at once widespread demands for greater social and gender mobility and a reactionary backlash that sought to reinforce hierarchies. Domestic and sexual roles were of particular concern to reactionary British moralists, as it was through such seemingly private channels that dangerous political temptations could corrupt the body politic. Despite the strength of this counter-revolutionary regulation, "the French Revolution released a kind of seismic affective energy," the so-called "affective revolution" that, according to Lynn Hunt and Margaret Jacobs, disrupted "any supposed lockstep progression of rigidly prescribed gender norms, [or] of enforced heterosexuality" via new forms of erotic and "affective experimentation."[1] Hunt and Jacobs explore this revolutionary affectivity in the erotic and diabolic correspondence between young men in radical Dissenting circles, though such affective experimentation is visible across the spectrum of letters in this volatile period: from explorations of taboo, anti-hierarchical intimacies in sentimental novels and Gothic romances, to philosophical writings on the somatic properties of the sublime, the empirical basis for sentiments, and the biological and social aspects of sexual difference.

The Romantic period as traditionally delineated (and the expanded Romantic Century, 1750–1850) falls squarely across this historical period of significant change in class, social, and sexual relations in Britain, and as a result, the imaginative literature at the turn of the century should be approached with these reevaluations of sex and gender in mind. Poetry enjoyed a special significance within these widespread new speculations on sexuality and gender. "Poetry is . . . a passion," declared William Wordsworth in his "Essay, Supplementary to the Preface," and proceeded to spiritualize this passion through narratives of maturation, wherein his poetry assumes a sacred status as "spousal verse" celebrating the union of male poet and female nature. Yet for Letitia Landon, Wordsworth is the "most passionless of writers," and it is instead Byron who is "our poet of passion."[2] Landon and Byron had scandalized London society with the rumors surrounding their private passions, fueling the sales of their poetry but also the hostility which they encountered in a literary establishment that was increasingly morally restrictive, especially for women. Wordsworth, in contrast, surrounded himself with sister-wives and cultivated a domesticated patriarchal image that sublimated the passion he believed necessary for poetry through intellectual and moral channels, achieving what Landon termed the "moral sublime."[3]

Wordsworth's model of poetry (in the Prospectus to *The Recluse*) as a "great consummation" between poet and nature in "spousal verse" represents an affective heterosexuality increasingly normative to the masculinity of British men of all classes. But this complementary heterosexuality coexisted with other Romantic-era masculinities: for example, intensely homophilic ones, like that shared by Sir Leoline and his estranged friend Sir Roland in Coleridge's "Christabel," or by Byron and his public-school friends; otherwise non-reproductive sexualities like that of the masturbator, an increasing concern in medical writings and visible in Keats's nineteenth-century reception, thanks in part to Byron's emasculating reading of him as "frigging his *Imagination*";[4] declining models like that of the aristocratic bisexual libertine, which Byron stubbornly maintained; and the exclusively homosexual "sodomites" associated with metropolitan molly houses, and derided by Mary Wollstonecraft as "equivocal beings," as unnatural, she believed, as women of leisure.

The sexualities available to women were also surprisingly diverse. Dissenting feminists like Wollstonecraft and Mary Hays insisted on women's active, explicitly politicized passions, toward both men and women, and typically charged them with a spiritual dimension via the radicalized religious enthusiasm revived at the end of the century. Moralists like Hannah More proliferated a normative heterosexuality drained of all pleasures save those of domesticity. A range of Sapphic identities was also visible by the late eighteenth century: from Anne Lister's encoded diaries detailing her erotic encounters with women, to Anna Seward's passionate sonnets to her friend Honora (and diary entries demonizing reputed lesbians), to the "English Sappho," Mary Robinson, who heterosexualized Sapphic passion in *Sappho and Phaon*, but with radical effects. Romanticism nurtured a promiscuous proliferation of sexualities, gender identities, and forms of intimacy even as it endured an intensifying codification of complementarity.

The Romantic period marks a borderland between recognized regimes of sex and gender, with competing historical models offering starkly different visions of the turn of the nineteenth century. Lawrence Stone's progressive model of the rise of affective individualism and the domesticization of sexuality throughout the eighteenth century, *The Family, Sex and Marriage in England, 1500–1800*, influential since its publication in 1979, has met with significant challenges. More recent anti-progressive studies, writing in the wake of Foucault's *History of Sexuality*, vol. I, have emphasized the increasingly rigid definitions of gender and sexuality characterizing the shift from the eighteenth to the nineteenth century. These histories of sexuality typically locate near the early eighteenth century the decline of a pluralistic continuum incorporating same-sex practices, and the rise of increasingly codified gender identities, for example the sodomite (later known as the homosexual). Recent histories of the body and of sexualities do agree broadly on the decline of an Aristotelean, one-sex/two-gender model in which the male sex was synonymous with the universally human, and "woman" was an inferior, inverted version of the male, different in degree but not in essence. Thomas Laqueur's controversial *Making Sex: Body and Gender from the Greeks to Freud* (1990) located the shift from this one-sex/two-gender model to the two-sex model of incommensurable difference in the late eighteenth century, and while historians have challenged a number of Laqueur's contentions (for example, his reliance on a stable "male" sex and gender against which to problematize woman and femininity), the broad outlines of Laqueur's argument that sex and gender were increasingly codified in the modern era are consistent with more recent work of historians like Londa Schienbinger, Randolph Trumbach, and Anna Clark. The rise of complementary sexual difference – the newer two-sex model that would dominate in nineteenth-century ideologies of domesticity – whether seen as nurturing affective individualism and female-centered bourgeois morality, or, conversely, as trapping women within a newly essentialist, medicalized identity as passionless and domestic, needs to be read as only one, albeit hegemonic, new development in the sexual landscape of the Romantic period. And increasingly the history of sexuality is theorized along affinitive, not medicalized lines (e.g., heterophilic instead of heterosexual), a useful strategy for resisting the anachronistic reification of Victorian categories in earlier periods. The paradox of affective and affinitive experimentation thriving at the same time as an intensification of sexual complementarity places Romanticism at a critical historical crossroads, not only politically, as is well known, but also for issues of gender and sexuality.

Drawing both on these historical perspectives on the shifts in sex and gender, and on modern queer theory, a new "queer Romanticism" increasingly available to us owes much to revolutionary changes in the history of sexuality and promises to revitalize gendered studies, particularly gender-complementary ones that consider only two fixed genders in relationship to an ahistorically "natural" two-sex model of difference. One could argue that gender-complementary models that seek to unify a feminine or woman's Romanticism reflect the (in this one respect) historically arbitrary rediscovery and anthologizing of Romantic women's writing beginning in the 1980s, which produced an illusorily coherent body of "Romantic women writers."[5] My aim in this chapter is thus to consider the poetry of both male and female Romantics, and specifically how characteristically Romantic poetic excesses and experiments illuminate the increasingly defamiliarized landscape of sexes and genders with which historians present us.

Gendering poetic identities

Byron's poetry and shifting sexual identities loom large in these new sexual landscapes of Romanticism. And yet situating Byron within this expanding new history of sexualities reveals that the cross-dressing Don Juan, lauded by some critics for his demystification of sexual privilege and essentialism, also seems to embody an "inexorably doomed notion of what it was to be a man," the aristocratic libertine.[6] Byron's aristocratic libertine masculinity is at home in an older one-sex model in which aristocratic men were understood to enjoy sex with age-appropriate male partners without threatening their masculinity or social status. *Don Juan* in particular may voice Byron's awareness of sexual oppression in such episodes as Julia's letter (Canto I, l. 194), bemoaning that love "is woman's whole existence," but the poet's misogyny is never wholly separate from his sympathy. Ultimately it is anachronistic class privilege that underwrites Byron's renowned *mobilité* through sin's long labyrinth, and authorizes his famous contempt for the "Gynocrasy" of women intellectuals and especially women poets.

Regarding the status of women, Wordsworth would perhaps agree with Byron that, as the latter remarked to Lady Blessington, the ideal woman should have "talent enough to be able to understand and value" his own "but not sufficient to be able to shine herself."[7] Wordsworth gathered around himself a group of women devoted to fostering his genius above all else, and grew noticeably uncomfortable when visited by women poets – for example, Felicia Hemans and Maria Jane Jewsbury – who sought poetic professionalization, something he repeatedly advised against for women. Never wholly at ease around women intellectuals (like Mary Shelley and Germaine de Staël, in Byron's case), these otherwise wildly different Romantic poets shared a fundamental investment in a poetic identity unshakeably masculine, whether domesticized (for Wordsworth), homoeroticized, or even queer (for Byron).

The persistence of a declining libertine male sexual identity in Byron is related to the thoroughly respectable and accurately "patriarchal" sexual identity of Wordsworth, even though Byron's looks backward through a homophilic tradition of civic humanism while Wordsworth's looks more at home in the long nineteenth century's domesticization of sex as a family affair. Both forms of male privilege, whether waning or waxing, combined with an intense sense of (different) class entitlement, underwrite these poets' unparalleled drive for self-possession in what they perceived as a feminized literary marketplace. The extent of these poets' sexualization of their craft raises the question of why they worked so hard to (re)masculinize a profession widely associated with women.

I wish to consider this question in the light of three features distinctive to the Romantic Century: new developments in the history of sexualities and the body, political demands for the "rights of woman," and the commercialization of print culture. First, as we have seen, the Romantic period enjoyed a plethora of contradictory models of sexual difference and gendered identities. Far from marking a smooth transition between well-defined, periodized regimes such as an early modern one-sex model and the nineteenth-century domesticization of essential sexual difference, the Romantic period is more fruitfully approached as a volatile borderland of competing discourses, which partly account for Romanticism's signature excesses, ambiguities and experiments. Despite the traditional focus on women's volatile sexual and gender roles in the long eighteenth century, increasingly historians have focused on the changes wrought in masculinity. Some historians even argue that "men possessed the less stable and more contested gender"[8] in the long eighteenth century, a conclusion compatible with Randolph Trumbach's ambitious *Sex and the Gender Revolution* (1998). Trumbach argues that an increasingly compulsory male heterosexuality demanded constant proofs of masculinity via the domination of women, which he documents in the sharp rise in domestic violence, prostitution, and illegitimacy throughout the eighteenth century. The literary aggression toward women readers and writers expressed by canonical male poets, like their aggression against increasingly democratized reading publics, should be read, I suggest, as evidence of the vulnerability of masculine literary identities, as well as of feminine ones.

Unprecedented demands on behalf of the "rights of woman," radicalized by the French Revolution, had further raised the stakes for all poets concerned with how poetic roles are sexualized and democratized (thus, for all poets). The 1793 Jacobin republic marked in some respects a high point for the legal rights of women and families, destined not to be regained until the twentieth century. The short-lived Jacobin republic also marked the low point in gender relations according to counter-revolutionary ideologues like Hannah More and Jane West, as well as republican feminists like Helen Maria Williams. More's and West's didactic poetry, fiction, and essays demonized the French as carriers of an infectious plague of Jacobin reforms, like women's right to divorce, inheritance, and child custody. Widely accessible to the working classes, broadside ballads like More's popular "Sinful Sally" defended domestic sexual values for the poor against such revolutionary temptations. With entirely different political intentions, Williams saw the Jacobin republic, which had ousted the bourgeois Girondins and banned women from public political clubs, as a dangerously masculine threat to what she idealized as a Revolution pursuing ideals seamlessly both middle-class and feminine.

Along with these ideological and "sexological" changes informing Romantic poetry came radical changes in print culture. The end of perpetual copyright in 1774, new technologies like machine-made paper and stereotyping, and increasing access through circulating libraries and rising literacy, significantly expanded the number of Romantic-era publications and readers. The resulting need for authors, especially poets, to grow more commercially and professionally astute had far-reaching implications for the content and form of the poetry produced. The sales of single-author volumes of poetry peaked in 1820, and afterwards were increasingly priced out of the market by new media like gift books and annuals, and many more periodicals with increasingly distinct audiences. Coleridge and Wordsworth, though they had begun their careers by publishing newspaper verse, ventured into the feminized terrain of the annual with considerable hand-wringing. All of the canonical male poets' impressive defenses of poetry's cultural capital (a defining feature of Romantic print culture) could also be read as their defense of male poetic privilege under threat by a perceived deluge of scribbling women.

Between 1780 and 1830, at least 2,584 volumes of poetry were published by women, with approximately 900 women poets publishing during roughly this same period.[9] The proliferation of women's poetry troubled to some extent all the canonical poets – from Wordsworth's complaint in the "Preface" to the *Lyrical Ballads* over the "deluges of idle and extravagant verse," to Keats's anxious distancing of his work from Mary Tighe's *Psyche*, to Byron's satirical attacks on Bluestockings as intellectual upstarts in *The Blues* (1821). In some respects, Keats and Byron persisted in a losing battle for the remasculinization of poetry in the 1820s; as Richard Cronin observes, "it may be significant that the years in which women poets were dominant coincided fairly precisely with the years in which the sale of poetry collapsed."[10] The overall number of individual volumes of poetry did decline after 1820, and some publishers refused to publish poetry a decade later (famously, John Murray, who had already made his fortune publishing Byron). Yet one could make a counterargument against this familiar decline of poetry model, using the publishing successes of women poets, whose number of volumes published seems relatively stable through the mid-1830s.[11] The "decline of poetry" thesis works in part by eclipsing the popularity of women poets, reviving a false (though Romantic) dilemma: "a choice between a vulgar popularity and an insubstantial isolation."[12] Hemans and Landon supported extended families through their poetry, which has recently begun to attract the serious intellectual debate that it deserves. Hemans's poetry in particular sold in the tens of thousands throughout the nineteenth century, making her one of the bestselling British poets.[13] To relegate these important Romantic poets to "vulgar popularity" is to replicate uncritically the anxieties of their male contemporaries. Moreover, if we consider the proliferation of poetry in the annuals and gift books, which sold in the tens of thousands in the 1820s and 1830s, and did so by targeting women readers, one could argue that poetry's readerships increased at the end of the Romantic period, though the cultural capital of poetry did not.

The rise of feminized new poetic media like annuals, though they may have priced much (hitherto male) poets' individual volumes out of the market, also produced new poetic identities like that of "poetess." This feminized model of a poet enjoyed a continuum of gendered associations – from a low point as emasculated, diminutive emanation of true poet, to its moralized apotheosis in the minds of literary critics like Alexander Dyce and Frederic Rowton, who imagined the poetess as the essentially feminine and sentimental poet of the domestic affections so popular with early Victorian readers. Poets like Hemans, Landon, and Mary Robinson assumed the role of "poetess" at various stages in their careers, but it is a mistake to identify any of them consistently as a self-declared "poetess." At the end of her career, Robinson

developed her Sapphic poetic ideal based on a politicized, historicized understanding of Sappho as "the unrivalled poetess of her time." Despite this
original association of "poetess" with the celebrated Sappho dating back
to the sixteenth century, by the eighteenth century the term "poetess" had
acquired a largely derogatory usage.[14] Hemans's and especially Landon's
shifting poetic identities in the first three decades of the nineteenth century
are too often simplified into that of "poetess," especially by scholars of Victorian literature eager to establish a narrative of feminist maturation from a
Romantic poetess of sentiment to a more socially engaged Victorian woman
poet. Hemans is now rightly credited with having expanded the so-called
"domestic affections" associated with poetesses to encompass and even sur-
pass the world of men, both geographically and historically. Landon also
profited from the persona of poetess in the 1820s poetry on which most critics focus, but in later poems like "The Fairy of the Fountains" (1833) and
in her novels she critiqued the gendering of poetic spheres in more complex
ways.

So labile was the identity of "poetess" that perhaps the author who perfected its poses of embowered femininity was Alfred Tennyson. As Hemans's
"ablest successor,"[15] Tennyson published a number of poems in the poetess
tradition, for example "Mariana," "The Lady of Shalott" (1832), and "The
Palace of Art." "The soul in 'The Palace of Art,'" writes Richard Cronin,

> abandons her gorgeous palace for a humble cottage in the vale, in a gesture
> that, not least in its ambivalence, closely echoes the self-abnegating eagerness
> with which Hemans and Landon imagine women poets such as "Prosperzia
> Rossi" and Eulalia ready to surrender their fame for a life of humble, loving
> domesticity. (p. 107)

The poetess remains a crucial figure in our efforts to continually challenge
the often unsatisfactory distinctions between poetry of the Romantic and
Victorian periods, a distinction that is too often built upon the elision of
women poets' considerable accomplishments in the transitional decades of
the 1820s to the 1840s. As recently as 2000, Victorian scholars were still
content to rely on familiar assumptions of poets and genres springing fully
formed out of that magical year, 1832:

> When Tennyson portrays the artist in "The Lady of Shalott" as enclosed *fem-*
> *inine* consciousness and figures her problems as both aesthetic and erotic, he
> inaugurates a century-long concern with the sex and gender of art and artistry.[16]

But Tennyson did not inaugurate this concern, just as 1832 did not inaugurate the nineteenth century. As a poet who wrote "quite uninhibitedly as
a woman,"[17] Tennyson *inherits* the concern with "the sex and gender of

art and artistry" from writers like Hemans (in "Prosperzia Rossi"), Letitia Landon (in *The Improvisatrice*), John Keats (in *Lamia*), and Mary Robinson in her 1796 volume, *Sappho and Phaon*. Sappho inaugurated this tradition, which nineteenth-century poets like Hemans and Tennyson continued, under the problematic sign of "poetess." Indebted to the aestheticized sentimentality of Hemans, the hypnotic metrics of Robinson,[18] and the autoerotic solitaries of Landon, Tennyson the poetess illustrates the queer shifts in the gendering of nineteenth-century poetic identities.

The poetess figure, whether male or female, remains fertile ground for self-reflexive meditations on the gendering of poetry and poetic identities. By the time Tennyson published his poetess poems in 1830 and 1832, the poetess phenomenon was beginning its decline, the subject of satirical attacks like the Countess Blessington's "The Stock in Trade of Modern Poetesses." Like Landon's many self-reflexive comments on the construct of "poetess" (too often read by modern critics as Landon's unmediated experience as a "poetess"), Blessington's poem was published in an expensive annual (*The Keepsake for 1833*) largely responsible for proliferating the poetess phenomenon. Blessington satirizes the mass-produced metaphors of poetess poetry that connected this phenomenon to both senses of *cliché* – new typeface technology, and the derivative verse that this technology proliferated:

> Stars and planets shining high,
> Make one feel 'twere bliss to die;
> Twilight's soft mysterious light;
> Suns whose rays are "all" too bright;
> Wither'd hopes, and faded flowers,
> Beauties pining in their bowers;
> Broken harps, and untuned lyres;
> Lutes neglected, unquench'd fires;
> Vultures pecking at the heart,
> Leaving owners scarce a part.[19]

Blessington's poem makes "poetess" available to both male and female poets: "'twere bliss to die" is a Hemans constant but also echoes Pope's patriotic translation of *The Iliad*, and even Keats's "Nightingale"; similarly, "beauties pining in their bowers" resonates equally well with Landon as with Tennyson. The neglected lutes littering the landscapes of Hemans and Landon, meanwhile, coexist with the Promethean torments of Byron. The point is not that poetess poetry is derivative of male-authored poetry, but that trademarks that we now associate with male poets were in 1833 the "stock in trade of modern poetesses." The heroes in these poetess poems are Byronic – "Half a brigand – half corsair" – or perhaps, inversely, Byronic heroes are so widely diffused throughout 1830s popular culture that they can no longer be designated by their author's proper name, but are now reabsorbed within a feminized popular culture in which Byron discovered them in the first place (i.e., the Gothic). Blessington's radical implication (compared to modern readings of the poetess) is that the poetess, not the Byronic poet, *is* the modern poet: "This now is all the stock in trade, / With which a *modern* poem's made," she concludes (p. 153, emphasis added). The feminization of poetry is so complete by 1833 that all "modern" poets, whether they published earlier like Byron or recently like Tennyson, appear to write in its shadow.

Gender and specularization

Hemans is widely credited as the central figure in this feminization of nineteenth-century British poetry. In *Records of Woman* (1828), Hemans had extended woman's domain internationally and transhistorically, elevating the domestic affections above all else as the ideal subject of poetry, and hence privileging women's roles as both poets and poetic subjects. In "The Grave of a Poetess," the final poem in *Records of Woman*, Hemans offers a complex meditation on the poetess phenomenon, one addressed to an important (and unnamed) predecessor, the Irish poet Mary Tighe, who had been, like Hemans, both unhappily married and highly gifted. Hemans's reflection on this earlier "poetess" figure, one admired by Keats and Landon as well, famously concludes by severing the "poet's eye" from "the woman's heart," implying that "poetess" embodies an awkwardly gendered hybrid:

> Where couldst thou fix on mortal ground
> Thy tender thoughts and high?
> Now peace the woman's heart hath found,
> And joy the poet's eye.[20]

This important meditation on the cultural codes gendering poetess and poet is typically read as Hemans's critique of earthly regimes of gender that make poet and woman incompatible, or conversely, as Hemans's compliance with these gendered codes that warn of disaster if women leave a female affective sphere to pursue a masculinized poetic vision.

As a meditation on the career of her predecessor Tighe, the closing of Hemans's "The Grave of a Poetess" – the severance of eye and heart, vision and desire – knowingly revives Tighe's central concern with the politics of vision, or specularization.[21] In her six-canto *Psyche* (1805/11), Tighe rewrites the legend of Psyche and Eros to suggest that sexual knowledge is potentially empowering for women, and specifically for women poets. Psyche's objectification of and desire for Eros is recounted in ornate Spenserian stanzas, foregrounding the poetic and philosophical conventions of desire for which women are typically the object, not the subject. According to Harriet Kramer Linkin, Tighe "reclaims the gaze for women's poetry through her representation of reciprocal objectification," and does this "before the second generation of masculinist Romantic poets anxiously examine comparable issues."[22]

Tighe was not alone in questioning the sexual politics of Romantic vision in her poetry – her contemporaries had also made the relationship of active sexual desire and poetic vision central in such early works as Robinson's *Sappho and Phaon* (1796), Dacre's "The Mistress to the Spirit of Her Lover" (1805), and Bannerman's "The Dark Ladie" (1802). Like *Psyche*, these poems reverse the prevailing poetic dynamic of desiring male subject and desired female object. Robinson, like Tighe, did this by eroticizing the Sapphic poet's gaze over the passive body of her male lover, as in "Sonnet X: Describes Phaon":

> Oft o'er that form, enamour'd have I hung,
> On that smooth cheek to mark the deep'ning dyes,
> While from that lip the fragrant breath would rise,
> That lip, like Cupid's bow with rubies strung!
> Still let me gaze upon that polish'd brow,
> O'er which the golden hair luxuriant plays.[23]

While some read the absence of female–female desire in *Sappho and Phaon* as a sign of Robinson's reluctance to associate her poetic ideal with a forbidden sexuality, Jerome McGann instead reads the poem as a prophetic manifesto of "'a woman speaking to women'" about the possibility of an enlightened sexuality.[24] As well as being the origin and end of the poetess identity, "Sappho" in the Romantic period could signify active female desire across a broad spectrum: from female–female desire (including pornographic uses), to revolutionary forms of ostensibly heteronormative desire for an allegorical Phaon, to increasingly politicized visions of Sappho's role inspiring other women, as in Catherine Grace Godwin's *Sappho* of 1824, wherein Phaon is wholly absent.

Active female desire, enacted through the woman's gaze, links Robinson's Sappho, Dacre's Mistress, Tighe's Psyche, and Bannerman's Dark Ladie. The work of Dacre, Bannerman, and Robinson shared a further connection via their embrace of Gothic, which in part accounts for their foregrounding of how poetic vision is gendered, and compels us to consider Romantic and Gothic traditions together. Like the better-known poems of Tighe and Robinson, Bannerman's Gothic ballad "The Dark Ladie" problematizes the specularization of desire that is central to the male poetic identities of, for example, Wordsworth and Coleridge. In Bannerman's ballad, which responds to an earlier poem by Coleridge, crusading knights are enthralled by the gaze of a captive Muslim woman, whose veil invites their scopophilia only to reverse it:

> But, from the Ladie in the veil,
> Their eyes they could not long withdraw,
> And when they tried to speak, that glare
> Still kept them mute with awe![25]

Moments of gazing and unveiling literalize and eroticize Romantic poets' accounts of poetic vision itself, from the Dark Ladie's supernatural resistance to the attempts to unveil her, to Sappho and Psyche's loving looks over the unclothed bodies of their lovers, to the poet's terror as Moneta, "curtained . . . in mysteries," unveils in Keats's *The Fall of Hyperion* (comp. 1819; Canto I, l. 289).

The climactic scene in which Geraldine disrobes before a spellbound Christabel in Coleridge's Gothic poem is one of the era's best-known instances of such specularization of desire, one uniquely lesbian. Coleridge's demonization of (female) desire in "Christabel," like Bannerman's in her volume of ballads, *Tales of Superstition*, demonstrates the necessity of placing Gothic at the center of our understandings of Romanticism and sexuality. Like his contemporaries Bannerman and Robinson, Coleridge distrusted the feminized and maternalized nature often visible in William Wordsworth's "spousal verse." The nightside of nature that Christabel inhabits suffuses her autoerotic and homoerotic experiences with a perversity immediately glimpsed by the poem's outraged critics in 1816, who famously dubbed Coleridge's masterpiece "the most obscene poem in the English language." Unlike Wordsworth's "Nutting," which put feminized nature violently in its place, and concluded with a characteristic admonition to a "dearest maiden," "Christabel" did not establish a narrative of (hetero)sexual maturation, or consummation, to contain the aggressive energies it revealed in the androgynous figures of Christabel and Geraldine. The poem's resistance against such heterocentric metanarratives is built into its formal structure as a heterogeneous fragment. The numerous contemporary conclusions to "Christabel" published after 1816 – typically focused on unveiling the "true" sexuality that the ambiguous Geraldine embodies – attest to Gothic's unique ability to frustrate the will to truth central to the expressive hypothesis of Romantic poetry. Given its aura of perversity, it is telling that "Christabel" had to wait for Byron, a fearless reinventor of the Gothic, to help see it into print in 1816, long after an anxious Wordsworth had removed the poem from the

Lyrical Ballads, worried that "Christabel" "could not be printed along with my poem with any propriety."[26]

The poetry of Byron and Shelley is traditionally associated with a sexual frankness that the earlier generation avoided, and their revived political radicalism often embraced sexual liberties (including feminist liberties, for Shelley). Shelley in particular would become the genteel, postrevolutionary herald of what Robert Southey in 1800 called "the orgasm of the Revolution,"[27] in such later works as *Prometheus Unbound* and *Laon and Cythna*. But Shelley's and Byron's radicalization of aristocratic male sexual privileges drew upon a larger cultural field, the affective revolution that included plebeian and female figures as well: from self-taught poets like Bannerman and Robert Burns, to well-connected genteel poets like Tighe, to socially mobile feminists like Robinson. Burns's bawdy verse is a good example of plebeian writing that reasserted the levelling properties of sex (here, to "mow") in a revolutionary context:

> An' why shou'd na poor bodies m[o]w, m[o]w, m[o]w,
> And why shou'd na poor bodies m[o]w;
> The rich they hae siller, an' houses, an' land,
> Poor bodies hae naething but m[o]w.[28]

Such radicalized heterophilia could coexist with homophilic and homophobic affinities, even within the same poem. Thus, sentimentalized homophilia, for example in Sir Leoline's nostalgia for his friendship with Sir Roland (William Hazlitt's favorite part of "Christabel") is as much a part of this affective revolution as the misogynist homophobia evident in Hazlitt's simultaneous insistence that "there is something disgusting at the bottom of his subject, which is but ill glossed over by a veil of Della Cruscan sentiment."[29] In Hazlitt's review of "Christabel," the republicanism and lush eroticism of cosmopolitan poets like Robert Merry and Mary Robinson (associated with the controversial "Della Cruscan" circle in the 1780s and 1790s) is no longer visible. Instead, as a vestige of "Della Cruscan sentiment," the lesbianism of "Christabel" is symptomatic of the feminization of poetry that a professional critic like Hazlitt sought to combat through such manly gestures as unveiling "disgusting" sentiment. For Hazlitt, young working-class women represented an appropriate erotic ideal for manly Englishmen like himself, a problematic (and safely heterophilic) ideal in light of the sexual dynamics of his infamous 1803 Keswick episode (involving rumors of rape) and his fascination with the young Sarah Walker in *Liber Amoris* (1823).

Sister lovers were the privileged objects of transgressive sexual energies for canonical figures like the early Wordsworth, Byron, and Shelley, and hence they have been widely discussed as a distinctive feature of the Romantic sexual landscape. Suggesting a revolutionary vision of the levelling powers of *fraternité*, the sister-lover ideal also indulges in a narcissistic nostalgia for prelapsarian feminine innocence that women poets did not idealize via sibling incest (though paternal incest did feature in women's fiction). In contrast to this critical emphasis on the radical potential of Romantic male sexualities, I wish to discuss an equally significant sexual ideal found throughout women's poetry, that of unearthly lovers. By considering this neglected feature of Romantic sexuality in relationship to early modern mystical marriage traditions (like reading the poetess forward across the Romantic/Victorian divide), my aim is to situate Romantic poetry, and women's central role therein, within larger developments in sexuality and gender.

From seraphic love to seraphic frenzy

The sexual graphicness of *Don Juan*, or of Burns's bawdy verse, does not typically appear in women's published poetry, yet the eroticized elements of women's verse to which I have referred were not lost on contemporary reviewers. Tighe's religious framework for *Psyche* followed the tradition in which Neoplatonists had reintroduced the myth at the turn of the nineteenth century (that is, as an allegory of the Christian soul's path towards divine love). Yet male reviewers of *Psyche* typically eroticized and secularized Tighe's ostensibly spiritual allegory, praising the poem's ability to "cast . . . a voluptuous and soothing trance."[30] An example of such voluptuousness is Tighe's description of Psyche gazing upon the sleeping Eros:

> o'er his guileless front the ringlets bright
> Their rays of sunny lustre seem to throw,
> That front than polished ivory more white!
> His blooming cheeks with deeper blushes glow
> Than roses scattered o'er a bed of snow.[31]

Part of a centuries-long reappropriation of Petrarchanism by European women poets, Psyche's gaze, like Sappho's, redirects Petrarchan conceits towards a male Beloved, revealing her unabashedly sexual desire:

> Speechless with awe, in transport strangely lost
> Long Psyche stood with fixed adoring eye;
> Her limbs immoveable, her senses tost
> Between amazement, fear, and ecstasy,
> She hangs enamoured o'er the Deity.[32]

The Gentleman's Magazine singled out the above passage for their female readers: "we trust the description of his manly form and features will excite many warm emotions in the breasts of the female readers of this poem."[33]

The uneasy embrace of the erotic and spiritual evident in *Psyche*'s reception was central to the traditions of enthusiasm, Della Cruscanism, Petrarchanism, and devotional verse that inform Romantic poetry of desire from Blake's *Visions of the Daughters of Albion* to Robinson's *Sappho and Phaon*, and Tighe's *Psyche* to Shelley's *Epipsychidion*. Unearthly lovers (e.g., Eros, the mythical Phaon, ghosts, Christ, or angels) allowed women poets to explore female desire with the license uniquely available to classical and mythological subjects. Compared to Byron's and Burns's celebrations of worldly sexuality, unearthly lovers may appear to twenty-first-century readers as instances of eroticism sublimated through religious or sentimental discourses, what Jean Hagstrum dismissed as an "unearthly *angélisme* that dissipated the physical."[34] Such a reading misses not only the "profoundly synaesthetic and transformational" nature of sensibility, according to McGann,[35] but also the Christian traditions of mystical marriage and devotional poetry (and the secular tradition of Petrarchanism), that these Romantic poets inherited and transformed.

Early modern and early eighteenth-century poets enjoyed a rich tradition of eroticized spirituality in verse that allowed women in particular to use an ostensibly heteronormative desire for Christ in order to resist sexuality channeled through domestic and reproductive duties. Well-known examples of this eroticized spirituality in the verse of early modern poets like Aemelia Lanyer often combined religious discourse with Petrarchan conventions in order to devise new ways of voicing desire for a Beloved: typically Christ (available as both a feminine and a masculine figure), but also in the form of other safe male figures such as dead husbands, fathers, or patrons.

Elizabeth Singer Rowe's "Seraphic Love," included in her enduringly popular *Miscellaneous Works* (1739), is a relatively late example of the mystical marriage informing Romantic poetry of desire:

> Thou beauty's vast abyss, abstract of all
> My thoughts can lovely, great, or splendid call;
> To thee in heav'nly flames, and pure desires,
> My ravish'd soul impatiently aspires.[36]

Popular with male and female early modern writers, such a celebration of mystical marriage would become increasingly difficult to evoke in the wake of the rise of rational religion and evangelicalism in the eighteenth century. Rowe's numerous reinterpretations of the Song of Songs included such erotic blazons of Christ as heavenly Bridegroom, in light of which we should reconsider the examples I discussed earlier from Robinson and Tighe:

> The roses that his lovely face adorn,
> Out-blush the purple glories of the morn.
> The waving ringlets of his graceful hair,
> Black as the shining plumes the ravens wear.
> His eyes would win the most obdurate heart,
> Victorious love in ev'ry look they dart.
> His balmy lips diffuse divine perfumes,
> And on his cheek a bed of spices blooms.
> His breast, like polish'd iv'ry, smooth and fair,
> With veins which with the sapphires may compare.
> ("CANT. Chap. V.")[37]

Such "erotic portraits of Christ" and evocations of mystical marriage to him were also "often written by male writers for the contemplation of male readers" in the early modern era, "and betray little if any anxiety that such language was sexually transgressive."[38]

The transgressive charge of such writings began to eclipse their religious conventionality in the eighteenth century, however, as Rowe's reception reveals. Rowe was a Dissenter known as a paragon of charitable piety, and yet by the time of her death in 1737 her contemporaries had begun to question the imbrication of the sexual and spiritual central to her religious vision. Isaac Watts, who had celebrated his mystical marriage to Christ in early writings, later distanced himself from such passion; in his "Preface" to Rowe's *Devout Exercises of the Heart* (1738) he noted that "it was much the fashion, even among some Divines of eminence, in former years, to express the Fervours of devout Love to our Saviour in the Style of the Song of Solomon."[39] Unfortunately, those, like Rowe, who are "raptur'd with such a Flame of divine Affection" are now liable to have their effusions "perversely prophaned by an unholy Construction."[40] By the end of the eighteenth century, such perverse prophanation had become the norm, typically expressed in politicized debates over the crisis in enthusiasm.

As the most important precedent for Romantic women poets' unearthly lovers, Christ had represented to earlier writers both "a male lover and a female beloved," attesting to the "fluidity of gender identifications in mystical marriage writing."[41] Thus, that Aemelia Lanyer in her passion poem *Salve deus* (1611) "offers a beautiful lover Christ," complete with eroticized blazoning of Christ's body, "to female readers does not mean that she is appealing to them solely on heteroerotic terms."[42] Similarly for Romantics, Phaon and Eros are safely male in one respect, but like Christ they are also dangerously unearthly and explicitly mythic figures, whose pre-Christian, pagan origins and non-reproductive sexuality signal their authors' departure from the heteronormative sexuality espoused, for example, by Hannah More's repentant "Sinful Sally" (1796):

> Courting days were thus beginning,
>   And I soon had proved a wife;
> Oh, if I had kept from sinning,
>   Now how blessed had been my life![43]

The unmarried, evangelical More enforced this exclusively reproductive sexuality throughout her popular works, an earthbound vision as alien to the raptures of Rowe's devotional verse as to the classical *frissons* of Robinson's *Sappho* and Tighe's *Psyche*. Writing nearly a century after Rowe, Tighe and Robinson had gained access to newly contentious eighteenth-century aesthetic traditions – for example, the increasingly secularized discourses of the sublime, associationism, and the Gothic – which effectively severed the connection between desire and the divine that earlier writers enjoyed.

While Rowe and other early eighteenth-century poets of "seraphic love" figured desire as seraphic ascent towards divine union, Romantic poets often imagined their supernaturalized desires as descent and alienation. Ann Batten Cristall's "The Enthusiast. Arla" (1795) evoked this earlier seraphic love only to invert it. Arla's "seraphic song" describes how "a cherub downward flew" to her:[44]

> Such hues empyreal his bright frame adorn,
> He seems a ray of the eternal morn!
> So fraught with living fires, his ardent eyes
> Shot forth long beams which sparkled through the skies;
> From him bright emanations darted round,
> And his waved pinions gave celestial sound!
> Entranced, nor doubting what her fancy saw,
> Her youthful bosom heaved with sacred awe.

> (p. 335)

Revising Petrarchan and mystical marriage conventions in this vision of Arla and her angelic beloved, Cristall's poem is unmistakably Romantic, and Blakean, in its allegiance to a fallen imagination. Cristall's angelology is precise, for in attempting seraphic ascent in her song, and seeming to succeed instead in drawing down a cherub, Arla has invoked the first fallen cherub, Lucifer. And indeed a Satanic seducer does exploit Arla's "seraphic frenzy": "Potent in ill, he bent his subtle powers / To draw young Arla in his wily snare": as "Her passions were already set on fire" by the angel, soon "Her sweet affections glide" to her seducer (pp. 336–7). Cristall's "The Enthusiast. Arla" illustrates the transformation that "seraphic love" had undergone in a new era of enthusiasm in crisis: seraphic love was now a dangerously sexualized "seraphic frenzy," associated in the 1790s with groundless political ideals and rebellion. While, like Rowe, a member of a prominent Dissenting circle, Cristall inhabited a radically altered cultural landscape in the 1790s, when the ancient embrace of the erotic and the spiritual was, as in "Christabel," "perversely prophaned by an unholy Construction."

Cristall imagines such an unorthodox union of human and (delusively) divine to illustrate Arla's "enthusiastic raptures blind" (p. 335), and also to purchase greater latitude in voicing women's desire. But Cristall's project is also more ambitious, and merits her frequent comparisons to Blake: the celestial lover offers the poet a tantalizing glimpse of post-Edenic sexuality reimagined, when humans commune once more with angels, and thus (as in early modern writings) also of women's transformation of the conditions of oppression traced to Eve's transgression. This spiritualized framework for desire became itself the subject of Romantic women's poetry of unearthly lovers, often evoking a wish that desire and sexuality be transformed from their fallen state. Unearthly lovers (sometimes "divine," usually fallen) represent a major, unexamined vein of sexualized poetic inspiration for Romantic poets, a motif resonant with its early modern roots in religious discourses, but one which had come unmoored from its religious context in an increasingly fragmented, naturalized, and supernaturalized Romantic poetics.

The canonical Romantics' obsession with rewriting the Fall is well known; as Lucy Newlyn has discussed, male poets offered new visions of the fortunate Fall as a means of "expressing sympathy with the female lot, and for presenting sex as growth" in works like *Don Juan*, "Christabel" and "The Eve of St. Agnes."[45] Blake offered the most elaborate revisions of this Miltonic theme in *Thel*, *The Visions of the Daughters of Albion*, and *The Book of Urizen*. In *The Visions*, composed while Blake moved in the same circles as Wollstonecraft (and perhaps Cristall), he takes this refashioning of female sexuality into new territory by figuring Oothoon's liberation from male violence and possessiveness as her desire to entice other women into her lover's bed, and her ability to enjoy watching "their wanton play, / In lovely copulation, bliss on bliss" (pl. 10). For Blake, liberation from the moral codes restraining sexual desires should not return us to the stasis of Eden, but transform the fallen world anew. Eve's trespass at the tree of knowledge would no longer bar fallen humanity from the immortality granted by the tree of life (see Genesis 3.24):

For the cherub with his flaming sword is hereby commanded to leave his guard at the tree of life; and when he does, the whole creation will be consumed and appear infinite and holy, whereas it now appears finite and corrupt.

(*The Marriage of Heaven and Hell*, pl. 14)

"This will come to pass by an improvement of sensual enjoyment," prophesies Blake's devil. Like Oothoon, Arla had imagined revolutionary possibilities for sensual enjoyment, but had been similarly betrayed by the oldest of male villainies. Cristall restored the fallen Arla to paternal affection and "cherished reason" (p. 341), and even followed Arla's narrative of repentance with a separate "Song of Arla, Written During her Enthusiasm," a first-person rhapsody that reaffirms the doomed vision that the omniscient narrator of "The Enthusiast" had chastened.

The corruption of seraphic love into seraphic frenzy did not eliminate from the Romantic period this ancient theme, and its potential intermingling of mystical marriage with older traditions of the loves of the sons of God for the daughters of man. In visions of fallen sexuality redeemed or reversed we can often find hints of the intercession of fallen angels, from the "Eden Lucifer" suggestively glimpsed in the utopian eroticism of Shelley's *Epipsychidion*, to his admirer Mary Ann Browne's oblique vision of a new Eden in "The Remembrance of a Dream":

> Yet we seemed from other mortals severed
> – We might have been in the world alone.
> There were none to watch us, and none to chide us,
>   No jealous fears, no curious eyes;
> Our love flowed on, the power to guide us,
> And 'neath its spell we were good and wise.[46]

A devout Christian, unlike Shelley and Byron, whom she admired, Browne similarly rejects God's mutually exclusive opposition between the tree of knowledge and the tree of life, seeing Eden instead through the Serpent's eyes, as a paradise where Eve could be simultaneously "good and wise." Like Coleridge, Tighe, and Robinson before her, Browne sets sexual knowledge at the heart of inspiration and intellectual liberation. "The Remembrance of a Dream" is a dubious vision of paradise diffracted, like the fragment "Kubla Khan: A Vision," through a series of formal prisms (memory, dream) that signal both the illusiveness and the intensity of her desire.

Waking from this dream of Eden reimagined, Browne's poet may be addressing her predecessor Shelley (whose grave famously designated him *cor cordium*, heart of hearts) as her absent beloved: "thy heart of hearts is blending / Its vital stream of love with mine." Shelley's *Epipsychidion* had offered a more elaborate vision of a new Eden suffused with sacred sexuality, wherein he might realize his utopian dream of fusion with an unattainable female "antitype": "The fountains of our deepest life, shall be / Confused in passion's golden purity . . . We shall become the same, we shall be one / Spirit within two frames, oh! wherefore two? One passion in twin-hearts" (ll. 570–5). Browne's poem "The Spirit-Tryst" reenacts Shelley's Edenic encounter in *Epipsychidion*:

> Kiss me, Mine Own, and I will lift
> My lips to answer thy caresses;
> Ay, freely shower the precious gift.[47]

The intense physicality of *Epipsychidion*'s eroticism is shared by Browne's poem, via the rhapsodic language of Canticles. Browne specifically addressed Shelley (and Byron) in several poems in *Mont Blanc* (1827), and in later works like "Spirit-Tryst" and "Remembrance" (following a Christian conversion in 1832) she once again reconnects seraphic love to the dubious forms it had acquired in the controversial works of unbelievers like Shelley (in *Epipsychidion*) and Byron (in *Heaven and Earth*).

"The Spirit-Tryst" may appear as the sublimated *angélisme* Hagstrum warned of, but in fact Browne, as committed a Christian as she seems a Shelleyan and Byronic poet, continued this epithalamic tradition that remained central to Romanticism, without shying away from the transgressive echoes that Byron and Shelley had reawakened in their treatments of this theme. Browne's friend Letitia Landon was even bolder in her transformations of female desire written in the shadow of Shelley and Byron, and her poetry would in turn significantly influence Barrett Browning and Tennyson. By the end of the Romantic period, "spousal verse" had wandered far from its Wordsworthian incarnation as the heterophilic male poet's consummation of his love of female nature. Vulnerable to the perverse profanations visited upon "Christabel," and embodied in the dubious forms of unearthly lovers, the embrace of poetry and sexuality has proven to be one of Romanticism's enduring legacies.

NOTES

I am grateful to James Chandler, Kari E. Lokke, Maureen McLane, and Sue Wiseman for helpful suggestions on different aspects of this chapter.

1 Lynn Hunt and Margaret Jacobs, "The Affective Revolution in 1790s Britain," *Eighteenth-Century Studies* 34/4 (2001), pp. 491–521, at pp. 497, 510.
2 Letitia Landon, in *Life and Literary Remains of L. E. L.*, ed. Laman Blanchard, 2 vols. (London, 1841), vol. II, p. 150; Landon, *Romance and Reality*, ed. F. J. Sypher, 3 vols. (Delmar: Scholars' Facsimiles and Reprints, 1998), vol. III, p. 181.

3 Landon, *Romance*, vol. II, p. 119.
4 Byron, *Byron's Letters and Journals*, ed. Leslie Marchand, 12 vols. (Cambridge, MA: Harvard University Press, 1973–82), vol. VII, p. 225.
5 Judith Pascoe, "'Unsex'd Females': Barbauld, Robinson, and Smith," in *The Cambridge Companion to English Literature 1740–1830*, ed. Thomas Keymer and Jon Mee (Cambridge: Cambridge University Press), pp. 211–26.
6 D. S. Neff, "Bitches, Mollies, and Tommies: Byron, Masculinity, and the History of Sexualities," *Journal of the History of Sexuality* 11/3 (2002), pp. 395–438, at p. 438.
7 Lady Blessington, *Conversations of Lord Byron*, ed. Ernest J. Lovell (Princeton: Princeton University Press, 1969), p. 110.
8 *English Masculinities*, ed. Michele Cohen and Tim Hitchcock (London: Longman, 1999), p. 8.
9 De Jackson includes approximately 900 female poets between 1770 and 1835 in *Romantic Poetry by Women: A Bibliography* (Oxford: Clarendon Press, 1993), p. xv; the number of volumes is from Stuart Curran's seminal essay, "The 'I' Altered," in *Romanticism and Feminism*, ed. Anne Mellor (Bloomington: Indiana University Press, 1988), pp. 185–207.
10 Richard Cronin, *Romantic Victorians: English Literature, 1824–1840* (Basingstoke: Palgrave, 2002), p. 97.
11 See de Jackson's "Note on the Annual Rate of Publication," in his *Romantic Poetry*, pp. 392–4.
12 Lee Erikson, *The Economy of Literary Form: English Literature and the Industrialization of Publishing, 1800–1850* (Baltimore: Johns Hopkins University Press, 1996), p. 25.
13 On Hemans's sales, see William St. Clair, *The Reading Nation in the Romantic Period* (Cambridge: Cambridge University Press, 2004), pp. 607–8, 715–19.
14 Laura Mandell, "Introduction: the Poetess Tradition," *Romanticism on the Net: The Transatlantic Poetess* 29–30 (February–May 2003), www.erudit.org/revue/ron/2003/v/n29/index.html (accessed April 15, 2008).
15 Herbert Tucker, "House Arrest: The Domestication of English Poetry in the 1820s," *New Literary History* 25/3 (1994), pp. 521–58, at p. 542.
16 Kathy Alexis Psomiades, "'The Lady of Shalott' and the Critical Fortunes of Victorian Poetry," *The Cambridge Companion to Victorian Poetry*, ed. Joseph Bristow (Cambridge: Cambridge University Press, 2000), pp. 25–45, at p. 39 (emphasis original).
17 Cronin, *Romantic Victorians*, p. 107.
18 Stuart Curran, "Mary Robinson and New Lyric," *Women's Writing* 9/1 (2002), pp. 9–23. Curran also made a case for considering Tennyson as poetess in his plenary talk at the Mary Robinson conference in 2000.
19 Blessington, "The Stock in Trade of Modern Poetesses," in *British Women Poets of the Romantic Era*, ed. Paula Feldman (Baltimore: Johns Hopkins University Press, 1997), p. 152.
20 Hemans, "The Grave of a Poetess," in *Romantic Women Poets*, ed. Duncan Wu (Oxford: Blackwell Publishing, 1997), p. 574.
21 Harriet Kramer Linkin, "Recuperating Romanticism in Mary Tighe's *Psyche*," in *Romanticism and Women Poets*, ed. Stephen Behrendt and Harriet Kramer Linkin (Lexington: Kentucky University Press, 1999), p. 159.

22 Linkin, "Recuperating," pp. 157, 152.

23 Robinson, in Wu, *Romantic Women Poets*, p. 194.

24 Jerome McGann, *The Poetics of Sensibility: A Revolution in Literary Style* (Oxford: Oxford University Press, 1996), p. 102.

25 Anne Bannerman, *Tales of Superstition and Chivalry* (Edinburgh: Vernor & Hood, 1802), p. 6. See Craciun, *Fatal Women of Romanticism* (Cambridge: Cambridge University Press, 2003), pp. 156–94.

26 William Wordsworth, in *Collected Letters of S. T. Coleridge*, ed. Earl Leslie Griggs, 6 vols. (Oxford: Clarendon Press, 1956–71), vol. I, p. 643n.

27 Robert Southey, 1800 letter to Coleridge, *New Letters of Robert Southey*, ed. Kenneth Curry, 2 vols. (New York: Columbia University Press, 1965), vol. I, p. 215.

28 Robert Burns, "Poor Bodies Do Naething But M[o]w" (comp. 1792), *The Merry Muses of Caledonia* (1799), facs. edn. with introduction by G. Ross Roy (Columbia: University of South Carolina Press, 1999), pp. 80–1.

29 William Hazlitt, review in the *Examiner* (June 2, 1816), in *Romantic Bards and British Reviewers*, ed. John Hayden (Lincoln: University of Nebraska Press, 1971), p. 146.

30 *Critical Review* 4 (June 1812), pp. 606–9, at p. 607.

31 Tighe, *Psyche*, in Feldman, *British Women Poets*, p. 767.

32 Ibid., pp. 767–8.

33 *The Gentleman's Magazine* 82 (1812), pp. 464–7, at p. 466.

34 Jean Hagstrum, *The Romantic Body: Love and Sexuality in Keats, Wordsworth and Blake* (Knoxville: University of Tennessee Press, 1985), p. 20.

35 McGann, *The Poetics*, p. 82.

36 Rowe, *Poetry of Elizabeth Singer Rowe*, "Introduction" by Madeleine Forrell Marshall (Lewiston/Queenston: Edwin Mellen Press, n.d.), p. 222.

37 Ibid., p. 206.

38 Erica Longfellow, *Women and Religious Writing in Early Modern England* (Cambridge: Cambridge University Press, 2004), p. 82.

39 Isaac Watts, "Preface" to Rowe's *Devout Exercises of the Heart* (London: 1738), p. xiii. Note that the pages in the British Library copy from which I quote are misnumbered, so that p. xiii is followed by p. vi.

40 Watts, "Preface", p. vi.

41 Longfellow, *Women*, p. 83.

42 Ibid., pp. 83–4.

43 Hannah More, "The Story of Sinful Sally" (1796), in Wu, *Romantic Women Poets*, p. 51.

44 Anne Batten Cristall, "The Enthusiast. Arla." in Wu, *Romantic Women Poets*, pp. 333, 335. Subsequent references in the text.

45 Lucy Newlyn, *Paradise Lost and the Romantic Reader* (Oxford: Oxford University Press), p. 7.

46 Mary Anne Browne, "The Remembrance of a Dream," *Dublin University Magazine* 26 (December 1845), pp. 690–1.

47 Mary Anne Browne, "The Spirit-Tryst," *Dublin University Magazine* 26 (December 1845), p. 689.

FURTHER READING

Craciun, Adriana, *Fatal Women of Romanticism* (Cambridge: Cambridge University Press, 2003)

Elfenbein, Andrew, *Romantic Genius: The Prehistory of a Homosexual Role* (New York: Columbia University Press, 1999)

Hofkosh, Sonia, *Sexual Politics and the Romantic Author* (Cambridge: Cambridge University Press, 1998)

Mellor, Anne, ed., *Romanticism and Feminism* (Bloomington: Indiana University Press, 1988)

Ross, Marlon, *The Contours of Masculine Desire: Romanticism and the Rise of Women's Poetry* (Oxford: Oxford University Press, 1989)

Sha, Richard, ed., *Historicizing Romantic Sexuality*, Romantic Circles Praxis Series, January 2006, www.rc.umd.edu/praxis/sexuality/index.html

Shiebinger, Londa L., *Nature's Body: Gender and the Making of Modern Science* (Boston: Beacon, 1993)

9

TIM FULFORD

Poetry, peripheries and empire

In 1768, when Captain James Cook set sail for Tahiti, Britain had only recently wrested control of Quebec from France. It still ruled its American colonies from London. Spain was still the imperial power in Mexico, California, and "Louisiana" – a vast area of which nobody knew the limits, for parts of America's northwest coast were still uncharted. Britons knew still less of Africa, and were second to the Dutch in the exploration of South East Asia.

By 1833 the picture had changed vastly: Britain had lost its first American empire and, after fifty years of intense exploration and conquest, acquired a new one. It had colonized Australia, spread its missionaries to Polynesia, and planted its manufacturers in South America. It had penetrated Africa, and charted much of the Polar seas and America's west coast. It had crossed Canada, taken possession of India, occupied Burma and founded Singapore. Unrivalled on the seas, it was the most powerful empire in Europe and its explorers were national heroes.

Global power changed culture at home and these changes helped precipitate Romanticism. From the 1780s, London became a city of shows, teeming with the products of empire. As a Russian visitor remarked, it was like a "continuous fair"; its shops offered spectacular displays of "absolutely everything one can think of."[1] Oriental muslins, Chinese porcelain, Javanese furniture, even caymans and leopards could be viewed, handled, and purchased. And many Britons, rich from the profits of colonial crops, including coffee, indigo, sugar, and, increasingly as empire in India was extended, opium, could afford to cultivate a taste for the exotic.

The poetry that we today call Romantic originated not in celebration of but in opposition to the results, at home, of profit made abroad. William Cowper, for example, recognized in consumerist London a culture of excess that put him in mind of the oriental fleshpots of the Bible:

> where has commerce such a mart,
> So rich, so throng'd, so drain'd, and so supplied,
> As London, opulent, enlarg'd and still
> Increasing London? Babylon of old
> Not more the glory of the earth, than she
> A more accomplish'd world's chief glory now.
> (*Task*, Book I, ll. 715–24)[2]

Wordsworth, who was deeply influenced by Cowper, also viewed London as an imperial storehouse, dazzling but ultimately shallow, as it uprooted people from their origins, turning them into deracinated shows in a huge fairground:

> The Swede, the Russian; from the genial south,
> The Frenchman and the Spaniard; from remote
> America, the Hunter-Indian; Moors,
> Malays, Lascars, the Tartar, the Chinese,
> And Negro ladies in white muslin gowns.
> (*Prelude* [1805], Book VII, ll. 239–43)[3]

The retreat from London to the country – that essential element of Romanticism – was a retreat to an idealized rural periphery not just from the urban centre but also from the effects of empire. Like Cowper before him, Wordsworth was rejecting the imperial metropolis, offended by the evidence everywhere visible in its streets of Britain's new power to exploit the furthest reaches of the globe for its own benefit. Like Cowper too, he preferred the morality that he detected in the peasant's relationship to the land – the peasants concerned being those in Wales, Scotland, and the Lake District, who were sufficiently remote not to be affected by the new capitalist agriculture.

The idealization of the rural fringes was an idealization of cultures and languages long colonized by England and English. Under way by the 1760s, it was, at its most shallow, simply a self-indulgent desire, on the part of urbanites, for a brief escape to an exotic, pastoral idyll. A new industry sprang up servicing English visitors' longing to see rugged landscapes from safe viewpoints and listen to blind harpists in Welsh inns.[4] Ancient cultures were packaged for tourists as part of a heritage experience. Needless to say, the recent history of cultural and linguistic dispossession was excluded from the tour – even though the Scottish Highlands were, after the rebellion of 1745, under military occupation. Writers did, however, romanticize the safely distant history of ancient Welsh and Scottish resistance to English rule: in Thomas Gray's "The Bard" (1757), a medieval Celtic leader laments the defeat of his Welsh tribal culture by English invaders. In Thomas Macpherson's Ossian poems (1760–63), another bard mourns the destruction of Scottish clans. In both texts, a patriarchal culture is idealized at the moment of its death; both, moreover, are offered as English versions of oral poetry originally performed in Celtic languages.[5]

The anti-English nationalism of Macpherson's poems was muted by their location in the remote past and their elegiac tone. They offered a sentimental admiration for a Gaelic past rather than an angry indictment of present English colonialism or an urgent advocacy of change. In this respect they influenced Walter Scott's chivalric romances and, later, his Waverley novels. Yet they laid the foundation for more radical writing, which brought their Romantic anti-colonialism into the context of present-day nationalist struggles. Ossian was enormously influential in the European countries trying to break free of the Hapsburg and Ottoman empires; it also prepared the ground for the reception of Burns, who adapted vernacular Scots and updated the folk ballad, often to republican effect, for he sympathized with the American and French revolutions (and thereby with the enemies of his own government). Burns became a key figure for English Romantics, for he demonstrated that rural culture and rustic language could give the poet a language of moral power and critical authority that the polite poetry produced in commercial, metropolitan London utterly lacked. Wordsworth effectively anglicized Burns's position, speaking for an English rural fringe against the spreading culture of capitalism just as Burns did for Scottish culture.[6]

In Wales, antiquarian interest in the bardic past sparked a cultural revival with contemporary nationalist implications. Scholar-poets such as Iolo Morganwg collected Welsh verse from the time of resistance to English domination. They interpreted and translated (and in Iolo's case, forged) medieval texts, creating a national canon for a Welsh nation to identify itself by. They codified the socioreligious role played by bards, and invented/revived cultural ceremonies in which that role was ritualized. By these means they created/renewed a native tradition through which the Welsh could reconnect themselves with the culture of their precolonial past, rediscovering a pride in themselves as they rediscovered the power and sophistication of their ancient literature. Like Burns, the Welsh nationalists sympathized with the American revolutionists' fight against rule from London; Iolo and many others argued for the historical truth of the legend that the medieval prince Madoc, fleeing from the domination of Wales by the English, sailed the Atlantic, landed in America before Columbus, and founded a colony there that intermarried with the Indians. Somewhere in newly independent America, they believed, there still survived a tribe of Welsh-Indians, living free from colonial domination in the kind of society the Welsh had once enjoyed in Wales itself.[7]

The example of England's colonies making common cause was inspiring for young English radical poets who were searching for a ground from which to resist their own commercial culture and arbitrary government. The young Robert Southey befriended Welsh scholars and used their revival of bardic culture in his epic poem *Madoc* (1794–1805), in which the exiled prince is the hero, the invading English the villains. Southey's Madoc emigrates to pre-Columbus America, only to discover that there, too, rural people suffer under the imperial tyranny of a city-culture – the Aztecs enslave the surrounding tribes. Madoc frees the tribes and defeats the Aztecs. The liberated Indians then intermarry with the exiled Welsh to found a free, hybrid culture that cannot be imagined in Britain. Thus Southey constructs an alternative, ideal history in which the actual oppression of rural Wales by England, and of rural America by the Aztecs (and later by the colonizing Spanish and English) is superseded by an interracial colonial utopia, as once oppressed peoples find liberty and pursue happiness together in a patriarchal, tribal and bardic society.

England's colonial domination of Scotland, Wales, and America consti-tuted a domination of fellow white people. Also a formative issue for Roman-ticism, though less commonly so, was Britain's domination of black people. In Parliament, Edmund Burke lambasted the British governors of Bengal for organizing the rape and pillage of Indian gentlewomen – treatment they would never have permitted white gentlewomen to suffer. In verse, Cowper developed these accusations into a general critique of British rule in India. "Hast thou," Cowper asked his nation,

> though suckled at fair Freedom's breast,
> Exported slavery to the conquer'd East,
> Pull'd down the tyrants India served with dread,
> And raised thyself, a greater, in their stead?
> Gone thither arm'd and hungry, return'd full,
> Fed from the richest veins of the Mogul,
> A despot big with power obtained by rapine and by stealth?
> With Asiatic vices stored thy mind,
> But left their virtues and thine own behind,
> And, having truck'd thy soul, brought home the fee
> To tempt the poor to sell himself to thee?
>
> (*Expostulation*, 365–75)

Here empire is corrupting: Britons are degenerating into Western replicas of the old Eastern conquerors of India, resembling the parasitic Mogul dynasty as they enslave and cheat the native people. Cowper is uncompromising: he does not simply condemn individual colonists for specific misdeeds but questions the imperial project *per se*, asking his nation whether it is not becoming alienated from the virtues of liberty and lawfulness on which it prides itself.

It was not only the colonization of the East Indies that worried Cowper and others like him. Increasingly through the 1780s Britons began to make objections to the enslavement of Africans in the West Indies. Many of those objecting were men and women who, appalled by the culture of consumption they saw spreading across Britain, participated in a religious revival of the Church of England. These Evangelicals attacked colonial slavery as a violation of Christian principles. Committed to reviving Britons' national morality, they campaigned in Parliament and the press. Those who possessed literary ability, Cowper and Hannah More among them, wrote propaganda verse that demanded readers' pity for black slaves. They wrote verse because it was a prestigious genre, taken seriously in the public sphere. Published in newspapers and magazines, it was respected by legislators such as Charles James Fox, the Whig leader and parliamentary opponent of the slave trade, who prided himself on his knowledge of the classics of English and ancient poetry. At the same time, verse also aimed to change the hearts and minds of the expanding bourgeoisie who increasingly read periodicals: it was emotively powerful as well as culturally authoritative. Abolitionist texts, however, were not necessarily anti-imperialist: More, for example, wanted an end to slavery in the West Indies but not to the plantation system or to Britain's occupation of the Caribbean. The sugar and coffee, it was hoped, would be harvested by the willing labor of emancipated former slaves.[8]

Some writers took the Evangelicals' verse in a more radical direction. Typically, these writers were from groups that faced social disadvantage or exclusion within British culture. The Unitarians were one such. Prohibited because of their unorthodox religious belief from holding public office, they regarded themselves as victims of unjust laws maintained by an unrepresentative Parliament. In their eyes, colonial slavery was not an anomaly in an otherwise peaceful mercantile empire, but the epitome of a system of arbitrary government that, at home and abroad, enriched a few at the expense of others' freedom. If Britain did not reform this system and grant liberty, then revolution was justified. Thus Robert Southey, one of a generation of intellectuals who embraced Dissenting religion, condoned the uprising of enslaved Africans against planters in his "To the Genius of Africa" (1797). His friend Coleridge, also a recent convert to Unitarianism, not only justified slaves' violent rebellion but also connected their treatment with that of the other native peoples ruled by Britain. In "Africa," he wrote, "the unnumbered Victims of a detestable Slave-trade – in Asia the desolated plains of Indostan and the Million whom a rice-contracting Governor caused to perish – in America the recent enormities of the Scalp-Merchants – the four Quarters of the Globe groan beneath the intolerable iniquity of this nation!"⁹ As a critic of government at home, Coleridge took it as his prophetic role to show his fellow Britons that their empire was a sham. Empire was the globalization of tyranny and brutality.

Southey and Coleridge were middle-class, university-educated intellectuals. The extremity of their rhetoric reveals their degree of disenchantment with the culture of "getting and spending" (in Wordsworth's words) that they saw in London, Bristol, and Liverpool – the cities enriched by imperial trade.¹⁰ But it also reveals the political confidence given to radical groups by events in America. When Britain's colonists there had rebelled against arbitrary government, they had won the support of English Unitarians – including Southey and Coleridge's heroes, Richard Price and Joseph Priestley – who likened the colonists' political disenfranchisement to their own. And when the colonists proved successful in their revolution against rule from London, Dissenters of all classes were quick to turn them into morale-boosting (and heroic) examples of how imperial government could be overthrown. The London artisan and antinomian Christian, William Blake, printed his own tribute to the colonial rebels. *America: a Prophecy* (1793) is an anti-imperialist allegory in which Blake predicts the destruction of his own nation's armies:

> at the feet of Washington down fall'n
> They grovel on the sand and writhing lie. While all
> The British soldiers thro' the thirteen states sent up a howl
> Of anguish: threw their swords & muskets to the earth & ran
> From their encampments and dark castles seeking where to hide
> From the grim flames . . .
>
> (pl. 15)¹¹

By the 1790s then, a new generation of poets was coming to public attention, a generation for which opposition to British rule in America, India, and the West Indies was formative. Romantic poetry was, in origin, anti-imperialist.

By 1814, matters had changed considerably. In that year, Wordsworth was in agreement with Coleridge and Southey when, in *The Excursion*, he declared Britain's mission to be the colonization of East and West with its surplus people. These were people from the rural peripheries of Britain who, stricken with poverty, as Wordsworth had earlier lamented in *Lyrical Ballads*, had better emigrate to Canada, Australia, and Africa than be sucked into the London that corrupted most who went there.

So the wide waters, open to the power,
The will, the instincts, and appointed needs
Of Britain, do invite her to cast off
Her swarms, and in succession send them forth;
Bound to establish new communities
On every shore whose aspect favours hope
Or bold adventure . . .
                                    . . . Your Country must complete
Her glorious destiny. Begin even now.
                        (*The Excursion*, Book IX, ll. 375–408)[12]

Wordsworth foresaw a global anglicization as British people carried their values to "savage" lands – a process already under way in North America, since a high proportion of the army comprised Welsh, Scots and Irish, many of whom remained in the colonies after their term of service or just plain deserted to live and trade with Indians. Having been an opponent of Britain's commercial empire, Wordsworth had now become a chief proponent of settlement colonization. How had this change come about?

One of the principal causes was compassion: Wordsworth thought emigration the only hope for the rural laborers against whose eviction and impoverishment in Britain he protested. But another factor in changing his mind was the Napoleonic Wars. From 1798, France embarked on a series of imperial conquests, invading Egypt, Spain, Portugal, Italy, Russia, and the Swiss cantons, and threatening Britain itself. Faced with an expanding martial France, even Britons who had initially welcomed the French Revolution realized it was taking a different course from its American predecessor. Coleridge, Southey, and Wordsworth were increasingly suspicious of Napoleon, a crucial issue being his reimposition of slavery in the French colonies and his edict removing people of color from France. In 1802, Wordsworth registered his disgust in two powerful sonnets, "Toussaint L'Ouverture" (in which he sympathized with the black liberator of Haiti who had been betrayed by French duplicity and left to rot in prison), and "The Banished Negroes" (in which he places the reader face to face with a black refugee, torn first from her homeland and then from her adopted France).

Hatred of despotism pushed Romantic poets to an accommodation with the established British order of which they had been so critical. Afraid of being colonized by the French, they added their weight to a defense of the realm – and, following from this, a defense of the British Empire, whose wealth and strength helped resist French advances. Moreover, in 1807 it became easier to defend Britain's empire because Parliament abolished the slave trade. This historic act, the culmination of the campaign that had helped turn Coleridge and Southey into poets, further reconciled one-time opponents of empire to its continuation. After 1807 liberal writers felt able (however myopically) to portray Britain's empire as one in which native peoples received liberty and law, in contrast to their enslavement and exploitation in the empires of Spain, Portugal, France and the Ottomans. And in this revised view of empire, the agents of civilization were not only naval officers (who now patrolled the seas to stamp out illegal slave-trading) but also missionaries.

The missionary movement began in 1795, when the London Missionary Society was founded and sent mostly preachers to the South Sea islands that Cook had recently visited. By the early nineteenth century the movement had expanded, with Southey's favorable reviews of missionary reports helping to bring the movement to the notice of the middle-class public. He worked in tandem with William Wilberforce, who led a parliamentary campaign on behalf of missions. By 1813, the campaign had succeeded in forcing a reluctant East India Company, afraid that attempts to proselytize might lead to disturbances among its Hindu and Muslim subjects, to support Christian missionaries in its territories.

A new justification of empire was now under way: British rule brought Christian civilization as well as liberty. This ideology in turn produced a modification of a popular genre that had itself been bound up with imperial issues since its origins – the verse romance. Ever since 1704, when the Arabian Nights Tales began to appear in French translation, poets had occasionally tried their hands at stories of love set in an exotic East. Until the 1820s, however, such stories usually displayed no more than a smattering of Oriental color. William Collins said of his "Persian Eclogues" (1742) that they might as well have been called Irish as Persian: their exoticism was non-specific. By the second half of the eighteenth century, a more detailed appropriation of Eastern culture was beginning. In France, Germany, and Britain a new generation of scholars was translating Arabic and Persian poetry from manuscript. In doing so, they brought far more precise and historically aware versions of Eastern cultures back to Europe than had previously been the case. These versions had their limitations since the scholars' understanding was largely textual, made from European libraries rather than after immersion in the contemporary Middle East.

William Jones was the foremost scholar to bring about this transformation in Britain. "Persian" Jones, as he was nicknamed, used his astonishing facility as a linguist to translate ancient Arabic and Persian poets.[13] And Jones was not only a translator, but a pioneering cultural historian who replaced Collins's vague and generic Orientalism with a sophisticated argument for the importance of Arabic and of Persian poetry as intense art emerging from distinct cultural traditions and specific geographic conditions. By 1783 Jones had been rewarded for his brilliant Orientalist scholarship with the position of judge in the supreme court in Britain's colony in Bengal. Once established there, he began in-depth study of Indian culture that was to transform Orientalism – and Orientalist poetry – irrevocably. Having rapidly acquired Sanskrit, Jones had by 1784 made his groundbreaking contribution to philology and anthropology, showing that there was a common Indo-European language family and that Indian civilization and philosophy were sources of the Egyptian and Greek culture to which Europe traced its roots. But Jones's studies were not only linguistic. With the Asiatic Society of Bengal, which he founded, he embarked upon a comprehensive assessment of India's religion, poetry, and natural history. This project, published annually in the *Asiatick Researches* from 1789, opened European eyes to the sophistication of Hindu culture. It produced a newly detailed view of India for European readers, a view that did not *simply* follow the priorities of colonial conquest and administration. Jones, that is to say, studied Indian tradition both in order to facilitate colonial rule *and* because he was delighted by a culture that, in several respects, he thought superior to that of Britain. As a consequence, his Orientalism did not merely strengthen imperial authority or solely move the so-called truth about the East to Europe. It also put that authority in question, at least implicitly, by asserting the value of Oriental literature as a tradition from which Europeans could learn aesthetic and moral values that they had formerly thought the exclusive legacy of Europe.

While Jones opened European eyes to India, the French savant Constantin Volney brought Egypt to its attention. After the publication of his *Les Ruines* in 1791, the grandeur of Egyptian antiquity and the vigor of Bedouin culture became objects of attention, so much so that when Napoleon invaded Egypt in 1798, he took with him a scientific expedition intended to record the manners and monuments of the country. Volney's travels thus helped precipitate a colonial venture with scientific knowledge as one of its aims.

Poets too were indebted to Volney. In *Gebir* (1796), Walter Savage Landor, following an Oriental tale by Clara Reeve, set a verse romance in a Volneyan Egypt ruled by a despotic court in the grip of superstitious priests. Gebir, the hero, is a European colonialist who intends to conquer, only to fall in love with the Egyptian queen. Romance overcomes imperial war, until Gebir is killed by priestly wiles. A harmonious union of East and West, the poet implies, can occur only after the defeat of Oriental priestcraft and despotism by enlightenment.

Landor's poem seemed prophetic in the 1790s because Napoleon's invasion of Egypt followed hard upon its appearance. And it certainly helped develop a genre. After Landor, the Oriental romance became *the* single most popular Romantic form, characteristically handling the interactions of East and West through the story of lovers whose paths are shaped by the politics of empire. Southey was Landor's first admirer, and the marks of that admiration are apparent throughout *Thalaba* (1801), an Arabian romance that paraded its verisimilitude to a specific Orient, vouchsafed by scholarly footnotes to the researches of Volney and Jones. Like Landor, Southey was antiimperialist: his hero was a destroyer of superstitious monarchs and priests. But Thalaba is also recognizably an Eastern version of a Wordsworthian rustic from the rural peripheries of Britain: born a shepherd in the desert, he is a pure-hearted wanderer, immune to the corruptions of court and city and an austere and self-denying man of God, who upholds spiritual fervor over sensual love. As such he is a figure embodying Southey's moral critique of the commercial, consumerist church and state as much as his distaste for Oriental court culture. He is also the first Muslim to feature as the hero of a British epic poem.

In 1810 Southey renewed his engagement with Orientalism in a still more radical romance, *The Curse of Kehama*, which, as he stated in the "Preface," "took up that mythology which Sir William Jones had been the first to introduce into English poetry," not just to add a dash of local color but also "to construct a story altogether mythological."[14] In developing Jones's presentation of Hindu myth, Southey aimed to reinvigorate what he regarded as the exhausted Western genre of epic. The "moral sublimity" of Indian myth would supply the great theme and lofty subject-matter that eighteenth-century imitators of "the great poets of antiquity" so clearly lacked.[15] By combining an Oriental content with an older Western style, Southey hoped to achieve what his fellow poets had not – an epic for an age in which Britain was in contact with Eastern cultures to a degree never before seen.

Southey took the epic eastwards and asked readers to see Hindu culture not just as an exotic other, or just as a decorative veneer, or even, as in Jones's own verse, as a fascinating anticipation of Western tradition. More radical than Jones, Southey treated it as a subject-matter, belief system, and poetic style as appropriate for the epic as were Trojan wars to Homer and the biblical fall of man to Milton. *The Curse of Kehama* constituted the apogee of the kind of Orientalism precipitated by Jones – a kind that neither solely appropriated the East and exported it westwards nor simply categorized it according to European knowledge systems, but used it to question the cultural forms that Europeans saw as proof of their superiority. By making the epic Hindu (albeit pseudo-Hindu), Southey left it radically altered.[16] He had made an imaginative leap beyond British convention and, even if he could not produce an authentic representation of Hindu scripture, the hybrid that he did create demanded that British readers be moved and awed by their likeness to the foreign.

The reviewers saw what Southey was doing and hated it. John Foster worried about the credibility conferred on "false religions"; *The Monthly Review* remarked on the "utter depravity of his taste."[17] Southey, they recognized, was deliberately innovative: he had "his own system of fancied originality, in which every thing that is good is old and every thing that is new is good for nothing."[18] This system was not his alone. Southey's "gross extravagancies" typified a "school of poetry" of which Wordsworth and Coleridge were members.[19] To contemporary reviewers, in effect, Romantic literature was a dangerous new movement epitomized by Southey's Jonesian and Hindu epic. Ironically enough, Southey half agreed with his reviewers, for he was not always prepared to endorse the innovations of his own text. He referred to the "monstrous . . . deformities" of the Hindu mythology that supplied his plot and his symbolism. He also attacked Jones.[20] It was as if Southey fought shy of the affiliation to a Jonesian India into which the imaginative process of writing verse led.

Southey's Eastern romances opened new possibilities for his admirers. It was under the influence of the travel narratives made available to him by *Thalaba* (when still a work in progress) that Coleridge wrote "Kubla Khan."[21] Coleridge's poem is much more subtle than his model: in "Kubla Khan" the disturbing blend of geographic exactitude and generic exoticism is not just a way of setting a moral tale in a notional East, but an essential part of the *modus operandi*: as Xanadu slips off the map into a "vision in a dream," the cultural function, in Europe, of imagining a fantasy Orient is brought into focus. Orientalism, Coleridge tells us in "Preface" and poem, emerges from a Western state of mind, from the poet's reverie consciousness, which converts his reading-matter into a dream-narrative in which his own creative hopes and fears can be viewed in dramatic form. The poet uses Orientalist books to feed his mind with material that it can turn into a story about his own poetic powers. The resulting Eastern tale is a projection – a sequence whose ostensible otherness allows the poet to recognize things about himself that he cannot usually see. And it is offered as such: Coleridge depicts his poem, that is to say, as a kind of magic mirror in which the dreaming poet, half believing in the reality of the Orient he dreams ("its images rose up before me as things"[22]), discovers what kind of dreamer he is – a khan, a demon lover, an inspired bard. The Orientalist exterior uncovers an occidental and psychological interior. It is only by understanding this, only by acknowledging the part of himself that he portrays as an Abyssinian maid, that the Western poet will gain sufficient awareness of his own pleasures and pains to gain control of his creativity. Coleridge, in effect, makes "Kubla Khan" both an example of and a commentary upon the psychological function of the myth of creativity that he shows the Oriental tale to be.

For Percy Shelley, both Southey's mythological imagination and Coleridge's internalized lyricism were inspiring. It was in *Alastor* (1816) that Shelley most successfully developed the themes and methods of *Thalaba* and "Kubla Khan." Shelley's whole quest-narrative follows Southey's almost exactly, as his poet-hero, like Thalaba, leaves the desert and the pastoral love of an Arab maiden:

> an Arab maiden brought his food,
> Her daily portion, from her father's tent,
> And spread her matting for his couch, and stole
> From duties and repose to tend his steps –
> Enamoured, yet not daring for deep awe
> To speak her love
>
> (ll. 129–34)[23]

Even the *Alastor* poet's route follows Thalaba's – first to Babylon and then on, by magic boat, through caverns that lead to death. Shelley, of course, internalizes the quest: his hero is searching within, and his external landscape, influenced by Southey's, Jones's, and Coleridge's luxurious and ornamented descriptions, allegorizes an internal one of sexual desire and intellectual longing. The internalization of the quest romance, that quintessential mark of Romanticism as twentieth-century critics defined it, had as its impetus the Oriental tale as modified by Southey and Coleridge and by the scholarship of Jones, which made themes, diction, and mythology available for a younger generation of poets. In other words, the Romantic lyric had as one of its sources the Orientalism that was itself made possible by Britain's empire.

Others also learned from Southey's Oriental tales, but took them in a less internalized direction than Shelley. "Stick to the East," Byron told Thomas Moore, "the public are Orientalising."[24] Southey had opened a new field but his own works were "unsaleables," being too long and too dense. Moore took Byron's advice and followed in Southey's footsteps, carefully avoiding, however, the error of making his poems depend on a complicated and unfamiliar mythology. The result, *Lalla Rookh* (1817), was far less demanding than Southey's works. Moore's story revolved around conventional romantic love and mortal conflict rather than around a mythical interpenetration of human and divine, as in *Kehama*. Moore used Orientalist texts to provide accurate local color, but did not ask readers to step outside their religious beliefs or poetic expectations.

There was, however, another, veiled location within Moore's Orientalist tale: Ireland. In *Lalla Rookh* Moore expressed his sympathies with Irish nationalism by moving a local colonial conflict and a newly internal border to the ancient East.[25] The context was this: after unsuccessful uprisings against Anglo-Irish and Protestant rule in 1798 and 1803, the Irish agreed to an Act of Union with Britain in return for trade advantages and emancipation of Catholics from restrictive laws. Thus Ireland, Britain's oldest colony, lost its separate parliament and was governed from London. But London's promises were not fulfilled: Catholics were not given full civil rights, and disenchantment, unrest, and violence followed. Union seemed to have enshrined Ireland's subordinate position rather than overcome it. Poverty and emigration gathered pace.

Moore did not protest against these developments in his homeland explicitly but instead glamorized Persian and Zoroastrian resistance to Arabian Muslim invasion. The allegory aligned Protestant Britain's designs on Ireland with Islam's on Iran: imperialism, Moore suggested, was driven by religious zeal and self-righteousness. This was to renew, critically, an alignment between Western Protestantism and Eastern Islam that Southey had made admiringly in *Thalaba*. But Moore's allegory was muted: the distance of his medieval and Eastern setting ensured that his poem did not raise current Irish issues strongly enough to disturb his potential purchasers, the English middle classes. Moore seduced them by surrounding his tale of violence with a perfumed frame narrative, and enjoyed immense popularity.

Byron not only advised Moore but worked on Oriental tales himself, using Southey as a point of departure. His bestselling Eastern Tales were more concise than Southey's epics, demanded no detailed knowledge of Eastern myth, and focused historical events through stories of cross-cultural love. Whereas Coleridge and Shelley internalized the Oriental romance, Byron sexualized it. In *The Giaour* (1813), he dramatized imperial competition by relating the desire of Turkish Muslim and Western Christian for the same Balkan woman. Locked in struggle, the two lords represent a world in which religion is a marker (and source) of imperial identity – an ideology rather than divine truth – and in which those caught between the endless, stalemated opposition of two faiths, at the point where East and West meet, are doomed to be stifled. No Western triumphalist, no Evangelical apologist, Byron neither lauded Britain's colonial gains nor relegated other religions below the Christian. He Romanticized, instead, a fatalistic and gendered worldview in which power-seeking men build empires in their image, subjugating and effeminizing the peoples caught between them, until they decay, to be succeeded by another. Byron was thus less optimistic than Shelley who, in "Ozymandias" (taking his text from Volney and Southey) welcomed time's destruction of an empire, but foresaw no inevitable rise of another in its place.

By 1816 Byron and Shelley were in exile, their radical scepticism marginalized to Europe (though more rhetorically direct as a result). After the final defeat of Napoleon at Waterloo (1815), Britain seemed, to most people at home, to have ended the era of imperial strife. With the French Empire destroyed, with Spanish America on the road to liberation, with the Ottoman Empire crumbling, Britons felt themselves to be rightful masters of a new world order. This new confidence was defined by a number of poems that adapted the Oriental romance to other areas of the globe and, in the process, portrayed British empire as a civilizing mission. William Lisle Bowles had already published *The Missionary* (1811–13), influencing Byron with a tale of Chile at the time of its conquest by the Spanish. His purpose was to praise native, Araucan, resistance to a brutal, enslaving, imperial power at a time when Creole South America was rebelling against colonial rule. The poem narrates colonial relations through a love story, with a kindly missionary father establishing a peaceful community in the Andes in which Spanish and Chilean youth – boy and girl – are united under his paternal blessing. The moral is clear: Christian paternalism will create lasting and peaceful colonies because childlike natives will welcome the authority of more technologically advanced Europeans if treated with compassion. Here Bowles endorsed the missionary movement that his friend Southey was promoting in the press and in his own poem *The Tale of Paraguay* (1825). Felicia Hemans did likewise in her "American Forest Girl" (1828), in which a Native American girl's compassionate love for a white-boy captive who was suffering torture leads to his release, allowing the poet to suggest the inevitable triumph of Christian ethics. If this sunny view of colonialism now seems almost culpably naïve (as many experienced colonial officials argued), nevertheless the romantic dress in which it disguised the business of empire, a business that was often too nakedly exploitative for public comfort, appealed to readers' consciences. Bowles, Hemans, and Southey envisaged empire without the economic exploitation that was its *raison d'être* and without the military force that was its foundation. Many Britons, happy to sleep easily in their beds, were keen to believe that their nation could redeem itself by bringing peace, prosperity, and salvation to "savages."

Ironically enough, it was contact with so-called savages that prompted the most searching as well as the most ideological Romantic poetry. Interaction between Britons and indigenous peoples was not always defined by prejudices or framed by the ideologies and institutions of empire. Nor was there always, on the ground, a power advantage on the British side, at least at the time contact was made. And when there was not, the interactions and impressions that British travelers recorded in their journals often slipped free of the existing stereotypes and conventions, prompting the poets who read these journals, in turn, to create more complex and challenging fictions such as Coleridge's *The Rime of the Ancyent Marinere* (1798), Wordsworth's "The Complaint of the Forsaken Indian Woman" (1798) and Blake's "Little Black

Boy" (1789). This process was especially noticeable in two areas – the South Pacific islands and North American forests – where Britons entered into more personal relationships than in India or the Caribbean. Why? Because in these places individual Britons were further away from the structures of imperial authority, often, indeed, vulnerable and dependent on, or companions with, local people, whose power they had to acknowledge and whose society they had to interpret.

In Tahiti, Tonga, and New Zealand, Cook's voyagers encountered people previously almost utterly unknown to Europeans. In 1768, 1772, and 1776 they spent enough time living among these islanders for close, if precarious, relationships to be formed. They and subsequent voyagers following in their wake were agents of empire, who occasionally used superior firepower, but they were also outnumbered and, as such, dependent on the hosts who received them as visitors, not conquerors, with a mixture of unease, curiosity, and hostility. All these responses are recorded in the Britons' narratives, which rapidly move on from general stereotypes to analyse individual differences as well as the many unique social and religious aspects of what they appreciated were complex cultures. The narratives caused a sensation when published after the voyagers' return, and they led some (Cowper, in Book I of *The Task*, for example), to revise their assumptions about civilized Europeans and savage Indians.

In North America too, soldiers, traders, and emigrants met indigenous people in multifarious circumstances. They were captured by them, fought alongside and against them, deserted to them, and married them, creating new generations of hybrid identity living in tribal society or even back in Britain. A few, a very few, of these people achieved English literary voices of their own, writing back to Britons in terms that matched neither the stereotypes nor the words used by white travelers. These writers were a new phenomenon, and they deserve further study, both in their own right and because their words reveal the unavoidable partiality of British writers' representations, be they ever so oppositional within British culture. The Mohawk chiefs Joseph Brant / Thayendanegea and John Norton / Teyoninhokarawen were their own men, even when influenced by the literary forms that an education in eighteenth-century English made available to them. So too the Indian/Persian visitor Mirza Abu Taleb Khan and the African writer Phillis Wheatley. Their texts, shaped by British culture yet oppositional to much of what that culture stood for, reveal that Romanticism was not only a British product of an imperial age, a product that, at different times, contested and celebrated empire, but also a discourse that the people subjected to British empire began to turn to their own needs – using some of its motifs while rejecting others vehemently.

NOTES

1 Quoted in James Walvin, *Fruits Of Empire: Exotic Produce and British Taste, 1660–1800* (Basingstoke: Macmillan, 1997), p. 158.

2 All quotations from Cowper are taken from *The Poems of William Cowper*, ed. John D. Baird and Charles Ryskamp, 3 vols. (Oxford: Oxford University Press, 1980–95).

3 *William Wordsworth: The Prelude: A Parallel Text*, ed. J.C. Maxwell (Harmondsworth: Penguin, 1971).

4 On this phenomenon see Malcolm Andrews, *The Search for the Picturesque: Landscape Aesthetics and Tourism in Britain, 1760–1800* (Aldershot: Scolar, 1989).

5 See Fiona Stafford, *The Last of the Race. The Growth of a Myth from Milton to Darwin* (Oxford: Clarendon Press, 1994); Katie Trumpener, *Bardic Nationalism: The Romantic Novel and the British Empire* (Princeton: Princeton University Press, 1997).

6 See *Robert Burns and Cultural Authority*, ed. Robert Crawford (Edinburgh: Edinburgh University Press, 1997).

7 See Gwyn A. Williams, *Madoc: The Making of a Myth* (London: Eyre Methuen, 1979).

8 For abolitionist writing see *Slavery, Abolition, and Emancipation. Writings in the British Romantic Period*, ed. Peter J. Kitson and Debbie Lee, 8 vols. (London: Pickering & Chatto, 1999).

9 Samuel Taylor Coleridge, *Lectures 1795, On Politics and Religion*, ed. Lewis Patton and Peter Mann (London: Routledge & Kegan Paul, and Princeton: Princeton University Press, 1971), p. 58.

10 From Wordsworth's sonnet "The world is too much with us."

11 See William Blake, *The Continental Prophecies*, ed. D. W. Dörrbecker, vol. IV of *Blake's Illuminated Books*, ed. David Bindman (Princeton: Princeton University Press and the Blake Trust, 1995).

12 William Wordsworth, *The Excursion 1814* (Oxford: Woodstock, 1991).

13 See *Sir William Jones: Selected Poetical and Prose Works*, ed. Michael J. Franklin (Cardiff: University of Wales Press, 1995), pp. 320–1.

14 *The Poetical Works of Robert Southey, Collected by Himself*, 10 vols. (London, 1838), vol. VIII, p. xv.

15 Ibid., pp. xvi–xvii.

16 On Southey's Orientalization of the epic, see Marilyn Butler, "Orientalism," in *The Penguin History of Literature: The Romantic Period*, ed. David Pirie (Harmondsworth: Penguin, 1994), pp. 395–447. Also, Javed Majeed, *Ungoverned Imaginings: James Mill's "History of British India" and Orientalism* (Oxford: Clarendon Press, 1992).

17 *The Eclectic Review* 8 (April 1811), pp. 334–50; quoted in *Robert Southey: The Critical Heritage*, ed. Lionel Madden (London: Routledge & Kegan Paul, 1976), p. 140; *The Monthly Review*, quoted in Southey's "Preface" to *Kehama*, in *The Poetical Works of Robert Southey*, vol. VIII, p. xxi.

18 *The Monthly Review*, quoted in Southey's "Preface" to *Kehama*, in *The Poetical Works of Robert Southey*, vol. VIII, p. xx.

19 *The Monthly Review*, quoted in ibid.

20 *Selections from the Letters of Robert Southey*, ed. J. W. Warter, 4 vols. (London, 1856), vol. II, pp. 75, 96.

21 As Elizabeth Schneider has shown in her *Coleridge, Opium and Kubla Khan* (Chicago: University of Chicago Press, 1953).

22 From Coleridge's "Preface" to the poem. In *The Poetical Works of S. T. Coleridge*, ed. J. C. C. Mays, 3 vols. (Princeton: Princeton University Press, 2001), vol. I, Part I, p. 511.

23 In *The Poems of Shelley*, ed. Kelvin Everest and Geoffrey Matthews, 2 vols. (Harlow: Longman, 1989–2000), vol. I, Part I, p. 469.

24 *Byron's Letters and Journals*, ed. Leslie Marchand, 12 vols. (London: John Murray, 1973–82), vol. III, p. 101.

25 See Majeed, *Ungoverned Imaginings*, pp. 93–100.

FURTHER READING

Bewell, Alan, *Romanticism and Colonial Disease* (Baltimore: Johns Hopkins University Press, 1999)

Fulford, Tim, Debbie Lee, and Peter J. Kitson, *Literature, Science, and Exploration in the Romantic Era: Bodies of Knowledge* (Cambridge: Cambridge University Press, 2004)

Fulford, Tim, and Peter J. Kitson, eds., *Romanticism and Colonialism* (Cambridge: Cambridge University Press, 1998)

Leask, Nigel, *British Romantic Writers and the East: Anxieties of Empire* (Cambridge: Cambridge University Press, 1992)

Lee, Debbie, *Slavery and the Romantic Imagination* (Philadelphia: University of Pennsylvania Press, 2002)

Said, Edward, *Orientalism*, 25th anniversary edn. (New York: Vintage Books, 2003)

10

KEVIS GOODMAN

Romantic poetry and the science of nostalgia

For the Reader cannot be too often reminded that Poetry is passion: it is the
history or science of feelings.
William Wordsworth, Note on "The Thorn"[1]

Introduction

For better or worse, Romanticism and nostalgia are so frequently associated as to be nearly synonymous. An influential account of Romantic
thought across Europe once characterized the movement by its "nostalgia
for the natural object, expanding to become nostalgia for the origin of this
object," and the longing for nature is but one of many returns associated
with the period.[2] These include, in addition, the retrieval of romance modes,
the renewed interest or imaginative investment in national and cultural pasts,
the turn from polite culture to the "very language of men" – at times con-
joined with a full-scale retreat from the anonymity of print culture and its
potentially hostile public – and the reanimation of oral cultures and orality, even when, or perhaps especially when, the bards were inauthentic and
technologically mediated.

The implicit or explicit understanding of nostalgia in each case casts the
phenomenon as a distancing, even a falsification, of the pressing realities
of modernity: urbanization, the vexed national politics within a newly but
uneasily united kingdom of Britain, the equally if not more vexed international politics, warfare and colonial endeavors, print technology and the
marketplace. This is the nostalgia familiar in common parlance today – the
sentimental and safe retrospect, the pleasing melancholy, the whitewashing
of less lovable aspects of history, past and present alike. Susan Stewart thus
writes that nostalgia testifies to "a longing that of necessity is inauthentic . . .
because the past it seeks has never existed except in narrative." The nostalgic,
she writes, "is enamored of distance, not of the referent itself."[3] Nostalgia,
writes one critic of postmodernity, "exiles us from the present as it brings
the imagined past near"; another, Fredric Jameson, argues that nostalgia, so
construed, is "an elaborated symptom of the waning of our historicity, of
our lived possibility of experiencing history in some active way."[4] And for
a recent literary historian of the Victorian novel, nostalgia became, in the

nineteenth-century *Bildungsroman* from Jane Austen on, a form of amnesia, an adaptable, affable winnowing of the specificity and disturbance of the past in the name of a largely conservative and curative narrative march toward the future.[5]

There is nothing entirely wrong with the theses about *Romanticism* summarized in my first paragraph – like all tested truisms, they test partly true for the initial purposes of description. However, the account or definition of *nostalgia* in my second paragraph postdates the Romantic period. For eighteenth- and early nineteenth-century readers, the term would have carried none of the cozy associations it now holds. Nor would it yet have had much to do with memory: its provenance would have been scientific. Having made its debut in medical texts, it signified a disease, specifically a disability of wartime and colonial mobility, a somatic revolt against forced travel, depopulation, emigration, and other forms of transience. Coined at the end of the seventeenth century by a Swiss physician, Johannes Hofer, the term described a dangerous and frequently fatal wasting illness among soldiers, sailors, and others forced to leave their homes permanently or temporarily. Nostalgia itself was soon on the move, for the international medical community seized Hofer's account, which then traversed all the major eighteenth-century nosologies (medical taxonomies) across Europe, picking up national associations and emphases as it moved along. The diagnosis seems to have answered a practical need during a century marked by persistent international and global warfare: the wars of the Spanish Succession (1701–14), the Polish wars of the 1730s, the Franco-Austrian wars of the 1740s, the Seven Years War carried out globally in the 1750s, the struggle for American independence, and then, from 1793 to 1815, the almost uninterrupted conflict with France. On home turf, there were also Scottish uprisings and the threat of Jacobite invasions. Moreover, since Britons were spread far and wide all over the over-extended and ever-extending maritime empire, the disease flourished at sea, and thereby received poignant articulation within naval or maritime medicine as well as in narratives of exploration and conquest. Many of the now forgotten names that one finds in the considerable clinical profile – Thomas Trotter, William Falconer, Joseph Banks, Robert Hamilton, Thomas Arnold, George Seymour, and others – belonged to men caught up in the flux of military, colonial, or expansionary process. Nostalgia was thus in its original sense no "symptom of waning historicity" (to return to Jameson's phrase) but quite the opposite. It represented a waxing attempt, within scientific discourse, to register the growing pains of historical existence.

The usual story is that this nostalgia disappears at the beginning of the nineteenth century, at least as a pathology; most scholarly accounts that mention it tend to treat it as a curiosity, a quaint anecdote from a now anti-quated stage of medicine. The disturbing disease – both illness and more general unease – of historical existence appears in modern scholarship, if it appears at all, as a colorful backdrop for what it became, the false conscious-ness that our own contemporaries distrust or disown. Yet the conditions of warfare, colonial conflict, and patterns of forced migration did not disappear with the onset of the Romantic period. Indeed, as Mary Favret, has reminded us, they became perpetual.[6] Even where the battles were not fought on home turf or the conditions of mobility experienced at first hand, the awareness of conflict and the condition of alarm were never far from the British imag-ination – war was "in the air," as Favret has put it – while at the same time the human casualties were carried home again: in displaced soldiers, retired sailors, and other returning travelers. We might wonder, therefore, whether reports of the original phenomenon's disappearance are premature.

What if the disturbing disease of historicity did not recede, even as it ceased to frequent clinical diagnoses and nosologies, but rather moved quietly into a new discipline, where it persisted, unnamed as such, as its troubling bedrock? What if nostalgia as we think of it today – that diffuse, sentimentalized ret-rospect – is the product of a kind of track-switching operation, whereby a more pleasing substitute, an adaptive memory function, took on the name of the troubling original phenomenon, while the initial sensory-physical disor-der, whose historical context was global warfare and expansion (as well as internal, domestic depopulation), continued on its way, thereafter negotiated or "treated" in a different venue from the medical treatises? Although my phrasing is a bit extravagant, that is the possibility this chapter will explore. The new "home" for the historical disease formerly known as nostalgia, I propose, lies in Romantic-era writings on aesthetics. More specifically, it came to reside in the period's discourse about Poetry – a curious category, which hovered between what Percy Shelley called "poetry in a restricted sense" (metrical verse, with lower-case and technical modesty) and Poetry "in a universal sense," with grand and upper-case ambitions as a distinctively human discourse, nothing less than "the creative faculty" (Shelley), or "the science of feelings" (Wordsworth).[7] The result of this discursive migration is consequential not only for the ways we think about the relation between sci-ence and poetry but also for the way we understand the history embedded – rather than suppressed – within literature.

What did Wordsworth mean when he used that well-known phrase "the science of feelings" as an epithet for Poetry in *Lyrical Ballads*? I analyze that note and its context in detail below, but here it is important to note that "sci-ence of feelings" is itself a Janus-faced phrase. The "of" may be objective or possessive, rendering the "feelings" either the focus or the agent of "science."

If the genitive is objective, are we to understand Wordsworth's "science of feelings" as a relative of the Scottish "science of man" – the systematizing philosophies of human nature charted by David Hume, Adam Smith, Lord Kames, and others? Yet it was Wordsworth, echoing contemporary formulations, who insisted categorically on the "philosophical contradistinction" between "Poetry and Science" (in the 1800 "Preface" to *Lyrical Ballads*), argued that "we murder to dissect" ("The Tables Turned"), and, in the *Prelude*, scoffed caustically at those who seek "to class the cabinet / Of their sensations." That he should place his narratives of passion in apposition with a scientific conception of his work would thus seem cause for curiosity. Or does the phrase instead attempt to elaborate a distinctive kind of affective cognition, with the feelings as possessors of their own "science," like the mode of sensuous perception and particularized knowledge already called "aesthetic" on the Continent, and defined by Alexander Baumgarten's *Reflections on Poetry* (1735) against logic or reason – against, that is, the contemplation of things removed from sensate representation?

Tracing the surprising genealogy of nostalgia as it leads from the medical and human sciences into the *Lyrical Ballads* and the prose commentary provided on that volume by Wordsworth and Coleridge, this chapter will offer a snapshot of the transition from one sense of the phrase (the sciences that try to systematize human nature and the operations of the human frame as objects of scrutiny) to the other – to a nascent understanding of "feeling as thought," as Wordsworth elsewhere wrote. This affective cognition emerges, furthermore, as more sensitive to the limits of such closed systems of human nature, registering or retaining, as the disease of nostalgia always had, a sense of the historical ghosts in the Enlightenment machine. One purpose of this focus, in other words, is to take a view of the relationship between "Science" and "Poetry" that offers something more nuanced than simple opposition or analogy. Opposition, we have seen, was the formulation of choice proffered by the Romantics themselves in their most high-flying statements, and not only by Wordsworth, Coleridge, and Shelley but also by numerous, often anonymous, contributors to the periodical press. Analogy or homology is the configuration more frequent in recent scholarship, as in the numerous studies that bear some version of the name *Romanticism and Science*. Here, while the "and" has the advantage of being less defensive than antithesis and therefore opening up more avenues of inquiry, it does not necessarily guarantee something more specific than correspondence or comparison, which may be retroactively imposed. The case of nostalgia analyzed in the following pages presents a picture or model more like that of a relay movement, a passing of the baton from the medical sciences to an emergent aesthetics. And the "baton," I will suggest, is the historicity, the pressure of the present that (modern, sentimental) nostalgia supposedly suppresses – in short, the history not "of" but *in* the feelings. As medical nostalgia moved outside the purview of scientific explanation and beyond the physician's treatment, the history of mobility – and history perceived as motion – came to lodge in the project and practice of poetry itself. A second main purpose of refocusing Romanticism around (a more historically accurate account of) nostalgia, then, is to offset some of the conservative associations that have clustered around Romantic poetry as return, retreat, a de-historicizing "exile from the present" – that is, nostalgic in the sense we assume today.

Motion sickness: medical nostalgia

Ian Hacking has reflected on the peculiar nature of the "transient" illness – one that appears in *a* time and *a* place or places, and later fades, at least in its original form and as an aberration to be negotiated within the medical community. He understands such outbreaks in terms of their "ecological niches," defined by a number of vectors – some medical (available frameworks or taxonomies of illness, criteria of observability), some cultural (polarities of virtue and vices within which the illness can lodge, conditions which call for some "release" into madness), and others more accidental. All of these elements collaborate to produce a "stable home" for the visibility of the illness as an illness.[8] How might we begin to specify nostalgia's niche? After all, there has always been homesickness – we have Odysseus and Ovid to remind us of it. What made this outbreak different and that difference visible?

What may now seem most remarkable, in the archive of eighteenth- and early nineteenth-century writing on the topic, is the disease's thorough somatic characterization. The anti-dualist human sciences of the period, whether mechanistic or vitalist, combined with the residues of Galenic medicine to provide quite a baroque profile. For Johannes Hofer, influenced by the Greco-Roman legacy and by the works of sixteenth- and seventeenth-century natural philosophy on the circulation of the blood and the operation of the nervous system, this disease of the "afflicted imagination" coincides with organic lesions in the brain, caused by the excessive "vibration of the animal spirits through those fibers of the middle brain in which impressed traces of ideas of the Fatherland still cling."[9] The brain "traces" are then "impressed more vigorously by frequent contemplations of the Fatherland," Hofer writes – with a symptomatically circular logic – and in turn "raises up constantly the conscious mind toward considering the image of the Fatherland." Hofer equivocates the question of whether the repeated thoughts of the Fatherland cause the organic lesions in his subjects' brains or whether the repeated motions of the animal spirits in the same pathways (then lesions) of the brain cause nostalgia and therefore the fixation on home. Either way – and he seems to want to have it both ways – the results are patho-physiological, and they take the form of strangely paralyzed and paralyzing organic "motions":

> [Nostalgia] brings back the animal spirits as though fixed or rather directed always toward the same motion . . . the spirits, busied excessively in the brain, cannot flow with sufficient supply and proper vigor through the invisible tubes of the nerves to all parts . . . In truth, when the animal spirits are regenerated in niggardly supply, and at the same time are devoured on account of the con-tinuous quasi-ecstasy of the mind in the brain, by degrees partly the voluntary motions and partly the natural [motions], grow quiet, langour of the whole arises, the circulation of the blood loses vigor . . . and becomes denser and thus apt to receive coagulation.[10]

Hofer's medical cases – including a country girl taken from home for hospi-talization, a young student from Bern transplanted to Basel, and Helvetian soldiers fighting abroad – tend first to be "moved by small external objects" and later possessed by the idea of home (*"Ich will heim, Ich will heim"* are the only words spoken by his country girl), so much so that in extreme cases they are rapt in a kind of "ecstasy," and they "feel little, nor see those present, nor hear them . . . even if their senses are twitched by these external motions."[11] In short, to anticipate a formula familiar to readers of Wordsworth, their minds are wholly occupied by absent things as if they were present, and their bodies absent to present things. Without prompt repatriation, or at least the restoration of mobility to the body and to the bodily spirits, fever, livid spots, and even death result.

The classical doctrine of animal spirits would be succeeded in British medicine by David Hartley's psychology of association, in which ideas con-sist of mechanistic vibrations, tremors along the medullary system extending from the brain, through the spinal marrow and nerves, to the extremities and back again, and prompting other vibrations/ideas with which they have been associated by contiguity or succession in the past. Hartley's much debated and reprinted *Observations on Man, His Frame, His Duty and His Expec-tations* (1749) would in turn be modified by the influential Scottish physi-cians William Cullen and John Brown, and by Joseph Priestley in England, one of Hartley's commentators. Yet in each case, the problem of disturbed "motions" remained absolutely central to the theorization of disease for the next hundred years, especially in Britain after John Locke, where the empiri-cal and anti-dualistic bent of the human sciences provided hospitable ground, and where Isaac Newton's model of gravitational forces moving inanimate bodies added both prestige and a powerful analogy for the laws of animal motion, active within animate ones.

There may be no more thorough or imaginative (even science-fictional) theorization of such "motions" than Erasmus Darwin's 1,200-page nosology and summa of British empiricism, *Zoonomia* (1794–6). For Darwin, absorbing Newton, Hartley, and others, ideas are nothing more or less than motions of the sensorium (hence they are called "sensual" or "sensorial motions"), analogous – Darwin even suggests they are identical – to the motor arousal that he designates "muscular motions." "Nostalgia" Darwin classifies among the "diseases of volition," along with reverie, somnambulism, and erotomania; each consists of the "violent exertions of ideas" to relieve the "accumulation of sensorial power" (*Zoonomia*'s phrase for pain). The nostalgic whose mind teems with ideas of home is thus swayed by involuntary "sensorial motions," and these, for Darwin, may at worst discharge themselves in muscular motion, even into a fatally ironic bid to control the body's placement and movement:

> III.i. i. 6. *Nostalgia*. **Maladie du Pais. Calenture**. An unconquerable desire of returning to one's native country, frequent in long voyages, in which the patients become so insane as to throw themselves into the sea, mistaking it for green fields or meadows. The Swiss are said to be particularly liable to this disease, and when taken into foreign service frequently desert from this cause, and especially after hearing or singing a particular tune, which was used in their village dances, in their native country, on which account the playing or singing this tune was forbid by punishment of death. Zwingerus.

> > Dear is that shed, to which his soul conforms,
> > And dear that hill, which lifts him to the storms.   Goldsmith.[12]

I will return shortly to Darwin's anglicization of the malady by combining Swiss with British examples, but first it is worth heeding the inadvertent insight of Darwin's choice of examples for classification: the "foreign serviceman" (i.e., Swiss mercenary), the sailor, or simply – for this is the title of the poem by Oliver Goldsmith that he is quoting from – *The Traveller*. "Nostalgia" was a disease of "motions" in more than just the anatomical or physiological sense. It was also a pathology of travel, a result of the compulsory motion *of* bodies, not just within them.

This point may seem obvious to us, blessed as we are with the happy perspicuity of hindsight. However, the medical taxonomist's license rarely extends to a consideration of such larger historical motions – geographical movements as well as their shifting political and economic determinants of war, depopulation, emigration, resettlement. Indeed, William Cullen, who occupied the prestigious Chair of Medicine at the University of Edinburgh,

where the young Erasmus Darwin studied, cautioned against a consideration of the "remote causes" of illness, arguing that practitioners and classi-
fier alike should focus on "external appearances" or symptoms only.[13] Yet
entries in such schemes as *Zoonomia* – or William Falconer's 1788 treatise,
"A Dissertation on the Influence of the Passions upon the Disorders of the
Body" (which gives nostalgia pride of place as its last and "most remarkable
instance" of such disorders), or even some of Cullen's own training manuals –
do seem to *misrecognize*, with a peculiarly insightful precision, the larger
world narratives whose determinants are so difficult to parse immanently, in
their unfolding. The vividly somatic imaginations map the world on to the
body and seem to grapple with it there, and while the body may offer a safer
space for analysis, the language of "powers," "extremities," and "principal
seats" in these texts nonetheless remains rife with potential as a metaphor
or heuristic space for adumbrating global or national systems. "The muscles of locomotion," if inactive, warns Thomas Beddoes's *Hygëia* (1802–3)
are "like troops insufficiently disciplined," and "will be easily thrown into
confusion," so that "accidents may break the connection between the ideas
and the single muscles, of which the sets are composed."[14] And for those
physicians who, like Beddoes and Darwin, were also poets, "inlisti[ng]," as
Darwin's *Botanic Garden* (1790–1) put it, "Imagination under the banner of
Science," recourse to the purple poetic diction of earlier eighteenth-century
poetry could locate shadows of the body politic in the operations of the
body natural – as in Darwin's typical description of passion in *The Temple
of Nature* ("Associate tribes of fibrous motion rise / Flush the red cheek or
light the laughing eyes") – while skirting, as such diction characteristically
had, crucial questions of causation and agency. Hints of the historical "case,"
or situation, infiltrate the medical case history, and trouble the medical diag-
nostician's and taxonomist's task.

In retrospect, we can see that nostalgia was therefore of a piece – a
"niche" – with the proliferating genre of medical geographies and disease
landscapes, those attempts to map global spaces by their pathogenic or salu-
brious qualities, which have received fine attention from Alan Bewell as the
discursive medium of colonial war.[15] If smallpox, cholera, malaria, etc., were
considered to be diseases of place – and a greater enemy to colonial conquest
or exploration, Bewell points out, than military opposition – so in its way
was nostalgia. It was the special instance of a disease of displacement, but,
no less than these other diseases, an obstacle to seamless expansion: that
sailor who throws himself overboard, the soldier who deserts, is one fewer
sailor, one fewer soldier. As a traveler's pathology, nostalgia was also, if
less obviously, of the same moment as its direct antithesis: the travel cure,
equally a proliferating cultural practice, with its own abundant literature

(Bath guides, etc.) and multiplying sites – the newly popular health spots and resorts. The spa-seeker who takes the waters, whether at Bath, Tunbridge Wells, Bristol, or other resorts, may be but the ironic counterpart of Darwin's nostalgic, who throws himself *into* them, as it were, as the last resort. After all, Matthew Bramble (the habitually convalescent protagonist of Tobias Smollett's *Humphrey Clinker*) and Roderick Random (the star-crossed sea doctor of Smollett's earlier novel by that name), share an author and set of concerns. In other words, the accounts of nostalgia, the medical geographies, and the literature of the resort all participate in the fiction or faith that place, air, and soil – or change of place, air, and soil – are therapeutic, differing only with respect to whether it is home, or leaving it, that favors health.

Yet the fact that they can differ so radically on this rather notable point suggests that the intensifying problem was not "motions" in and of themselves but a newly delicate relationship between mobility and liberty, and the vexed questions that accompany that relationship: problems of volition, a keyword of the medical discourse of "motions" (and, we will see, inherited as such by Romantic discussions of meter), and volition's antithesis, compulsion. Movement, when free, is healthful – a form of exercise; when forced, perilous. Why are naval shipmen, pondered the ship doctor Thomas Trotter, prone to nostalgic illness when they are impressed while, as volunteers or bounty-men, they remain in healthful and active spirits? Sir James Pringle, tending to the British army fighting in Napoleonic France, noted the greater prevalence of disease among foot-soldiers, whose lives are marked by "excess of Rest and Motion," than in the cavalry, who, controlling their horses, "lead a more uniform life . . . and a constant and easy exercise."[16] The questions that the medical literature negotiates with varying degrees of explicitness are: how much and what sorts of movement are salutary, and what sorts malignant?

From medical nostalgia to poetic tautology: the "Thorn" principle in the *Lyrical Ballads*

Just as surely as the smallpox, or malaria or cholera – or the drifting clouds – the disease of nostalgia travels. And it came home, but not, or not just, in the safe or sentimental ways we are used to considering it.

Look again at Erasmus Darwin's composite entry in *Zoonomia*. There are three quotations here, only two of which Darwin identifies. The ones with attribution are from the Swiss doctor Theodore Zwinger's ("Zwingerus") 1710 reprint and revision of Hofer's dissertation on nostalgia and, after that, Goldsmith's *The Traveller*. The first, unidentified piece of prose comes from Samuel Johnson's *Dictionary* definition of "calenture," or tropical fever (in Johnson's 1755 entry: "a distemper in hot climates wherein they [sailors] imagine the sea to be green fields"), for medical nostalgia's fortunes in Britain had become hitched to this nautical disease. They also gained momentum from one other, less likely, accomplice – the scurvy – since, as two kinds of appetite or longing (for home and for the fruits thereof), nostalgia and scurvy merged in the frequent diagnosis of "scorbutic nostalgia." Thomas Trotter's *Observations on the Scurvy* (1792), which influenced Beddoes and, through Beddoes, Coleridge and Wordsworth, offered this account:

> I consider these longings [the "desire of being on land"] as the first symptoms and constant attendants of the disease [scurvy] in all its stages. The cravings of appetite, not only amuse their waking hours, with thoughts on green fields, and streams of pure water; but in dreams they are tantalized by the favourite idea; and on waking, the mortifying disappointment is expressed with the utmost regret, with groans and weeping, altogether childish . . . This scorbutic Nostalgia, *"in absentibus a patria, vehemens eundum revisendi desiderium,"* belongs to the second species of Doctor Cullen's Genus.[17]

Trotter (another Cullen student) has green fields "and" streams of pure water, but the topos, which is remarkably widespread, usually appears in the form we find in Johnson and Darwin: the hallucination of green fields *in* the seas, a wishful collapse of distance that conflates land and water and turns pastoral into psychopathic fantasy. One meets it again in William Cowper's extremely popular *The Task* (1785), whose narrator, reading travel narratives and newspapers by the hearth, spends a fair amount of that poem imaginatively at sea, with the mariner:

> his blood inflam'd
> With acrid salts; his very heart athirst
> To gaze at Nature in her green array.
> Upon the ship's tall side he stands, possess'd
> With visions prompted by intense desire;
> Fair fields appear below, such as he left
> Far distant, such as he would die to find –
> He seeks them headlong, and is seen no more.[18]

Wordsworth, in turn, borrowing his "description of Calenture" from "an imperfect recollection of an admirable one in prose, by Mr. Gilbert, Author of the Hurricane" (*LB*, p. 137n.), offers this elaboration in "The Brothers," one of the 1800 *Lyrical Ballads*, whose protagonist, the returned mariner Leonard, is possessed like the nostalgics who precede him, by the recurrent presence of absent land, of home at sea:

> [He] would often hang
> Over the vessel's side, and gaze and gaze,
> And while the broad green wave and sparkling foam
> Flashed round him images and hues, that wrought
> In union with the employment of his heart,
> He, thus by feverish passion overcome,
> Even with the organs of his bodily eye,
> Below him, in the bosom of the deep
> Saw mountains, saw the forms of sheep that graz'd
> On verdant hills, with dwellings among trees,
> And Shepherds clad in the same country grey
> Which he himself had worn.
>
> ("Brothers," ll. 51–62)

As other readers of the poem have noted, Leonard's double is his now dead brother James, who suffers from the complementary problem: waiting at home for Leonard, we are told, he suffered from the disorder of somnambulism (another of Darwin's diseases of volition, we recall), so that, sleepwalking, he seeks Leonard in dreamed distant lands. Where Leonard no longer attends to the foreign spaces around him, James is abstracted from the native world around *him* and, not as lucky as Leonard, he falls off a precipice and dies, in a sense, away from home. "The Brothers," argues Bewell, seeks to convey that "'being at home, isolated from the outside world, is no longer possible." A rewriting of Coleridge's "The Rime of the Ancient Mariner" without the supernatural machinery (poor Leonard ends up going back to sea and finishes his life as a "grey-haired mariner"), "The Brothers" is a critique of colonial war and an "exploration of the psychological dimensions of the new world brought into being by global commercial expansion – the 'profitable life' – intimating that it is one in which . . . the familiar presents itself as foreign and vice versa."[19]

Yet "The Brothers" is no isolated case in the *Lyrical Ballads*. One finds returned mariners, failed homecomers, and closeted clinical nostalgics everywhere in the collaborative project of Wordsworth and Coleridge, who put their avid reading of travel narratives and, in Coleridge's hypochondriacal case in particular, medical literature to good use. There is *the* Ancient Mariner himself – indeed one reader has even diagnosed the "Rime" as a "Tale of the Scurvy" and its characters as scorbutic nostalgics,[20] and I will return to that poem below. There are also the son of the "Old Man Travelling," the "Female Vagrant," and the narrator of "The Thorn." Let us follow the last of these, for he will take us beyond thematic analysis.

As Wordsworth informed readers in his sustained prose note to "The Thorn," his narrator has been a "Captain of a small trading vessel," and is now "past the middle of life"; while he has come home to England, he has "retired to some village or country town of which he was not a native, or in which he had not been accustomed to live" – which is to say that he, too, is neither foreigner nor native but both at once (*LB*, p. 288). The captain himself relates that he comes "with his telescope, / To view the ocean wide and bright," when a storm arises, and through "mist and rain, and storm and rain," his eye is caught by "a woman seated on the ground," a hill of moss, a thorn, and next to them all, a notably reduced version of the haunted sea in the nostalgia-calenture topos whose provenance we have followed – he sees, that is, a pond ("The Thorn," ll. 181–2, 188, 198). This pond, we are told no fewer than three times by a refrain that has generated considerable mirth and contempt since 1800, measures "three feet long and two feet wide": "I've measured it from side to side: / 'Tis three feet long and two feet wide" (ll. 32–3), chants the captain. The precision of its dimensions notwithstanding, it is no less a delusive screen than Leonard's flashing scene which reflected back to him images of his own earlier self. "The Thorn"'s sea-captain puzzles:

> Some say, if to the point you go,
> And fix on it a steady view,
> The shadow of a babe you trace,
> A baby and a baby's face,
> And that it looks on you;
> Whene'er you look on it, 'tis plain
> The baby looks at you again.
> ("The Thorn," ll. 225–31)

The minds of men like the narrator, Wordsworth's note informs us, "are not loose but adhesive"; as he adds, in a well-known phrase, they "*cleave* to the same ideas" (emphasis added). They are, one might add, like the medical nostalgics from Hofer on (nostalgia, we recall from Hofer, "brings back the animal spirits as though fixed or rather directed always toward the same motion"). Such minds as the captain's circle around an *idée fixe*, where the emphasis falls on the "fixed" and the small – "'Tis three feet long and two feet wide" – out of which impressive effects are built.

All of this would be illuminating in a passing way, but we need not play "name that theme" or "diagnose that nostalgic." The important point instead is that in "The Thorn" and its explanatory note the effects of nostalgia are no longer just a subject of representation – they have become a defining principle of representation. Wordsworth's note, that is, absorbs the disorder that the *Ballads* render topically into the very groundwork of his aesthetic theory. Hence the following portion of the note's discussion includes some of his most important statements about "Poetry," including the phrase that provides this chapter's epigraph:

> There is a numerous class of readers who imagine that the same words cannot be repeated without tautology; this is a great error: virtual tautology is much oftener produced by using different words when the meaning is the same. Words, a Poet's words more particularly, ought to be weighed in the balance of feeling, and not measured by the space which they occupy upon paper. For the Reader cannot be too often reminded that Poetry is passion: it is the history or science of feelings; now every man must know that an attempt is rarely made to communicate impassioned feelings without something of an accompanying consciousness of the inadequateness of our own powers or the deficiencies of language. *During such effort there will be a craving in the mind, and as long as it is unsatisfied the speaker will cling to the same words, or words of the same character.* There are also various reasons why repetition and apparent tautology are frequent beauties of the highest kind. Among the chief of these reasons is the interest which the mind attaches to words, not only as symbols of the passion, but as THINGS, active and efficient, which are of themselves part of the passion.   (*LB*, pp. 288–9, emphasis added)

Trotter's and others' "cravings of appetite" may find their lineal descendant here, in that "craving of the mind." Coleridge's acidic comment about "The Thorn" – "It is not possible to imitate truly a dull and garrulous discourser, without repeating the effects of dullness and garrulity"[21] – is on target in a way that even Coleridge did not quite mean. Repetition is the point: *not only* the repetition of the narrator's chattering qualities in the haplessly prosy "Mr. Wordsworth," but also the reproduction of the sea-captain's "cleaving" and "adhesive" mind in the reader, whose mind is to be marooned upon words as things. The poet, it seems, wants to make craving nostalgics of us all – that is, to correct our eyes from skimming the "space upon paper" by catching our minds in the same repetitive motion, to induce or encourage thought's tendency to return to the same grooves, grooves which the period's science had rendered quite literally. "To the thorn, and to the pond / Which is a little step beyond, / I wish that you would go," chants the narrator, and – like the "*Ich will heim, Ich will heim*" of Hofer's patient – that is indeed the effect of tautology over and over again: "And that it looks on you; / Whene'er you look on it, 'tis plain / The baby looks at you again." Here, the once dangerous disease, the threatening immobility amid mobility, has come to describe the sort of sensuous cognition induced by reading, characterized here as a mindfulness of the affective weight ("balance of feeling") rather than the semantic or informational content of words.

What do the feelings know, or "balance," in their "science"? That question is inseparable from what we make of the arrested locomotion – the logo-motion – that the poem, according to Wordsworth, seeks both to recreate and to induce by means of tautology and other forms of repetition or repetitive motion. Notwithstanding the attempt to convert the dangerous passions into more profitable "interest" in the later part of the note, there remains something frightening, and altogether resistant to the discourse of profit, about this clinging, here no less than in the case of "We Are Seven" or the "Last of the Flock."[22] This is a cleaving that brings out the full antithetical senses of the verb "to cleave": to join (as in Genesis's "a man shall cleave unto his wife, and they shall be one flesh") and to sunder, tear apart. It is a clinging-to that attempts precariously to fend off a profound separation or endless circulation, just as (and at the same time as) words as things are preferred to words valued for their exchangeability – either as "symbols of the passion" or as spaces on the paper. This is not the distancing of the present associated with sentimental nostalgia. What is transported or revealed in the passage from the medical accounts into Wordsworth's deliberately cultivated pathology of communication – in short, in the movement from medical nostalgia to poetic tautology – is something of that other term in the full phrase "the *history* and science of feelings": the history that lies behind both "sciences" and which doctors faced with cases of nostalgia sought vainly to cure – the pathos of motion, or a certain kind of endless, unfree motion.

Wordsworth's conception of "Poetry" as the "science of feelings" thus intervenes where the medical writings on nostalgia had previously lodged: as an attempt at once to register and to address the pathologies of motion that emerge in response to increased mobility, expansion, exploration, and the underside of all of these, war. His understanding of such a charge I take to underlie the peculiar (and ludic) comments about meter a few sentences earlier in the "Note on the Thorn": "It was necessary that the Poem, to be natural, should in reality move slowly, yet I hoped that, by the aid of the metre . . . it would appear to move quickly. The Reader will have the kindness to excuse this note, as I am sensible that an Introductory Poem is necessary to give this Poem its full effect." The over-explanation here may reflect not just the spreading infection of the captain's "garrulity" but, more urgently, the poet's own sense that something quite important but unresolved is at stake in achieving the proper readerly "motions" – neither too quick nor too slow – although it remains entirely and symptomatically unclear whether the poem moves slowly or quickly. (Try, reading those lines, to discern an answer!) In this respect, as I have tried to suggest, there remains an important difference between Wordsworth's "science of feelings" and the medical treatments. Where the former had been intent on restoring healthy motions, or at least an adaptive equilibrium thereof, Wordsworth – notwithstanding his later, Victorian reputation as a physician to the feelings – seems more willing to court the disease, to inculcate a kind of cognitive fixation, and to stage the dialectic between cleaving to and apart. Hence, here even the grandest claim for poetry as a human science, rival and heir apparent to the Enlightenment systems of human nature, is inseparable from a description of various effects of compulsory movement – inseparable from poetry as repetitive motion syndrome. Indeed, even the declaration itself ("Poetry is . . .") becomes subject to near-compulsive utterance ("the Reader cannot be too often reminded"). Tautology not only provided, as Celeste Langan has suggested in an important reading of the note, a defamiliarizing brake – a technique for challenging what the Advertisement to the 1798 ballads had called "our own pre-established codes of decision."[23] It also acts as a thorn in the side of ideologies of progress, forward mobility, and cure, a resistance in the finite mind to infinite motion.

Free spirits and forced motions: Coleridge's response

Coleridge, initial collaborator in the *Lyrical Ballads* project, is in this as in most instances a particularly canny reader of Wordsworth's poetry, and I would suggest that the *Biographia Literaria* grasps the implications of Wordsworth's earlier resistance to comfortable or healing "motions." For here it is worth recalling that alongside Coleridge's more frequently discussed disagreements with his estranged coauthor – his acute skepticism toward Wordsworth's claims about the "real language of men" and his unsentimental demystification of the "Preface"'s idealization of rustic life – the problem of poetic motion also resides at the core of the dispute waged rather unilaterally by the *Biographia Literaria*. By poetic motion I mean, as both poets did, two things, clearly inseparable: the motion simulated and induced by the poem and the techniques of meter, which contribute, along with other verbal effects, to that overall motion.

In one of the two chapters that discuss "The Thorn," Coleridge parts from Wordsworth's claim in the "Preface" to *Lyrical Ballads* that meter effects no difference between the language of poetry and that of prose. It does make a difference, responds Coleridge, because the artificial superaddition of meter to the elements of diction constitutes, or should constitute, a "*voluntary* act," so that "traces of *volition* should throughout the metrical language be proportionally discernible" (*BL*, vol. II, p. 65, emphasis original). "There must be," he continues, "an interpenetration of passion and will, of *spontaneous* impulse and of *voluntary* purpose." "The legitimate poem," he had argued three chapters earlier (also in response to Wordsworth), "must be one, the parts of which mutually support and explain each other," and if they do, that "interpenetration" of passion and will, spontaneous impulse and voluntary purpose, will transfer itself to the reading process:

> The reader should be carried forward, not merely or chiefly by the mechanical impulse of curiosity, or by a restless desire to arrive at the final solution, but by the pleasureable activity of the mind excited by the attractions of the journey itself. Like the motion of a serpent, which the Egyptians made the emblem of intellectual power; or like the path of sound through the air, at every step he pauses and half recedes, and from the retrogressive movement collects the force which again carries him onward. "Precipitandus est *liber* spiritus" says Petronius Arbiter most happily.   (*BL*, vol. II, p. 14, emphasis original)

"The free spirit must be hurried onward": Coleridge's happy or, at the least, wishful model of a partial regression that acts as forward propulsion seeks an alternative to tautological circularity – to such "unmeaning repetitions" that, the *Biographia* comments suspiciously, can resemble the place-keeping and face-saving antics of a poor play-actor who "in the scanty companies of a country stage . . . pops backwards and forward, in order to prevent the appearance of empty spaces, in the procession of Macbeth, or Henry VIII" (*BL*, vol. II, p. 57). Turning back to earlier eighteenth-century art criticism – to Hogarth (whose *Analysis of Beauty* is the source for the serpent analogy) and to Kames, whose *Elements of Criticism* (1762) praised "undulating motion, as of waves, of a flame, of a ship under sail" because "such motion is more free" – Coleridge would restore to reading the pleasures of travel – the tour, the freely chosen trip to the resort.[24]

That possibility, however, rests on the premise that meter and the poetic motions it seeks to induce are a "voluntary act" and not mere "mechanical impulse," nor – recall the classification of nostalgia – a disease of volition. Coleridge may here protest too much. First of all, he may be protesting against more than Wordsworth, or at least a different opponent. All the insistence on "voluntary purpose," "traces of volition," and interpenetration of the will might remind us that the main or at least the first antagonist of the *Biographia Literaria* is Hartley – and, under the rubric of "Hartley," much of the associationist psychology and materialist brain science that negotiated disease as disordered bodily motion, including Erasmus Darwin. From the point of view of the *Biographia*, the problem with physiological schemes like Hartley's and Darwin's is that they take all "traces of volition" out of the free spirit's happy forward precipitance, rendering us all subject to spontaneous impulses and external stimuli. The image that Coleridge chooses for the life of the will in such a system where "ideas are themselves . . . nothing more than their appropriate configurative vibrations" may be resonant by this point:

Again, from this results inevitably, that the will, the reason, the judgment, and the understanding, instead of being the determining causes of association, must needs be represented as its *creatures*, and among its mechanical *effects*. Conceive, for instance, a broad stream, winding through a mountainous country with an indefinite number of currents, varying and running into each other according as the gusts chance to blow from the opening of the mountains. The temporary union of several currents into one, so as to form the main current of the moment, would present an accurate image of Hartley's theory of the will.

(*BL*, vol. I, p. 110, emphasis original)

Coleridge's concerns about tautology and other forms of involuntary motion merge very precisely in the *Biographia* with his protest against the materialist bent of the eighteenth-century sciences of man. Behind all of these lies the nightmare image of the body, buffeted by currents that come from indefinite sources, subjected to motions beyond its control.

Yet this is, in case after case, the defining scenario of so much of Coleridge's poetry: from the tortured vision of life as a "becalmed bark, / Whose Helmsman on an ocean waste and wild / Sits mute and pale his mouldering helm beside," in "Constancy to an Ideal Object," and the longing desire for some distant "breeze that play'st on Albion's shore" in "Homesick, Written in Germany," to the dramatic enactment of both of these agonized lyric stances in Coleridge's most famous contribution to the *Lyrical Ballads*, "The Rime of the Ancient Mariner," certainly a tale of nostalgia if not also of the scurvy. For readers in search of that poem's meaning, Coleridge was on the surface all too ready to oblige by multiplying easy answers, whether in the form of the culminating apothegm of its earliest version ("he prayeth best, who loveth best / All things both great and small") or the later archaizing addition of prose narrative glosses. Yet against the various readings the *Rime* has occasioned in its stages of reception, from a "cock and bull story" (Charles Burney), "a Dutch attempt at German sublimity" (Robert Southey), to an exploration of the consequences of "maritime expansion of the Europeans" (William Empson), we might simply pose its main plot action: the recurrence of objects alternately set and stopped in motion by forces that can be neither identified or controlled from within the poem. I offer the following collage from the poem, with apologies for the pastiche but with remarkably little detriment to the story: "The ship was cheer'd, the Harbour clear'd, / Merrily did we drop"; "Day after day, day after day, / We stuck, ne breath ne motion; / As idle as a painted Ship / Upon a painted Ocean"; "A speck, a mist, a shape, I wist! / And still it ner'd and ner'd: / And, an it dodged a water-sprite, / It plung'd and tack'd and veer'd"; "But in a moment she 'gan stir, / With a short uneasy motion / Backwards and forwards half her length / With a short uneasy motion"; "Upon the whirl, where sank the Ship, / The boat

spun round and round" and so on. The "Ancyent Marinere," "Christabel" –
such poems and protagonists are each *so* very poorly described by Petronius
Arbiter's happily precipitant "free spirit" that we should realize how very
wishful the *Biographia*'s description of poetic legitimacy is, how much more
honored in the breach than in the acceptance. Coleridge's theory may argue
strenuously for meter as a form of voluntary motion, but his verse practice
suggests his fascination with poetry as a "disease of volition," enacting and
thematizing compulsory motion.[25]

"Motions that are sent he knows not whence": history, or feelings beyond science in *The Prelude*

Wordsworth did not offer a formal riposte to the *Biographia Literaria*,
although it is an interesting thought exercise to imagine what that would have
been. I would like to propose that had he done so, the form of his response
would be a passage he had written for the 1805 *Prelude* and preserved for
the 1850 *Prelude*. It will look familiar by now, since it is a transposition of
the nostalgia/calenture topos:

> As one who hangs down-bending from the side
> Of a slow-moving Boat upon the breast
> Of a still water, solacing himself
> With such discoveries as his eye can make
> Beneath him in the bottom of the deeps,
> Sees many beauteous sights, weeds, fishes, flowers,
> Grots, pebbles, roots of trees, and fancies more,
> Yet often is perplex'd, and cannot part
> The shadow from the substance, rocks and sky,
> Mountains and clouds, from that which is indeed
> The region, and the things which there abide
> In their true dwelling; now is cross'd by gleam
> Of his own image, by a sun-beam now,
> *And motions that are sent he knows not whence*,
> Impediments that make his task more sweet;
> – Such pleasant office have we long pursued
> Incumbent o'er the surface of past time
> With like success.[26]

Recollection is rendered here as the kind of mental travel Coleridge advised
as an effect of reading poetry – the mind excited by the attractions of the
journey, purposeful without a purpose. This is also therefore the moment
when the former disease of mobility (signaled by the residue of the green
fields in the sea subplot) is turned into a figure of speech, and the symptom

of the present is converted into a simile about temporal distance and pleasing recollection – that "sweet task" and "pleasant office" in the passage. Gone, too, is the hallucinatory but dangerous clarity of the watery screen in the earlier versions of this scene, which beguiled the boatman to leap in and seek death with fatal longing. What emerges, as a result, is closer to the more familiar and safe nostalgia that others have described, the nostalgia that is "enamored of distance" (see my introduction, above). This viewer cannot see beneath the "surface of past time."

What preserves this benign indeterminacy, and keeps the bottoms from resolving into a deathly invitation? One answer is the very movement of the boat, that recurrent and conventional image in the *Prelude* for what Wordsworth called the "progress of my song" – that is, for the poem propelled gently by its meter, here represented as "slow-moving," and more like the half-receding-fully-forward progressing motion of Coleridge's dreams than the alternately static and madly kinetic unpiloted bark of "The Ancyent Marinere," Coleridge's nightmare. However: the bark is not the only source of movement: there are also those "motions that are sent he knows not whence." They intrigue, precisely because they are represented as arriving from outside the boat-poem and because they are strangely sourceless, with no identifiable origin. A word search for Wordsworth will remind us that "motions" is a word of considerable complexity, as complex and ubiquitous in the *Prelude* as "sense."[27] And for the most part, Wordsworth would like to interpret them either in benign and pantheistic terms, like the "motion and . . . spirit that . . . rolls through all things" in "Tintern Abbey" (ll. 101–3) or else benignly and physiologically, like the "motion of our human blood" in that same poem (44), or the "hallowed and pure motions of the sense" in the first book of the *Prelude* (1805, 1, l. 551).

Yet these "motions that are sent he knows not whence" in the *Prelude* 4 passage do not fit such available patterns easily. As impulses without an identifiable source, they have the unpredictable potential of the arbitrary eddying currents that Coleridge deplored in his discussions of Hartley's passive will. At the same time, though, they are also no longer bodily motions, as in Hartley, or in Darwin's sensuously rising "fibrous motions," or in the medical literature on nostalgia and other diseases of the will. Wordsworth is drawing on this literature, just as he is drawing on the specific nostalgia/calenture topos, but the physiological motions from the medical literature *have moved outward*, into the arena of context, "atmosphere," air or environment. The apperception of mobility that emerges from the relay of figurations (from the scientific to the poetic) is not the same that went into the medical dissertations and nosologies we started with. The dialectical movement of history through its articulations – as I have tried to suggest, the movement whereby a waning medical discourse waxes as a nascent aesthetic one – is not tautological or repetitive in the static sense. The awareness here seems different and relatively clearer, even if it is as apparently minimal as the difference between attending to a particular "case" history (this sick sailor, that unhappy soldier, etc.) and widening the frame to apprehend *as external* the motions that partly guide the boat's ways – forces in excess of any single pilot, voyage plan, or act of volition, forces that Marxist historiography has sometimes called an "absent cause." (They do not, however, preclude steering the boat – Wordsworth's nuanced version yields neither to total determinism nor to a simple faith that the free spirit precipitates itself forward.)

I would suggest, then, that those physiological motions, or more precisely those motions that the earlier writings had rendered in organic terms, here yield up an image or figuration of the historical content they misrecognized there (see "Motion sickness," above). It is as if we catch a physiological materialism (in this case, the waning medical discourse of "motions") yielding its place to, yet also producing, the grounds of a proto-historical materialism, a nascently historicist kind of thinking. Of course, from a tidy and positive historiographical perspective, one might want a fuller account or contextual mapping of the conditions of a modern mobility. Yet historians are rarely in the boat – the owl of Minerva, as Hegel observed, takes flight at dusk, and the historian's perspective, like necessity, is apparent only after the fact, or from the shore. They have a harder time identifying what Raymond Williams, with an aptly scientific metaphor, called history "in solution," or what I have called, with an intentionally double sense, history in motion.[28] But it is in just such a situation, where a full view of history lies beyond immediate sense experience at the same time that its conditions exert a tangible, if mediated, pressure on sense, that figures can carry on a particular and important kind of semantic work. The point here is that the choice of figure is not arbitrary, for the nostalgia subplot supplies a kind of context – a long and charged genealogy of voyagers parted from their true dwelling and therefore crossing everywhere the gleam of its image.

NOTES

1 William Wordsworth and Samuel Taylor Coleridge, *Lyrical Ballads*, ed. R. L. Brett and A. R. Jones, 2nd edn. (London and New York: Routledge, 1991), p. 288. Hereafter *LB*.

2 Paul de Man, "The Intentional Structure of the Romantic Image," in *The Rhetoric of Romanticism* (New York: Columbia University Press, 1985), p. 6. First published in 1960 (in French).

3 Susan Stewart, *On Longing: Narratives of the Miniature, the Gigantic, the Souvenir, the Collection* (Durham, NC: Duke University Press, 1993), pp. 23, 145.

4 Linda Hutcheon, "Irony, Nostalgia, and the Postmodern," in *Methods for the Study of Literature as Cultural Memory*, ed. Raymond Vervliet and Annemarie Estor (Atlanta: Rodopi, 2000), p. 195; Fredric Jameson, *Postmodernism, or, the Cultural Logic of Late Capitalism* (Durham, NC: Duke University Press, 1999), p. 21.

5 Nicholas Dames, *Amnesiac Selves: Nostalgia, Forgetting, and British Fiction, 1810–1870* (Oxford: Oxford University Press, 2001).

6 Mary A. Favret, "War in the Air," *Modern Language Quarterly* 65 (2004), pp. 531–59; "Everyday War," *English Literary History* 72 (2005), pp. 605–33.

7 For a discussion of Poetry as a discourse or "anthropologic," see Maureen N. McLane, *Romanticism and the Human Science: Poetry, Population, and the Discourse of the Species* (Cambridge: Cambridge University Press, 2000), especially ch. 1.

8 Ian Hacking, *Mad Travelers: Reflections of the Reality of Transient Mental Illness* (Cambridge, MA: Harvard University Press, 2002).

9 Johannes Hofer, *Dissertatio Medica de nostalgia* (Basel, 1688); trans. Carolyn Kiser Anspach, *Bulletin of the History of Medicine* 2 (1934), pp. 381, 384.

10 Ibid., p. 387.

11 Ibid., p. 385.

12 Erasmus Darwin, *Zoonomia, or the Laws of Organic Life*, in *The Collected Writings of Erasmus Darwin*, introd. Martin Priestman, 9 vols. (Bristol: Thoemmes Continuum, 2004), vol. IX, pp. 82–3.

13 From William Cullen's lectures on pathology, quoted in John Thomson, *The Life, Lectures, and Writings of William Cullen*, 2 vols. (Bristol: Thoemmes Press, 1997), vol. I, pp. 329–30.

14 Thomas Beddoes, MD, *Hygëia: or Essays Moral and Medical*, 3 vols. (Bristol: J. Mills, 1803), vol. III, p. 168.

15 See Alan Bewell, *Romanticism and Colonial Disease* (Baltimore: Johns Hopkins University Press, 1999).

16 Trotter, quoted in *The Health of Seamen: Selections from the Works of Dr. James Lind, Sir Gilbert Blane, and Dr. Thomas Trotter*, ed. Christopher Lloyd (London: Navy Records Society, 1965), p. 269. Sir James Pringle, *Observations on the Diseases of the Army, with Notes by Benjamin Rush, MD* (Philadelphia, 1810), p. 81.

17 Thomas Trotter, *Observations on the Scurvy, with a Review of the Opinions Lately Advanced on that Disease*, 2nd edn. (London: printed for T. Longman and J. Watts, 1792), pp. 44–5.

18 William Cowper, *The Task* 1.447–54, quoted from *The Task and Other Poems*, ed. James Sambrook (New York: Longman, 1994).

19 Bewell, *Romanticism and Colonial Disease*, pp. 56–7.

20 See Jonathan Lamb, "'The Rime of the Ancient Mariner,' a Ballad of the Scurvy," *Pathologies of Travel*, ed. Robert Wrigley and George Revill (Atlanta: Rodopi, 2000), pp. 157–77; and *Preserving the Self in the South Seas, 1680–1840* (Chicago: University of Chicago Press, 2001), pp. 117–18, 126, 128.

21 Coleridge, *Biographia Literaria*, ed. James Engell and W. Jackson Bate, 2 vols., Bollingen series (Princeton: Princeton University Press, 1983), vol. II, p. 49. Hereafter *BL*.

22 On this point, see Geoffrey H. Hartman, *Wordsworth's Poetry, 1787–1814* (Cambridge, MA: Harvard University Press, 1987), p. 143.

23 Celeste Langan, *Romantic Vagrancy: Wordsworth and the Simulation of Freedom* (Cambridge: Cambridge University Press, 1995), p. 124.

24 Henry Home, Lord Kames, *Elements of Criticism*, 6th edn., ed. Peter Jones, 2 vols. (Indianapolis: Liberty Fund, 2005), vol. I, p. 180.

25 For a similar treatment of compulsory motion, speech, and meter in "Christabel" and the *Biographia*, see Celeste Langan, "Pathologies of Communication from Coleridge to Schreber," *South Atlantic Quarterly* 102 (2003), pp. 117–52.

26 William Wordsworth, *The Thirteen-Book Prelude*, ed. Mark L. Reed, 2 vols. (Ithaca: Cornell University Press, 1991), vol. I, p. 157 (1805 *Prelude* 4, ll. 247–64) (emphasis added).

27 For a famous discussion of "sense" in *The Prelude*, see William Empson, *The Structure of Complex Words*, reprint edn. (Cambridge, MA: Harvard University Press, 1989), pp. 289–305.

28 For Williams, see, e.g., *Marxism and Literature* (Oxford: Oxford University Press, 1977), p. 133. For an extension of this argument about history on the move, see Kevis Goodman, *Georgic Modernity and British Romanticism: Poetry and the Mediation of History* (Cambridge: Cambridge University Press, 2004).

FURTHER READING

Cheeke, Stephen, *Byron and Place: History, Translation, Nostalgia* (New York: Palgrave Macmillan, 2003)

Christensen, Jerome, *Coleridge's Blessed Machine of Language* (Cornell: Cornell University Press, 1981)

Colley, Linda, *Captives: Britain, Empire and the World 1600–1850* (London: Jonathan Cape, 2002)

Cunningham, Andrew, and Nicholas Jardine, eds., *Romanticism and the Sciences* (Cambridge: Cambridge University Press, 1990)

Fox, Christopher, Roy Porter, and Robert Wokler, eds., *Inventing Human Science: Eighteenth-Century Domains* (Berkeley and Los Angeles: University of California Press, 1995)

Fulford, Tim, Debbie Lee, and Peter J. Kitson, *Literature, Science, and Exploration in the Romantic Era: Bodies of Knowledge* (Cambridge: Cambridge University Press, 2004)

Manning, Susan, "Antiquarianism, the Scottish Science of Man, and the Emergence of Modern Disciplinarity," in *Scotland and the Borders of Romanticism*, ed. Leith Davis, Ian Duncan, and Janet Sorensen (Cambridge: Cambridge University Press, 2004)

Richardson, Alan, *Romanticism and the Science of the Mind* (Cambridge: Cambridge University Press, 2001)

Starobinski, Jean, "The Idea of Nostalgia," *Diogenes* 54 (1966), pp. 81–103

11

WILLIAM KEACH

Rethinking Romantic poetry and history: lyric resistance, lyric seduction

Now look around, and turn each trifling page,
Survey the precious works that please the age;
This truth at least let Satire's self allow,
No dearth of Bards can be complained of now:
The loaded Press beneath her labour groans,
And Printer's devils shake their weary bones,
While SOUTHEY's Epics cram the creaking shelves,
And LITTLE's Lyrics shine in hot-pressed twelves.[1]
Byron, *English Bards and Scotch Reviewers*

I

Lyric poetry was long accorded paradigmatic status within the cultural formations we call Romanticism. But for more than a decade now this paradigm has been the focus of intense, productive rethinking. The older consensus prioritized a poetry – and a poetics – of private subjectivity and reflexive interiority, with its formal achievements motivated primarily by a distinctive psychological and philosophical agenda and by a commitment to imaginative transcendence over social engagement. This consensus has now given way to more varied accounts that emphasize generic diversity, canonical openness, and historical determination.

Lyric's status within Romantic scholarship has shifted gradually but decisively since the 1980s. The historicist interventions of that decade by Jerome McGann, Marilyn Butler, Marjorie Levinson, Clifford Siskin, Alan Liu, James Chandler, and others established fresh possibilities for assessing the centrality of lyric in Romantic culture. More recently Chandler has shown that in the case of Shelley especially, lyric is constitutive of – not just constituted by or within – the historicity of Romantic discourse. Anne Janowitz has explored the powerful "communitarian" current in Romantic lyric poetry that developed alongside – sometimes in tension with, sometimes as an extension of – the traditionally privileged "individualist" current. And Sarah Zimmerman, arguing that recent historicist work has actually been less consequential for our assumptions about lyric than about other prominent genres, has advocated "collapsing" such habitual distinctions as private/public, personal/social, and autobiographical/historical as part of grasping more fully "the social responsiveness of lyric poems." Zimmerman's interest in the "social responsiveness" of "poems that seem to resist historical engagement and thereby to uphold conventional views of the mode as inherently asocial" is particularly relevant to the questions I will pursue here.[2]

Even a cursory survey of lyric poetry in the Romantic period reveals its often overt critical resistance to social conditions in Britain in a moment of sustained historical crisis. From the older generation of Romantic writers there is Blake seeing signs of apocalyptic change in the "marks of woe" and "mind forged manacles" of "London," Wordsworth recognizing the significance of the Haitian revolution in "To Toussaint L'Ouverture," Coleridge agonizing over Britain's war with France in "Fears in Solitude." And from the younger Romantics there are Byron's and Shelley's sustained poetic attacks on imperialist war abroad and political corruption at home, as well as Clare's laments over the devastating effects of agricultural enclosure. My agenda in this chapter presupposes a recognition of such explicitly historical and political Romantic poetry but extends it to include a less obvious alternative conception of lyric resistance, a conception most incisively developed (with differing emphases) in the writing of Theodor Adorno and Walter Benjamin.

What Adorno and Benjamin have to say about lyric is philosophically subtle and sometimes elusive. But it is indispensable to the difficult and unfinished work of reading the historicity of a Romantic poetry that is *not* overtly historical or political in its modes of reference and representation – a poetry that privileges moments of autonomous affective intensity and reflexive subjectivity in ways that we still take to be definitive of the lyric mode. Such poetry may be engaged not in an escape from history, they argue, but in an aesthetic resistance to it. This alternative sense of resistance combines affective intensity with an intrinsic formal difficulty that refuses unimpeded, habituated cultural appropriation – including appropriation by explicitly liberatory ideological projects. It enables us to avoid the impoverishing constriction of understanding as historically and socially significant only those lyric poems that explicitly claim such significance – and of consigning lyrics that are not explicitly historical or social to a realm of mystified escapism. That Adorno and Benjamin are primarily concerned with modernist lyric and its advent in the mid-nineteenth-century decline of Romanticism gives their work an additional pertinence to the questions on which this chapter is focused. From this perspective, Romantic lyric does not just give way to the depersonalized formal discipline we associate with modernism; it often manifests a demanding stylistic difficulty that both anticipates and challenges modernist poetry's techniques of resisting the dominance of bourgeois culture.

II

In his 1957 essay "On Lyric Poetry and Society," Adorno conceives of lyric as the supreme literary site of the aesthetic itself in its self-defining resistance to capitalist mass culture. Adorno's argument makes its way via characteristic gestures of negation: the opening is all about expectations that he has no intention of meeting, assumptions that he has every intention of exposing as fallacious. At the same time, also characteristically, the essay advances a series of audaciously universalizing claims. The most striking of these holds that the social dimension of lyric writing cannot be grasped through reading practices that simply prioritize social context and historical situatedness. Lyric texts must "not be abused by being made objects with which to demonstrate sociological theses."[3] They must instead be read so that "the social element in them is shown to reveal something *essential* about the basis of their [aesthetic] quality" (pp. 37–8, emphasis added). To grasp the social dimension of a lyric poem, we "must discover how the entirety of a society, conceived as an internally contradictory unity, is manifested in the work of art" (pp. 38–9). The "approach must be an immanent one. Social concepts should not be applied to the works from without but rather drawn from an exacting examination of the works themselves" (p. 39). In its most extreme moments of immanent aesthetic essentialism and purity ("the demand that the lyric word be virginal," p. 39), as Adorno himself acknowledges, the essay borders on a kind of methodological perversity: "it is precisely what is not social in the lyric poem that is now to become its social aspect" (p. 42).

Adorno regards lyric as a paradigmatic mode of the aesthetic in its reflexive inwardness, its commitment to "the priority of linguistic form" (p. 43), its intrinsic relation to music. The guiding principle – inclusive yet nonetheless paradoxical in its articulation – is that "the lyric work is always the subjective expression of a social antagonism" (p. 45). There may be an allusion here to Leon Trotsky's remarkable polemic in *Literature and Revolution* against Proletkult demands that poetry always explicitly represent the experience of the working class. Writing in the aftermath of the 1917 Russian Revolution and the devastating civil war fought to defend its gains, Trotsky insists that it is nonsense to say that we demand that the poets should describe inevitably a factory chimney, or the uprising against capital! . . . Personal lyrics of the very smallest scope have an absolute right to exist within the new art . . . the new man cannot be formed without a new lyric poetry. But to create it, the poet himself must feel the world in a new way.[4]

With a later and far more pessimistic sense of the determining "social antagonism[s]" of his own historical moment, Adorno too emphasizes that lyric reveals its most important social significance through the formal articulation of interiorized and individuated experiences that emerge, through a necessarily antagonistic process of articulation, from a "collective undercurrent" (p. 45) of social experience.

It is at the level of form and style that lyric enacts what Adorno takes to be its defining resistance to hegemonic ideologies and to commodification. Robert Kaufman is right to question any tendency to locate Adorno within a "critique of aesthetic ideology" tradition, and to insist instead that "On Lyric Poetry and Society" "is dedicated to immersion in poetic form, to full experience of and engagement with its textures, syntaxes, rhythms, and tonalities."[5] What Kaufman terms "lyric formalism" is intrinsic to Adornian resistance – to a resistance that generates effects of "estrangement" or "alienation" through stylistic "difficulty" and "complexity." In "On Lyric Poetry and Society" we get a glimpse of what such formalist resistance means for critical practice in Adorno's brief readings of a Romantic text – Eduard Mörike's "Auf einer Wanderung" ("On a Walking Tour") – and of a modernist text by Stefan George ("Im windes-weben," "In the winds-weaving," from the song cycle *Seventh Ring*), a poem at once linked to and separated from Mörike's by the "remains of Romanticism" (p. 51). Of particular significance for the possibilities of using Adorno's "lyric formalism" to read stylistic resistance in British Romantic lyric is the trajectory Adorno follows from Mörike's Romanticism into modernist lyric's negative work of recognizing, by resisting, historical circumstances and social forces that threaten to deny the possibility of lyric aura.

"Aura" is Benjamin's crucial term for that specifically aesthetic sense of the unique "authority of the object" that derives from our belief in authorial originality as the basis of "authentic" artistic production. Benjamin's brilliant, divagating commentary "On Some Motifs in Baudelaire" (1939) begins by accentuating a kind of lyric resistance that runs counter to but also complements Adorno's later argument: "Baudelaire envisaged readers to whom the reading of lyric poetry would present difficulties."[6] The "difficulties" Benjamin has in mind here are in one sense antithetical to Adorno's emphasis on the formal difficulty of poetry that refuses easy appropriation by capitalist culture. Baudelaire's mid-nineteenth-century readers are too bored and distracted by urban life for lyric to matter, not (as in Adorno's scenario) too eager for and credulous of the nostalgia and sensuous escapism that most readers imagine lyric poetry offers. As Benjamin continues, however, this resistance in Baudelaire's readers inverts and transforms itself into a resistance within the lyric text itself, particularly into poetic gestures that reveal Baudelaire's "defensive reaction" to the perverse "attraction and allure" of the urban masses (p. 167). Among these gestures is an enacted collapse of aesthetic perception, grasped figuratively by Benjamin as a collapse of the reciprocated human look or gaze. The more intensely Baudelaire longed for such social and aesthetic reciprocity, "the more unmistakably did the disintegration of the aura make itself felt in his lyrical poetry" (p. 189). The advent of modern European lyric poetry appears, for Benjamin, through an introjection of the denial of the social and psychological conditions that make lyric possible in the first place. It is partly in response to Benjamin's analysis that Adorno affirms, almost two decades later, his version of an aesthetic of lyric resistance.

More emphatically than Benjamin, Adorno regards lyric as the supreme case of art's precarious ability to assert its claim to autonomy and critical agency through acts of resistance that articulate themselves as stylistic difficulty, risk, experimentation. Referential and ideological content matters to Adorno at the level of style; it matters insofar as it is trans-formed into textual materiality. Furthermore, and with more problematic implications, Adorno's poetics – and his aesthetics more comprehensively – posit a process of cultural recognition and valuation that operates through the elaboration of deductive analytical principles. The contingent pressures of cultural production at a given historical moment usually have little bearing on his critical judgments. For Adorno, it would seem, there is no such thing as bad or shallow or self-indulgent lyrics, or lyrics that accept established poetic conventions and regimes of social power. Verse texts that fail to meet his criteria of formal difficulty and resistance do not count as lyrics at all. The idea that lyric poetry might meet Adorno's aesthetic criteria and, for example, attempt to engage a broad readership on commercially viable and popular terms is theoretically impossible.

To amplify and also to complicate what is at issue in Adorno's and Benjamin's conceptions of lyric resistance, I turn to Frank Lentricchia's "Lyric in the Culture of Capital" (1991), an extrinsically oriented, anti-essentialist essay that stands in especially productive contrast to Adorno's poetics of immanent essentialism. Although Lentricchia's main concern is with the careers of Pound, Frost, and other American modernist poets, he identifies an investment in lyric among these writers that emerges in contradictory ways from what he calls "the anticapitalism of Romantic literary theory" and its resistance to the production of lyric poems as marketable commodities.[7] Lentricchia's assumptions about Romantic "anticapitalism," though not the critical uses to which he puts this idea, have much in common with those of Michael Löwy and Robert Sayre in *Romanticism against the Tide of Modernity*.[8] Lyric resistance comes into existence, Lentricchia shows, as an inevitable counterforce to the circumstances of poetic materialization in captalist culture: to be published, read, reviewed, and recognized is to submit to a process of commodification regarded as both destructive and seductive. Literary commodification is subject, of course, to the class position and gender of both author and reader, and to the range of specific institutional circumstances in which particular forms of writing were published and sold. Lentricchia's account is centered on twentieth-century male poets who needed to sell their poems to acquire economic as well as cultural capital; the terms would have to shift significantly for women poets of the Romantic era – or for men, such as Byron, with enough wealth and social power to forgo (for a time) dependence on the market for literature.[9]

The key mediation in the development Lentricchia follows out of Romanticism into high modernism is provided by the mid- and late nineteenth-century anthologies of poetry – preeminently by Francis Palgrave's *Golden Treasury of the Best Songs and Lyrical Poems* (first published in 1861, expanded and reissued into the twentieth century). Palgrave's title, unwittingly or otherwise, echoes the opening line of Keats's 1816 sonnet about access to literary riches, "On First Looking into Chapman's Homer": "Much have I travelled in the realms of gold." Keats's lyric transmutation of monetary and eventually of imperial gold ("stout Cortez" presides over the sonnet's final lines) into unforeseen aesthetic value provides an ideological and figurative point of reference within Romanticism for Palgrave's project of making the "Best . . . Lyrical Poems" available to a new range of Victorian readers whose struggle for economic success threatened to deprive them of great poetry's civilizing power. Palgrave aimed, Lentricchia maintains, at nothing less than "liberating the spiritual life of the capitalist subject" (p. 198). Central to this project was an ideology of lyric purity and "disengagement" that, ironically, issued in anthologized "commodities of lyric sameness," "snippets of lyric grace" (p. 199) that brilliantly succeeded in becoming the very kind of marketable things to which they were imagined as ideal alternatives.

Modernists such as Pound repudiated Palgrave's attempt to accommodate the lyric tradition to the perceived needs of a mass readership while failing to resolve the dilemma of poetry's socioeconomic viability. Pound and Frost moved in radically divergent directions in responding to this dilemma, with correspondingly divergent strategies for preserving lyric's capacity for resisting the relentlessly seductive pressure to produce what book and magazine publishers would sell. Lentricchia's account makes evident, as Adorno's does not, the inevitable provocation of and counterforce to lyric resistance – the seductive power of commercial success and popular cultural reception. In Romantic culture, in ways that anticipate a high modernist moment often assumed to have constituted itself through a repudiation of Romanticism, the allure of commercial success and mass popularity often threatened and sometimes succeeded in appropriating a poetic determination to be socially and historically resistant – or indeterminate.

For Adorno, cultural production recognizable as art maintains its identity *as art* through its resistance to and implicit critique of what is culturally normative and dominant. But it can only enter the sphere of culture in the first instance by reifying itself, by becoming a materialized aesthetic object susceptible of collapsing into the very commodity form that it deploys its formal integrity to oppose. How does Romantic lyric perform and survive within the forcefield of this version of Adorno's "negative dialectic"?

III

The dynamic of resistance and seduction I have been foregrounding is different from, though it often exists in intriguing relation to, representations of erotic resistance and seduction that have always been fundamental to lyric poetry. From the Song of Songs to Sappho to Ovid to Provençal song to Petrarch to Sidney to Donne to Byron and Keats, desire as seduction and desire as resistance to seduction have been among lyric's most recurring and recurrently troped configurations. The specific forms of cultural resistance and seduction I am concerned with can have contradictory as well as obvious connections to the erotic rhetoric of the broader lyric tradition. In Blake and Shelley and Keats – and on quite different stylistic and social grounds for each of these writers – the language of erotic seduction may articulate, not the kinds of transparent design upon a reader's desire satirized in Byron's joke in *English Bards and Scotch Reviewers* about Thomas Moore's hot little duodecimo lyric volumes, but rather forms of resistance itself, aesthetic and political. We need to be open to reading some forms of seduction as gestures of lyric resistance.

Turning now from the theoretical possibilities opened up by Adorno, Benjamin, and Lentricchia to the vast range of lyric writing in British Romanticism, I begin with an unlikely but historically important pair of lyric poets. It is impossible to imagine a more unAdornian writer than Mary Robinson. She was, as Judith Pascoe aptly observes, both an innovator "in the literary delineation of emotional extremes" *and* a poet in "frank pursuit of commercial success."[10] Precisely because Robinson's accomplishments are so antithetical to Adorno's ideas of aesthetic integrity, her lyric writing is worth considering from the perspective of a paradigm of resistance and seduction. Recognized in the 1790s for her poetry of emotive extravagance and formal facility (Coleridge exclaimed about "The Haunted Beach" from *Lyrical Tales* [1800], "the metre – ay! that Woman has an Ear"),[11] Robinson is also remarkable for the contradictory variety of her lyric identities – for the array of fictive subject positions and affective performances she invents. Famous in the pages of the *Morning Post* and other papers for writing as Sappho and Lesbia, Robinson performs male lyric voices too – such as the one she adopts in "Oberon to the Queen of the Fairies," first published on June 3, 1790, in an upstart paper called the *Oracle and Public Advertiser*. Oberon tells Mab how he decked himself out in miniature natural finery to visit Maria on behalf of a spurned lover called "Il Ferito," a pseudonym of Robert Merry, the founding figure of the Della Cruscan movement that flourished in the 1780s and early 1790s:

> The am'rous air
> Snatch'd nectar from her balmy lips,
> Sweeter than haughty JUNO sips,
> When GANYMEDE her goblet fills
> With juice the citron bud distills.
>
> (ll. 22–6)

This witty kind of seduction as resistance recalls Robert Herrick's "Oberon's Feast," and also Mercutio's tribute to Queen Mab in Act I of *Romeo and Juliet*. The conventional gender drama of Oberon's facilitating seduction of Maria is resistingly reversed in its being Juno, not Jupiter, whose cup is filled by Ganymede (Rosalind's disguise identity in another Shakespeare play). This is lyric writing with a glissando intensity different from the extravagant abjection staged in Robinson's *Sappho and Phaon* sonnet sequence and other poetry from the 1790s – poetry that has been read by Jerome McGann and others as articulating its own kind of coded political resistance to Tory establishment values.[12] The nectar snatched from Maria's lips here may be sweeter than that served up by Ganymede for the "haughty JUNO," but the logic of the simile leads us to infer that it also has more citric acidity.

Thomas Moore's career as Irish favorite in London Whig social circles began just as Mary Robinson's career came to an end with her death in 1800. Moore's *Odes of Anacreon*, dedicated to Robinson's most famous lover, the Prince of Wales, appeared in this year, followed quickly by the *Poetical Works of Thomas Little* in 1801. Moore immediately developed a reputation as a lyric seducer so trashily suspect that Coleridge refused to have a poem of his own included in a memorial volume for Robinson because the volume was also to include some of Moore's poetry: "I have a wife, I have sons, I have an infant Daughter – what excuse could I offer to my own conscience if by suffering my name to be connected with those of Mr Lewis, or Mr Moore, I was the *occasion* of their reading the Monk, or the wanton poems of Thomas Little Esqre?"[13] For Coleridge, Moore's lyrics are all seduction, no imaginative or formal resistance. This is at bottom Hazlitt's assessment as well – except that for him, particularly in the earlier account given in the 1818 lecture "On the Living Poets," Moore's gift for poetic seduction demands its own recognition: "Mr. Moore's Muse is another Ariel, as light, as tricksy, as indefatigable, and as humane a spirit. His fancy is for ever on the wing, flutters in the gale, glitters in the sun. Every thing lives, moves, and sparkles in his poetry." Moore's most significant "fault," consequently, is the corollary of this very energy – "an exuberance of involuntary power," a "facility of production" that "lessens the effort of . . . what he produces."[14] There is nothing in Moore's lyrics that resists and, in resisting, would become capable of "grappling with the deep-rooted prejudices of the mind, its inveterate habits." Hazlitt sees Moore as simultaneously "heedless, gay, and prodigal of his poetical wealth" and – far more successfully than Robinson – given to turning this very prodigality into profit: "Mr. Moore ought not to have written Lalla Rookh, even for three thousand guineas." "Even" is there in Hazlitt's sentence to indicate that it is not the allure of making money out of the fad for Orientalism that is objectionable, but rather a form of poetic "execution" that "still turns to the effeminate and voluptuous side."

That Moore should be found seductive *and* "effeminate" is a point worth pondering, not least because the posture of seduction in the Thomas Little lyrics is sometimes resistant to any such characterization. There is, for instance, "Did Not," the poem with which W. H. Auden chose to open his selections from Moore in the 1966 anthology *Nineteenth-Century British Minor Poets*:

> 'Twas a new feeling – something more
> Than we had dared to own before,
>   Which then we hid not;
> We saw it in each other's eye,
> And wished, in every half-breathed sigh,
>   To speak, but did not.
>
> She felt my lips' impassioned touch –
> 'Twas the first time I dared so much,
>   And yet she chid not;

But whispered o'er my burning brow,
"Oh! Do you doubt I love you now?"
  Sweet soul! I did not.

Warmly I felt her bosom thrill,
I pressed it closer, closer still,
  Though gently bid not;
Till – oh! The world hath seldom heard
Of lovers, who so nearly erred,
  And yet, who did not.

The predictable masculine urgency in this poem is surrounded by a projection of shared excitement and reciprocal caution. The speaker's "did not" in the middle stanza is framed by shared but differently inflected "did nots" in the first and third. What is shared at the end includes a kind of joke with and on "The world" about just saying no. Moore's lyric enacts a moment of mutual seduction that ends in a gesture of playfully resistant deferral.

It would be easy to dismiss or condescend to this kind of lyric writing from the early 1790s. We do not need Adorno's lofty ideal of lyric integrity or Benjamin's soberly ironized retrospective sense of where Romanticism was heading to discount such lyric wit and return to Blake's *Songs* – or to Burns's, for that matter. My point in beginning with Robinson and Moore is to indicate possibilities of lyric performativity that include finely turned gestures of resistance within a poetry of public literary seduction – seduction practiced upon the British reading public by a *déclassée* actress and royal consort and by the son of a Dublin grocer. Wordsworth and Coleridge had to locate themselves a few years later in a cultural environment attuned to a more complicated and varied lyric spectrum than we are accustomed to recognizing. The aura of early British Romantic lyric could be engendered through evocations of playful urban fancy as well as by expressions of radical apocalyptic subjectivity and reflexively cultivated returns to what the speaker in Wordsworth's "Lines Written in Early Spring" calls "Nature's holy plan." And some features of what we have briefly located in these lyrics of Robinson and Moore survive into later Romantic poetry – in Byron and Percy Shelley, and with a very different affective inflexion in the "Cockney" poetry of Leigh Hunt and Keats.

The case of Byron's lyric poetry is particularly worth reconsidering in this regard. Here, the dynamic of lyric resistance and seduction attains a level of socially and historically constituted intensity that we are not just invited but compelled to read as the function of a uniquely empowered authorial aura. Yet the basic stylistic idiom often recalls Moore, to whom Byron sent the earliest of his four lyrics entitled "Stanzas for Music" on May 4, 1814:

> I speak not – I trace not – I breathe not thy name,
> There is grief in the sound – there were guilt in the fame;
> But the tear which now burns on my cheek may impart
> The deep thought that dwells in that silence of heart.
>
> (ll. 1–4)

"Thou hast asked me for a song," Byron wrote in sending these "Stanzas" to Moore, "and I enclose you an experiment, which has cost me something more than trouble."[15] The "trouble" in question is usually assumed to refer to Byron's sexual intimacy with his half-sister Augusta Leigh, the addressee of "Stanzas." But it may also refer to the kind of lyric "experiment" that Byron is engaging in here. A year after the first two cantos of *Childe Harold's Pilgrimage* had made him unprecedentedly famous, Byron enacts an unspeakably private lyric defiance through a characteristic rhetoric of expressive resistance that reveals as it conceals – and also through the anapestic cadences of Moore's elegiac tribute to Robert Emmet from *Irish Melodies*:

> Oh! Breathe not his name, let it sleep in the shade,
> Where cold and unhonor'd his relics are laid.
>
> (ll. 1–2)

In contrast to Moore's deferential gesture of refusing to name, Byron's is at once imperious and self-exposing. The speaker/singer's passionate connection with and commitment to the "thou" of the poem is at the same time an act of public defiance. Lyric subjectivity here becomes a function of the ways in which this public defiance gets turned back into wished-for, denied, and impossible intimacy. At the end of the poem

> the heartless may wonder at all we resign,
> Thy lip shall reply not to them – but to mine.
>
> (ll. 19–20)

This lyric was not published until five years after Byron's death, so we have to read its construction of fraught private intensity out of conflicted celebrity by projecting beyond the immediate circumstances of Byron's actual relations in 1814 with his newly conquered readership. In this respect the poem is a lyric "experiment" with a delayed public reception.

Yet the implications of these "Stanzas" for an exploration of lyric resistance and seduction are all the more suggestive for the poem's being withheld from publication. Among other things, they put under revealing critical pressure John Stuart Mill's classic pronouncement that "eloquence is *heard*; poetry is *over*heard." What Byron's readers both hear and overhear in this poem is a seductive challenge to their own right to listen. And what about the question of this lyric's "music"? Byron sent the poem to Moore untitled but in response, he says, to a request for a "song," so it is fair to ask: what actual music could these "Stanzas" be "for"? I can think of no nineteenth-century composer – not even Robert Schumann, creator of the brilliant sequence of song-settings for Heinrich Heine's passionate and bitterly ironic "Dichterliebe" ("Poet's Love," 1840) – whom we can imagine producing music appropriate to Byron's "Stanzas." The poem may be an anti-lyric lyric in this literal as well as in other figurative senses. Its disturbing metrical aura has more to do with a troping of conventions and expectations peculiar to the speech rhythms of popular verse such as Moore's and Robinson's than it does with writing that in some sense aspires to the condition of music.

The dimension of lyrical musicality would appear to be quite differently and more predictably present in an 1816 poem that also came to bear the title "Stanzas for Music" when it was published by John Murray in the collected *Poems* of that year:

> There be none of Beauty's daughters
> With a magic like thee;
> And like music on the waters
> Is thy sweet voice to me:
> When, as if its sounds were causing
> The charmed ocean's pausing,
> The waves lie still and gleaming,
> And the lull'd winds seem dreaming:
> (ll. 1–8)

This first stanza spins out its sequence of similes – the first negative, the next two positive – to approximate in words the effect on the speaker's feelings of the addressee's singing. All we can know about the singing itself is registered, ironically, in terms of a deepening quietness and suspension of agitation in the speaker's emotions: the singer's voice moves by producing stillness. The lyric subject's voice, by contrast, moves the reader through a contrapuntal rhythm that expands as it thwarts prosodic habits. It is worth looking back here to W. W. Robson's 1966 essay on Byron and its attentiveness to connections between a lyric's articulation of subjective depth and "the individuality of its verse-rhythm." The thematic substance of "There be none of Beauty's daughters," he observes, "is no more than a gravely conventional compliment, in the Regency manner . . . The imagery . . . is of the same quality as Byron's friend Tom Moore's." But, Robson continues, through "subtle abrogations of regularity" in the rhythm and tempo of the opening lines "(Everything is lost, if we make the semantically insignificant change [in the second line] to 'With a magic *like to* thee')," Byron's poem "may be said to achieve [its] own kind of decorum, a decorum not deriving from any impersonal convention or established mode."[16] This quirky notion of a "decorum" peculiar to a specific lyric event – a "decorum" established through departure from and therefore resistance to conventions that negatively define the rhetorical occasion – strikes me as a valuable way of understanding how Byron's lyrics work to determine the terms on which they enter Regency literary culture.

Different as it is from the 1814 "Stanzas for Music," "There be none of Beauty's daughters" is linked to the earlier lyric through one of Byron's signature figures, the "chain." The pent-up violence of "We repent – we abjure – we will break from our chain" (1814, l. 7) is transmuted rather than dissolved at the beginning of the later poem's second stanza:

> And the midnight moon is weaving
> Her bright chain o'er the deep;
>
> (ll. 9–10)

Byron extends a sense of powerful agitated desire held in momentary affective suspension in the images of a "breast . . . gently heaving" (l. 11), of "a full but soft emotion, / Like the swell of Summer's ocean" (ll. 15–16). Historically this poem may be about John Edelston, Byron's young Cambridge lover whose singing he adored and who died tragically in 1811, or about Claire Clairmont, Mary Shelley's half-sister and Byron's lover during the spring and summer of 1816. Or it may be about both of them: a lyric of transferred reference to two relationships in which singing produced and came to stand for the modulation of tumultuous desire and attachment. The range of referential possibilities in this poem needs to be grasped in terms of a stylistic performance that seduces its readers by inviting but also resisting complete identification with the lyric moment, and that achieves a self-determining aura through what it makes of the determinations of poetic tradition.

What the dialectic of resistance and seduction in Byron's lyrics cannot do is prevent their acquiring the status of literary commodities as they become part of cultural history. In stark contrast to the overtly commercial ambitions of Robinson and Moore, Byron refused to accept payment generated by the sale of his poetry until near the end of his career. Yet the poems were sold nonetheless – and made huge profits for his publisher. (For later publishers as well: the 1816 "Stanzas for Music" was included in Book Fourth of Palgrave's *Golden Treasury*, positioned between lyrics by Scott and Shelley entitled, respectively, "Outlaw" and "Lines to an Indian Air.") A consequence of this process, as Jerome Christensen has argued, was that "Lord Byron" inevitably became a commodified cultural identity, notwithstanding Byron's own efforts inside and outside his writing to use his aristocratic privilege as a resource for attacking the commercial literary production he was already satirizing in *English Bards and Scotch Reviewers*.[17] More certainly than any of his contemporaries, Byron would have grasped the force of Adorno's paradox: "unless [art] reifies itself, it becomes a commodity." The question for him was not whether this was his and every other poet's fate, but whether in becoming commodities, poems necessarily surrender their potential for expressive and critical self-determination.

IV

The history of lyric poetry has always included a resistance to history; it has always valued the momentary suspension, if not the ultimate transcendence, of historical determination. Some of the greatest poems of British Romanticism – Wordsworth's "Tintern Abbey," Shelley's "Mont Blanc," Keats's "Ode to a Nightingale" – express a desire for such suspension or transcendence within contexts that include the defining counter-pressures of transpersonal circumstances and constraints. From the vantage point of the Adornian theory of lyric that I have been working with and against in this chapter, we need to understand how the resistance to history in these and other Romantic lyrics is itself historical – a defining aspect of the terms on which such lyrics become what Benjamin calls "documents of civilization." We also need to understand how such lyric resistance to history is integral to Adorno's principle that all art stands in an inherently contradictory relationship to the social: "art becomes social by its opposition to society, and it occupies this position only as autonomous art."[18]

Adorno's aesthetic of dialectical negation runs counter to much of the recent historicist work on Romantic lyric, with its affirmative emphasis on the evident and elaborated historicity of poetic representation, production, and reception. Under the conditions of capitalist modernity, "subjective expression," the ostensibly traditional term in Adorno's conception of lyric, constructs itself as textual materiality through its formal resistance to and distance from the "social antagonism" that constitutes all art's contextual grounding. This kind of essentialist approach to lyric, as we have seen, significantly limits our ability to read the full range of Romantic poetry's relationship to commodity culture. It has the advantage, however, of insisting on an anti-historical, counter-social impulse that remains extremely important to Romantic lyric, even if it does not – as Adorno would have it – establish a universal defining criterion for what the entire lyric mode can be.

I conclude this chapter by looking briefly at a sequence of textual examples that invite us to read with an Adornian awareness of the historicity of lyric's resistance to history – and with an adjusted sense of the seductions of the literary marketplace. My examples are drawn not from familiar Romantic lyric genres such as the ballad and the sonnet, which have been re-examined recently in work that emphasizes their openness to historical determination and their embracing of "social antagonism" and political agendas, but from a less obvious generic location.[19] Lyric poetry is not limited to the individual lyric poem or lyric sequence. Some of the period's most remarkable experiments in lyric writing, and some of its most challenging opportunities for exploring the dynamic of lyric resistance, are to be found within more extended and ambitious narrative and dramatic forms. In the examples that follow, lyric's traditional privileging of affective intensity and reflexive interiority is distinctively at issue, as is its traditional relation to music. These familiar effects can function within epic mythopoeic narrative as moments of lyric condensation that resist by arresting the narrative's inescapable, historically determined telos.[20]

The most complex transitional moment in Wordsworth's *The Prelude* comes at the beginning of Book VII, following the medial crisis of the visit to revolutionary France and the Alps in Book VI and anticipating the tumultuous experience of London and the return to France in the books that follow.[21] Here, in the longer 1805 version, are the lines that stage Wordsworth's renewed epic undertaking as lyric epiphany:

> But I heard
> After the hour of sunset yester-even,
> Sitting within doors betwixt light and dark,
> A voice that stirred me. 'Twas a little band,
> A quire of redbreasts gathered somewhere near
> My threshold, minstrels from the distant woods
> And dells, sent in by Winter to bespeak
> For the old man a welcome, to announce
> With preparation artful and benign –
> Yea, the most gentle music of the year –
> That their rough lord had left the surly north,
> And hath begun his journey. A delight
> At this unthought-of greeting unawares
> Smote me, a sweetness of the coming time,
> And, listening, I half whispered, "We will be,
> Ye heartsome choristers, ye and I will be
> Brethren, and in the hearing of bleak winds
> Will chaunt together." And, thereafter, walking
> By later twilight on the hills I saw
> A glow-worm, from beneath a dusky shade
> Or canopy of the yet unwithered fern
> Clear shining, like a hermit's taper seen

Through a thick forest. Silence touched me here
No less than sound had done before: the child
Of summer, lingering, shining by itself,
The voiceless worm on the unfrequented hills,
Seemed sent on the same errand with the quire
Of winter that had warbled at my door,
And the whole year seemed tenderness and love.

(Book VII, ll. 20–48)

A lyric representation of lyric's own restorative power, this passage evokes historical duration and age and seasonal change in the process of their yielding momentarily to an unforeseen sense of the "sweetness of the coming time" (l. 33), to an intimation that "the whole year seemed tenderness and love" (l. 48). As so often in *The Prelude*, "seemed" here is the rhetorical mark not of illusion but of visionary phenomenology ("the sky seemed not a sky / Of earth," ll. 349–50). Through a familiar paradoxical merging of "sound" and "Silence" (ll. 42–3), "music" and "shining" light, lyric interrupts and transforms the poem's record of its own historical genesis – "Five years are vanished since I first poured out / . . . A glad preamble to this verse" (ll. 1–4) – and projects its generative potential into the immediate future, as "last night's genial feeling overflowed / Upon this morning" (ll. 49–50).

The beautiful performative enjambment in "Last night's general feeling overflowed / Upon this morning" – the line overflows its own prosodic termination – is characteristic of Wordsworth's blank verse and suggestive of this lyric moment's arresting influence on the poem's autobiographical and historical diegesis. It is a formal effect generated out of an intense lyric responsiveness to nature's "music" – but it is not itself an instance of musical form. Neither, however, is it an instance of what Paul Fry sees as "lyric ostension's" defining discursive register, "language viewed strictly as pure sound and as graphic trace" (p. 21). Fry is rightly skeptical, as was John Hollander in his 1975 study *Vision and Resonance*,[22] of poetry's aspiration to the condition of music, since this aspiration usually "results in the reduction of music to sound" (p. 44). "It is not *music* that poetry hears," Fry continues, "but rather *sound*, with its emphasis on resonance, pitch, and timbre, and an implication even of monotony." The "mesmerization by sound of the will to signify," he says, "must be a permanent resource of poetry" (p. 45). But in Wordsworth's lyric epiphany at the beginning of Book VII of *The Prelude*, the sounds of nature are transfigured into a "gentle music" that quickens rather than mesmerizes the will to signify: the resulting overflow of renewed energy spills over from lyric interruption into resumed autobiographical narration via a textual event that summons up the full range of language's semiotic and syntactic resources. Wordsworthian lyric here empowers by interrupting and resisting the poet's life history, at a moment when he is about to narrate his wanderings "among / The unfenced regions of society" (Book VII, ll. 61–2).

For an instructive contrast to this instance of lyric resistance within Wordsworth's autobiographical epic, consider the following passage from Keats's anti-Wordsworthian epic fragment, *Hyperion*. The narrative context is inescapably historical and political: Saturn and the other Titans gathered around him are lamenting their anticipated fall – the giving way of one ruling order to a new emergent power. The sea goddess Clymene tells how her effort to deflect the misery with "melody" produced by blowing through a shell provokes a musical response from Apollo, the new Sun-god of music and poetry:

> from a bowery strand
> Just opposite, an island of the sea,
> There came enchantment with the shifting wind,
> That did both drown and keep alive my ears.
> I threw my shell away upon the sand,
> And a wave fill'd it, as my sense was fill'd
> With that new blissful golden melody.
> A living death was in each gush of sounds,
> Each family of rapturous hurried notes,
> That fell, one after one, yet all at once,
> Like pearl beads dropping sudden from their string:
> And then another, then another strain,
> Each like a dove leaving its olive perch,
> With music wing'd instead of silent plumes,
> To hover round my head, and make me sick
> Of joy and grief at once.
>
> (Book II, ll. 274–89)

In the odes, Keats interrupts immersions in lyric intensity with the claims of historical temporality and struggling mortality. Here, the mythically allegorized narrative of historical and cultural change is interrupted by a represented experience of lyric that absorbs into itself and places in momentary suspension the anxieties of anticipated loss. The notes of Apollo's music come to Clymene both inside and outside time – "one after one, yet all at once"; they are experienced simultaneously as the breaking of previously constructed sequence ("Like pearl beads dropping sudden from their string") and as a hovering duration that is the fleeting dialectical resolution of determined sequence and free indeterminacy. Clymene is momentarily suspended between her resistance to loss and her joy in irresistibly seductive beauty. It is when her resistance eventually asserts itself most strongly – "Grief overcame, / And I was stopping up my frantic ears" (Book II, ll. 289–90) – that the power of Apollo's music is most overwhelming – "A voice came sweeter, sweeter than all tune" (Book II, l. 292). The passage enacts the power of lyric to arrest historical consciousness within an allegorical unfolding of poetry's own crisis of historical change.

Focusing as I have done on individual moments of lyric intensity in *The Prelude* and *Hyperion* may seem to disregard, even falsify, the more pervasive lyric textures of narration in these poems. But there are advantages to paying especially close attention to the effects such performative thematizations of lyric have on these poems' epic ambitions and trajectories. With Shelley's *Prometheus Unbound*, the last of the grand Romantic undertakings I offer for fresh consideration from this perspective, we are faced with a still more challenging deployment of lyric. As an experiment in "Lyrical Drama" (the designation in Shelley's subtitle) motivated by a radical utopian politics and by a radically idealist set of philosophical convictions, *Prometheus Unbound* pervasively subordinates to lyric form not only narrative but the fiction of dramatic voice itself. It could be argued that Shelley's *Prometheus* is one continuous exploration of lyric's potential to resist the history of things as they are and of society as it is, and that it accomplishes this resistance as remarkably through its "lyric formalism" (Kaufman's Adornian term) as through its explicit political vision.

Within this sustained lyric register are textual utterances identified exclusively as lyric functions – "Chorus" and "Semichorus," "Voice" and "Echo." Shelley's experimenting with these lyric fictions presents important opportunities for reading in terms of a paradigm of resistance/seduction. Consider the sequence that emerges out of Panthea's astonishing exchange with Asia about her prophetic dreams in Act II, scene 1. They eventually envision being able to "read" – on the blossoms shed from a "lightning-blasted almond tree" and in "the shadows of the morning clouds" – variations on the words "O follow, follow." First written and read, then spoken and heard, these words will eventually lead Asia and Panthea to Demogorgon's realm of necessity. But the inscribed words must first be re-articulated as natural echo and song.

> ECHOES
> O follow, follow,
>   As our voice recedeth
> Through the caverns hollow
>   Where the forest spreadeth;
>   [*More distant.*]
>   O follow, follow,
>   Through the caverns hollow,
> As the song floats, thou pursue

> Where the wild-bee never flew,
> Through the noontide darkness deep,
> By the odour breathing sleep
> Of faint night-flowers, and the waves
> At the fountain-lighted caves,
> While our music, wild and sweet,
> Mocks thy gently-falling feet,
>   Child of Ocean!
>   (Book II, Act I, ll. 173–87)

Shelley is exploring a power of song that is simultaneously seductive and resistant – literally seductive, in that it will eventually lead Asia and Panthea "Down, Down! / . . . Through the veil and the bar / Of things which seem and are" (Book II, Act II, ll. 55–60); dramatically resistant, in that it refuses to limit its significance to existing historical discourses of "things which seem and are." The Echoes in Act II anticipate and make possible the condition of utopian attainment celebrated in Act IV, when language is imagined as "a perpetual Orphic song" (l. 415). In *Prometheus Unbound*, the imagination of utopian self-liberation and self-realization assumes the form of perpetual lyric – the form human language assumes as it confronts its own historicity in the impossible effort to extend itself beyond the historical.

The experimental lyricism of *Prometheus Unbound* is everywhere shaped by Shelley's critical utopianism: from within history as we presently know it, the "good place" (*eu-topos*) is "no place" (*ou-topos*). In this respect especially, Shelley's poetic "experiment" is convergent with Adorno's and Benjamin's efforts to rethink for modernist poetry Romanticism's belief in the utopian dimension of lyric discourse.[23] One difference marking the lyric utopianism of *Prometheus Unbound* – and of *The Prelude* and *Hyperion* as well – is that the seductions of commercial success so important to the cultural status of shorter lyric poems in the early nineteenth century are much less directly in play. "SOUTHEY's Epics" may have "cram[med] the creaking shelves" in Byron's day – eventually alongside editions of Byron's own poetry – but there was no danger of this becoming the fate of Wordsworth's, Keats's, and Shelley's epic undertakings. In these daringly ambitious poems, lyric is dislocated from its most readily commodifiable forms and from the probability of mass readership; its power of aesthetic resistance is self-consciously placed in the service of personal and cultural desires that are at once more ambitious and more selective in their anticipated reception. Any adequate assessment of Romantic lyric poetry needs to attend to the distinctive functions of lyric within such epic environments. In them, lyric works – through its characteristic dialectic of resistance and seduction – to expand its capacity for realizing its own conditions of existing in history.[24]

NOTES

1 Robert Southey (1774–1843), who became Poet Laureate in 1813, wrote a number of long, elaborate narrative poems including *Joan of Arc* (1796), *Thalaba the Destroyer* (1801), and *The Curse of Kehama* (1810). "Thomas Little" was the pseudonym under which the Irish poet Thomas Moore published his earliest lyrics, many of which had a seductively erotic aspect. These lyrics were published in duodecimo volumes colloquially called "twelvemos" or "twelves."

2 See Sarah M. Zimmerman, *Romanticism, Lyricism, and History* (Albany: State University of New York Press, 1999), p. xii; James Chandler, *England in 1819: The Politics of Literary Culture and the Case of Romantic Historicism* (Chicago and London: University of Chicago Press, 1998), especially the opening section of ch. 10, "Lyricism and Historicism"; Anne Janowitz, *Lyric and Labour in the Romantic Tradition* (Cambridge: Cambridge University Press, 1998).

3 Theodor W. Adorno, "On Lyric Poetry and Society," in *Notes to Literature*, ed. Rolf Tiedemann, trans. Shierry Weber Nicholsen, 2 vols. (New York: Columbia University Press, 1991), vol. 1, p. 37. Subsequent references in the text. Subsequent page references are given parenthetically within the text.

4 Leon Trotsky, *Literature and Revolution*, ed. William Keach (Chicago: Haymarket Books, 2005), p. 144. The "Proletkult" against which Trotsky's polemic is directed was an organization (and also a journal), founded during the early years of the Russian Revolution, that promoted what its proponents thought of as "proletarian" literature and art.

5 Robert Kaufman, "Adorno's Social Lyric, and Literary Criticism Today: Poetics, Aesthetics, Modernity," in *The Cambridge Companion to Adorno*, ed. Tom Huhn (Cambridge: Cambridge University Press, 2004), p. 355. Kaufman's other impressive articles rethinking Adorno's relation to Romantic theory and poetics include "Red Kant, or The Persistence of the Third *Critique* in Adorno and Jameson," *Critical Inquiry* 26 (2000), pp. 682–724; "Negatively Capable Dialectics: Keats, Vendler, Adorno, and the Theory of the Avant-Garde," *Critical Inquiry* 27 (2001), pp. 354–84; "Aura, Still," *October* 99 (2002), pp. 45–80; "Sociopolitical (i.e. Romantic) Difficulty in Modern Poetry and Aesthetics," *Romantic Circles Praxis Series* (2003), www.rc.umd.edu/praxis/poetics.ns/kaufman; "Lyric's Expression: Musicality, Conceptuality, Critical Agency," *Cultural Critique* 60 (2005), pp. 197–216.

6 Walter Benjamin, *Illuminations*, ed. Hannah Arendt, trans. Harry Zohn (New York: Schocken Books, 1969), p. 155. Subsequent references in the text.

7 Frank Lentricchia, "Lyric in the Culture of Capital," in *Subject to History: Ideology, Class, Gender*, ed. David Simpson (Ithaca and London: Cornell University Press, 1991), p. 195. Subsequent references in the text.

8 Michael Löwy and Robert Sayre, *Romanticism against the Tide of Modernity* (Durham, NC, and London: Duke University Press, 2001). Original French edition 1992.

9 For the specific terms on which women writers entered the realm of commercial literary production during the Romantic period, see Sonia Hofkosh, *Sexual Politics and the Romantic Author* (Cambridge: Cambridge University Press, 1998).

For additional work on the distinctive role of magazines, gift-books, and albums in the publication of women's poetry, see *Women's Poetry, Late Romantic to Late Victorian: Gender and Genre, 1830–1900* (New York: Macmillan-St. Martin's, 1999).

10 Mary Robinson, *Selected Poems*, ed. Judith Pascoe (Toronto: Broadview, 2000), p. 20. Quotations of Robinson's poetry are from this edition.

11 Quoted by Pascoe in Robinson, *Selected Poems*, p. 58.

12 See Jerome J. McGann, *The Poetics of Sensibility: A Revolution in Literary Style* (Oxford: Oxford University Press, 1996).

13 Samuel Taylor Coleridge, *Selected Letters*, ed. Earl Leslie Grigg, 6 vols. (Oxford: Oxford University Press, 1956–71), vol. I, p. 905.

14 *The Complete Works of William Hazlitt*, ed. P. P. Howe, 21 vols. (London: J. M. Dent, 1931–4), vol. V, pp. 151–2.

15 *Byron's Letters and Journals*, ed. Leslie A. Marchand, 12 vols. (Cambridge, MA: Harvard University Press, 1973–82), vol. IV, p. 114.

16 W. W. Robson, "Byron as Poet," in *Critical Essays* (London: Routledge & Kegan Paul, 1966), p. 276.

17 See Jerome Christensen, *Lord Byron's Strength: Romantic Writing and Commercial Society* (Baltimore: Johns Hopkins University Press, 1993).

18 Theodor W. Adorno, *Aesthetic Theory*, ed. and trans. Robert Hullot-Kentor (Minneapolis: University of Minnesota Press, 1997), p. 225.

19 For recent work on the ballad tradition and historiographical discourse, see Maureen N. McLane, "Tuning the Multi-Media Nation, or, Minstrelsy of the Afro-Scottish Border ca. 1800," *European Romantic Review* 15 (2004), pp. 289–305, and "The Figure Minstrelsy Makes: Poetry and Historicity," *Critical Inquiry* 29 (2003), pp. 429–51. For an overview of developments in the sonnet that includes insightful commentary on its intensified openness to politics and history, see Stuart Curran, *Poetic Form and British Romanticism* (New York and Oxford: Oxford University Press, 1986), pp. 29–55.

20 The discussion that follows is informed by Paul Fry's account of poetic "ostension" in *A Defense of Poetry: Reflections on the Occasion of Writing* (Stanford: Stanford University Press, 1995). Subsequent references in the text.

21 See Alan Liu's observations on the opening verse paragraph of Book VII as at once a "rebeginning" – a reworking of the "glad preamble" at the beginning of the poem – and a consolidation of the poet's project of subordinating historical determination to the self-determining workings of transcendent imagination in *Wordsworth: The Sense of History* (Stanford: Stanford University Press, 1989), pp. 221–3.

22 John Hollander, *Vision and Resonance: Two Senses of Poetic Form* (Oxford: Oxford University Press, 1975), pp. 3–4 and *passim*.

23 Kaufman, "Lyric's Expression," p. 209, identifies as "language's greatest possibility . . . its utopian vocation as lyric."

24 In *Poetic Form and British Romanticism*, Curran observes that the radical stylistic practices of *Prometheus Unbound* "enlarge the frames of reference so as to mediate between an internal psychological state and its enveloping political organization, between one mind and the whole of human culture, between time and eternity, spatial fixity and the infinite" (p. 199).

FURTHER READING

Armstrong, Isobel, *The Radical Aesthetic* (Oxford: Blackwell Publishers, 2000)

Easthope, Anthony, *Poetry as Discourse* (London: Routledge, 1983)

Jackson, Virginia, *Dickinson's Misery: A Theory of Lyric Reading* (Princeton: Princeton University Press, 2005)

Pyle, Forrest, *The Ideology of Imagination: Subject and Society in the Discourse of Romanticism* (Stanford: Stanford University Press, 1995)

Rooney, Ellen, "Form and Contentment," *Modern Language Quarterly* 61/1 (2000), pp. 17–40

Wolfson, Susan, *Formal Charges: The Shaping of Poetry in British Romanticism* (Stanford: Stanford University Press, 1997)

12

CELESTE LANGAN AND MAUREEN N. McLANE

The medium of Romantic poetry

"The recognition that every form is a form-in-a-medium dates
back to romanticism."
Niklas Luhmann, *Art as a Social System*[1]

Preliminaries

Among the questions confronting students of literature in the twenty-first
century is the place of the word – and of "letters" – in the era of electronic media. Should university departments of "English" be subsumed into
the more general category of "Media Studies"? Are authors mere "content
providers" for owners of iPods and computers? Should poetry be shelved
next to other forms of audio entertainment in media megastores? In the context of the Age of Information, the so-called "Age of Wordsworth" seems
to retreat into the distant past, and to make the concept of a Romantic
revolution in poetic language and form seem remarkably quaint. This chapter begins from the quite different premise that Romantic poetry is both
strikingly illuminated by, and capable of illuminating, our multi-mediated
situation. We suggest, in fact, that the study of Romantic *poiesis* – poetic
making in its broadest sense – belongs as much to media history as to literary scholarship. Defined by its relation to print culture even when it existed
in and insisted on oral and manuscript forms, Romantic poetry might even
serve as a synonym for what we mean by multimedia. For decades, media
theorists and historians have grappled with the impact of new media on our
bodies, imaginations, and sensoria; inasmuch as man is the "learning, creating, and communicating being," new technologies for communication have
put pressure on our ideas of "Man" and his or her imaginative ventures, not
least poems.[2]

That British Romantic poetry might have something to tell us about the
situation of media: such a premise is implicitly encoded in the titles of two
familiar mid-twentieth-century books: Geoffrey H. Hartman's *The Unmediated Vision* (1954) and Harold Bloom's *The Visionary Company* (1961). On
the face of it, of course, these titles seem to establish an opposition between
the "unmediated vision" of poetry and the various mediating apparatuses
of communication technologies. The vision invoked by Bloom and Hartman

describes a process of seeing *through* rather than *with* the bodily eye; a kind of viewless seeing, if not of "a blind man's eye" (as Wordsworth put it in "Tintern Abbey") then at least of "an eye made quiet" by a profoundly inward gaze.[3] Scholars have rightly suggested that to explore Romantic poetry in terms of "vision," "imagination," and correspondent breezes is to obscure the more concrete, technical, and material mediations of poetry. Yet those same terms, subjected to reinterrogation, yield evidence of historically specific forms of mediation, including the regimes of pedagogy that produced subjects capable of generating and receiving such "visions." Under such reinterrogation, Bloom's *Visionary Company* evokes a kind of Romantic Broadcasting Company, an "RBC" before the fact – the "viewless wings of poesy" gone wireless. Similarly, Hartman's reference to the Romantic poet's dream of *Unmediated Vision* is likely to remind scholars and students by contrast of their own profound obligations to the Trianon Press (which between the late 1940s and 1980s produced beautiful facsimiles of William Blake's books) and more recently to the William Blake Archive (www.blakearchive.org/blake), to say nothing of the syndical corporate bodies – universities and their presses – that have made the lines of Romantic poets available to historically and geographically dispersed readers.

The most obvious evidence of the idealization or dematerialization of poetry as "unmediated vision" might be the tendency of both Romantic poets and their critics to disregard one primary task of vision in 1800: reading books. (This is not to suggest that Romantic literati were not preoccupied with the status and nature of reading: anxieties about reading, new kinds of readers, reading materials, and readers' institutions abound and intensify in this era. Coleridge among others offered a description of reading with immense pertinence to this discussion: "For as to the devotees of the circulating libraries, I dare not compliment their *pass-time*, or rather *kill-time*, with the name of *reading*. Call it rather a sort of beggarly day-dreaming, during which the mind of the dreamer furnishes for itself nothing but laziness and a little mawkish sensibility."[4]) The Romantic era coincided with, though should not be prematurely reduced to, a certain regime of print with specific technical-material writing practices. As scholars have reminded us, letterpress printing was the dominant technology of the Romantic moment.[5] Between 1789 and 1824, some 5,000 books of original verse were published in Britain.[6] Yet the relation between these two variables has been insufficiently examined. What are we to make of the profusion of poetry, that "distressed genre," in the era of print capitalism?[7] To the extent that we regard "Romantic" as naming a specific kind of poetry or poetics, can we attribute that specificity to its media situation, to which David E. Wellbery has given the ungainly but useful name of "mediality" ("the general condition within which, under certain circumstances, something like 'poetry' or 'literature' can take place")?[8] Would we be justified in regarding the poetry of the period as at least as much the product of a "media revolution" (famously, if reductively, characterized by Wordsworth as "the rapid communication of intelligence"[9]) as of democratization, urbanization, and other formations of modernity?

At first, these suggestions may seem counterintuitive: after all, print was hardly a new medium *circa* 1800. Yet Friedrich Kittler has made a powerful case that in Germany massive "alphabetization" – new modes of learning to read which made *silent* reading a normative value – did indeed constitute a media revolution, and scholars of British Romanticism have observed a similar transformation. (One need not subscribe to Kittler's emphatic techno-determinism to find his bracing diagnoses of Romanticism, modernism, and the horizons of the regime of print, now closing, to be conceptually useful.) Driven by and driving the greater availability of letterpress printing, the generalization of silent reading promoted an effective interiorization of the medium of language. The difference between reading aloud and reading silently is considerable: reading aloud requires the complex "translation" of a visual stimulus, writing, into the medium of speech. Reading silently, however, typically elides the question of medium. As Kittler, quoting Schlegel, puts it, "one believes one hears what one merely reads."[10] But in fact the illusion may be even more profound than that of vocal presence: as if imitating the "silent thought"[11] that preceded its verbal articulation, silent reading appears to offer immediate access to the thoughts of another.

As even this brief glance at the practice of reading makes clear, it is by no means easy to settle the question of which "medium" of thought – speech or writing – is more "immediate"; in fact, the question seems nonsensical on its face. But the possibility that a media revolution might allow a return to immediacy is nonetheless a recurrent argument in literary history as well as in more recent media studies. So too is its opposite: the suggestion that only by foregrounding mediations, exposing techniques for achieving the effect of immediacy, does literature – or art in general – distinguish itself from popular entertainment. Here we confront what media theorists have called "the double logic of remediation"[12] – a simultaneous drive toward immediacy on the one hand, hypermediacy on the other. Each available or invented medium claims to remedy, but also to "remediate," the perceived gap between experience and representation. Thus for example perspectivalism "corrects" the flatness of painting and film "animates" the image; but also, painting returns to trump photograph and film, insisting by its flatness and stillness that depth and motion belong not to the object but to perception. "Remediation" in this sense seems to offer a valuable corrective to our tendency to think of media and technology as successive regimes – "steam, electric, electronic, microchipped," as John Hollander puts it.[13]

It is in the context of such procedures of remediation that Romantic poetry offers an especially fascinating case. "Immediacy" as a desired aesthetic effect is of course a prominent keyword in Romantic discourse and scholarship, yet hypermediacy – the conspicuous marking of mediation, a kind of "busyness"[14] – flourished as well in the Romantic era, as even the barest acquaintance with Chatterton's, Blake's, or Walter Scott's work suggests. To consider how poetry mediates itself – whether through the apparatus of a poet's body and voice, composition-in-performance, a transcription, a printed text, or their overlappings – is to examine, in the broadest sense, the means through and historical conditions under which human imagination materializes itself. Poets' claims on behalf of poetry cast their long shadows on our own differently mediated present, and may help to illuminate what is at stake in debates about "reading" in a post-literate, hypermediated age. The Romantics' concern to liberate poetry from the status of mere verse can be understood not simply as a rivalry with the novel, or with prose, or "science," but more broadly as an attempt to develop and demonstrate the capacity of poetry to function across media; or, to put it another way, we find in this period a sustained effort to reimagine poetry not as a genre – a literary kind among kinds – but as a medium.

Before moving forward, it is worth acknowledging explicitly the slipperiness of the terms we here deploy – a slipperiness the attentive reader may well have already observed, and which we believe is diagnostic and productive. "Medium," "media," and other related nouns are notoriously labile, as the *Oxford English Dictionary* suggests and as debates in media theory show. "Medium" may connote, among other things, a middle layer; a means; an intermediary; a transmitting conduit; an impeding conduit; a solution or solvent; a physico-technical apparatus; a route; a conductor; an instrument; a means of communication; a physical object for the storage of data. There is moreover a modern tendency to subsume the plurality of "media," however construed, into a monolithic singular, "The Media."[15] We believe that an exploration of "poetry" through the grid of "medium" brings home the complexity, suppleness, and historical specificity of these categories in the Romantic era, and that such a double-sided inquiry holds promise for reflections on our own moment.

Romantic poetry and historical media analysis: problems and potential payoffs

The configuration of a historical media regime is often recognizable only after a profound break. Perhaps this is why, since the mid-twentieth century, as the full impact of electronic media has begun to be felt, critics and historians have been increasingly attuned to the stakes of previous media formations – particularly the status of the book. Such reassessments are vital, for unless we think comparatively – along temporal and geographical axes – we risk a technological determinism. That writing, the printing press, or the worldwide web exist tells us almost nothing about their social uses, distributions, and effects. Failing to study the whole media situation, literary scholars and historians tend to universalize their accounts of a medium's benefits and drawbacks, despite historical and ethnographic evidence that the same medium can be used and valued differently in different times and places. When Jerome McGann writes of the web as having restored language "to something like the richness that it possessed in the Middle Ages," he rightly suggests that the history of media is not sequentially progressive; any given historical culture may offer information- and sensation-rich media environments.[16] But he might also seem to suggest – mistakenly, we believe – that the period *between* the illuminated medieval manuscript and the worldwide web – that is, when print served as a general medium – was a "dark age" for language, and for poetry.

Evincing nostalgia for a tradition of oral performance, proclaiming opposition to the *mass* medium of print, Romantic writers of verse draw attention to the striking elasticity of the term "poetry." Small wonder that Wordsworth recognized it was a word "of very disputed meaning" in the Advertisement to the 1798 edition of *Lyrical Ballads* (p. 7); poetry broadly considered spanned everything from antiquarian ballad collections to popular songs and national airs, from highly wrought odes to verse romances, those long narrative poems that rivaled novels as the most popular print genre of the period. The category of poetry was destabilized by far more than questions of genre, meter, and rhyme. Though print had long established its hegemony, oral and manuscript forms of poetry publication persisted in the Romantic era; and if these forms often flowed into print, print often found itself re-oralized (as poems passed back into "tradition," or were recited) and rewritten (as poems were entered by hand in commonplace books, for example). Romantic poetry thus moved through a variety of complex feedback loops. Several of Robert Burns's poems and songs, often brilliantly fashioned out of oral-traditionary materials, moved into print but also back into oral tradition (and now thrive on the web). By the time Coleridge's "Christabel" found its way into print, he had to defend himself against the impression of servile copying, so successfully had the poem been circulated by the oral performance of John Stoddart and others. Nor were such complex oral-literate transactions the only site of remediation. Keats and Byron seem to have developed their distinctive poetic styles partly through having so frequently "lapsed" into rhyme in their extensive epistolary correspondence.

John Stuart Mill famously proposed – with Wordsworth in mind – that lyric poetry was not heard but rather overheard: this might be seen not simply as a conceit – that of Romantic apostrophe, say, in Wordsworth's "Solitary Reaper" ("Will no one tell me what she sings?"), or in Shelley's "Ode to the West Wind" ("O wild west wind!") – but as a dimension of social fact: poems were indeed heard, overheard, misheard, and re-heard throughout this period in ways hard for us to imagine – though the ascendance of electronic media has retuned our ears, perhaps, to some aspects of the more orally/aurally saturated soundscape we encounter in memoirs of the Romantic period. As David Perkins observes, "In their daily lives the Romantics heard poetry more than most of us do; when they read silently, they heard it more in the ear of the mind; and they heard it differently. In the Romantic age schools emphasized memorizing and reciting."[17] The oral remediation and transmission of written and printed poems were and are crucial to their afterlife, or apparent immortality. Whether in the form of coterie performance (Thomas Moore's singing *Irish Melodies* in the drawing rooms of London), or in the "elegant extracts" that were print culture's version of the commonplace book, or in the pedagogy of recitation (e.g., of Felicia Hemans's "Casabianca," or when little Johnny Wordsworth learns "to repeat" the ballad "Chevy Chase" "by heart" for Thomas De Quincey), the oral mediation of Romantic poems is an important part of their history.[18]

One important reason that Romantic-era poetry rewards historical media analysis is that it captures the difficulty of deciding what we mean by *reading*. On the one hand, Romantic poets read their own and other poems *aloud*; on the other, they insisted that the "poetry" of Shakespeare could be appreciated only in the silent study. A generative confusion over the phenomenology of the reading experience is a crucial context, we believe, within which to understand Romantic interest in the human sensorium. Note how often, for example, Romantic "vision" is mediated by the ear. The "Introduction" to Blake's *Songs of Experience* (1794) tells us to "*hear* the voice of the Bard / Who present, past and future sees."[19] But, just as often, music is mediated by the eye: "A Damsel with a dulcimer / In a vision once I saw."[20] This foregrounding of sensory mediation is compounded nowhere so brilliantly as in Keats's "Ode on A Grecian Urn," where we encounter a virtual museum of the several arts, and where virtual, "unheard" melodies are preferred to actual songs.[21] But the architectural form of this museum bears attention: it is a "leaf-fring'd legend" – that is, a form of writing, which, like the urn itself, we may consider to be a "foster-child" of silence.

Romantic poetry *qua* poetry further rewards historical media analysis because its invocation of orality seems to represent the goal of immediacy in art; yet the whole point about meter, which remained the index of poetry in this period, is that it exhibits precisely the process Niklas Luhmann describes as "the impression of . . . immediacy, while the brain is actually executing operations that are highly selective, quantitatively calculating, *recursively operative*, and hence always mediated."[22] When readers "hear" – or, through whatever organ, somatically perceive – a pattern in sounds, they engage in analysis as well as register a synthetic whole. Such analysis is at the heart of what we mean by communication, according to Gregory Bateson: "We might regard patterning or predictability as the very essence and *raison d'être* of communication . . . communication is the creation of redundancy or patterning."[23]

The notorious elaboration in British (and German) Romanticism of such vocal and somatic tropes as apostrophe (the figure of address), prosopopoeia (personification), and exclamatio aim to generate such "an impression of their immediacy" – to abolish our consciousness of the print (and writerly and alphabetic) media through which a poem typically comes to us. Consider Wordsworth's proposal in his "Preface" to *Lyrical Ballads* of the poet as a "man speaking to men" (p. 255); his re-purposing of "the real language of men" (p. 241) as that suitable for poetry; his ceaseless, vexed inquiries into vocal presence and auditory immanence: all instances of his life-long project to conjure immediacy (typically figured as oral, or as speech) in writing and print. In this line we might also consider any number of Shelley's poems, flush with the urgency of represented immediacy: his homage to the skylark's "unpremeditated art" in his ode is a phantasy as well of un(pre)mediated art.[24]

Yet the same poets who describe the poet as "a man speaking to men" and poetry as a kind of super-medium of imagination just as frequently call attention to the book, the page, the line, the drop of ink – which, "falling like dew upon a thought," but also upon paper, "makes thousands, perhaps millions think" (*Don Juan*, Canto III, stanza 87). Byron describes the power of the print medium as "strange" – "'Tis strange, the shortest letter which man uses / Instead of speech, may form a lasting link / Of ages" – even supernatural, since "paper, even a rag like this, / Survives himself, his tomb, and all that's his!" (ibid.). Here the "supernatural" effect of speech's afterlife is insistently a product of technology, not transcendence.

If Byron was perhaps the poet most attuned to the "strange" situation of poetry *circa* 1800, many other poets exhibit a similar self-consciousness about the problem of poetry's medium and the status of its mediation. Thus Wordsworth's "Solitary Reaper," whose overheard song – conspicuously marked as linguistically as well as musically mediated, sung in Erse (Scottish Gaelic) – inspires the poet's question, "Will no one tell me what she sings?" *That* she sings, he conveys in his own English ballad stanzas; *what* she sings remains obscure, its possible contents lovingly itemized and remediated into his verse.

> Perhaps the plaintive numbers flow
> For old, unhappy, far-off things,
> And battles long ago:
> Or is it some more humble lay,
> Familiar matter of today?[25]

Here opacity breeds reverie; and we observe as well a striking transmediation of her "song" into his "numbers" – poetry emerging not only as a potentially communicative act but as an information processing system. We might say, following Roman Jakobson on the poetic function, that Wordsworth posits his singer as addresser, her singing as channel, himself as inadvertent addressee; her song, the "message" – the semantic verbalizable content, in Jakobson's model of poetic functions – is ostentatiously obscured.[26] Immediacy (emotional, linguistic, and otherwise) would seem always to be "far-off," elsewhere – the fantasized property of Gaelic singers, or idiot boys (see poem of same in *Lyrical Ballads*), insentient birds, and biddable breezes. Rather than offering us consistent expressivist renditions or blasts of immediacy, then, Romantic poets more often flag just how subtly and multiply their poems mediate any supposedly transparent experience they seem to proffer.

From the mid-eighteenth century onward, poets working in various Englishes became increasingly conscious of, and experimental with, the medial status of their art. We might trace the growth of this media-consciousness in part to the aftermath of the appearance in the last decades of the eighteenth century – just prior to the Romantic revolution, in other words – of two purported "mediations" of poetry of the "middle ages" between classical and modern poetry: we mean the appearance in print of poetry said to be by Ossian and Rowley. The Ossian poems, purported third-century CE Scottish Gaelic fragments and epics, were published by James Macpherson between 1760 and 1763, with an annotated "collected edition" published in 1765; the first published collection of Rowley poems – allegedly the work of a fifteenth-century Bristol monk – appeared in 1777. The controversies over Ossian, Chatterton's Rowley, and other related "scandals of the ballad,"[27] fueled a new interest in the status of oral tradition, oral culture, oral composition and performance, and their literary simulations. Both forgery scandals launched an extended literary-cultural debate about the possibility of dating and historicizing media – of theorizing oral poetries *v.* manuscript evidence *v.* print cultural artifacts. Were there necessary and detectable differences between poetry that began its life on lips rather than paper? Could poets from different places and eras hit independently on the same verse form? (Chatterton claimed that Rowley's quasi-Spenserian stanza form "was in use 300 years before" Spenser wrote.[28]) Were parchment and manuscript to be read differently than foolscap (watermarked paper) and black-letter – the former as evidence of historical authenticity, and therefore of literary greatness, the latter as evidence of popularity and therefore of literary baseness? How were readers to judge the difference, when they were reading poems ostensibly derived from such disparate origins through the homogenizing medium of wire-wove and hot-pressed paper?[29] Why was oral poetry of the past more valuable, popular song of the present less valuable, than poetry in print? Forced to assess and evaluate the ratios among these media, poets and antiquarians began to reckon with them as media.

To emphasize a Romantic nostalgia for immediacy is to run the risk of reinforcing still-prevailing myths that Romanticism is backward-looking, anti-technological. The situation is, as we have hoped to suggest, more complicated. Walter J. Ong, a pioneer in considering literature's relation to media, argued that technological advances in communication and Romantic claims for the empire of imagination were two sides of the same historical coin: a new "noetic abundance" emerged, in which poetry no longer had to serve the needs of information storage but could rather range more freely, untethered by age-old requirements of mnemonic repetition.[30] From a different, Marxist frame of reference, Jacques Rancière reinforces this claim: "Wordsworth vindicates and defines for an entire era a subjective revolution of poetic writing" – "the possibility for the poet to withdraw from *the duty of representation.*"[31] It could be said, however, that alongside this ballooning of subjectivity, poets in this period eagerly embraced the duty of representation and markedly broadened its scope – representing Highlanders, Spaniards, Egyptian monuments, battles, plants, travel, diseases, mountains, rivers, Greeks, Native Americans, Scottish border-raiders, dairy-maids, languid ladies, fops, rustics, rubes, and radicals. To explore Romanticism as a question of representation or its refusal keeps us perhaps too strictly within the domain of virtual contents: representations *of what?* Subtending this matter of poetic contents, shifting though they were, is that of poetic medium: poetry *by means* or *as means* of what?

We suggest that Romantic poets discovered that they needed to invent a "middle" for poetry, or rather, to reinvent poetry *as* a middle – to mediate between orality and print, as well as between an imagined "barbarism" and the triumph of commercial society. Thus it is possible to understand controversies surrounding the disputed term "poetry" as precisely an attempt to generate both media theory and media history. Nor is it surprising that attempts to historicize poetry should founder (and thus require a supplementary theorization) upon a Scottish case, that of Macpherson. For the Scottish Highlands – that "ancient" or primitive culture whose very air or atmosphere seemed to be successfully channeled in Macpherson's prose "translations" – posed a similar problem for the "conjectural" or stadial history pioneered by the Scottish Enlightenment. For writers like Adam Smith and Dugald Stewart, history was not only a progressive narrative – it was also *successive*: a commercial society essentially *replaced* a pastoral economy.

Like the feudal structure of the clans, the persistence of poetry in print culture represented the problem of uneven development. Thomas Love Peacock, poet, satirist, and employee of the British East India Company, wittily observed as much in his *The Four Ages of Poetry* (1820), the essay which provoked Shelley's famous response, *A Defence of Poetry* (1821). As Peacock saw it, poetry emitted a dim, anachronistic light; it had entered a decrepit Iron Age (its fourth, decadent age) while history and enlightenment marched on. Peacock indicted poetry as residual frippery idiotically pursued in an era of progress, change, and technological know-how: "A poet in our time is a semi-barbarian in a civilized community. He lives in the days that are past."[32]

How and whether poetry might feel out viable presents and futures as well as usable pasts: this was the crux of Romantic *poiesis*. Preoccupied with poetry's historicity, alive to its mediality, poets in the Romantic era launch a wide range of transmedial investigations.

Experiments in the medium of poetry: *Lyrical Ballads* and other forged middles

When the Advertisement to the 1798 edition of *Lyrical Ballads* expressed a hope that readers "should not suffer the solitary word Poetry, a word of very disputed meaning, to stand in the way of their gratification," Wordsworth seemed to offer an account, at least, of poetry's opposite: "pre-established codes of decision" (p. 7). To have already established, to know from the start what poetry is or does, would make the volume misfire. It might be said, in other words, that the Advertisement itself disputed the meaning of the word "poetry," and that the dispute may be read in the very title. For that famous title does two important things. First: rather than develop a new poetic form, or merely rework generic conventions, it poses a question, suggests a possibility: what would it be like, the poems ask, to "hear" oral-formulaic poetry (ballads) through the medium of written poetry (lyric)? Such a question had been posed and answered, in one key, in the collections of vernacular ballads proliferating in the period. Ballads had of course long existed in many media: oral tradition, broadsides, chapbooks, bookform. As a poetic "kind," ballads intriguingly ran the gamut from anonymous orality to highly elaborate, authored literary productions; and antiquarians from Thomas Percy to Joseph Ritson and later Walter Scott and William Motherwell dedicated themselves to re-mediating this manuscript, early print, and oral material into books. In these ballad collections we also encounter a poetic medium too often ignored in conventional literary histories, though conspicuous in the literary poetry of the era (cf. Wordsworth's Solitary Reaper): the native singer, the oral informant, the reciter who appears as medium of song and culture. Wordsworth's many rustic informants in *Lyrical Ballads*, "Resolution and Independence," *The Excursion, The Recluse*, etc., might be linked to the many informants – often, notably, women – who populate ballad collections: Mrs. Hogg, mother of James Hogg, himself both oral informant and man of letters; Anna Gordon Brown (cited in Scott's *Minstrelsy* and Robert Jamieson's *Popular Songs and Ballads*); Mrs. Arrot of Aberbothrick (hailed by Jamieson); Agnes Lyle of Kilbarchan and Widow Nichol of Paisley, solicited by William Motherwell for his 1827 *Minstrelsy: Ancient and Modern*. Such notes and citations point to the embodied background mediations of poetry, the complex transactions that brought poetry "out of the mouths" of singers into printed books, alongside other source materials including manuscripts, broadsides, and previously printed books.

Lyrical Ballads exploits from another direction the transmedial potentialities of balladry. Consider how many of the poems have in their title the words "Lines written." Such titles seem designed to draw attention to poetry's use of the material support of paper, of chirography – more particularly, of the letter ("Lines written at a small distance from my House, and sent by my little Boy to the Person to whom they are addressed"). But the real point may be the obvious disjunction between the particularized time and place of the writing and its "record" in the printed volume; it is as if the anonymous author of *Lyrical Ballads* were none other than James Macpherson, claiming to possess but withholding the manuscript proofs. And what are we to make of the entirely etherealized locations alluded to in "Lines written *a few miles above* Tintern Abbey" or (here indeed lies one whose name is writ in water) "Lines written near Richmond, *upon the Thames*, at Evening"? Well in advance of media theorist/guru Marshall McLuhan's *aperçu* about media change – that the content of one medium is another medium – *Lyrical*

Ballads demonstrates how this might be so. But its demonstration is considerably more complex than McLuhan's influential formula would suggest, for the relations between, on the one hand, "form" and "content," and on the other, form (or genre) and medium, become unsettled. What, for example, is the proper "form" of a *lyrical* ballad? If it employs ballad meter, is it then merely a (faux) ballad? Or, merely by abandoning black-letter and broadside for the "interiority" of the three-dimensional *book*, do poems become lyrical, giving priority to "feeling" over "action and situation"? Which, in other words – the meter or the paper – corresponds to poetry's "form"? And does it matter if the poem is *read*, or *read aloud* – if in the case of a poem like "Goody Blake and Harry Gill" Wordsworth employs a "more impressive metre than is usual in Ballads" ostensibly to enable the *oral* transmission of information first reported in Erasmus Darwin's *Zoonomia* ("it has been communicated to many hundreds of people who would never have heard of it, had it not been narrated as a Ballad")? To read the poem aloud is to hear the "chatter" of its insistent rhymes but not the *virtual* music – the oxymoronic "chatter still" of the neighbors – that connects the poem thematically to "the still, sad music of humanity, / Nor harsh, nor grating" of "Tintern Abbey." Wordsworth described "Tintern Abbey," moreover, as an attempt to make blank-verse paragraphs function as analogues of the strophe, antistrophe, and epode of an ode. By asking us to "hear" one poetic kind through another, the volume insists on posing a central question: what is the medium of poetry?

To ask that question is to ask two questions at once, for "the medium of poetry" is a phrase that can be read as both objective and subjective genitive: poetry's medium and/or poetry-as-medium. To the extent that one imagines poetry as a notional content, an essence or virtual message that requires transmission, the poem-as-message might be hosted by a variety of media – the mouth, the hand (chirography), the printed page, the web; each is a medium of/for poetry. But insofar as "poetry" names a technology, poetry itself may be understood as a conduit, a channel – as the "medium" for some defined content. This content might be conceived of as "information" (the "facts" reported in Erasmus Darwin's *Zoonomia* or Hearne's *Journey from Hudson's Bay to the Northern Ocean*, cited in Wordsworth's "The Complaint of a Forsaken Indian Woman") or even as mere feeling. In both of these latter cases, poetry "itself" is not a *content*; it is the medium which transmits a content. And this transmission is by no means transparent: Wordsworth's "Goody Blake and Harry Gill," after all, "supernaturalizes" the instance of *mania mutabilis* reported by Darwin, and the poet "superadds" even to "the spontaneous overflow of powerful feelings" the "charm" of meter (those "continual impulses of pleasurable surprise" that constitute the "particular movement of metre"). The medium of poetry in this second sense is itself a kind of digital code, of stress patterns.

It is this double sense suggested by "the medium of poetry," perhaps, that helps to determine the specific character of Romantic poetic experiment. In order as it were to solve the problem of poetry's medium, Romantic poets often make poetry the explicit subject – and transmitted content – of the poem. Sometimes this is obvious. Coleridge's "The *Rime* of the Ancyent Marinere" and Scott's *The* Lay *of the Last Minstrel* make the verse narratives of their eponymous narrators *almost* coincident with the poem itself, though in each case the "frame" narrative serves to mark those verse narratives *as* a content. A similar logic might be seen at work in that other famously "doubled" book of the Romantic period, Blake's *Songs of Innocence and of Experience.* The "states" of Innocence and Experience act to frame the songs, which are the "contents" of a book ("that all may read"[33] – yet note how the presumably pre-literate children in the frontispiece to *Innocence* are *being read to*). Other, similar gestures toward making poetry the "content" of the poem can be found almost at will: Wordsworth's "Song at the Feast of Brougham Castle" offers a contemporary poet's "translation" of late medieval minstrel's song; while in *Childe Harold's Pilgrimage*, the lay of "Sir Childe" in Canto I is surrounded by Spenserian stanzas as an island by the ocean, and in Canto II, a translated Albanian war cry serves as a poetic "content." Here we see the double logic of remediation in full explicit operation – oral contents notionally repurposed into Harold's relation, further glossed by Byron's ethno-linguistic notes *in propria persona.*

Now, perhaps such doublings and framings and enfoldings seem less radical on their face than the axiom, "The content of one medium is always another medium." After all, in each of these cases, one could argue, the medium of poetry (in both senses) is *language.* To wonder about the relation of poetry to that linguistic medium is perhaps the central project of the Romantic period, for the privilege accorded to poetry in the hierarchy of the arts depends upon the argument that its "material" – the equivalent of painting's pigments and music's strings – is nothing but *language itself.* As Shelley observed in his *Defence of Poetry*:

> Language . . . is a more direct representation of the actions and passions of our internal being, and is susceptible of more various and delicate combinations, than colour, form, or motion . . . For language is arbitrarily produced by the Imagination and has relation to thoughts alone; but all other materials, instruments and conditions of art, have relations among each other, which limit and interpose between conception and expression. The former is as a mirror which reflects, the latter as a cloud which enfeebles, the light of which both are mediums of communication.[34]

Shelley privileges language because it is "more direct" – less mediated, in other words – than other artistic materials: color, form, motion (dance). All the "instruments and conditions of art," linguistic and otherwise, aspire to function as "mediums of communication" of the mind's "light." Language as mirror *v.* all other materials as enfeebling clouds: here we have not only a version of M. H. Abrams's "mirror and lamp" aesthetics but a media theory. Language, according to Shelley, by being "arbitrarily" produced, by being made of the same stuff as thought itself, is therefore thought's purest channel: language subjects thought to the least distortion. While such a declaration is typical in the period – similar arguments are put forward by Coleridge, as well as by several of the German Romantics – it nonetheless raises as many questions as it presumes to answer. Shelley appears to assume, for example, that the various arts – employing different media – attempt to communicate the same content: "the actions and passions of our immortal being." But suppose the avowed aim of a medium is to communicate (as its content) *another medium*?

Can it truly be said, moreover, that language "has relation to thoughts alone"? Or do not the various "media" of language – the vocal apparatus, the alphabet, the air that carries sound, the "vellum or wild Indian leaf" (l. 5) that saves Imagination from "dumb enchantment" (l. 10) in Keats's "The Fall of Hyperion"[35] – demonstrate language's dependence on "other materials, instruments, and conditions"? Lamenting this dependence, Wordsworth in Book V of *The Prelude* famously asks, "why hath not the Mind / Some element to stamp her image on / in nature somewhat nearer to her own?" (ll. 45–7).[36] And when Blake reminds us that "Even Milton and Shakespeare could not publish their own works" ("To the Public," 1793),[37] he effectively underscores the extent to which print, that remediation of writing, may "interpose between conception and expression." In short, definitions of poetry as an expressive art (or a mnemonic device) that identify language as its medium only defer or deflect the question of poetry's medium to the problem of *language's* medium.

In addition to answering the question "What is the medium of poetry?" by making poetry at once the form and the content, the message and the channel of the communicative act, *Lyrical Ballads* might be said to intend its own intervention in the history of poetry – and the history of media – to serve as a provisional answer. It is as if Wordsworth and Coleridge wish to supply a missing link – a *medium* in the sense of a middle term – between the supposedly ancient oral forms so recently collected by Percy, Ritson, and Scott, and the literate, polite verse that had assumed the title of Poetry. (This line of thinking could illuminate Walter Scott's several romances as well, as these long poems are conspicuous orchestrations not only of historical material but also of historicizable *media* – especially oral and manuscript poetries, those preserved in that living archive that Scott, the "last minstrel," purports to remediate.) By supplying (forging) a missing link between a notional orality and print literature, these poets produce something more than a mere *hybrid*. When Walter Ong called "oral literature" a conceptual "monstrosity,"[38] he retroactively illuminated the sense of contemporary reviewers of *Lyrical Ballads* that here was "[some]thing out of nature's certain course."[39] In *The Monthly Review* of June 1799, Charles Burney denounced what he saw as the perversely regressive avant-gardism of the poems:

> Though we have been extremely entertained with the fancy, the facility, and (in general) the sentiments of these pieces, we cannot regard them as *poetry*, of a class to be cultivated at the expense of a higher species of versification, unknown in our language at the time when our elder writers, whom this author condescends to imitate, wrote their ballads. – Would it not be degrading poetry, as well as the English language, to go back to the barbarous and uncouth numbers of Chaucer? Suppose, instead of modernizing the old bard, that the sweet and polished measures, on lofty subjects, of Dryden, Pope, and Gray, were to be transmuted into the dialect and versification of the xivth century? Should we be gainers by the retrogradation? *Rust* is a necessary quality to a counterfeit old medal: but, to give artificial rust to modern poetry, in order to render it similar to that of three or four hundred years ago, can have no better title to merit and admiration than may be claimed by any ingenious forgery. None but savages have submitted to eat acorns after corn was found.[40]

Burney's classification of "species" of verse underscores the narrative of historical progress that is at work in most theories and histories of media. Wordsworth's and Coleridge's retro-neo project violates the proper evolutionary development of verse. By suggesting that different patterns of versification succeed one another, Burney implies that even the "polished measures" of eighteenth-century poetry will become obsolescent in their turn. And the horizon of that obsolescence is already legible in the next paragraph, when Burney avers that the success of *Lyrical Ballads* – its "realism," more or less – owes nothing to its metrical experiment:

> When we confess that our author has had the art of pleasing and interesting in no common way by his natural delineation of human passions, we must add that these effects were not produced by the *poetry*; we have been as much affected by pictures of misery and unmerited distress in *prose*.   (p. 713)

For Burney, then, the volume of *Lyrical Ballads* is something like an embarrassing transitional object.

But what is most interesting is the fact that such a transitional object is *forged*; that the "retrogradation," to use Burney's term, is intentional. Why do Wordsworth and Coleridge seek to insert themselves, as it were, at the end of the fifteenth century? The answer: they are exploring the "medium of poetry" in another sense: neither its origin nor its end but rather its *middle* – and by extension, perhaps, its *essence*. For it may be that the question of a medium and the question of an essence are always bound together: the very possibility of multiple "mediations" produces in turn the question, "mediations of *what [thing]*?"

In remarking that the "language" adopted in "The Rime of the Ancyent Marinere" "has been equally intelligible *for these last three centuries*" (emphasis added), Wordsworth and Coleridge signal to us that the horizon of their project is that of the book, of print, and print-language. The intelligibility of the language of the "Rime" appears to depend on a fixation of a linguistic form around the time of Gutenberg and Caxton. And as the notoriously antiqued spelling of that poem suggests, Wordsworth and Coleridge owe a debt in this procedure to Thomas Chatterton, who similarly intervened to provide a "medium" for literary history – namely, the fictitious fifteenth-century priest, poet, and collector of antiquities, Thomas Rowley. By supplying (false) information about the existence of oil painting in England prior to the sixteenth century, by suggesting that Rowley could independently hit upon a stanza like Spenser's, the documents Chatterton produced "forged" a stronger link between past and present. Indeed, he even offered a rationale for the development of the print medium:

> Me thynketh ytt were a prettie devyce yffe the practice of oure bakerres were extended further. I merveille moche, our *scriveynes* and *amanuenses* doe not gette lytel letters cutt in wood, or caste in yron, and thane followynge by the eye, or with a fescue, everyche letter of the boke thei meane to copie, fix the sayde wooden or yron letters meetelie disposed in a frame or chase; thanne daube the same over with somme atramentous stuffe, and layinge a thynne piece of moistened parchment or paper on these letters, presse it doune with somme smoothe stone or other heavie weight: by the whiche goodlye devyce a manie hundreth copies of eche boke might be wroughte off in a few daies, insteade of employing the eyen and hondes of poor clerkes for several monthes with greate attentyon and travaile. (vol. I, p. 60)

The ostentatious orthographic deviance forces us – as it did Chatterton's first readers – to look at, and not through, print, even as the content of the passage conceives of letterpress print as it were "before" letterpress print. (Here Chatterton reminds us that "invention" is both ideational and material.) Chatterton explicitly situates his project in a history of media technology as well as literature, and by "forging" both, he distresses both, asking us to consider the relations between poetry, the printing press, and their dialectical engagement. Such flagrant experiments in hypermediacy are as characteristic of the age as Aeolianism.

Chatterton, Wordsworth, and Coleridge have an unlikely ally in their attempt to forge connections between "middles" and essences – and to locate the essence of poetry in its "middle age." In the first stanza of Canto XII of *Don Juan* (a place that might have been its middle), Byron seems to identify the printed ballad as an artifact peculiarly fitted to capture or express the essence not only of art but of humanity "itself":

> Of all the barbarous middle ages, that
>   Which is the most barbarous is the middle age
> Of man! it is – I really scarce know what;
>   But when we hover between fool and sage,
> And don't know justly what we would be at –
>   *A period something like a printed page,*
> *Black letter upon foolscap*, while our hair
>   Grows grizzled, and we are not what we were.
>   (Emphasis added)

In what is perhaps the most unusual, certainly the most unrecognized, Romantic account of the aesthetic as a kind of Kantian "purposiveness without purpose," Byron here suggests that early print literature – "black letter upon foolscap" – is sufficiently removed from origin and destination to achieve a kind of autonomy. We note that, while the "period" of the printed page is that of letters, the letters are not converted into a discernible *content*; the medium, in short, is the only legible message. Here the possibility that poetry might have a purpose – whether conceived in relation to an "original intention" (to preserve cultural memory, *à la* Ossian) or an end (to affect the reader "by pictures of misery an unmerited distress") – is obviated by the textual object's equal distance from these "real" contexts.

This preoccupation with print, its historicity, and its conventions (orthographic and otherwise) is one index of a Romantic preoccupation with mediality *tout court*. The oral turn so prominent in Romanticism allowed one such liberation, or complication, of poetry's status; the circulation of poems in manuscript (Mary Tighe's "Psyche," Keats's letters) and via recitation (most famously, "Christabel") suggested alternate means of publication than the press; and the theorization of poetry as an imaginative project whose origins lay in the far, oral past ensured that poetry, unlike, for example, the novel, had a stronger claim to be considered a supermedial, transhistorical venture: it had preceded writing, preceded print, and could indeed outlast them.

We can see, then, that when Burns and Wordsworth and Scott and Hogg (for example) oriented poetry toward oral and notionally oral modes, they participated in a complex venture, reflecting and cocreating a complex medial-linguistic reality. Scott's ostentatious repurposing of prior contents and prior media offers an exemplary Romantic case of remediation: the scenes, plots, genres, and tropes of traditional balladry fueled his enormously popular romances, from *The Lay of the Last Minstrel* (1805) through *The Lady of the Lake* (1810), on to his historical novels, themselves stuffed with fragments of poetry, Highland set-pieces, bards, and minstrels. Scott began as a translator of German balladry, became a bestselling poet and then a bestselling novelist and was also a prolific biographer, editor, and essayist: his transmedial potentials have been further released in twentieth-century adaptations of his novels to film and TV. Of all Romantic poets, he was perhaps the one most indifferent to poetry as a medium, and to literature itself, as David Hewitt observes: "There is a sense in which Scott's work is literature only because of the need for a medium, and that it is closer to performance, a permanent negotiation between tale teller and audience, in which the excitement of the moment takes both parties through to the end."[41]

Conclusion: Shelleyan outsoarings, or romantic poetry as media theory

Scott's indifference to poetry *per se* reminds us of the broader vexing of that category, a vexing that should be read as a crucial episode not only in the history of poetry and poetics but as a signal and perhaps unfinished moment in the history of media and media theory. In this light, certainly Shelley's poems look newly (or continually) vital, of particular theoretical and sensual-technical interest. In much criticism, Shelley appears (if he does appear) as the least grounded of poets, still a version of Matthew Arnold's "ineffectual angel" or Eliot's "puerile" failure, the poet most liable to outsoar materiality and to elude a reader's grasp;[42] William St. Clair is only the most recent critic to observe that *Prometheus Unbound* referred not only to Shelley's poem but to its material fate: few chose to buy, much less to bind, its pages.[43] Yet if to unsympathetic critics his ideas lacked efficacy and his pages did not merit binding, his language acquires a stunning materiality.

If transportation is a communication technology, an aspect of a total media situation, Shelley's "cars" (chariots and coaches) and numerous "barks" (boats) suggest his preoccupation with conveyance in all aspects. The medium is at least part of the message. How to get there from here? This was the paramount question of all radicals and reformers. It is striking how often magic or mythical cars appear in Shelley – from the "magic car" of *Queen Mab*, his first major poem, to the celestial transportation offered to Asia in *Prometheus Unbound*, to the terrifying chariot of his last, unfinished great work, *The Triumph of Life*.[44] The problem of Romantic transport acquires new specificity when subjected to a historical media analysis. The postal system, the network of roads, the emergence of new critical journals as a signal "medium of culture" (in Marilyn Butler's phrase[45]): these materials and ideational networks, these modes of transport and contact, were crucial to the formation of a literary public sphere, a communicative zone of inquiry, exchange, debate, a zone strongly marked – especially during the Napoleonic Wars – by government repression. The revolution may or may not be televised, but Shelley's imagined revolution – the overriding thematic of his poetry – was incessantly audiovisualized, its movements virtually kinesthetic, propelling spirits and readers ever onward in a shared dream in an optative mode. In *Prometheus Unbound*, Shelley pictures revolution as a stunning sound-and-light show: curses, songs, ringing voices, personified voices in the air, visions rolling on brains, light illuminating reconstructed man. So too in *The Mask of Anarchy*, "voice" travels great distances in order to bear radical political messages: "As I lay asleep in Italy / There came a voice from over the Sea."[46]

How to communicate ideas, to make them sensible, to impress them on our sensorium, via poetry? Shelley's poetry often makes such operations the content of his verse. Thus the "Ode to Liberty" begins: "A glorious people vibrated again / The lightning of the nations: Liberty / From heart to heart, from tower to tower, o'er Spain, / Scattering contagious fire into the sky, / Gleamed."[47] The transformation of a populace into a singly vibrating medium, its content the lightning of liberty: here the telegraphic imagery of instantaneous communication has a political content. It is not irrelevant that Napoleon early on appreciated the use of the telegraph, just as he understood newspapers as military material (we refer here to optical or semaphoric telegraphy, not the electromagnetic telegraphy realized with Morse's innovations in the 1830s).[48] As if anticipating twentieth-century information theorists, Shelley plays with light pulses as significant data bits. In *The Triumph of Life* an ambiguous "shape all light" appears[49] – light affording the very condition of perception, as McLuhan reminds us in his discussion of electric light in *Understanding Media*.

Such meditations run the risk of appropriating Romantic poetry to a media futurity it has no knowledge of; we run the further risk of reinserting Romanticism into a progressive narrative of media (if not necessarily historical or political) evolution. Yet as Blake ringingly declared in one of the "Proverbs of Hell," "What is now prov'd was once only imagin'd."[50] Romantic poets and theorists established a horizon for thinking the conditions of mediality, not least the neuro-sensory *a priori* of the human body. As Niklas Luhmann observes, "Without eyes one cannot read, without ears one cannot hear.

Communication must be highly conspicuous in the perceptional field if it is to be perceived at all. It must captivate perception – by means of some striking noise, through bodily postures explicable only as expressive behavior, or by employing special conventional signs in writing" (p. 15).

When Harold Bloom described Romanticism as the internalization of quest-romance, he pointed to a prominent feature of Romantic poetic discourse: its focus on operations of internalization, the synapses of interiority, what we might today call the network of the nervous system.[51] The "Chorus of Spirits" in *Prometheus Unbound* announces: "We come from the mind / of human kind / which was late so dusk and obscene and blind" (Act IV, ll. 93–5). Such lines gloss not false (or true) consciousness but the very apparatus *of* consciousness: mind as general human medium, mind unbound to the "ratio of the five senses," in Blake's phrase. The mind-mapping of Romanticism offers us a media allegory, a kind of neural imaginary, a phantasy of unmediated plugged-in transport. Yet if Shelley offers a transcendent dematerialized imaginary, the human mind alone as *sine qua non* for mediation, we find in Keats the techno-material correlative for such poetic instantaneity: building a fane in his brain for Psyche in his ode, Keats turns hidden mental intricacies into a physiological architecture, a network of and for poetry that poetry itself repeats.

What had seemed flights into the unreal may now look peculiarly predictive, as when Shelley salutes the nameless immortals coming to pay homage to the dead Keats in *Adonais*: "And many more, whose names on Earth are dark / But whose transmitted effluence cannot die / So long as fire outlives the parent spark, / Rose, robed in dazzling immortality."[52] Celebrating the contingently "transmitted effluence[s]" of dematerialized poets, here Shelley liberates us from a merely literary history (whether underwritten by the name of the author, the work, genre, period, or even the discourse of poetry). He ushers us into a broader "history of our species":[53] a history of media transmission, its conditions, impasses, and potentially "transmitted effluences." That the human mind might effortlessly "render and receive" such transmissions, "Holding an unremitting interchange / With the clear universe of things around" (as Shelley put it in "Mont Blanc"[54]): this is the Romantic poetic phantasy *par excellence* – the imagination of a pure, noiseless, static-free, perfectly transmitting medium. It is the same aspiration that underwrites the dream of fiber optics – which aims to reduce the plurality of media to one – as well as the promise of virtual reality. Yet amid all these phantasies of media transparency and immediacy, perhaps we would do well to recall the words of the American poet Charles Bernstein, a keen student of Romantic predecessors, the powerful hopes sedimented in "poetry," and the peculiar status of language-as-medium: "We have to get over, as in getting over a disease, the idea that we can 'all' speak to one another in the universal voice of poetry. History still mars our words, and we will be transparent to one another only when history itself disappears."[55]

NOTES

The authors are grateful to James K. Chandler, Kevis Goodman, Ann Wierda Rowland, and especially to Laura M. Slatkin for reading and commenting upon drafts of this chapter.

1 Niklas Luhmann, *Art as a Social System*, trans. Eva M. Knodt (Stanford: Stanford University Press, 2000), p. 127.

2 For this definition of "Man," see Raymond Williams, *The Long Revolution* (Orchard Park, New York: Broadview Press, 2001), p. 118.

3 William Wordsworth, "Lines written a few miles above Tintern Abbey," in William Wordsworth and Samuel Taylor Coleridge, *Lyrical Ballads*, ed. R. L. Brett and A. R. Jones, 2nd edn. (London and New York: Routledge, 1991), ll. 25, 48, p. 114.

4 Samuel Taylor Coleridge, *Biographia Literaria*, ed. James Engell and W. Jackson Bate, Bollingen series (Princeton: Princeton University Press, 1983), p. 48n.

5 See, e.g., Morris Eaves, "The Sister Arts in British Romanticism," in *The Cambridge Companion to British Romanticism*, ed. Stuart Curran (Cambridge: Cambridge University Press, 1993), p. 243.

6 See Stuart Curran, "Romantic Poetry: Why and Wherefore?," in Curran, *The Cambridge Companion to British Romanticism*, p. 216.

7 See Susan Stewart's important essay on emergent modern literary problematics, "Notes on Distressed Genres," in *Crimes of Writing: Problems in the Containment of Representation* (Durham, NC, and London: Duke University Press, 1994), pp. 66–101.

8 See David E. Wellbery, foreword to Friedrich A. Kittler, *Discourse Networks, 1800/1900*, trans. Michael Metteer, with Chris Cullens (Stanford: Stanford University Press, 1900), p. xiii.

9 Wordsworth, 1800 "Preface" to *Lyrical Ballads*, p. 249.

10 Friedrich Kittler, *Gramophone, Film, Typewriter*, trans. Geoffrey Winthrop-Young and Michael Wutz (Stanford: Stanford University Press, 1999), p. 9. The quotation is from Schlegel's *Critical Fragments*.

11 *Viz.* William Wordsworth, "Simon Lee," l. 74, in Wordsworth and Coleridge, *Lyrical Ballads*, p. 62.

12 See Jay David Bolter and Richard Grusin, *Remediation: Understanding New Media* (Cambridge, MA: MIT Press, 1999), especially "Introduction: The Double Logic of Remediation," pp. 20–5, and ch. 1, "Immediacy, Hypermediacy, and Remediation," pp. 20–50. See too *Rethinking Media Change: The Aesthetics of Transition*, ed. David Thorburn and Henry Jenkins (Cambridge, MA: MIT Press, 2003), "Introduction," pp. 1–16.

13 John Hollander, "Literature and Technology: Nature's 'Lawful Offspring in Man's Art,'" *Social Research* 71/3 (Fall 2004), p. 753.

14 For this astute gloss on "hypermediation," and for a penetrating account of hypermediacy (especially in eighteenth-century newspapers) as a route to

generating a "reality effect" and "illusion of immediacy," see Kevis Goodman, *Georgic Modernity and British Romanticism: Poetry and the Mediation of History* (Cambridge University Press, 2004), pp. 77–8.

15 See ibid., ch. 1, pp. 17–37, for a crucial genealogy of "media" and "mediums" from Aristotle through the Restoration and into Addison's *Spectator* papers.

16 Jerome J. McGann, *Radiant Textuality: Literature after the World Wide Web* (New York: Palgrave, 2001), p. xiii.

17 David Perkins, "How the Romantics Recited Poetry," *Studies in English Literature, 1500–1900* 31/4, Nineteenth Century (Autumn 1991), pp. 655–71, at p. 656.

18 On Hemans's "Casabianca," see Catherine Robson, "Standing on the Burning Deck: Poetry, Performance, History," *PMLA* 120/1 (January 2005), pp. 148–62; on John Wordsworth's learning "Chevy Chase," see Letter 160, W. W. and S. H. to Thomas De Quincey, Wednesday, 24 May [1809], *The Letters of William and Dorothy Wordsworth*, vol. II, *The Middle Years*, Part I, *1806–1811*, arranged and ed. Ernest de Selincourt, 2nd edn., rev. Mary Moorman (Oxford: Clarendon Press, 1969), p. 342.

19 William Blake, "Introduction" to *Songs of Experience*, in *The Complete Poetry and Prose of William Blake*, ed. David V. Erdman (New York: Doubleday, 1988), p. 18.

20 Samuel Taylor Coleridge, "Kubla Khan," ll. 37–8, in *Coleridge: Poetical Works*, ed. Ernest Hartley Coleridge (New York and Oxford: Oxford University Press, 1980).

21 Philip Fisher, "A Museum with One Work Inside: Keats and the Finality of Art," *Keats-Shelley Journal* 33 (1984), pp. 85–102.

22 Luhmann, *Art as a Social System*, p. 8.

23 Gregory Bateson, *Steps to an Ecology of Mind* (New York: Ballantine Books, 1972), p. 412. Quoted in N. Katherine Hayles, *How We Became Posthuman* (Chicago: University of Chicago Press, 1999), p. 25.

24 Percy Bysshe Shelley, "To a Sky-Lark," l. 5, in *Shelley's Poetry and Prose: Authoritative Texts, Criticism*, 2nd edn., ed. Donald H. Reiman and Neil Fraistat (New York: W. W. Norton, 2002), p. 304.

25 Wordsworth, "The Solitary Reaper," in *"Poems, in Two Volumes," and Other Poems, 1800–1807, by William Wordsworth*, ed. Jared Curtis (Ithaca: Cornell University Press, 1983), p. 185.

26 See Roman Jakobson's seminal essay, "Closing Statements: Linguistics and Poetics," in *Style in Language*, ed. Thomas A. Sebeok (Cambridge, MA: MIT Press, 1960), pp. 350–77.

27 Susan Stewart, "Scandals of the Ballads," in *Crimes of Writing*, pp. 102–31.

28 *The Complete Works of Thomas Chatterton*, ed. Donald S. Taylor, 2 vols. (Oxford: Clarendon Press, 1971), vol. I, p. 272. Subsequent references in the text. See also Margaret Russett and Joseph A. Dane, "Everlastinge to Posterityie: Chatterton's Spirited Youth," *Modern Language Quarterly* 63/2 (2002), pp. 141–65.

29 The allusion is to the first chapter of Sir Walter Scott's *Waverley*: "It is from the great book of Nature, the same through a thousand editions, whether of black-letter, or wire-wove and hot-pressed, that I have venturously essayed to read a chapter to the public" (New York: Penguin, 1985), p. 26. For the relevance of such questions specifically to poetry, see Alan D. Boehm, "The 1798 Lyrical Ballads

and the Poetics of Late Eighteenth-Century Book Production," *English Literary History* 63/2 (1996), pp. 453–87.

30 Walter J. Ong, *Rhetoric, Romance, and Technology: Studies in the Interaction of Expression and Culture* (Cornell University Press, 1971), p. 279.

31 Jacques Rancière, *The Flesh of Words: The Politics of Writing*, trans. Charlotte Mandell (Stanford: Stanford University Press, 2004), pp. 9, 13 (emphasis added).

32 Thomas Love Peacock, *The Four Ages of Poetry*, in *The Works of Thomas Love Peacock*, vol. VIII: *Essays, Memoirs, Letters, and Unfinished Novels* (New York: AMS Press, 1967), p. 20.

33 William Blake, "Introduction," *Songs of Innocence*, in *Songs of Innocence and of Experience*, introd. Geoffrey Keynes (London: Oxford University Press, 1967), pl. 4, l. 14.

34 Percy Bysshe Shelley, *A Defence of Poetry*, in *Shelley's Poetry and Prose*, p. 513, para. 5.

35 In John Keats, *Complete Poems*, ed. Jack Stillinger (Cambridge, MA: Belknap Press of Harvard University Press, 1991), p. 478.

36 William Wordsworth, *The Prelude: 1799, 1805, 1850*, ed. Jonathan Wordsworth, M. H. Abrams, and Stephen Gill (New York: W. W. Norton & Co., 1979), p. 155.

37 William Blake, *The Complete Poetry and Prose of William Blake*, rev. edn. by David V. Erdman, with commentary by Harold Bloom, rev. edn. (New York: Doubleday, 1988), p. 692.

38 Walter J. Ong, *Orality and Literacy: The Technologizing of the Word* (London and New York: Methuen, 1982), p. 10.

39 The allusion is to *The Prelude* (Book IX, l. 253).

40 Charles Burney's review appeared in *The Monthly Review*, 2nd series, 29 (June 1799), pp. 202–10. Repr. in *The Romantics Reviewed: Contemporary Reviews of British Romantic Writers*, ed. Donald H. Reiman (New York: Garland, 1972), Part A, vol. II, p. 713.

41 David Hewitt, "Scott, Sir Walter (1771–1832)," in *The Oxford Dictionary of National Biography*, ed. H. C. G. Matthew and Brian Harrison (Oxford: Oxford University Press, 2004); online edn., ed. Lawrence Goldman, May 2006, www.oxforddnb.com/view/article/24928 (accessed October 17, 2006).

42 T. S. Eliot, "Shelley and Keats," in *The Use of Poetry and the Use of Criticism: Studies in the Relation of Poetry to Criticism in England* (Cambridge, MA: Harvard University Press, 1933), p. 82.

43 See William St. Clair, *The Reading Nation in the Romantic Period* (Cambridge and New York: Cambridge University Press, 2004), p. 192.

44 For iterations of the "magic car," see Percy Bysshe Shelley, "Queen Mab," ll. 208, 237, 249, in *Shelley's Poetry and Prose*, ed. Reiman and Fraistat, pp. 22, 23.

45 Marilyn Butler, "Culture's Medium: The Role of the Review," in Curran, *The Cambridge Companion to British Romanticism*, pp. 120–47.

46 Percy Bysshe Shelley, *The Mask of Anarchy*, ll. 1–2, in *Shelley's Poetry and Prose*, p. 316.

47 Percy Bysshe Shelley, "Ode to Liberty," st. 1, ll. 1–5, in ibid., p. 307.

48 See Patricia Crain, "Children of Media, Children as Media: Optical Telegraphs, Indian Pupils, and Joseph Lancaster's System for Cultural Replication," in *New Media, 1740–1915*, ed. Lisa Gitelman and Geoffrey B. Pingree (Cambridge, MA: MIT Press, 2003), p. 67.

49 Shelley, "The Triumph of Life," l. 352, in *Shelley's Poetry and Prose*, ed. Reiman and Fraistat, p. 494.

50 William Blake, *The Marriage of Heaven and Hell*, in *The Complete Poetry and Prose of William Blake*, ed. Erdman, p. 36.

51 See Harold Bloom, "The Internalization of Quest-Romance," in *Romanticism and Consciousness: Essays in Criticism*, ed. Harold Bloom (New York: W. W. Norton, 1970), pp. 3–24.

52 Percy Bysshe Shelley, *Adonais*, st. 46, ll. 406–9, in *Shelley's Poetry and Prose*, ed. Reiman and Fraistat, p. 403.

53 Shelley, "A Defence of Poetry," in ibid., p. 488.

54 Shelley, "Mont Blanc," ll. 38, 39–40, in ibid., p. 90.

55 Charles Bernstein, "State of the Art," in *A Poetics* (Cambridge, MA: Harvard University Press, 1992), p. 5.

FURTHER READING

Abrams, M. H., *The Mirror and the Lamp: Romantic Theory and the Critical Tradition* (New York: Oxford University Press, 1953)

Fielding, Penny, *Writing and Orality: Nationality, Culture, and Nineteenth-Century Scottish Fiction* (Oxford: Clarendon; New York: Oxford University Press, 1996)

Galperin, William, *The Return of the Visible in British Romanticism* (Baltimore: Johns Hopkins University Press, 1993)

Havelock, Eric A., *The Muse Learns to Write: Reflections on Orality and Literacy from Antiquity to the Present* (New Haven: Yale University Press, 1986)

Hayles, N. Katherine, *Writing Machines* (Cambridge, MA: MIT Press, 2002)

Headrick, Daniel R., *When Information Came of Age: Technologies of Knowledge in the Age of Reason and Revolution, 1700–1850* (New York: Oxford University Press, 2000)

Hollander, John, *Vision and Resonance: Two Senses of Poetic Form* (New Haven: Yale University Press, 1985)

Langan, Celeste, "Understanding Media in 1805: Audiovisual Hallucination in *The Lay of the Last Minstrel*," *Studies in Romanticism* 40/1 (Spring 2001), pp. 49–70

McLane, Maureen N., "Tuning the Multi-Media Nation; or, Minstrelsy of the Afro-Scottish Border ca. 1800," *European Romantic Review* 15/2 (June 2004), pp. 289–305

McLuhan, Marshall, *Understanding Media: The Extensions of Man*, Introduction by Lewis Lapham (Cambridge, MA: MIT Press, 1994)

Mitchell, W. J. T., *Picture Theory* (Chicago: University of Chicago Press, 1994)

Stewart, Garrett, *Reading Voices: Literature and the Phonotext* (Berkeley: University of California Press, 1990)

Trumpener, Katie, "'The End of an Auld Sang': Oral Tradition and Literary History," in *Bardic Nationalism: The Romantic Novel and the British Empire* (Princeton: Princeton University Press, 1997), pp. 67–127

13

ANDREW BENNETT

Romantic poets and contemporary poetry

The Romantics among the English poets

John Keats's assertion in a letter that he would be "among the English Poets" after his death is usually understood to be a proudly defensive declaration, against attacks on his poetry in the *Quarterly Review* and elsewhere, that once he was dead his genius would be properly recognized and his work would become a prominent part of the canon of English Literature. "This is a mere matter of the moment," Keats declares of his detractors' aspersions: "I think I shall be among the English Poets after my death."[1] One might think of Keats's sense that he will be properly recognized only after death as no more than an acknowledgment of the idea that, as Samuel Johnson put it in his 1765 "Preface to Shakespeare," a century is "the term commonly fixed as the test of literary merit":[2] Keats would be recognized after his death for the simple reason that he could not be recognized before it. And some critics have argued that his comment specifically alludes to a relatively new kind of publishing venture: canon-forming, and nation-building multi-volume collections of poems by the English (or British) poets such as the 44-volume edition of *The British Poets* overseen by Hugh Blair (1773–6), *The Works of the English Poets, with Prefaces, Biographical and Critical, by Samuel Johnson* (68 volumes, 1779–81); John Bell's 109-volume *The Poets of Great Britain* (1777–83); and Alexander Chalmers's 21-volume *The Works of the English Poets* (1810). According to this reading, Keats was imagining that after his death his poems would literally take their place within the covers of such volumes alongside, or "among," those of his beloved Shakespeare, Spenser, and Milton. But we might also understand Keats to be proposing something rather different – something that is nevertheless consequential upon the desire for his poems to be bound together with those of Shakespeare. Keats's desire to be posthumously placed among the "English Poets" involves the prospect of another kind of bookish afterlife in which his poetry will survive in the language of later poets. For a poet to thrive in posterity means, after all, not only to be read and anthologized but to be rewritten. Keats may be saying that his poetry will live on, intertextually, in the very language of future poets. In other words, the English poets to whom he refers include those who were still to be born.

This chapter will examine the accuracy of such a prediction for Keats and for the Romantic poets more generally by considering their residual or posthumous presence in contemporary poetry in English; it will examine the survival of the British Romantic poets as a vital, energizing force in later twentieth- and twenty-first-century poetry. And it will contemplate contemporary poets as in some sense the "second selves" that William Wordsworth spoke of in "Michael: A Pastoral Poem" (1800): in a sentence that lurches somewhat awkwardly but perhaps rather hopefully from the plural to the singular, Wordsworth refers to the "youthful Poets, who among these Hills / Will be my second Self when I am gone."[3] The prospect of such a survival may be understood to be coded more generally within the poetry and poetics of the major Romantic poets because already intensely desired by them. What we call "Romanticism" can be conceived of in terms of a reconceptualization of poetry around just such a proleptic desire to be "among the . . . Poets" after one's death. This chapter examines the nature of that legacy in some aspects of contemporary anglophone poetry.

Charles Rzepka has recently argued that Wordsworth is "like the air we breathe," that the presence of his writing "circulates throughout the space that surrounds us as readers of verse in English."[4] And the same might be said for the Romantic poets more generally, with regard both to their poetry and to their poetics. Contemporary culture, indeed, is pervaded by developments in conceptions of poetry and art that are associated most fully with the Romantic period. Developed in part out of classical and Renaissance sources, and out of the neoclassical thinking of the earlier eighteenth century, "Romanticism" involves a powerful conglomeration of ideas that remain influential today. These ideas include newly invigorated notions of imagination, inspiration, genius, and the sublime; the celebration of Nature as an antidote to the rapid industrialization and urbanization of society; the production of the modern sense of the author as a unique, original, and autonomous individual resisting increasingly commercialized pressures of the publishing industry; the paradoxical conception of literature or art as "disinterested" (as Kant, Hazlitt, and others would have it) and the idea, at the same time, that poetry is a "passion" (as Wordsworth argues, after John Dennis); the idea that the poet should be a "camelion" figure, changingly absorbed by and absorbing what he writes about, an individual that expresses or lives in "negative capability" (to use Keats's phrases),[5] together with the apparently contradictory sense that the identity and subjectivity of the poet are themselves central to the poem; the conception of reading or literary reception as involving a "willing suspension of disbelief" (in Coleridge's famous phrase); the uncanny idea that, as Shelley argues in his *A Defence of Poetry*, poetry makes the familiar strange; and, perhaps most importantly, the equally uncanny possibility that what is most powerful and strange, most powerfully strange, about poetry is that it is just the crafted deployment of "ordinary" language – that poetry is a "selection of the language", as Wordsworth puts it, "really used by men."[6]

But if Romanticism is, therefore, often in only vaguely defined and barely acknowledged ways, part of the "air we breathe," part of the way that we conceive of poetry, it is also more directly and more explicitly a source of poetic material. And one of the most interesting ways that readers, critics, and poets have directly engaged with Romantic poetry over recent decades has been to blur the distinction between writer and writing, between poet and poem. One way to approach the question of the significance of Romantic poetry in contemporary culture is to examine the often rather contradictory ways in which contemporary poets directly express their interest in, as well as their distance from and resistance to, the lives as well as the work of their eminent predecessors.

John Keats's afterlives

John Keats is the Romantic poet who is perhaps most often and most intimately evoked by contemporary poets, just as it was Keats, along with Shelley, who was most often mourned and memorialized in nineteenth-century poems.[7] And what is most striking about contemporary evocations of Keats is the intensity with which they often figure a particular kind of affiliation and even personal identification, however guarded, with the youthful poet. "I think I half believed I was him," Anne Stevenson comments of her first encounter with the poet's work in Miss McKinney's twelfth grade English class in 1950, in "John Keats, 1821–1950" (2000).[8] Although the American writer Constance Urdang declares in her poem "Keats' (1990) that "It isn't Keats I love but the incorruptible / Purity of his words,"[9] contemporary poets tend nevertheless to recall Keats on account of his tragically curtailed life as much as on account of his writing, or of what Tom Clark calls his "intense language drive."[10] Keats's life, of course, lends itself to retelling on account of the way that it constitutes a particular kind of "allegory"[11] – the allegory of the fate of poetic genius and the poet's suffering, neglect, and necessarily early death. Keats instantiates, in other words, the very being of the poet or at least a certain archetype or ideal of the poet that we have inherited and in some ways still cling to, albeit in somewhat attenuated form: what we have inherited from Keats and others is one of the dominant senses of what it means to be a poet, to have poetic sensibility, to be or to have the strangeness of genius ("Genius is so strange," Ian Crichton Smith opines of Keats in "For Keats" [1972][12]), and crucially to suffer critical neglect or even scorn in one's lifetime before going to an early grave. Tom Clark makes a similar point in a prefatory note to his "poetic novel" or "biography in verse" on Keats's life, *Junkets on a Sad Planet* (1994), when he remarks on the way that Keats's "conceptual proposals of the figurative aspects of a poet's life" – proposals which emphasize "the problem of suffering" as a theme both "within and without the work" – present "a unique readout of the experience and meaning of being a modern poet."[13]

Recent poetic responses to Keats also tend to suggest that the division of poet and poetry is itself something of a fragile and unstable fiction: loving the "incorruptible purity" of Keats's words, loving his language – however we construe or describe it – is, in a sense, loving Keats, since Keats (like any other dead poet, indeed) just is language. Three notable poetic sequences – Amy Clampitt's "Voyages: A Homage to John Keats,"[14] Andrew Motion's prose and poem sequence "Sailing to Italy,"[15] Clark's *Junkets on a Sad Planet* – suggestively explore the inescapable imbrications of life with language, of suffering and genius with writing, emphasizing the fact that what we have of Keats, what remains of him, is only language, only the words he wrote in letters to friends and the words he wrote as poems. Concerned as these collections are to question or deconstruct the oppositions between history and fiction, the present and the past, life and writing, original and copy, performance and authenticity, self and other, they seem to produce a kind of linguistic resuscitation: Clampitt, Clark, and Motion incorporate the language of Keats's letters and his poems into their own modern texts, making new poetry out of a dead poet's words.

Perhaps the most striking of these evocations is that of Amy Clampitt. In "Voyages: A Homage to John Keats," the twentieth-century poet's response to Keats's life is mediated by the words of his poetry and letters – as in the final two stanzas of the second poem, "Teignmouth," for example, which describe

> an *annus mirabilis* of odes before the season
> of the oozing of the cider press, the harvest done,
> wheatfields blood-spattered once with poppies gone
> to stubble now, the swallows fretting to begin
>
> their windborne flight toward a Mediterranean
> that turned to marble as the mists closed in
> on the imagination's yet untrodden region –
> the coal-damps, the foul winter dark of London.[16]

What stands out here is the intimacy, the intensity of affiliation, with which the passage records, recreates, and reorders the language of Keats, the language of the letters and the poems. After the conventional description of Keats's extraordinarily productive year between September 1818 and September 1819 as his "*annus mirabilis*," almost everything in the first stanza cited here consists of a reordering of the words of Keats's "To Autumn": "season" is from the first line's "Season of mists and mellow fruitfulness";[17] the "oozing of the ciderpress" is a collapsing of two lines at the end of Keats's second stanza ("Or by a cyder-press, with patient look, / Thou watchest the last oozings hours by hours"); Clampitt's "harvest done" and "stubble" both allude to the "stubble-plains" in the final stanza of "To Autumn" and to its general sense that harvesting has finished; the reference to poppies alludes to the "drowsing" effect of the "fume of poppies" in Keats's poem; and "the swallows fretting to begin" reworks the ode's final line, "And gathering swallows twitter in the skies." The final stanza of Clampitt's poem is a little more diverse in its references but still entirely Keatsian: "windborne" is condensed from "To Autumn"'s gnats in stanza three, which are "borne aloft / Or sinking as the light wind lives or dies"; "mists" is a word which, in its unmistakable plurality, is taken from the first line of Keats's poem; "the imagination's yet untrodden region" is from another Keats poem, "Ode to Psyche"'s "untrodden region of my mind" (l. 51); "marble" is from, among other things, the "marble men and maidens" that seem so to disappoint the speaker at the end of "Ode on a Grecian Urn" (l. 42); and the description of the mists closing in on London's "foul" air might seem to echo the sentiments of a letter dated just before Keats wrote "To Autumn."[18] Even the seemingly un-poetic "blood-spattered" in the earlier stanza of Clampitt's poem can be read as an allusion to one of the commonly cited historical contexts of "To Autumn," since, as critics have pointed out, the poem was written soon after and arguably in response to or in protest against a famously bloody charge by government troops on unarmed protesters at St. Peter's Field in Manchester (the so-called "Peterloo Massacre" of August 16, 1819); or it could be interpreted more directly as an allusion to the blood that spattered out of Keats's lungs over the next eighteen months as he slowly died from consumption. There is little here that originates with Clampitt, then, except the crucial matters of selection, of syntax, and of the reordering of words. And what is remarkable about these stanzas is, as I say, the intimacy of affiliation with which they embrace Keats's words, his language, in a poem that does so in order to intimate a sense of his life (and, more importantly, perhaps, his death, the manner of his dying after his voyage to Italy); what strikes one is the apparent ease of identification that a late twentieth-century female

American poet can express toward an early nineteenth-century London Cockney writer.

While these stanzas may be remarkable for their exclusive appropriation of Keats's language, they are certainly not unique in Clampitt's sequence, or indeed, in one respect at least, in contemporary poetry more generally: rather, they are in some ways characteristic of a certain tendency in twentieth-century responses to Keats. What poets often do when they write on Keats, on the man, is to repeat and rework his poetry and letters, incorporating his writing into theirs, making his words their own, affiliating their own work and ultimately themselves with the Romantic poet. This is not to deny that, from Lord Byron on, other poets have also responded to the intense and somehow intensely youthful luxuries of Keatsian poetry by distancing themselves through humor or satire; nor is it to deny that the figure of the youthful, yearning poet dying tragically early from consumption has become something of a cliché, a model that can only have credibility for a certain kind of aspirant to poetic fame; nor indeed that a major part of the critical response to Keats from the middle of the twentieth century has involved something like a deconstruction of the class- and gender-determined charge of Keatsian desire, and of the Keatsian sense of beauty, and of truth. But there is a strong and continuing strand of poetry that, like Clampitt's poems, responds most strongly by a kind of linguistic incorporation – even while Clampitt's writing is alive to the fact that Keats's words are not, never were, his own words, that his poetry is itself imbued with that of his contemporaries (with Wordsworth, for example, and Coleridge) as it is with the words of dead poets such as Spenser, Milton, and above all Shakespeare. Clampitt's poems indeed suggest that in engaging with Keats, with his life, his letters, and his poetry, one is also engaging with certain literary traditions, with Keats's traditions as well as with one's own (with the way that Keats can be read through the poetry and the lives of Walt Whitman and Hart Crane, Osip Mandelstam and Wallace Stevens), and with a sense that Keats's poetry, his language, is the language of other poets and that more generally poetry *is*, in a sense, those traditions, that it is a reworking or re-embodiment of the words of both the dead and the living poets.

"Mountains, monuments": William Wordsworth

Wordsworth is a far less tempting subject for later poets, and poets' identifications and affiliations with him are, perhaps understandably, rather less secure, rather more tentative, wary. His poetry may, as Rzepka argues, be "like the air we breathe," but contemporary poets tend to be rather more guarded in their response to the man.[19] In fact, only a relatively

small number of contemporary poets have explicitly engaged with –
rather than echoed or alluded to or indeed "breathed" as their literary
atmosphere – William Wordsworth. And some of these evocations are distinctly troubled and troubling. Despite Ted Hughes's evident admiration for
Wordsworth, for example, his "On Westminster Bridge" (1963) involves
a violently punning de-pastoralization of Wordsworth's "Composed upon
Westminster Bridge, September 3, 1802," in which the poet's head is imagined as floating along the Thames only to be "eaten" by the Isle of Dogs.[20]
There is a perhaps rather more subtle distancing of the Lake Poet in Geoffrey
Hill's "Elegiac Stanzas: On a Visit to Dove Cottage" (1957), in which Hill
expresses elegiac ambivalence towards Wordsworthian language as he contemplates Wordsworthian topics ("Mountains, monuments"), a Wordsworthian dwelling place (the tourist-ridden Dove Cottage), Wordsworthian
speech ("The tongue broody in the jaw"), and an uncannily inhuman
Wordsworthian presence ("Greatly-aloof, alert, rare / Spirit . . . near-human
spouse and poet"), before, at the end of the 24-line poem, adopting a kind of
heavy-handedly ironized Wordsworthian rhetoric of vapid exclamation and
acclamation ("O Lakes, Lakes! / O Sentiment upon the rocks!").[21] Another
response, prefigured by Hughes and Hill, is Tony Harrison's undercutting
of the culturally and institutionally exacerbated perception of Wordsworthian complacency and self-importance in "Remains" (1984): in a poem
that may be said to owe as much to Thomas Gray's "Elegy Written in a
Country Churchyard" as to Wordsworth, Harrison suggests that in a visit
to Dove Cottage one's interest might be redirected from the venerable poet
and his domestic accoutrements to an unknown and unnoticed Victorian
paper-hanger, whose note nailed to a shutter in "Wordsworth's Lakeland
shrine" seems somehow more poignant and more telling to Harrison than
the objects officially on view.[22] The possibility that the found Art of graffiti –
this time the contemporary obscene graffiti on a toilet wall – can challenge
the canonized authority of an institutionalized and politically conservative
Wordsworth appears again in Bob Perelman's "Fake Dream: The Library"
(1998). In this poem, the speaker and his lover, searching for a quiet place to
have sex in a library, notice some obscene graffiti on the wall of an occupied
men's room as they retreat, and move instead into the deserted book stacks,
next to Wordsworth's *Poetic Works*. But instead of sex we get poetry, and
politics. The speaker contemplates the way that Wordsworth's "later leaden
writing" betrays the "intensity" of his earlier work (in which Wordsworth's
"need / to express his unplaced social being / in sentences had produced
publicly verifiable / beauty") – a thought that somehow seems to connect
in the speaker's mind to the liberated pleasures of (illicit) sex, to unstable syntax (to the subversive telegraphic syntax of, and the subversion of

syntax in, obscene graffiti), and to the possibility of a bodily resistance to the "tyranny of / elemental words" (again, the resistance to a monumentalized Wordsworth and Wordsworthian diction is at work in this response).[23] When Perelman reprinted the poem in the "Introduction" to his collection *Ten to One*, he used it to illustrate his sense that for "living poets" writing is "closer" to graffiti than to the canonized, book-based poetry of a writer like the later Wordsworth[24] – perhaps recalling that the early Wordsworth, at least, was himself not averse to producing graffiti, a delinquent impulse addressed with a certain amount of ambivalence in his poem "To Joanna."

As each of these poems might in their different ways suggest, the very status, the monumental status, of Wordsworth leads to a modern or postmodern difficulty in taking him entirely seriously, so that when they respond to his poetry directly, contemporary poets are prone (like nineteenth-century poets) to employ satire in order to undermine the politically and poetically reactionary values that (the later) Wordsworth seems to embody. Wendy Cope's "A Nursery Rhyme as it might have been written by William Wordsworth" (from *Making Cocoa for Kingsley Amis* (1986)) is exemplary: Cope explores the pretensions of a certain idea of Wordsworth through a wittily accurate parody that humorously turns "Baa Baa Black Sheep" into a poem of ponderous and humorlessly pedantic encounter that has as much to do with the received idea of the later Wordsworth as it does with the immediate target of its satire, the *Lyrical Ballads* and other early Wordsworth poems of encounter. If, as the poet and theorist of Language Poetry, Charles Bernstein, suggests, "absorption" (the quality of encouraging the reader to accept unquestioningly the literary and political values and conventions of a poem, to construe the "artifice" of a poem as no such thing) "characterizes" Romantic poetry, and if by "Romantic" Bernstein means, as he seems to, Wordsworth above all, then it is clear that resistance to absorption, or to what Jerome McGann calls the "Romantic ideology," is as much part of Romanticism's contemporary reception as its acceptance is.[25]

The question of identification is nevertheless acute for one of the best-known and undoubtedly one of the most Wordsworthian of contemporary poets, Seamus Heaney. By some accounts, Heaney has made a career of being – and therefore perforce of not being – Wordsworthian, of both identifying with the Lake Poet and resisting that inevitable identification. His first collection, *Death of a Naturalist* (1966), is often seen as particularly Wordsworthian, with its closeness to land and landscape, its concern with memory and the poet's own genesis, its sometimes troubled intimacy with nature, and its allegiance to a certain plainness of poetic diction. Both Wordsworth and Heaney articulate a sense of displacement from the very place, the very nature, that inspires them. Heaney's collection involves, as its title announces, the *death* of the naturalist, the ending of a boyhood experience of affiliation with nature; and as Neil Corcoran has put it, poems such as "Death of a Naturalist," "The Barn," and "Blackberry Picking" are "written in the margin" of such passages as Wordsworth's "Nutting," "Winander Boy," and the boat-stealing episode from *The Prelude*.[26] In both Heaney and Wordsworth there is the evocation of a boyhood engagement with nature that also involves a subsequent alienation from it and an obscure sense of possible guilt.

Heaney has commented repeatedly on Wordsworth in his critical prose, acknowledging what he refers to as Wordsworth's "power over us"[27] and making of Wordsworth and his writing something of a poetic model. Heaney's allegiance to a Wordsworthian sense of self, as well as to a Wordsworthian sense of the "redress" or redemption of poetry or the imagination, is presented in a relatively early lecture, "Feeling into Words" (1974), which begins by quoting Wordsworth's lines on the "hiding places of my power" from *The Prelude*: "Implicit in those lines," Heaney comments, "is a view of poetry which I think is implicit in the few poems I have written that give me any right to speak: poetry as divination, poetry as revelation of the self to the self, as restoration of the culture to itself."[28] Ten years later, in "Place and Displacement: Recent Poetry from Northern Ireland" (1984), Heaney reiterated his sense of the centrality of a Wordsworthian vision when he suggested that Wordsworth's sense of the "bliss" of political hope immediately after the French Revolution and the divided loyalties that the subsequent war with England engendered in him in the later 1790s offered a model for the condition of the contemporary Nationalist poet in Northern Ireland: "Like the disaffected Wordsworth, the Northern Irish writers I wish to discuss take the strain of being in two places at once, of needing to accommodate two opposing conditions of truthfulness, simultaneously."[29] A few years later, introducing his selection of Wordsworth's poems, Heaney argued that *Lyrical Ballads* was "the volume of poetry that initiates the modern enterprise."[30] And in the same year (1988), he published an essay on Sylvia Plath in which he suggested that the "Winander Boy" episode from *The Prelude* can be read as a "parable" of the three stages of "poetic achievement."[31] In his prose, then, Heaney has made it unmistakably clear that Wordsworth is the preferred model not only for his own poetry but, in his view, for contemporary poets more generally.

It might therefore seem surprising that few of Heaney's poems actually make explicit reference to – rather than echoing, alluding to, or more generally expressing intellectual and poetic indebtedness to – Wordsworth or his poetry. Indeed, at the opening of the Jerwood Centre to house the

Wordsworth Library in Grasmere in 2005, it was notable that Seamus Heaney read a new poem not on the poet but on his sister Dorothy – on her youthful vitality and her later morbid insanity.[32] Such a resistance to an assertion of identification with the poet might be explained by the one well-known reference to Wordsworth that there undoubtedly is in Heaney's poetry, an un-Wordsworthianly self-deprecating and lightly ironic comment that is precisely concerned with the question of Heaney's allegiance or poetic identification with the Lake Poet. Heaney's "Glanmore Sonnets" (1979) is a sequence of ten poems describing the poet's withdrawal from the city and from the conflicts of political engagement to the contemplative life in the country. Withdrawal from society and from political engagement is itself, of course, a Wordsworthian trope or theme – expressed most clearly in "Home at Grasmere" – as well as in many ways an archetypically Wordsworthian act, and the "Glanmore Sonnets" are haunted by that poetico-historical fact.[33] The opening line of the second sonnet ("Sensings, mountings from the hiding places") echoes *The Prelude*,[34] but the third sonnet tests this affiliation more explicitly. The speaker addresses his wife, asserting that he will not "relapse / From this strange loneliness I've brought us to." He then begins what looks to be a potentially clarifying or self-justifying sentence with the words "Dorothy and William –," only to be cut off in mid-sentence by his wife's refusal to contemplate such an analogy: "You're not going to compare us two?" she demands mockingly of her poet-husband.[35] And he relents, leaving unfinished the potentially self-aggrandizing comparison between himself and his wife on the one hand and Wordsworth and Dorothy on the other. In other words, the poem makes dramatically clear Heaney's conflicted sense of identification with and resistance to his English poetic predecessor. This is a dialogue between a poet and his wife but it is also a dialogue of the poet with himself. The poem seems to question the viability of a twentieth-century poet's sense of unequivocal affiliation with Wordsworthian conceptions of poetic identity and with Wordsworth's particular way of conceiving of the poet's relationship with nature and memory, with the self and others, with geographical locus and political responsibility.

"Awe in the Ordinary": John Clare

Seamus Heaney's poetry also bears marked allegiance to that of John Clare, as does the work of poets as diverse as Theodore Roethke, R. S. Thomas, Michael Longley, and Tom Paulin. Perhaps somewhat surprisingly, given their geographical, cultural, temporal, and ethnic distance from the Northampton peasant-poet, the New York poet John Ashbery and the West Indian poet Derek Walcott have written tellingly in recent years about his poetry and both have made explicit their individual identifications with his writing, if not with his troubled life. The affinity of Ashbery with John Clare involves, in particular, a shared fascination with what the later poet identifies as his precursor's exacting sense of the "pointlessness" of the natural world. Of Clare's long poem of rural life, *The Shepherd's Calendar*, Ashbery comments in an essay on Clare that it takes "a special kind of reader to appreciate it for what it is," and then goes on to describe just what he thinks Clare's poetry is: "a distillation of the natural world with all its beauty and pointlessness, its salient and boring features preserved intact . . . the point is that there is no point."[36] Remove "natural" – since he is a poet concerned as much with the *polis*, with urban, social, industrial, or commercial life, as with the stringencies, the comforts, and the solitude of nature – and this could be a description of Ashbery's own poems. Clare, he says, "grabs hold of you"

> – no, he doesn't grab hold of you, he is already there, talking to you before you've arrived on the scene, telling you about himself, about the things that are closest and dearest to him, and it would no more occur to him to do otherwise than it would occur to Whitman to stop singing you his song of himself. It is like that "instant intimacy" for which we Americans are so notorious in foreign climes. Clare bears you no ill will and doesn't want to shock or pain you, but that isn't going to make him change his tale one whit . . . He is apt to show his wounds and crack a joke in the same moment; he is above all an instrument of telling.[37]

The early-nineteenth century Northampton poet is here encompassed within a Whitmanesque American sensibility and, in particular, an Ashberyan poetic voice – one that produces a sense of unabashed intimacy, one that talks of hurt and cracks jokes at the same time, one that is already speaking when we arrive. Precisely such a sense of intimacy and insouciance, of someone already telling you about himself before you have arrived on the scene, is indeed captured in a poem in which Ashbery characteristically embraces a Clare-like sense of the quotidian, the prose-poem "For John Clare" (1970):

> Kind of empty in the way it sees everything, the earth gets to its feet and salutes the sky. More of a success at it this time than most others it is. The feeling that the sky might be in the back of someone's mind. Then there is no telling how many there are. They grace everything – bush and tree – to take the roisterer's mind off his caroling – so it's like a smooth switch back.[38]

There is much here that is more Wordsworthian, if anything, than like John Clare – the feeling of the sky at the back of a mind in particular might be a prose paraphrase of the "Winander Boy" ("What will it all be like in five years' time when you try to remember?," Ashbery asks a few lines later, as if thinking of Clare leads to thinking about memory in "Tintern Abbey"). But there is also, as the poem goes on, a sense of the quotidian, of the non-hierarchical and inconsequential in the observation of nature. "There is so much to be said," as the poet says in an exquisite and un-Clare-like verbal quibble at the end of this first paragraph that says as much about Clare as it does about Ashbery, "and on the surface of it very little gets said": little gets said, on the surface of it, that is to say, which is to say that much might get said. But, in fact, Ashbery's postmodern poetry is all about surfaces, at least on the surface of it, and it is poetry in which, on the surface of it and much like Clare's, little gets said. And this – and it is just this for which Clare has been criticized in the past, and part of the reason for his relative neglect even in contemporary literary culture – is what Ashbery sees in him. The point is the poetry's pointlessness, the kind of empty way it sees and says everything, like a poet looking at a bird or a nest or a tree or a field – and just describing it.

Derek Walcott's elegy for his mother, "The Bounty" (1997), is a seven-part poem written in Dantesque *terza rima*. The "bounty" of the poem's title refers to the gifts – of life, of education, of poetry, and of religion – that his mother gave the poet, as well as to the abundance of nature in the Caribbean, to the name of Captain Bligh's ship (a ship that brought the bounty of the bread-fruit tree to the West Indies in the 1780s but that was also at the centre of a famous mutiny in 1789), and even to the Nobel Prize for Literature, awarded to Walcott in 1992 and described by W. B. Yeats in 1923 as the "bounty of Sweden."[39] But the "bounty" to which Walcott refers is also, above all, the gift of poetic language, the linguistic plenitude that allows Clare and after him Walcott to represent their plentiful, bountiful surroundings – a gift that Walcott values in John Clare and sees as his own West Indian inheritance. Walcott is particularly clear about this in the first section of "The Bounty":

> . . . the bliss of John Clare,
> torn, wandering Tom, stoat-stroker in his county
> of reeds and stalk-crickets, fiddling the dank air,
> lacing his boots with vines, steering glazed beetles
>
> with the tenderest prods, knight of the cockchafer,
> wrapped in the mists of shires, their snail-horned steeples
> palms opening to the cupped pool . . .
>
> (p. 3)

In later life John Clare wandered in mind as well as along the roads and in the fields, and was, as such, "torn" like "wandering Tom" – like wandering

Edgar in *King Lear* as he plays the part of "mad Tom," the mythical wandering beggar Tom O'Bedlam. But Walcott suggests that despite being torn, being mad, Clare allows us, still, a quasi-religious and undoubtedly idealized sense of natural plenitude in an English landscape, with its shires and mists and steeples, its beetles and snails and streams; he allows us what Walcott punningly refers to as a sense of "awe in the ordinary."[40] And this inspires from the Caribbean poet, torn as he is, wandering in mourning for his mother, a counter-colonial turn as he appropriates England for the West Indies and figures Clare blessing his own tropical landscape. John Clare – or "John Clare," the poetry of Clare – is like an autumn field, like a tree:

> Frost whitening his stubble, he stands in the ford
> of a brook like the Baptist lifting his branches to bless
>
> cathedrals and snails, the breaking of this new day,
> and the shadows of the beach road near which my mother lies,
> with the traffic of insects going to work anyway.
>
> (p. 3)

Clare is like John the Baptist, lifting his branch-like arms as he "blesses" both cathedrals and snails, both the monumental house of God and the fragile housing of the humble mollusc. And crucially, Clare is imagined as "blessing" *both* the nineteenth-century English landscape and the here-and-now of St Lucia, "the breaking of this new day" over the place near the Atlantic Ocean where Walcott's mother is buried. John Clare, the English poet, "blesses" St Lucia in the sense that he allows Walcott to see it, to appreciate it – to write it, invent it – and to bless it even in mourning for his mother: the bounty that Walcott accepts and records – the *everything* that is given from mother to son, the very life the mother engenders – is also that of John Clare, whose bounty is poetry as he helps the West Indian poet to see, and to write:

> I am moved like you, mad Tom, by a line of ants;
> I behold their industry and they are giants.
>
> (p. 4)

Beholding the ants – or the beetles or snails of the shires – makes of them giants in this madness of mourning, this madness of poetic vision, of metaphor and poetry, poetry that suggests that what we call "nature" encompasses madness, poverty, labor or industry, and mourning. Walcott is moved like mad Tom is moved, like Clare is moved, by a line of ants – and by "gi/ants", by a line of poetry and the aural resonance, the rhyme, of poetry's line-endings: he writes poetry out of nature and its "industry," and out of the poetry of John Clare.

Romantic poets' second lives

To suggest that contemporary poets are concerned to establish identifications and affiliations with the Romantic poets is not to suggest that they are
only concerned with those poets' intriguing, tragic, moving and sometimes
scandalous lives: their poems engage in the first place with Romantic poetry.
But it is to suggest that many contemporary poets focus or filter their interest
in Romantic poetry through those lives – and it is to suggest that there is,
that there can be, no "pure" response to the writing of the Romantics, that
there is no such thing as the "incorruptible purity" of a poet's words, no
response that is not bound up with a sense of the poets' messy, quotidian,
and often extraordinary lives. And this itself should come as no surprise
when we think of the ways in which the Romantic poets projected their
selves, their constructed or "fashioned" selves, into the poetry – and when
we remember how much they invested emotionally and professionally in a
sense of their own posterity, in the sense that they were writing, finally, for
an audience of future readers and for younger poets, for Wordsworth's "second Self when I am gone." What contemporary poets so often respond to,
in their identifications and affiliations, as well as in their resistance to such
allegiances, is the fact that Romantic poetry involves a haunting sense of
the poet's presence. It is, in the end, the temptations and dangers of poetic
allegiance and personal identification that determine contemporary poets'
encounters with their Romantic precursors. And thinking about such poets'
varied engagements with the Romantics might help us to think more clearly
about the constitution, the force, and the poetic effects of Romantic poetry
and about the Romantic poet's desire to survive among the English (which
also means, of course, among the Scottish, Irish, American, Caribbean . . .)
poets.

NOTES

1 *The Letters of John Keats, 1814–1821*, ed. Hyder Rollins, 2 vols. (Cambridge,
   MA: Harvard University Press, 1958), vol. I, p. 394.
2 Samuel Johnson, "Preface to Shakespeare," in *Rasselas: Poems and Selected
   Prose*, ed. Bertrand H. Bronson, 3rd edn. (New York: Holt, Rinehart &
   Winston, 1971), p. 262.
3 William Wordsworth, "Michael: A Pastoral Poem," ll. 38–9, in *Lyrical Ballads
   and Other Poems, 1797–1800*, ed. James Butler and Karen Green (Ithaca: Cornell
   University Press, 1992), p. 253.
4 Charles J. Rzepka, "Poetry," in *Romanticism: An Oxford Guide*, ed. Nicholas
   Roe (Oxford: Oxford University Press, 2005), p. 607.
5 Keats, *Letters*, vol. I, pp. 387, 193.
6 Wordsworth, *Lyrical Ballads*, p. 750.

7 For this claim, see Samantha Matthews, *Poetical Remains: Poets' Graves, Bodies, and Books in the Nineteenth Century* (Oxford: Oxford University Press, 2004), p. 115.

8 Anne Stevenson, "John Keats, 1821–1950," in *Poems, 1955–2005* (Tarset: Bloodaxe, 2004), p. 294.

9 Constance Urdang, "Keats," in *Alternative Lives* (Pittsburg: University of Pittsburg Press, 1990), p. 34.

10 Tom Clark, *Junkets on a Sad Planet: Scenes from the Life of John Keats* (Santa Rosa: Black Sparrow Press, 1994), p. 46.

11 Keats, *Letters*, vol. II, p. 67.

12 Ian Crichton Smith, *Selected Poems, 1955–1980*, selected by Robin Fulton (Loanhead: Macdonald, 1981), p. 158.

13 Clark, *Junkets on a Sad Planet*, n.p.

14 In Amy Clampitt, *What the Light Was Like* (London: Faber & Faber 1986), pp. 47–68.

15 In Andrew Motion, *Salt Water* (London: Faber & Faber, 1997), pp. 59–112.

16 Clampitt, *What the Light Was Like*, p. 50.

17 Quotations from Keats's poems are taken from *The Poems of John Keats*, ed. Jack Stillinger (London: Heinemann, 1978).

18 Keats, *Letters*, vol. II, pp. 155–6.

19 In "Poetry," Rzepka considers the influence of Wordsworth on Heaney, Hughes, Elizabeth Bishop, Charles Tomlinson, and others.

20 Ted Hughes, *Collected Poems* (London: Faber & Faber, 2003), pp. 104–5.

21 Geoffrey Hill, "Elegiac Stanzas," in *Collected Poems* (Harmondsworth: Penguin, 1985), p. 42.

22 Tony Harrison, *Selected Poems*, 2nd edn. (Harmondsworth: Penguin, 1987), p. 180.

23 Bob Perelman, "Fake Dream: The Library," in *Ten to One: Selected Poems* (Hanover, NH: University Press of New England, 1999), pp. xiv–xvi [the poem was originally published, as "The Library," in *The Future of Memory* (Buffalo: Roof Books, 1998)].

24 Perelman, *Ten to One*, p. xvi.

25 See Charles Bernstein, *A Poetics* (Cambridge, MA: Harvard University Press, 1992), p. 21; and see Jerome McGann, *The Romantic Ideology: A Critical Investigation* (Chicago: University of Chicago Press, 1983).

26 Neil Corcoran, *The Poetry of Seamus Heaney: A Critical Study* (London: Faber & Faber, 1998), p. 5.

27 Seamus Heaney, "Introduction" to *The Essential Wordsworth* (New York: Ecco Press, 1988), p. 4.

28 Seamus Heaney, *Preoccupations: Selected Prose, 1968–1978* (London: Faber & Faber, 1980), p. 41; see *The Prelude* (1805), Book 11, 335.

29 Seamus Heaney, *Finders Keepers: Selected Prose, 1971–2001* (London: Faber & Faber, 2002), p. 115.

30 Heaney, "Introduction," p. 6.

31 Heaney, "The Indefatigable Hoof-taps: Sylvia Plath," in *Finders Keepers*, pp. 220–7.

32 Seamus Heaney, "A Scuttle for Dorothy Wordsworth," in the *Guardian*, June 4, 2005, p. 8; the poem is reprinted in *District and Circle* (London: Faber & Faber,

2006), p. 70, where Heaney also has a short poem that does directly allude to William and to his poetry, "Wordsworth's Skaters" (p. 22).

33 This point is made by Anne Stevenson in "*Stations*: Seamus Heaney and the Sacred Sense of the Sensitive Self," in *The Art of Seamus Heaney*, ed. Tony Curtis, (Dublin: Wolfhound Press, 1994), p. 47.

34 See Wordsworth, *The Thirteen-Book Prelude*, ed. Mark L. Reed, 2 vols. (Ithaca: Cornell University Press, 1991), vol. I, p. 20 ("Trances of thought and mountings of the mind") and vol. II, p. 336 ("hiding places of my power").

35 Seamus Heaney, "Glanmore Sonnets," in *Opened Ground: Poems 1966–1996* (London: Faber & Faber, 1998), pp. 164–5.

36 John Ashbery, *Other Traditions* (Cambridge, MA: Harvard University Press, 2000), pp. 11, 17.

37 Ibid., p. 16.

38 John Ashbery, "For John Clare," in *Selected Poems*, 2nd edn. (London: Paladin, 1987), p. 107.

39 The phrase is quoted in poem 28 of *The Bounty* (London: Faber & Faber, 1997), p. 61; all quotations are from this edition. Subsequent references in the text.

40 This phrase is from section iii of "The Bounty," *The Bounty*, p. 7.

FURTHER READING

Davies, Damian Walford, and Richard Marggraf Turley, eds., *The Monstrous Debt: Modalities of Romantic Influence in Twentieth-Century Literature* (Detroit: Wayne State University Press, 2006)

Easthope, Anthony, *Wordsworth Now and Then: Romanticism and Contemporary Culture* (Buckingham: Open University Press, 1993)

Gelpi, Albert, "The Genealogy of Postmodernism: Contemporary American Poetry," *The Southern Review* 26/3 (Summer 1990), pp. 517–41

Larrissy, Edward, *Reading Twentieth-Century Poetry: The Language of Gender and Objects* (Oxford: Basil Blackwell, 1990)

"Modernism and Postmodernity", in Nicholas Roe, ed., *Romanticism: An Oxford Guide* (Oxford: Oxford University Press, 2005), pp. 665–74

Larrissy, Edward, ed., *Romanticism and Postmodernism* (Cambridge: Cambridge University Press, 1999)

Mandell, Laura, and Michael Eberle-Sinatra, eds., *Romanticism and Contemporary Culture* (Romantic Circles Praxis Series website), www.rc.umd.edu/praxis/contemporary

Robinson, Jeffrey C., *Reception and Poetics in Keats: "My Ended Poet"* (Basingstoke: Macmillan, 1998)

Ruoff, Gene W., ed., *The Romantics and Us: Essays on Literature and Culture* (New Brunswick: Rutgers University Press, 1990)

Sita, Melissa J., and Neil Fraistat, eds., *Fictional Representations of Romantics and Romanticism* (Romantic Circles Resource), www.rc.umd.edu/reference/misc/ficrep/nassr-sf.html

Steinman, Lisa M., ed., *Romanticism and Contemporary Poetry and Poetics* (Romantic Circle Praxis Series website), www.rc.umd.edu/praxis/poetics/toc.html

INDEX

Cambridge Companions to...

AUTHORS

TOPICS